Pere Johnstone

REHEARSAL FOR
DESTRUCTION

STUDIES IN PREJUDICE

EDITED BY MAX HORKHEIMER
AND SAMUEL H. FLOWERMAN

THE AUTHORITARIAN PERSONALITY
by T. W. Adorno, Else Frenkel-Brunswik,
Daniel J. Levinson and R. Nevitt Sanford

DYNAMICS OF PREJUDICE
A PSYCHOLOGICAL AND SOCIOLOGICAL STUDY OF VETERANS
by Bruno Bettelheim and Morris Janowitz

ANTI-SEMITISM AND EMOTIONAL DISORDER
A PSYCHOANALYTIC INTERPRETATION
by Nathan W. Ackerman and Marie Jahoda

REHEARSAL FOR DESTRUCTION
A STUDY OF POLITICAL ANTI-SEMITISM IN IMPERIAL GERMANY
by Paul W. Massing

PROPHETS OF DECEIT
A STUDY OF THE TECHNIQUES OF THE AMERICAN AGITATOR
by Leo Lowenthal and Norbert Guterman

Other Volumes in Preparation

SPONSORED BY
THE AMERICAN JEWISH COMMITTEE
SOCIAL STUDIES SERIES: PUBLICATION NO. II

REHEARSAL FOR DESTRUCTION

A Study of Political Anti-Semitism

in Imperial Germany

by

PAUL W. MASSING

HARPER & BROTHERS · NEW YORK

FOREWORD TO STUDIES IN PREJUDICE

At this moment in world history anti-Semitism is not manifesting itself with the full and violent destructiveness of which we know it to be capable. Even a social disease has its periods of quiescence during which the social scientist, like the biologist or the physician, can study it in the search for more effective ways to prevent or reduce the virulence of the next outbreak.

Today the world scarcely remembers the mechanized persecution and extermination of millions of human beings only a short span of years away in what was once regarded as the citadel of Western civilization. Yet the conscience of many men was aroused. How could it be, they asked each other, that in a culture of law, order and reason, there should have survived the irrational remnants of ancient racial and religious hatreds? How could they explain the willingness of great masses of people to tolerate the mass extermination of their fellow citizens? What tissues in the life of our modern society remain cancerous, and despite our assumed enlightenment show the incongruous atavism of ancient peoples? And what within the individual organism responds to certain stimuli in our culture with attitudes and acts of destructive aggression?

But an aroused conscience is not enough if it does not stimulate a systematic search for an answer. Mankind has paid too dearly for its naive faith in the automatic effect of the mere passage of time: incantations have really never dispelled storms, disaster, pestilence, disease or other evils; nor does he who torments another cease his torture out of sheer boredom with his victim.

Prejudice is one of the problems of our times for which everyone has a theory but no one an answer. Every man, in a sense, believes that he is his own social scientist, for social science is the stuff of everyday living. The progress of science can perhaps be charted by the advances that scientists have made over commonsense notions of phenomena. In an effort to advance beyond mere commonsense approaches to problems of intergroup conflict, the American Jewish Committee in May, 1944, invited a group of American scholars of various backgrounds and disciplines to a two-day conference on religious and racial prejudice. At this meeting, a research program was outlined which would enlist scientific method in

v

the cause of seeking solutions to this crucial problem. Two levels of research were recommended. One was more limited in scope and geared to the recurring problems faced by educational agencies; e.g., the study of public reaction to selected current events, and the evaluation of various techniques and methods such as those involved in mass media of communication as they impinge upon intergroup relationships. The other level suggested was one of basic research, basic in that it should eventually result in additions to organized knowledge in this field. The first level frequently consists of a large number of small studies, limited in scope and focused sharply on a given issue. In practice, we have found that the "goodness" of our smaller studies was proportional to our ingenuity in so devising them that they, too, could contribute basically to knowledge. The chief difference between the two levels of research—sometimes loosely called "short-range" and "long-range" research—seems largely to be due to the immediacy of implementation of findings as program-related or unrelated, rather than to differences in methodology, skills and techniques. On both levels, it is necessary to pursue an interdisciplinary approach to research problems.

To further research on both levels, the American Jewish Committee established a Department of Scientific Research, headed in turn by each of us. The Department saw its responsibility not only in itself initiating fundamental studies in the phenomenon of prejudice, but also in helping to stimulate new studies.

The present series of volumes represents the first fruits of this effort. In a sense, the initial five volumes constitute one unit, an integrated whole, each part of which illuminates one or another facet of the phenomenon we call prejudice. Three of the books deal with those elements in the personality of modern man that predispose him to reactions of hostility to racial and religious groups. They attempt answers to the questions: What is there in the psychology of the individual that renders him "prejudiced" or "unprejudiced," that makes him more or less likely to respond favorably to the agitation of a Goebbels or a Gerald K. Smith? The volume on *The Authoritarian Personality* by Adorno, Frenkel-Brunswik, Levinson and Sanford, based upon a combination of research techniques, suggests one answer. It demonstrates that there is a close correlation between a number of deep-rooted personality traits, and overt prejudice. The study has also succeeded in producing an instrument for measuring these traits among various strata of the population.

Within a more limited range of inquiry, the same question was asked with respect to two specific groups. The study on *Dynamics of Prejudice*, by Bettelheim and Janowitz, considers the connection between personality traits and prejudice among war veterans. Here the investigators were able to examine the impact of the war experience, with its complex anxieties and tensions, as an added factor of major significance affecting tens of millions of people. *Anti-Semitism and Emotional Disorder*, by Ackerman and Jahoda, is based upon case histories of a number of individuals, from different walks of life, who have received intensive psychotherapy. The special significance of this study lies precisely in the analytical source of the material, in the availability of a body of evidence dealing with phenomena beneath the realm of the conscious and the rational, and illuminating the correlation established in more general terms in the basic investigation of the authoritarian personality.

The other important factor in prejudice is of course the social situation itself, i.e., the external stimuli to which the predispositions within the individual have reacted and continue to react. Nazi Germany is the vivid example of the effect of the social situation, and it is to the understanding of the roots of Nazi anti-Semitism and thence to the present task of democratic reorientation in Germany that *Rehearsal for Destruction* by Massing is directed. As mediator between the world and the individual psyche, the agitator molds already existing prejudices and tendencies into overt doctrines and ultimately into overt action.

In the *Prophets of Deceit*, by Lowenthal and Guterman, the role of the agitator is studied. The agitator's technique of persuasion, the mechanism of mediation that translates inchoate feeling into specific belief and action make up the theme of that volume.

It may strike the reader that we have placed undue stress upon the personal and the psychological rather than upon the social aspect of prejudice. This is not due to a personal preference for psychological analysis nor to a failure to see that the cause of irrational hostility is in the last instance to be found in social frustration and injustice. Our aim is not merely to describe prejudice but to explain it in order to help in its eradication. That is the challenge we would meet. Eradication means re-education, scientifically planned on the basis of understanding scientifically arrived at. And education in a strict sense is by its nature personal and psychological. Once we understand, for example, how the war experience may in some cases have strengthened personality traits predisposed to group hatred, the educational remedies may follow logically. Similarly, to expose the psychological tricks in the arsenal of the agitator may help to immunize his prospective victims against them.

Since the completion of these studies the Department of Scientific Research of the American Jewish Committee has moved ahead into areas of research in which the unit of study is the group, the institution, the community rather than the individual. Fortified by a better knowledge of *individual* dynamics, we are now concerned with achieving a better understanding of *group* dynamics. For we recognize that the individual *in vacuo* is but an artifact; even in the present series of studies, although essentially psychological in nature, it has been necessary to explain individual behavior in terms of social antecedents and concomitants. The second stage of our research is thus focused upon problems of group pressures and the sociological determinants of roles in given social situations. We seek answers to such questions as: Why does an individual behave in a "tolerant" manner in one situation and in a "bigoted" manner in another situation? To what extent may certain forms of intergroup conflict, which appear on the surface to be based upon ethnic difference, be based upon other factors, using ethnic difference as content?

The authors of the volumes and the many colleagues upon whose experience and assistance they have been able to draw have widely differing professional interests. This is immediately reflected in the various techniques they have used, even in the way they write. Some of the books are more technical, others more "readable." We have not sought uniformity. A search for the truth conducted with the best techniques of the contemporary social sciences was our sole aim. Yet through all this diversity of method a significant measure of agreement has been achieved.

The problem requires a much more extensive and much more sustained effort than any single institution or any small group such as ours, could hope to put forth. It was our hope that whatever projects we could undertake would not only be contributions in themselves, but would also serve to stimulate active interest in continued study by other scholars. With deep satisfaction we have watched the steady increase in scientific publications in this field in the past few years. We believe that any study that bears upon this central theme, if carried out in a truly scientific spirit, cannot help but bring us closer to the theoretical, and ultimately to the practical, solution for reducing intergroup prejudice and hatred.

This foreword to *Studies in Prejudice* would not be complete without a tribute to the vision and leadership of Dr. John Slawson, Executive Vice-President of the American Jewish Committee, who was responsible for calling the conference of scholars and for establishing the Department of Scientific Research. Both editors owe Dr. Slawson a debt of gratitude for the inspiration, guidance, and stimulation which he gave them.

MAX HORKHEIMER
SAMUEL H. FLOWERMAN

CONTENTS

FOREWORD TO STUDIES IN PREJUDICE   v

INTRODUCTION BY SAMUEL H. FLOWERMAN   xiii

PREFACE   xv

PART ONE

ANTI-SEMITISM IN BISMARCK'S REICH

I.   THE LIBERAL ERA (1871–1878)   3
The liberal paradise—The depression places "Jewish liberalism" on trial—Spokesmen of the *Mittelstand:* Wilhelm Marr, Otto Glagau—Anti-Semitism, a political weapon for Bismarck's enemies—The Conservative-Catholic alliance—Bismarck's dilemma

II.   CONSERVATIVE-CLERICAL REACTION (1879–1886)   21
Two areas of social unrest—Court Chaplain Stoecker's Christian Social movement—First phase: against Marxist labor—Second phase: against the Jews—The context of Stoecker's success—The agrarian and industrial coalition—Bismarck strikes against liberalism and Social Democracy

III.   THE STATE AND THE RABBLE-ROUSERS   37
The Reich's rulers attracted and repelled by anti-Semitism—Tacit encouragement from above—The Bleichröder incident—Apex of the Berlin Movement—Bismarck and Stoecker—Public opinion weakens Stoecker's prestige—The future Kaiser rescues Stoecker—Summary

PART TWO

RACIAL ANTI-SEMITISM

IV.   STOECKER'S DECLINE (1886–1890)   51
The *"Kartell"* alliance of Liberals and Conservatives—Stoecker's movement an obstacle to the new political coali-

tion—Bismarck's wrath—Stoecker forced out of politics—
The new Kaiser compels Bismarck to resign—Stoecker
dismissed from office

V. THE CAPRIVI ERA (1890–1894)   60
The new Chancellor adopts a policy of moderation—The
Conservatives move to the counterattack—Stoecker re-
turns—The Conservatives' Tivoli program—The Agrarian
League—Socialists and anti-Semites score election gains
—A new attempt to outlaw "sedition"—Caprivi dismissed

VI. THE FIRST WAVE OF RACIAL ANTI-SEMITISM   75
The philosophy of despair—Racism and nationalism—
The metaphysics of blood—Abortive anti-Semitic parties
in Berlin—Anti-Semitism moves to the provinces—Success
in Hesse: "Peasant King" Otto Boeckel—Hermann Ahlwardt, "Rektor of all the Germans"—The racists' revolt
against law

VII. THE RATIONALE OF RACIAL ANTI-SEMITISM   99
Racial anti-Semitism judged by contemporaries—Reconcil-
ing the irreconcilable—Partners in duplicity—The Conservatives' cynical strategy—The racists' mixed feeling for
the Conservatives—The manipulators and the manipulated

PART THREE

ANTI-SEMITISM AND IMPERIALISM (1895–1914)

VIII. POLITICAL ANTI-SEMITISM ON THE WANE   113
The racist agitators disappear from the scene—Left-wing
opposition within the Stoecker movement—Stoecker's
"pyre" letter and von Hammerstein's downfall—The Conservatives jettison Stoecker—The Kaiser and Protestant
Church disavow Christian socialism—The Conservatives
"go modern"—The Mittelstand organizes

IX. NEW DIRECTIONS AND NEW TARGETS   127
The Stumm era—Paternalistic despotism—The attack
veers toward labor—The coup d'état again—For a Greater
Germany—The integration of the Mittelstand—The Federation of Commercial Employees—The Pan-German
League—Naumann's democratic imperialism—Government by bureaucracy—Imperialism and anti-Semitism

PART FOUR

SOCIALIST LABOR AND ANTI-SEMITISM (1863–1914)

X. THE SOCIALIST VIEWPOINT   151
Labor's alienation from political liberalism—Anti-Semitic
tendencies among the Lassalleans—Karl Marx's *Zur Judenfrage*—The Marxist interpretation of anti-Semitism—
The make-up of the Jewish group—Marxist criticism of
the Liberals' defense of the Jews

XI. MARXISM IN ACTION   170
The Social Democratic Party and the Stoecker movement
—The Social Democrats and racial anti-Semitism—Friedrich Engels and the radical Social Democrats—The controversy over the agrarian question—Anti-Semitism viewed
as an immature form of rebellion

XII. THE CASE OF FRANZ MEHRING   184
The disciple of Lassalle—Originally repelled by Marxism
—Attacks Stoecker's demagogy—Breaks with liberalism—
Turns radical—Denounces both anti-Semitism and "philo-
Semitism"

XIII. THE SOCIAL DEMOCRATIC PARTY IN THE ERA OF IMPERIALISM   190
(1895–1914)
The Social Democratic Party becomes integrated in the
national structure—Controversy over Zionism: utopia or
necessity?—The efficacy of socialist indoctrination—Jews
in the Social Democratic Party—The burden of the revolutionary ideology

NOTES AND REFERENCES   209

DOCUMENTS   277
    I. The Anti-Semites' Definition of Capital
    II. Adolf Stoecker's First Anti-Semitic Speech
    III. Anti-Semitism, Liberalism, and the Prussian Govern-
       ment
    IV. The Catholic Center Party's Argument Against Anti-
       Jewish Legislation
    V. Social Democratic Criticism of Anti-Semitic "Reform"
    VI. Hermann Ahlwardt on the Semitic versus the Teu-
       tonic Race
    VII. The Racists' Decalogue

VIII. Autobiographical Explanations of Anti-Semitism
        a. The *Junker*
        b. The Racist
  IX. A Private Letter of Friedrich Engels
   X. On the Intellectual History of Franz Mehring
        a. The Humanitarian Conservative
        b. The Theoretician of the Class Struggle
  XI. The Marxist Appraisal of Zionism: A Review of
       Theodor Herzl's *Der Judenstaat*
 XII. A Jewish Socialist on Jews and German Social De-
       mocracy

INDEX   331

INTRODUCTION

Rehearsal for Destruction is not another recital of Nazi horrors. I
think the people of the Western democracies are surfeited with these
horrible tales; the human organism seeks protection against such continued barrages of sadism and their hidden connotations of "collective"
guilt. Paul Massing has eschewed the macabre aspects of Nazi anti-
Semitism as well as individual-psychological interpretations of anti-
Semitism; other volumes in this series deal with anti-Semitism as a
psycho-cultural phenomenon. His book rests upon a social and political
framework. It attempts to show how anti-Semitism, always lurking in
the background of German social structure, could be conjured forth to
serve those who understood its political potentialities. Wisely he points
out that although in Germany a recrudescence of anti-Semitism accompanied economic distress it would be a mistake to assume that economic
distress alone was responsible.

To me, perhaps the most startling revelation of Massing's work—
startling because studies of anti-Semitism in America seem to point to
different relationships between anti-Semitism and such background factors as education, geographical location, etc.—is the disclosure that the
implacable enemies of Jews were more often urban than rural, and
members of higher-educated rather than lower-educated classes. The
most virulent anti-Semitism was spread by teachers, students, white collar workers, petty officials, the free professions and all kinds of "life-
reform" movements. In contrast, conservative Junkers, peasants and other
rural inhabitants had no special love for Jews but their dislike was circumscribed. Attacks on Jews were often linked with attacks on Junkers
and on Christianity. Anti-Semitism was inextricably tied to German nineteenth-century nationalism; its destructive nature derived from the peculiar social and political crises through which Germany struggled.

What are the implications from the lessons of Germany for the problem of anti-Semitism in the United States today? Reasoning by analogy
from one political-cultural setting to another is not without risk. Especially important is the difference in class structure of the United States
from what it was—and seems still to be—in Germany. Class structure
in Germany was relatively frozen and rigid, and upward mobility severely
limited. Whereas the term "class" when used in the United States re-

fers largely to economic divisions, class—almost the synonym of *Stand* —in Germany connoted status and caste. American class structure has permitted considerable vertical mobility, although such mobility may become far more circumscribed as our economic frontiers become increasingly "stabilized." The United States, despite the arguments of Marxist critics, does not have the solidified class structure—ruled by an old guard—as did pre-Hitler Germany, and hence does not afford the same opportunities for manipulation of masses as obtained in Germany. Nor do there appear to be signs that we are developing a *Mittelstand* ideology. Too, there is our long history of liberalism, of fair play, of championing the little man—despite our frequent and often severe lapses into mythology.

To Paul Massing the tragedy of Germany is personal as well as historical. A fighter against Nazism, he suffered—although a non-Jew—at its hands. Truly remarkable then is the objectivity and dispassion with which he has analyzed the political and social adumbrations of anti-Semitism and the undercurrents of which it was symptomatic; if anything his passion was his desire to be dispassionate. During the time he wrote the book I was close to Massing. I watched him labor, for labor it was, to distill the hundreds of manuscripts, documents, books, which provided the basis for an analysis that is both incisive and timely.

Rehearsal for Destruction, although a historical study, is of today. Surely it gives us a sounder basis for determining our policy toward Germany and the problem of its reeducation. This is not propaganda; it pleads no cause. It is an analysis of political and social movements, of a causative structure which we must understand if we are to deal intelligently with a nation which still cherishes an authoritarian way of life.

SAMUEL H. FLOWERMAN

PREFACE

This study deals with the historical forerunners of Nazi anti-Semitism in imperial Germany, during the period between the emancipation of the German Jews and the outbreak of the first World War. It is hoped that thereby a contribution may be made toward the comprehension of the political developments which eventually culminated in the mass murder of Jews as a national policy. By concentrating on the political aspects of anti-Semitism in Germany, on problems of power, group privileges, and group antagonisms, we also hope to further the understanding of modern anti-Semitism elsewhere.

Political anti-Semitism is not confined to national boundaries; nevertheless, it takes its specific features from a definite national environment. The area to be covered in this case history of political anti-Semitism in imperial Germany is, therefore, necessarily large. It includes political parties, religious and professional organizations, the government and the opposition, individuals and social groups. Treating the subject matter in such a broad setting involves considerable difficulties of selection and evaluation. There is the danger of giving too little and too much. The complex historical picture may easily become distorted if attention is focused on a single one of its features. There was not only anti-Semitism in Germany. Eminent and positive phases of Germany's intellectual, cultural, and even political life were neglected or entirely omitted if they seemed to have no bearing on the specific problem; no attempt has been made to give a comprehensive account of the times. On the other hand, the phenomenon is such that it cannot be detached from the sociopolitical fabric of German life. Understanding German anti-Semitism requires an understanding of German society.

Modern Germany never was able to develop a bourgeois society patterned after the models of Western liberalism. The fact that Germany never made a radical break with its feudal past was the most important single factor that determined the course its history was to take. Long after England and France had achieved national unity, a democratic government, and imperial possessions, long after the middle classes had become the centers of the cultural and economic life of these countries, Germany remained economically backward and politically undeveloped, with its middle classes too weak to take power and remake the nation, as the French and English middle classes had done. Throughout the existence of imperial Germany, the old feudal groups remained at the wheel. In the struggle for the preservation of their position they obtained support from the large prebourgeois strata between the middle classes and labor, which German sociology usually refers to as the Old *Mittelstand*.[1] The old ruling powers and the *Mittelstand* shared an antipathy to the kind of liberalism sponsored by the middle classes, and all these strata combined shared the fear of rising labor. Anti-Semitism became part of the ensuing sociopolitical configuration.

In the history of anti-Semitism in Germany, therefore, elements of reaction, in the conventional sense of the word, are curiously intermingled with elements of social rebellion. The nationalistic glorification of the German past and the repudiation of "acquisitive" Western society,[2] often stigmatized as Jewish, are linked with anti-Semitism as a manifestation of social protest. As early as the period of the Prussian "Wars of Liberation" against Napoleon, hatred of the Jews was coupled with ideals of liberty and freedom. The democratic revolution of 1848 again witnessed a recrudescence of popular anti-Semitism.[3] A leaflet which circulated at that time in Baden proclaimed, as the goals of the revolution, the annihilation of the aristocracy; the expulsion of the Jews from Germany; the deposal of all kings, dukes, and princes; and the murder of all government officials. It declared that "Germany must become a free state like America."[4] Not infrequently, the leveling of castles and the looting of Jewish homes took place together. In the 1880's, a social reformer organized the Hessian peasants on the basis of anti-Semitism and rural cooperatives, and in the 1890's, anti-Semitic agitators carried the fight against the landed aristocracy into the *Junkers'* own territory.

The dual nature of anti-Semitism as a political tool and as a confused expression of social protest may account for some of the popular misconceptions about its role in modern German history. The ruling groups did not use the tool incessantly. There were periods when they, and with them the majority of the German people, looked upon Jew-baiting as irresponsible and uncouth and expressed their protest against the persecution of Jews in other European countries. In the two decades prior to World War I, organized anti-Semitism was on the decline in Germany. The memory of these years has favored the erroneous belief that German anti-Semitism was negligible prior to the rise of the Nazi movement. The fact is that there were movements in Germany which made the fight against Jews the mainstay of their activity long before Hitler rose to power. Measured in terms of the number of their adherents, organizational strength, or political representation, the pre-Hitler anti-Semites never achieved the status of major political parties. But their significance cannot be judged by such criteria alone. They kept alive and disseminated anti-Semitism throughout German culture. They formulated the racist ideology long before the Nazis came into existence and helped pave the way for a political alliance of social forces that proved fatal to the German Republic and disastrous to the world.

That anti-Semitism was at times so unmistakably a manifestation of social protest, led to still another fallacious evaluation of its eventual function. As late as the first decade of the twentieth century, liberal historians and socialist writers were convinced that anti-Semitic agitation could not help but awaken the political interests of dormant social groups which, once they had been aroused to political thinking, would soon join the forces of progress. The impact of recent history should have dispelled the last remnants of such illusions.

However, the pendulum may again have swung too far. The events of the last decade have encouraged the belief that Germany was a unique case. It certainly was. But we would take Nazi theories of the German *Volksgeist* more seriously than the Nazis did themselves were we to attribute anti-Semitism to an innate German character. The Nazis found the "indigenous" product sufficiently exportable.

Just as an individual's anti-Semitism may have most complex psychological functions, political anti-Semitism can serve in a multitude of conflict situations. History shows how it was, at one time or other, used by clerical feudal interests against secular liberalism; by governments against the opposition; by reaction against labor; by imperialist forces against the peoples of coveted territories; by nationalistic resistance against foreign intervention. But history also shows the forces which resisted it and the circumstances which hindered its growth. Any fruitful analysis of the phenomenon, therefore, must be concrete and sensitive to its varied and often contradictory manifestations.

I wrote the present book as a member of the Institute of Social Research, New York, and I am deeply indebted to the Institute's director, Dr. Max Horkheimer, who first conceived of it and advised me throughout the period of writing. Other members of the Institute, Dr. Leo Lowenthal, Dr. Frederick Pollock, Dr. Felix J. Weil, and Dr. Karl A. Wittfogel, read the manuscript at various stages of completion, and I have freely drawn on their knowledge and experience. Dr. A. R. L. Gurland helped me greatly with his severe and constructive criticism. It is with a particular feeling of obligation that I thank Mr. George Fuchs for his untiring assistance. His knowledge of German society and politics and his passion for understanding the development of Germany's recent history have been a constant source of inspiration.

To Dr. John Slawson, Executive Vice-President of the American Jewish Committee, and to Dr. Samuel H. Flowerman, Director of the Committee's Scientific Department, I am thankful for having shown much patience with an author's procrastination.

I am anxious to express my gratitude also to Mrs. Lore Kapp and Miss Nina Rubinstein for assisting me in research work, and to Mrs. Edith Kriss for preparing the manuscript.

Messrs. Herbert and William Poster edited the manuscript. Mr. John I. Shields made the Index. Mr. Heinz Norden translated Documents I-XI and Miss Florella Haas of the American Jewish Committee Document XII. I want to thank them all for their assistance.

PAUL W. MASSING

Rutgers University
New Brunswick, New Jersey
September 15, 1949

PART ONE

Anti-Semitism in Bismarck's Reich

CHAPTER I

THE LIBERAL ERA (1871–1878)

In Germany, as in other European countries, the fight for Jewish emancipation was part of the greater conflict between the old feudal powers and the rising middle class. The gains and setbacks in the Jews' struggle for civil equality run parallel with the fortunes of German liberalism in its fight for democracy and national unification. The final emancipation law was not passed until 1869. But well before that time, Germany, on her way toward urbanization and industrialization, offered Jews economic, social, and cultural advantages which they did not find in eastern and southeastern European countries. Between 1816 and 1848, from the end of the Napoleonic Wars to the revolution, the Jewish population increased from 300,000 to 400,000. Jewish names were prominent in trading and banking as well as in literature and politics. When Germany's first national parliament, the National Assembly, convened in Frankfurt am Main in May, 1848, four of its members were Jews,[1] among them its vice-president Gabriel Riesser, a leader in the fight for Jewish rights and a democratic Germany. In the period of political reaction that followed the defeat of the revolution, the legal rights of Jews again were curtailed in practically all German states. The counterrevolution, however, did not entirely erase the changes which the revolution had introduced, nor did it forever suppress the aspirations that had been voiced in 1848. Economically and politically, the forces that stood for German unification and a liberalized regime were too strong to be ignored.

Bismarck's plan of unifying Germany under the king of Prussia called for political concessions and guarantees. The statesman had to overcome age-old suspicions and grievances against orthodox Protestant, semi-absolutistic, feudal Prussia. The Southern Catholics, the Hanoverians —"Prussians by annexation"—the Western liberals demanded protection against encroachments of the state. Without granting equality before the law and the right to participate in the government Bismarck could not hope to bring together the disparate members of the nation.

It was in the train of the necessary concessions to liberalism that Germany's Jews achieved the status of equal citizenship. On July 3, 1869,

3

all Jews within the territories of the North German Federation were pronounced free of all civic restrictions. The law, promulgated by the king of Prussia and countersigned by Bismarck, read:

All still existing limitations of civil and civic rights based on differences of religious creed are hereby abolished. Particularly the right to participate in municipal and state government, and to hold public office shall not be dependent on religious creed.

Of the southern German states, Baden had rescinded the last restrictions on Jewish civil rights in 1862, and Württemberg in 1864. The Jews of Bavaria received equal civil status when Bavaria joined the North German Federation during the Franco-German War (1870–71).

The historical circumstances of the emancipation had a lasting influence on the position of the Jews in German society. The various dynasties, Protestant orthodoxy, and the Prussian aristocracy had yielded to political pressure when they granted Jews equal rights as citizens but they expected gratitude and obedience for what appeared to them as an act of pure generosity. The bitterness of their later accusations against liberal Jews was of the kind a benefactor feels toward an ingrate. Moreover, as the emancipation had not resulted from a revolutionary political and social change, it retained the character of a government grant. The application of the emancipation law revealed the nature of its origin. In Prussia, for example, the government, so as not to offend feudal tradition, refrained from opening civil service careers to Jewish applicants. Jews were readily admitted to the bar but rarely to judgeship; to positions in the elementary schools but infrequently in the academic world. An unwritten law kept them out of the administration, the professional army, and nearly all offices of public authority unless they documented by baptism their willingness to surrender their religious identity.

Despite these limitations, political emancipation opened new avenues to German Jews. In politics and the arts, in journalism and science, as lawyers, bankers, businessmen, and writers, Jews took their place in public life. It was a baptized Jew, Eduard Simson, who at Versailles, as President of the North German Reichstag, presented the crown of the Kaiser to the king of Prussia. Two outstanding liberal parliamentarians and supporters of Bismarck in his efforts to unify and consolidate the Reich were Jews—Ludwig Bamberger and Eduard Lasker. Bismarck's personal financial adviser, who had helped finance the war against Austria in 1866, was a Jewish banker, Gerson von Bleichröder. Even a historian as skeptical of the possibilities of Jewish assimilation as Dubnow[2] comments favorably upon the circumstances under which German Jews lived during these years:

After the consolidation of the Reich, it appeared as if the specter of the Jewish question had once and for all been driven out of the united Germany. This was the time when Jews found access to the highest German circles and secured a firm position in all spheres of economic life. Jewish capital had a leading part in railroad building, in the construction of industrial plants and the organization of gigantic commercial enterprises. The Jewish intelligentsia asserted itself in the free professions as well as in those government services which were not closed to Jews.

Jews made these gains at a time of economic and national buoyancy. Rapid and reckless business expansion seemed to justify the claim that unfettered capitalism would ultimately work in the interest of all, even its temporary victims. The legal and technical instrumentalities required by liberal capitalism were created in quick succession. The industrial law of 1869 (Gewerbeordnung) had already established the principle of freedom of trade. The new stock corporation law of 1870 (Aktiennovelle) abolished the system of strict regulations which had hampered the development of joint stock companies. The introduction of the gold standard (Reichsmünzgesetze of 1871 and 1873) encouraged German business to go after a larger share of the world market.

The optimism of German entrepreneurs, already inflated because of the extraordinary advances in the coal, iron, and chemical industries, in railroad building, banking, and foreign trade, knew no bounds after the successful war with France. The unexpectedly quick payment of the French war reparations totaling five billion gold francs added to the prevailing confidence of the nation and especially of the middle class. From 1866 to 1873, industrial consumption of pig iron more than doubled. During 1872 more than twice as many stock companies were founded in Prussia as had been organized during the entire period from 1790 to 1867, among them 49 banks and 61 chemical plants. In 1871 the Deutsche Bank was established and in 1873 the Dresdener Bank.

It was the heyday of free enterprise in Germany. New economic possibilities multiplied generating a feverish desire to exploit them and get rich by the quickest rather than the soundest methods. Financial speculation was frantic and unrestrained and Germans of all classes plunged heavily on the stock market.[3] The economic and political ideology of the period was supplied by the two liberal parties, the Progress Party (Fortschrittspartei) and the National Liberal Party (Nationalliberale Partei).[4] The latter was the strongest party in the Reichstag and constituted Bismarck's most reliable ally.

In 1873 a world-wide depression set in which struck this eager, striving, speculating Reich as if with lightning. A financial crash came first and many quickly acquired fortunes were wiped out along with a host of small, painfully accumulated savings. The economic debacle that followed developed into one of the most prolonged and disastrous depressions in German history.[5] In the six ensuing years of economic disorder, the prestige and chances of German liberalism—never too good because of the country's belated economic and confused political development—were seriously if not fatally impaired. The position of the Jews in Germany was also immediately affected. Liberalism as a whole was placed on trial and the very name of "liberal" acquired a distinctly opprobrious connotation. To the enemies of the new era, liberalism was identified with the Progress Party and the National Liberal Party, both stigmatized as "Jewish."

At this juncture in German history, the two strongest political opponents of Bismarck's Reich policy were the Old Conservatives[6] and the Catholic Center Party.[7] The former felt their semifeudal powers to be threatened by the reforms which the Chancellor had undertaken for the sake of national unification. Against the Catholic hierarchy, Bismarck had been waging a determined war, seeking to establish the authority of the state over the church and abolishing many of its traditional privileges. Both these parties cast about for support in their struggle. It was only natural that they should turn to those social groups, the members of which had suffered most in the recent catastrophe and had, indeed, already begun to air their disillusionment and grievances against Bismarck and "Jewish liberalism."

One of the first articulate voices of discontent was that of Wilhelm Marr, a journalist who, at the beginning of the depression, published a pamphlet entitled *Der Sieg des Judentums über das Germanentum* (Jewry's Victory Over Teutonism).[8] It was not Marr's first venture of this kind. Ten years before, "aroused by the consequences of Jewish emancipation,"[9] he had published his first anti-Semitic pamphlet, *Judenspiegel*[10] which apparently had not attracted much attention. This time, he decided not to repeat the mistake he thought he had previously made of entering into polemics against Jewry. "My polemics were anachronistic; they came many centuries too late."[11]

Marr's pamphlet, often mentioned but seldom analyzed, is invaluable for the study of both the history of German anti-Semitism and modern fascist agitation in general. It is an unusual document and had a sensational effect. To begin with, Marr refrained from attacking the Jewish religion and professed himself as enlightened with respect to the function of all religion. "It is human nature to involve Providence and religion every time people want to commit stupidities or infamies. Men have rarely strangled each other in wars without first appealing to their respective gods and inflicting upon them the honor of becoming their

allies. In the same way God and religion had to be dragged in whenever
Jews were persecuted. . . ." He finds it "idiotic" to saddle the Jews with
the responsibility for Christ's crucifixion, "a performance staged, as we
know, by the Roman authorities which yielded in a cowardly fashion
to the howling mob of Jerusalem." He declares himself for "the unconditional defense of the Jews against all 'religious' persecution."

No less remarkable is his characterization of the Jewish people.
"Highly gifted and talented," "tough," "of admirable endurance and
resilience," are the attributes he bestows on them. He borrows arguments
from liberal defense and Jewish self-defense to explain the status and
economic role of the Jews in the Middle Ages. "Officially suppressed
from above, they found material compensation in their dealings with
the lower classes. The people were not permitted to grumble against
the exploiters on top, who used Jewry as their go-between." Popular
hatred, therefore, turned against the Jews, he writes in full acceptance
of the scapegoat theory. "The 'big shots' were by no means inconven-
ienced by occasional outbreaks of Jew-baiting. It perpetuated the Jews'
dependence and made them willing to go on with their job as middlemen. Besides, it stifled their will to demand, as 'brokerage,' the emancipation of their people." Marr seems to reach the highest degree of
objectivity when discussing the merits of the charge that Jews are revolutionaries. Of course they are, he argues, but "who wants to blame
them for greeting joyously the revolutions of 1789 and 1848 and eagerly
taking part in them? 'Jews, Poles, and literati,' were the conservative
catchwords in 1848. Why naturally. Three oppressed groups: The fortunate and contented of this earth don't revolt!"

Dismissing the complaints usually raised by anti-Semites, bowing to
the fortitude and genius of the Jewish group, Marr redefines the nature
of the "Jewish question" and puts it in a new perspective. He wants to
destroy an old and misleading stereotype. The Jews are not a small and
weak group, they are a world power! They are much stronger than the
Germans! The display of fairness and generosity in Marr's appraisal of
Jewish virtues serves to mould the new image of the Jews as a most
formidable opponent. Due to their racial qualities, he claims, the Jews
"triumphantly resisted the occidental world for 1,800 years," "rose in the
nineteenth century to the position of the first major power in the West,"
and have now in Germany become "the sociopolitical dictator despite
having been politically persecuted for centuries and without once resort-
ing to force." To be faced by an opponent of such caliber is a matter of
life and death. In such a fight, Marr thinks, it is altogether useless to
raise the question of guilt. Historical events once threw the Jews into
the Western world where they encountered "an element that was as alien

to them as they were to this element." Therefore don't hate individual Jews, he admonishes. His anti-Semitism is totalitarian. The Jewish group is attacked; not some of its members. The Jews, he insists, are a racially determined people; they cannot change and cannot be changed. Living with them on an equal footing is impossible because of their superior qualities. The alternatives being only "we or they," both sides are forced to use all means at their disposal. Fate has willed that Jews and Teutons, "like gladiators of cultural history," should meet face to face in the arena. The individual on either side has no choice but to follow his group in attack and defense. Acting under the orders of fate he cannot be held to account for his deeds.

The hour is late, Marr writes. The Germanic state is in rapid disintegration, the Germans' morale is sapped. They no longer have the physical and intellectual powers it would take to "de-Judaize" themselves. With an air of resignation characteristic of the pamphlet's spirit and style, he concedes the defeat of the Teutons. "Of tougher and stronger fiber than we, you [Jews] remained the victor in this peoples' war which you fought by peaceful means while we massacred and burnt you but did not possess the ethical strength to confine you to yourselves and to intercourse among yourselves." Is everything lost then? Probably, Marr says. But he manages to leave a few possibilities open in this constricted scheme of historical tragedy and doom.[12] A last desperate European counterattack against Jewry might yet take place, possibly led by Russia.[13] In Germany, a "catastrophe," an "explosion" is likely to happen before the Teutonic peoples capitulate. "Passionate popular indignation" is rising against the "Semitic aliens" and "Judaization of society."[14] The general pogrom, unavoidable and uncontrollable, is announced.

The evidence which Marr offers to substantiate his sweeping conclusions and gloomy predictions transfers us abruptly from the realm of historical destiny to the desk of a frustrated journalist. The big press, the liberal newspapers do not publish Marr. The complaint that the press is in Jewish hands and discriminates against all who are not allied with "Jewish liberalism" is recurrent and always the basis of the most dire prophecies.[15] Jewish monopoly of the press, "the result of the Thirty-Years War which Jewry officially has been waging against us ever since 1848," makes it impossible to write and to participate in Germany's political life. In the "New Palestine" that is Bismarck's Reich, "alien domination" has been legally recognized with the emancipation act. Its agent is National Liberalism, the party to which Jews flocked "because it was furthest advanced in the spirit of Judaization, in the philosophy of expediency and pragmatism, in a general lack of principles." Jews have "corrupted all standards, have banned all idealism from society, dominate commerce, push themselves ever more into state services, rule the theater, form a social and political phalanx . . . have degraded talent to glittering virtuosity, have made procuring advertisement (*die Kupplerin Reklame*) the goddess of public opinion and rule today." Marr's assault upon the founder and leader of this Judaized Reich is oblique and leaves open the possibility of a reconciliation. "As German and fellow-vanquished, it is not up to me to criticize the domestic statesmanship of Prince Bismarck. But if I were a *Jew* I would say: 'The Prince has understood his time as no statesman before him. He has the clear historical vision of a bankrupt and dying Germanic people and looks for forces of greater vitality.'" "What really," he continues, "could such men mean to him as we who cannot be the 'Reich's friends' any more because we no longer have a *German* Reich and who ask the Prince for nothing more than a modest space for a small quiet community which has not yet lost all ideals."

Occupational and political frustrations are cumulatively expressed in the closing sentences of the pamphlet. "What are we to do?" Marr asks. "Shall we throw ourselves into the arms of Rome? Shall we go 'to Canossa' and lay at the Pope's feet all our scientific achievements? That would be a harder journey than Luther's to Worms! Shall we join ranks with the Protestant bigots and hypocritically indulge in religious hatred? Just as impossible. The 'progressive' press is closed to us because you [Jews] have succeeded in monopolizing it. Indeed, sacred liberty itself has become a Jewish monopoly and must abide by sociopolitical Jewish dogmas. . . . Let us submit to the inevitable if we are unable to change it. Its name is: *FINIS GERMANIAE*."

Reliable biographical data on this forerunner of German racial anti-Semitism are scanty.* A scarcity of information on the life stories of leading anti-Semites, on their character and personality confronts us again and again. The fact is worth noting although the lack of such data does not seriously impede the progress of the present study. These individuals interest us primarily as representatives of social groups. The intensity of the sting of failure in their personal life, the psychological mechanisms set in motion for the sake of ego defense certainly are relevant factors if we ask why X and not Y rose to prominence in the anti-Semitic movement. Our problem, however, is broader; it is set by the historical facts that individual frustration, insecurity, resentment, and aggression found social expression in political anti-Semitism at certain times rather than others; that specific social groups were attracted more strongly than others by anti-Semitic agitation; that within the

* See reference 8.

affected groups diversified character and personality types were represented. In Marr's case, his charge of having been maneuvered out of
German journalism for the benefit of Jewish competitors might or might
not have been true. That he lost his job was perhaps due to greater requirements which the flourishing liberal press demanded of newspapermen. But it is· possible that he may really have become the victim of
office intrigue. In any case, Marr's violent outburst would have appeared paranoic and would have probably passed unnoticed had there not
been similar experiences too frequent in number and too unusual to be
written off as "normal" casualties in the competitive routine. Instead of
disappearing into oblivion, his pamphlet went through twelve editions
between 1873 and 1879 and created a sensation.

Marr's arguments permit us to trace the contours of the groups for
whom he speaks. He declares himself unwilling to sacrifice the achievements of modern science to the dogmas of Catholic religion; and he
has, allegedly, no taste for Protestant bigotry. He counts himself as one
of the "former radicals" now driven into the camp of forces which
"Judaized 'liberal' Germany" likes to call "reactionary."[16] The Social
Democratic Party appears to him as "the coarse, brutal but completely
blind protest against materialistic Judaization of society";[17] Germany, in
his opinion, was particularly defenseless against Jewish invasion because
"there was in the [various] Germanic states no developed sense of a
German nationality, let alone German national pride." Marr thus comes
originally neither from Catholicism nor Protestant conservatism, nor
from socialist labor. As a radical who once longed for a great German
nation but is now looking to the opponents of the current Reich policy
for protection against the powers of money, his development and behavior was typical of the members of disillusioned and uprooted *Mittelstand* groups in search of new alliances. At once boasting of their cultural and moral values and threatening to discard them as luxuries in
the venal world of "Jewish liberalism," these groups now offered themselves on the political market places. "Whoever helps us can have us."[18]

Marr's *Sieg des Judentums über das Germanentum* had hardly fired
the opening gun when a broader attack followed. In 1874, *Die Gartenlaube,* a literary magazine for the *Mittelstand,* published a series of anti-
Semitic articles on "The Stock Exchange and Speculation Fraud in Berlin." The articles, written by Otto Glagau,[19] expressed even more clearly
than Marr's pamphlet the grievances of groups whose livelihood and
status were in jeopardy—artisans, small entrepreneurs and merchants,
petty officials, and peasants. Glagau blamed Jewish legislators, particularly Lasker and Bamberger, for the passage of laws which favored
trade, the stock exchange, and big business to the detriment of handi-

craft and agriculture. His views on Jews, liberalism, Manchester theory, political parties, the modern bourgeoisie, and the role of the superior statesman likewise show extraordinary similarities to later Nazi doctrines. There is the same biting critique of liberal hypocrisy and conservative narrow-mindedness, the courting of industrial workers, the demand for social reforms—typical ingredients of fascist propaganda some fifty years later. There is even the unmistakably Marxist terminology, later sported by "left-wing" Nazis, in Glagau's description of the workings of the capitalist system.

Under the rule of economic liberalism, industrious and prosperous handicraft cannot survive; it is mercilessly uprooted by big industry; and in the same way as the big trader squeezes out the small one, the peasantry disappears more and more and is devoured by the large estates. In the new German Reich as in the Rome of antiquity, the healthy middle class disintegrates, and a destitute proletariat grows like an avalanche.[20]

Manchesterism is the King Midas doctrine of money, it wants to transform everything into money—the soil, labor and human ability; it glorifies egoism, and rejects all sense of solidarity, humanity and all ethical principles. It preaches crass materialism. Its motto is the notorious "laissez faire et passer.". . . The foremost demand of Manchesterism is therefore unrestricted freedom of trade and movement. Through this it believes it has done everything possible for the worker, but, as the latter has understood, this is only the freedom to choose the occupation and the place where he may starve to death. This very freedom to move and to trade provides the industrialist with an unending stream of cheap hands, by depopulating the countryside and overcrowding the cities.[21]

Jewry is applied Manchesterism in the extreme. It knows nothing any more but trade, and of that merely haggling and usury. It does not work but makes others work for it, it haggles and speculates with the manual and mental products of others. Its center is the stock exchange. . . . As an alien tribe it fastens itself on the German people and sucks their marrow. The social question is essentially the Jewish question; everything else is swindle.[22]

The social groups which Glagau defended had not as yet been able to build up an independent political organization which would effectively protect their interests. The attempts made by artisans during and after the revolution of 1848 were sporadic and unsuccessful. Glagau paid tribute to what he called the socialistic agitation they had carried on and expressed regret that, unlike the workers, they had not produced an organization of their own. The difficulty lower middle-class groups have in banding together for effective political action is a common phenomenon. It stems from their position between capital and labor as

well as from the heterogeneous socioeconomic interests prevailing within
the various segments of the lower middle class itself. These groups are
inclined, therefore, to look for a leader who does not seem to depend
on the support of established political parties. In times of acute tension
their political ideal is Bonapartism. The longing for the strong man, for
the "honest broker," who is above party politics, and for the "unpolitical"
state, is at the core of German lower middle-class politics from Bismarck
to Hitler. Not to have recognized the political potential of these groups
was German society's disaster. Liberalism had nothing to offer them but
the wisdom of the successful competitor; conservatism nothing but praise
of their moral virtues; socialism wrote them off the books as doomed by
the laws of capitalism. It took National Socialism to organize them for
action.

The economic philosophy of National Socialism, however, had long
been prepared. The concept of "predatory capital," for instance, that
figured so prominently in early Nazi economic theory, was a common
property of the anti-Semitic writers of the 1870's.* Otto Glagau, spokesman of the *Mittelstand*, applied it. Adolf Stoecker, exponent of Christian
Social anti-Semitism, a few years later took pride in the fact that he
warred only against "mobile capital," "stock-exchange capital." "Marx
and Lassalle," he said, "looked for the roots of the [social] problem not
in the direction of the stock-exchange, but of industrial production; they
made the industrialists responsible for all social ills and directed the
workers' wrath toward them. Our movement corrects this. We show the
people that the roots of their plight are in the power of money, in the
mercenary spirit of the stock-exchange."[23]

A stable income and a "just return for honest work" were at all times
the economic ideals of the German urban and rural *Mittelstand*. These
groups feared and hated the dynamism of capitalist economy, its mobility and speculative aspect. To them, the exchange of commodities and
money, wherein capital appears in its most abstract and anonymous form,
symbolized the immoral, usurious, and uncanny character of the system, with high finance its most sinister agency. The further removed
they were from any concrete knowledge of the workings of finance and
from personal contact with its world, the more mysterious and threatening it appeared.[24] This whole sphere of activity they saw as eminently
Jewish. The stereotype of the Jewish middleman, banker, and international financier—"swindlers all"—was certainly nurtured by the recollec-
tion of medieval Jewish money practice and the traditionally high proportion of Jews in trade and commerce. But the stereotype's longevity is

* Cf. Liebermann von Sonnenberg's definition of "useful" and "harmful" capital,
Document No. I.

likely to be related also to real economic conflicts which are distortedly expressed by the distinction between financial, that is "Jewish," and industrial-agrarian, that is "German" capital. The distinction was so readily accepted by lower middle-class groups because it provided them with a social critique that did not touch the foundation of the given order, private property, nor involve conflicting loyalties. Anti-Semitic agitators, therefore, found it most useful. This kind of anticapitalism did not alienate the anti-Semites' followers from the ruling groups. On the contrary, it made for the pseudo solidarity of the Christian state, and later for the myth of the racial community. How great the tactical need for such a departmentalizing of capitalism was may be judged by Hitler's reaction when he first heard Gottfried Feder speak on "Breaking the Slavery of Interest." "I knew at once," he wrote, "that this was a theoretical truth which must be of immense importance for the future of the German people. Sharp separation of finance capital from the national economy made it possible to oppose the internationalization of German economy without threatening the whole foundation of independent national self-preservation in the process of fighting against capital."[25]

The attacks upon "Jewish" financial swindles which were among the earliest reactions to the big crash of 1873 must be placed in this broad economic and ideological contest. It made little difference that Lasker, the liberal leader, in speeches in the Prussian Diet on January 14 and February 7, 1873, and in the Reichstag on April 4, 1873, had sounded a warning and disclosed that several Conservative members had given their support to dubious stock transactions. Among those he named was Geheimrat Hermann Wagener, a leader of the group behind the ultra-conservative newspaper, the *Kreuzzeitung*,[26] who became one of Adolf Stoecker's friends and a sponsor of the anti-Semitic Christian Social Party. Far from serving to absolve the Jewish group from the charge of having brought about the general collapse of business, Lasker's speeches were construed as a Jewish attempt to saddle the Conservatives with the responsibility. In the social configuration of the time, no participation of Conservatives in speculative swindles could make the era appear as a child of conservatism. With its new laws and business morals, enhanced social polarization, and political and religious tensions, this was an era of bourgeois progress, and it coincided with obvious gains in the status of the Jewish group. In this atmosphere the ludicrous assertions of Glagau and others that according to statistics ninety per cent of the speculators were Jewish, were gladly believed.

The anti-Semitism of men like Marr and Glagau—the list of agitators could be continued without much gain to the analysis—registered as an expression of private opinion which the public mind did not associate with specific organizations. The turn came in 1875. Anti-Semitism became a political issue, a matter of high strategy, when it was taken up by two politically defined newspapers, the *Kreuzzeitung*, which was the voice of orthodox Prussian Protestantism and conservatism, and *Germania*, the organ of the Catholic Center Party.

In a series of articles,[27] the *Kreuzzeitung* violently attacked the "pathetic mess of new German economic policies," for which it blamed men in Bismarck's confidence, among them his financial adviser, Bleichröder. The paper charged that just as this "governing banker" was a Jew, Bismarck's whole National Liberal era amounted to nothing but a banker's policy made for and by Jews. It contended that "fellow citizens of Semitic race" dominated the National Liberals through Lasker and Bamberger; that through the National Liberals they controlled the legislature; and that they ruled the German people through the National Liberal press. The threat was explicit and pointed. The position of Jews in German public life, the Conservative paper announced, would not remain unchanged once the Christian German people came to realize the nature of the "Jew-policy" carried on by the politically dominant groups.

In the summer of 1875 the leading Catholic paper, *Germania*, took over and reinforced the *Kreuzzeitung* accusations. The anti-Semitic articles in *Germania*[28] excelled in skillful demagogy. The paper needled Bismarck by reprinting a speech against Jewish emancipation which he had made in the Prussian Diet of 1847.[29] It ransacked the German classics, the writings of Goethe, Herder, Kant, and Fichte, for anti-Jewish statements, a procedure followed decades later in Theodor Fritsch's *Handbuch der Judenfrage*, and perfected by the Nazi Institute for the Study of the Jewish Question. *Germania* drew attention to the occupational distribution of Jews and argued with the aid of statistics that they were meagerly represented in the "productive strata" but were crowded together in "lucrative businesses," where they accumulated wealth at the expense of the Christian population. Attention was called to the "truly stupendous disproportions" in the number of Christian and Jewish pupils in schools of higher learning, an unmistakable hint to apply quota laws. The government's campaign against the Catholic Church, Bismarck's *Kulturkampf*,[30] was interpreted as a Jewish war to take revenge on Rome for having trampled the Jewish people underfoot 1,800 years before, but also as a smokescreen behind which Jewry could go ahead, unmolested, with its job of swindling and exploiting the German people.

Germania's program for an "emancipation of the Christians from the Jews" recommended Christian economic unity,[31] introduced slogans like

"Don't buy from Jews," "Don't borrow from Jews," and advised that savings institutions and credit institutions be organized as a step toward economic liberation from Jewish usury. In retaliation for liberal accusations that the Catholics were unpatriotic, *Germania* charged that during the Franco-German War, Jewish financiers had eagerly subscribed to the war loan of the French government but had remained cool toward the loan of the North German Federation. Moreover, the Catholic organ advanced a theory of anti-Semitism which operated with racial concepts. Hatred and persecution of Jews, it declared, were never caused by religious fanaticism, but were, rather, a protest of the Germanic race against the intrusion of an alien tribe. Catholic publications all over Germany took the cue from *Germania*, and the anti-Semitic press campaign which followed was interpreted by the editors of that paper as proving "how severely many people have been suffering under the pressure of the Jews."

After the concerted attack of the leading Conservative and Catholic papers had ceased, the fight was kept going by a group known as "the Anti-Chancellor League," which brought together Catholics and Conservatives, included many powerful aristocrats, and enjoyed the patronage of the Imperial Court. They put out a newspaper, sarcastically called the *Deutsche Eisenbahnzeitung* (railroad building was one of the *Gründer* industries in which fortunes were made and lost), and published a number of books[32] and pamphlets most of which were taken up with violent attacks against Bismarck and the Jews. The *Eisenbahnzeitung* referred sardonically to the Jews as Bismarck's "warriors for culture" and claimed that, following the age-old strategy of divide and rule, the Jews were making a bid for power by deliberately provoking a struggle against the Catholics. The Jewish question, the paper held, was a question of life and death for the German people and could be solved only after Bismarck and his Jewish system of government had been ousted.[33]

There were cultural as well as political motives for this startling Conservative-Catholic alliance. Bismarck had started the *Kulturkampf* in order to curb the political power of Catholicism in which he saw a danger to the Reich. The details of the bitter, drawn-out conflict are not relevant here but an acquaintance with its broad features is essential for an understanding of the situation.

The Catholic Center Party, founded in 1870, championed the rights of the Church against the State, and the interests of the individual member states against the Reich. Bismarck had called this new party "a mobilization against the state," that is, against his Reich which was based on the hegemony of the Protestant-Prussian monarchy. The Chancellor and the National Liberals regarded political Catholicism as the center of the *grossdeutsche*, pro-Austrian, anti-Prussian opposition against Bismarck's *kleindeutsche* solution of Germany's unification. Nationalist suspicion of political Catholicism was enhanced by the fact that the leader of the Catholic Center, Ludwig Windthorst, was a loyal friend of the king of Hanover whom Bismarck had dethroned after the war with Austria in 1866, and whose territory he had incorporated into the State of Prussia. It was for political rather than religious considerations that Bismarck engaged in the *Kulturkampf*. He introduced a number of bills, passed by both the Prussian Diet and the Reichstag, which transferred school supervision from the clergy to the government; outlawed the Jesuits and other religious orders; gave the government decisive influence over the appointment and dismissal of the Catholic hierarchy in Germany; placed Catholic seminaries under state authority; made civil marriage mandatory and established the marriage registrar's office. In Prussia, the constitutional privileges of the churches were revoked. Although directed against the Catholic Church, the *Kulturkampf* was taken by many Conservatives as a dangerous general advance of secular authority and as an indirect assault on one of the bulwarks of old Prussianism, the Protestant Church.

Protestant orthodoxy was built into the structure of the monarchic Prussian State. The authoritarian concepts of Lutheran theology found a home in the authoritarian principles of Prussian power. From the end of the eighteenth century on, under the shadow of the French revolution, the bonds between Church and State had been strengthened in many continental nations. Since the years of Prussia's wars against Napoleon I, when the divine rights of monarchy and ecclesiastic orthodoxy had been in common jeopardy, State and Church had entered into a close alliance. The Church's authority was to ensure the subject's obedience toward the State; in turn, Protestant orthodoxy relied on the authority of the State to suppress liberal tendencies in ecclesiastic as well as secular matters. Bourgeois movements and later socialist movements drew their strength from opposing State religion and a philosophy of government which taught that God was the source of monarchic sovereignty and that the existing social hierarchy was society's natural order.[34] When Bismarck, with the help of the liberal bourgeoisie, whittled down the power of the Catholic Church in the Reich, it was natural that Prussian Protestant orthodoxy should have felt itself under attack. The *Kulturkampf* evolved into a struggle between clerical and secular authority in general.

Antagonism to Bismarck's policies alone, however, could hardly have been the immediate reason for the concerted Conservative-Catholic attack on the Jews. In 1875, when the anti-Semitic campaign began, the *Kulturkampf* had been going on for four years. Nor could it have been generated spontaneously by the economic collapse. The shock of the big crash had come almost two years before. The stored-up aggressions seemed to have been set free by specific political events and political considerations.

The elections of January, 1874, gave an overwhelming victory to the National Liberals, "the party of Bismarck and the Jews." The Conservatives were the chief losers. Their percentage of the total vote declined from fourteen to seven; the number of their seats in the Reichstag from 57 to 22. The Catholic Center, on the other hand, withstood the *Kulturkampf* agitation and even increased the number of its representatives in the Reichstag from 70 to 91. Catholicism was now the only major political force with which the decimated Old Conservatives could align themselves. The initiative in the attack upon "Jewish liberalism" came from them; the anti-Semitic articles of the *Kreuzzeitung* preceded those of *Germania*. Here, for the first time in the history of the modern Reich, the "small but mighty party," as the Conservatives liked to call themselves, gave notice that it would have recourse to every political expedient to preserve its traditional prerogatives.

The motivations that prompted the Catholic Center Party to follow suit in the anti-Semitic campaign are somewhat more complex. As the party of a denominational minority, it could not hope, as the Conservatives did, to tap the large *Mittelstand* vote. But it could and did anticipate indirect political benefits from its onslaught against "Jews and Liberals." By weakening the National Liberals, Bismarck's most powerful supporters in the Reichstag, the Catholics could, to some extent, undermine the Chancellor's *Kulturkampf*. Moreover, Catholic Center influence in the Reichstag was contingent on its ability to form coalitions with either the Right or Left as long as either was unable to form a stable majority by itself. Despite the fact that the Catholics had increased the number of their seats in the Reichstag, the 1874 elections had seriously weakened their position by making the Left strong enough to dispense with their support. It was unquestionably to the interest of the Catholic Center to restore a more even balance by an alliance with the now outnumbered Right.

Such practical considerations were in all likelihood influential in their decision to participate in the anti-Semitic campaign. Nevertheless, the degree of hostility, the sheer vehemence of the *Germania* articles, does not seem wholly explicable by these factors alone. The sudden reversal of the position of the two minorities and the exasperation and resentment caused by it must also be taken into account. The Jews, who until recently had been considered as pariahs, members of a second-class group of citizens by law, were now prominent in public life, closely associated with the Chancellor himself and government policy. The Catholics, on the other hand, found themselves harassed officially and attacked from many sides at once. "What a pleasure this *Kulturkampf* is to the Jews!" the Catholic publicist, Constantin Frantz, remarked contemptuously in 1874.[35] "They have every reason in the world to whip it up as much as they can and to participate in it enthusiastically. And one cannot deny they make a really good job of it."

This Catholic vexation with Jews and Liberals was not entirely without cause. The Liberals had willingly taken part in an undemocratic government from the very beginning of the second Reich and had, ever since, basked complacently in the sun of the Chancellor's favor. Prominent Jews, such as E. Lasker, had taken a vigorous part in the parliamentary struggle for the anti-Catholic legislation of 1873. The Berlin liberal press, with which many Jews were associated, had crusaded against Conservative and Catholic "enemies of the Reich," helping to make "ultramontane" one of the most popular epithets of the period, blending, as it did, enlightened liberal opposition to established dogma with nationalistic hostility to an authority seated, "beyond the mountain," in the Vatican.

The Catholic anti-Semitic venture ended abruptly and in peculiar circumstances. A provincial Catholic newspaper, the *Schlesische Volkszeitung*, started reprinting the *Germania* articles but suddenly discontinued the series and published a statement dissociating itself from the content of the articles.[36] It declared hatred of Jews to be irreconcilable with the belief in Christian tolerance. It wondered whether *Germania* had not been duped by the *Kreuzzeitung*, hinted that the author of the *Germania* articles could very well have been Hermann Wagener, an intimate of Bismarck's, and that the articles might have been directly inspired by the Chancellor to lay the groundwork for a change of policy. Whether the *Schlesische Volkszeitung* was right cannot be ascertained. Wawrzinek[37] suspects that the *Germania* articles were written by Joseph Cremer, later a leader and Bismarck's agent in the anti-Semitic Berlin Movement. But officially inspired or not, the articles served their purpose. Two erstwhile political opponents had discovered a mutual enemy. In the anti-Jewish, antiliberal campaign Catholic anti-Prussianism and Protestant-Conservative ultra-Prussianism learned how much they had in common. The community of interests propelled the two major antiliberal forces toward further political cooperation.[38] An alliance was in the making in which Bismarck saw his great opportunity.

In the effort to develop a unified, industrialized German Reich, Bismarck had been compelled to rely on the forces of liberalism because the semifeudal Prussian aristocracy had been unwilling to relinquish any of its privileges. However, in the seventies, it became increasingly plain that he could not continue to govern the Reich with a liberal majority unless he were prepared to face drastic changes in the power structure of the state. From the very beginning of the new Reich, the egalitarian tendencies of trade and industry and the interests of the Prussian aristocracy and monarchy were in sharp conflict. The structure of the state itself contained rather than eliminated these tensions. Germany had been unified under a constitutional, not a parliamentary government. The executive power resided in a cabinet in whose appointment or dismissal the Reichstag, the people's representative body, had no voice. However, the cabinet could not govern against a hostile Reichstag, if and when laws had to be passed. National sovereignty was vested in the *Bundesrat*, the representation of the 25 states, convoked by the Kaiser and presided over by the chancellor. Without the *Bundesrat's* sanction no law could become effective. This government functioned under a constitutional theory which had as its central axiom the belief in the divine right of kings, a belief treated with derision by the sophisticated nineteenth century but essential for the uneasy compromise between the old and new powers upon which the Reich rested.

Throughout his chancellorship it was Bismarck's foremost concern to prevent the constitutional regime from giving way to parliamentary government under liberal and socialist pressure. Universal franchise, the necessary concession to liberalism, made this an ever-present danger and the Chancellor's dependence on the National Liberals rendered it more acute. Their support was not given gratuitously. They pressed for the liberalization of the administrative setup, and for opening up the executive branch, still a monopoly of landed and service nobility. They pursued an economic and social policy which met with growing opposition and made the business of governing more difficult and complicated. It was altogether detrimental to the position of the Chancellor as the "honest broker" between contending interests that he should have to depend on a single party. The nature of his office and the tasks of statesmanship under the circumstances called for the frequent reshuffling of the majority groupings in parliament. Without a realignment of Conservative and Catholic forces, however, only the Liberals could provide the majority he needed.

The social and political tensions of the depression were making Bismarck's course more difficult to maintain, when a new threat appeared. In the mid-seventies the two main organizations of socialist labor merged in the Social Democratic Party. Although in theory the new party was sharply opposed to the tenets of bourgeois liberalism, it functioned politically as the ally of the left-wing Liberals and shared their aspirations toward a parliamentary government. To defend the authoritarian state against the incursions of this powerful combination became Bismarck's most urgent pursuit and his political strategy was now redirected towards weakening the Liberals and suppressing the Socialists.

A program of social legislation and economic protectionism, he hoped, would enable the government to capitalize on the popular discontent caused by the depression. State intervention, he calculated, would embarrass and weaken the liberal champions of free trade. It would strengthen the powers and prestige of the Christian state and cut the ground from under the Social Democrats. To realize this design, however, Bismarck required the cooperation of a friendly Reichstag majority, which, by the very nature of his aims, he could only hope to obtain from the Conservatives and Catholics. A suitably reactionary coalition was rung in by the violent anti-Semitic, antiliberal campaign. That Bismarck himself thereby came in for a measured share of abuse did not blind him to his political needs and opportunities.

CHAPTER II

CONSERVATIVE-CLERICAL REACTION
(1879-1886)

Between 1873 and 1878, five years of economic stagnation and national malaise, a complex sociopolitical reorientation took place in Germany. The hardships of the working classes and their growing disaffection with Church and State became a matter of national concern and "the social question," a convenient label for these phenomena as a whole, became the topic of the hour, the subject of prolonged discussions in the press and pulpit. Reformism was the fashionable creed of the day and demands and proposals were heard on all sides. Inspired by Rudolf Todt, a Protestant parson, the *Zentral-Verein für Sozialreform* called attention to the distress of neglected urban and rural groups and urged the government to alleviate it. Reform organizations of every variety multiplied under such names as the "Tax and Business Reformers" and the "German Industrialists' Central Association for the Betterment and Protection of National Labor." In the academic world, the *Kathedersozialisten*, "socialists of the chair"[1] as they were nicknamed, were the most prominent reform group. Frequently the programs of these movements and organizations were tinged with anti-Semitism.[2]

All this reform activity essentially aimed at restoring the confidence of the working man in the government and at making the position of the lower middle classes more secure. But the response the reformers received in the two main areas of social unrest differed sharply. United by a common revolutionary belief, economically indispensable to the nation, the industrial workers had begun to challenge the existing order with increasing self-confidence and to participate in national life through professional, political, and cultural organizations of their own. They expected to improve their lot only by their own power and did not look for concessions from a state which refused to sponsor full parliamentary government. The discouraged, displaced, and amorphous *Mittelstand* groups, on the other hand, were unaccustomed to rely on themselves and had always been ready to accept the leadership of stronger powers. Earlier in the century, when the bourgeoisie had radically opposed the Christian Conservative state, the *Mittelstand* had rallied to its side and supported the liberal cause. Disappointed in liberalism and under severe economic duress, more and more of their number began to look toward the state for protection and patronage. Without a political organization or a program of its own the *Mittelstand* voiced its confused grievances and claims through a host of spokesmen: priests and professors, quacks and crusaders, embittered journalists and romantic reactionaries. It was a Protestant parson, Adolf Stoecker, who first succeeded in channelizing these diffuse resentments and aspirations, in giving them a name, a direction, and a political organization.

Stoecker himself came from a very modest *Mittelstand* family. His father was a blacksmith who signed up with the army, served as a non-commissioned officer for twenty-seven years and was recompensed with the civil service job of jail warden. He managed to send the son through college and university. "It still moves me to the bottom of my heart when I think of the sacrifices my parents made for it, how they scrimped, how simply they ate and dressed," Stoecker once explained.[3] The youth studied theology, earned his living at first as tutor in aristocratic eastern families, and was, after the usual apprenticeship in a number of small communities, promoted to the position of army chaplain. In Metz, the main city of recently annexed Lorraine, his patriotic fervor caught the eye of the Kaiser's entourage and in 1874 he was called to the Berlin Cathedral.

From early youth Stoecker was fascinated by the old Prussian aristocracy. He yearned to be accepted in high society, to enjoy its trust and emulate its mores. He embodied the *Mittelstand's* desire for authority and a strong state, its deep-rooted aversion to an "open" society. By character and station he was ideally suited to lead the lower middle classes back into the fold of Protestant conservatism. As chaplain of the Imperial Court, his word seemed to have the sanction of the highest authority, and as a devoted patriot[4] his claim to speak for the nation was easily accepted. His close relations with the *Kreuzzeitung* gave him great influence in the most respectable social circles, and his office as head of the Berlin City Mission, a charitable organization of the Protestant Church, brought him in contact with the lower classes. He was a man of strong character, of whom his onetime disciple Hellmut von Gerlach said that one had to hate or love him, that no one could face him with indifference.[5] Within a few years, Stoecker forged a powerful movement out of the social grievances of the *Mittelstand*, hatred of the Social Democratic Party, and fear of "Jewish" capital.

There is no doubt as to the purpose with which Stoecker began his political career in 1878. His original enemy was Marxism. He had been deeply disturbed by the spread of socialist ideas among industrial work-

ers long before he was appointed chaplain to the Imperial Court. As
early as 1869 he had written of labor as "the threatening danger that
moves through our time like a flood between weak dykes."[6] In 1871,
stirred by the events connected with the Paris Commune, he exhorted
the populace of the big cities to have more of the Christian spirit. Socialism was to him "an offspring of materialism, created in the palaces of
atheist wealth," and he set out to defeat the "International of hatred"
through Protestant charity, "the International of love."[7]

A letter[8] Stoecker wrote to Crown Prince Friedrich in 1878 to justify
his social and political agitation gives an excellent insight into his
motives:

. . . . what impelled me was the despair felt for my poor people whom
I saw hurtling toward an abyss, and the love for the souls I wanted to save
. . . . For almost ten years I have been devoting lively and continuous
effort to the study of the social question. In Berlin I became fully aware of
the urgent need of doing something to call the people back from the abyss.
I found that men who stood by the church, and with whom I entertained
friendly relations, nevertheless voted for the Social Democratic Party because
they felt that this party represented the workers' interest. In prayer and
meditation I then made up my mind to walk right into the Social Democratic
den, to take the wild bull by the horns and to wrestle with it. . . . For fifteen
years socialism has been the bait by means of which the workers were
cheated out of their belief and their patriotism. Whoever wants to reach their
hearts, must also speak about social problems.

Stoecker really "took the wild bull by the horns" in a mass meeting
which became as famous in the history of the Berlin Movement as the
first Hitler mass meeting in Munich did for the chroniclers of the Nazi
movement. Throughout the nineteenth century the mass meeting as an
expression and instrument of political will had been the prerogative of
anticonservative forces and regarded as appropriate only to the aspirations of the third, later of the fourth, estate. The idea of a Christian Conservative political meeting in a workers' district was so incongruous that
a sensation was created when posters appeared in North Berlin inviting
the public to attend a meeting for the purpose of establishing the Christian Social Workers' Party. Emil Grüneberg was announced as the main
speaker.

Grüneberg was a former tailor whom the director of the Berlin City
Mission had sent to Stoecker as an apparently reformed Social Democrat.
On the lookout for suitable aides to help him disorganize the Social
Democratic Party, Stoecker gladly took him in, although he had been
apprised of Grüneberg's shady character and criminal record. Accord-
ing to police information, Grüneberg, while a socialist agitator, had so-

licited money in high circles and been expelled from the Social Democratic Party; he had been in jail, once for *lèse majesté* and once for begging. His strained relations with the Seventh Commandment were a
matter of record. Did this deter the chaplain of the Imperial Court from
using Grüneberg? "Without the assistance of a man from the world of
labor I could not have started on the job," Stoecker commented in
retrospect.[9]

The people who came to the *Eiskeller* hall to listen to Grüneberg were
mostly members of the Social Democratic Party. Among them was the
Reichstag representative Johann Most, one of the party's best orators, a
firebrand known for his militant atheism.[10] The Social Democrats immediately took over the meeting but permitted free discussion. Grüneberg's
pious platitudes were received in good humor. The meeting was about to
become the grave rather than the cradle of the Christian Social Workers'
Party when Stoecker took the floor. His speech[11] instantly showed
him to be a demagogue of stature. He first made sure to ingratiate himself with the audience by pointing to his own humble background.
Although he had the high rank of Court Chaplain, he told them, he had
come from the working class and understood its miseries. He dramatically
described the distressing effects of the current depression on workers'
lives. He attacked capitalism, "this system of unlimited competition, of
crassest egotism" which leads "from crisis to crisis." He called for
remedy through social reforms—care for the disabled, restriction on fe-
male labor, the prohibition of Sunday work. Finally, he urged the
workers to join him in a new organization.

I have in mind a peaceful organization of labor and of the workers. Once
this exists people can get together and work in common for that which
has to be done. It is your misfortune, gentlemen, that you only think of
your Social State and scornfully reject the hand extended to you for reform
and help; that you insist on saying "we will not settle for anything less than
the Social State." This way you make enemies of the other social classes,
and hatred spoils everything.

Yes, gentlemen, you hate your fatherland. Your press shockingly reflects
this hatred. That is bad. To hate one's fatherland is like hating one's mother.
Besides, there is no reason why you should do so. Surely, not everything is
as it should be in our country, but we live on earth, not in heaven. The
German Reich of its own free will gave you universal suffrage for the very
reason that it wants you to consult with others peacefully and decide what is
best. You must not abuse this right by aiming at the destruction of your
fatherland. This is unreasonable and ungrateful.

But you also hate Christianity, you hate the gospel of God's mercy. They
teach you not to believe. They teach you atheism and you trust these false
prophets. . . .

A Social Democrat, who became a convert to the new political faith at this meeting, later set down his impressions. The audience, he reported, grew restless as Stoecker spoke, yet, well-disciplined, let him finish what he had to say. After him, Johann Most, wildly acclaimed, launched into a violent oration attacking Christianity and denouncing the clergy for their subservience to the exploiting classes.

By a large majority, the meeting carried a motion which rebuffed the "Christian Social" overtures. It read:

Whereas Christianity which has lasted for almost 1,900 years has not been able to mitigate the most extreme want of the overwhelming majority of humanity, much less to put an end to it; *whereas* today's clergy and servants of the Church show no intention of changing their traditional attitude; *whereas,* finally, any economic achievement, large or small, is completely worthless without the simultaneous unlimited enjoyment of political freedom, and *whereas* even the consummation of the Christian Social program would not bring about any change,

Be it resolved that this meeting expects a thorough elimination of all existing political and economic restrictions solely through the Social Democratic Party, and that it is our duty to support and to spread with all our strength the teachings of that party.

Not discouraged by his initial failure, Stoecker subsequently held a series of weekly meetings at which the Christian Social Workers' Party was finally organized. The party declared that it was founded "upon the Christian belief and the love of king and country"; it rejected Social Democracy as "impractical, un-Christian and unpatriotic"; advocated "a peaceful organization of labor in order to prepare, together with the other elements of national life, the necessary practical reforms"; and aimed "at narrowing the abyss between rich and poor and ensuring greater economic security."

More specifically the party urged the government to establish compulsory nationwide trade corporations which would regulate apprenticeship, represent the workers' interests and rights toward their employers, and vouch for workers' contractual liabilities under a system of compulsory arbitration. It advocated a government-controlled insurance scheme for widows, orphans, and disabled and aged persons. Under the caption "Protection of Labor" the program included demands for the prohibition of Sunday work; the elimination of factory work for children and married women; a standard working day, varying according to the needs of the different trades; international recognition of protective labor laws and adequate protection of national labor pending such recognition; protection of the workers from unsanitary conditions in shops and homes; reestablishment of laws against usury. Government plants were to be managed in a way friendly to labor; public ownership was to be extended "as far as economically advisable and technically admissible." The party also espoused a progressive income tax as a counterweight to existing or future indirect taxation, a progressive inheritance tax, stock exchange tax, and high taxes on luxuries.

The party platform appealed to the clergy to make every effort to improve the people's physical and cultural conditions and their ethical and religious welfare. It admonished the wealthy classes "to meet readily the justified demands of those who possess nothing" and not to oppose "feasible increases in wages and shorter working hours." It gave wholehearted support to the trade corporations as the new embodiment of all that had been good and useful in the old guilds. Finally, the party insisted that personal and professional honor be upheld, that all vulgarity in pleasure be shunned, and that family life be cultivated in the Christian spirit.

Stoecker readily admitted that this party platform was eclectic. "When formulating it," he wrote, "we proceeded in a very simple manner. . . . We had before us the demands of the Social Democratic and of the Catholic Social parties. We examined these demands and asked ourselves which ones we could accept and which ones we had to reject. Then we made the necessary additions." What political considerations guided him in his borrowing from other parties and making "the necessary additions"?

Although eclectic, Stoecker's platform was not arbitrary. The program of the new party had to be radical enough to lure the workers away from Social Democracy; but it also had to be innocuous enough not to antagonize the powers of the state, government, and business. Resistance from these quarters was considerable and Stoecker repeatedly complained about the lack of understanding exhibited by his conservative friends. The novel spectacle of a court chaplain noisily participating in political agitation could not fail to evoke objections. The dignity of the throne was involved; moreover, by virtue of his high office, Stoecker seemed to commit the Protestant Church to a stand on controversial socioeconomic matters which could not easily meet with conservative approval; finally, a new party was considered detrimental to the traditional interests of the Conservative Party.

To overcome the distrust of his conservative friends, Stoecker had to impress upon them the consequences of universal suffrage. In Prussia, it is true, the preponderant influence of the Conservatives was guaranteed by a highly inequitable electoral procedure for the lower chamber and by the feudal composition of the upper chamber.[12] However, one road only was open if the power of the Conservatives was to be extended beyond Prussia and securely established in the Reich, where parliament was chosen by general elections based on universal male suffrage. The party of the landed Prussian aristocracy, of the court circles, of the army, and of the Protestant hierarchy, had to become a nationwide mass party. To accomplish this end, concessions would have to be made, even if they went somewhat against the grain of this conservative group with its traditional values and prejudices, its rooted opposition to democratic "mob rule." But even if they had desired to remodel their party along "democratic" lines it would still have been difficult for the Conservatives to take up a new role as sincere friends of the lower classes. Their methods of dealing with their opponents in 1848 and the period of reaction which followed had not been forgotten. Stoecker, therefore, wisely insisted on an organization of his own, friendly to the Conservative Party, and actually its ally, but formally free and unhampered in carrying out its decision "to oppose the atheist organization of Social Democracy by a Christian coalition of workers" and to build a rallying point for the "worthy element in the realm of labor."

The relationship between Stoecker and the Conservatives was by no means of the servant-master type (nor was this true of the relationship between Hitler and the German Nationalist Party half a century later). To conceive of the agitator's function in such terms would be dangerously to oversimplify matters. To achieve its purpose the Christian Social Workers' Party needed ample freedom of action as did Hitler's National Socialist Workers' Party later. It had to be free to criticize and oppose the privileged classes. Success was impossible if the Christian Social Workers' Party appeared "as a fraction of the Conservative faction." The workers wanted an independent organization to protect their interests. This Stoecker could not promise unless he was free to push social demands that conflicted with privileges which the Conservatives were determined to defend. In the relationship between agitators and those whom they propose to assist, such conflicts are inescapable. They make for constant friction and suspicion and actually reflect the clash of interests among the divergent forces which the agitator has undertaken to unite.

Paradoxical though it may seem, it was democratization of government that gave the greatest impetus to political anti-Semitism by virtue of Germany's prevailing social hierarchy. The enemies of democratic rule now had to make use of the democratic process to maintain the old structure of power. The "mob," despised and feared by the aristocracy, had become the indispensable arbiter to the extent that political decisions depended on the popular ballot. The organization of the masses could no longer be safely left to liberalism or socialism. Stoecker saw this clearly. "There are conservative circles," he said in a public meeting,[13] "which are so withdrawn and superior that they consider it bad taste to go into mass meetings and take up the fight there. . . . We have left the strategic positions of public life to the enemies; now they hold the heights equipped with all the heavy and small arms of the press and the mass meeting while we have to reconquer one position after another. . . . What the Conservatives lack are big, exciting, stirring, all-embracing ideas. The other parties had such ideas. National Liberalism had [the idea of] national unity, it had the great concept of personal liberty. . . . [Now] we have unity and more liberties than we need. Today we must try to re-establish more order on the basis of liberty. Today other ideas will have to be impressed upon the mind of our people than those liberal ones. I believe they center around the two words: Christian Social."

Democratization of government likewise enhanced the chances of organizing a "mass movement from the Right"[14] with which to offset democratic rule by majority. The ballot, anonymous and indiscriminate, seemed the expression of social *Gleichmacherei*. The vote of the worker, the Social Democrat, the Jew, the good-for-nothing unemployed was equal to that of respectable people—the official, teacher, merchant, and peasant. Caste-conscious and status-conscious *Mittelstand* groups refused to accept the painful fact that industrial Germany did not grant them any longer the position they had enjoyed in the pastoral times of *Kleinstaaterei*. For the loss they had suffered in social status they could compensate by defensive ideologies. But what they had lost in economic security they only could hope to retrieve by political pressure exerted through political organizations of their own. The Conservatives, in need of mass support, found ready to hand, as it were, these lower middle-class groups eager to "go into politics."

In this first phase of his political career Stoecker had clearly defined the fight against Social Democracy as the main purpose of his Christian Social Workers' Party. In 1878 he wrote in a confidential letter to the Crown Prince: "We are on the eve of an election. I do not for a moment expect to get a Reichstag seat but I think in the three electoral districts where the Social Democrats are strong we will split the labor vote sufficiently to prevent Social Democracy from winning. Should we succeed in this, everybody would have to recognize the correctness of our strategy." Stoecker's hopes were dashed as the elections turned into a dismal defeat for the Christian Social Workers' Party. In all the Berlin districts combined, Stoecker's candidates obtained less than 1,500 votes, as compared to 56,000 for the Social Democratic Party. This marked the end of Stoecker's attempt to deliver Berlin's industrial proletariat back to

Church and State, and to replace the workers' revolutionary organization with one pledged to political subserviency.

The Stoecker movement entered a new phase. The demand for social reform in the interest of labor remained part of the Christian Social program but the nature of the party changed after 1878 in such a way as to make the designation "Christian Social" synonymous with anti-Jewish. The party's social appeal shifted with the target of its attack. In 1881 it officially dropped the word "Workers" from its name and henceforth was known simply as the Christian Social Party. In renaming his movement Stoecker conceded that his assault on the Social Democrats had failed, and that the party had become almost entirely lower middle class in composition.

Stoecker's program had called for a reconciliation between the state and the proletariat through the workers' submission to governmental control. The state, he had insisted, should abandon economic *laissez faire* and take a hand in revamping the relationship between capital and labor; in return the workers were to accept the benevolent authority of the Christian state. In its philosophy the program was directed against economic liberalism. Specific demands—tax on stock exchange operations, restoration of the law against usury—hinted at the identification of liberalism with the economic ills commonly attributed to Jewish business practices. But as long as Stoecker wooed the industrial population, anti-Semitism was not in the foreground of his agitation though it certainly was inherent in the orthodox Protestant concept of the Christian state. Occasionally, even in the early stages, statements of anti-Semitic principles were injected into the party literature. A leaflet which Stoecker had distributed during the election campaign of 1878 stated:

We respect the Jews as our fellow citizens and honor Judaism as the lower level of divine revelation, but we are firmly convinced that no Jew can lead German workers either in religious or economic matters. The Christian Social Workers' Party marches under the banner of Christianity.

On the whole, however, it would have been inexpedient for Stoecker to make use of anti-Semitism in appealing to the workers. The Social Democratic Party made it a point to teach the workers that it did not matter whether their exploiters were Jewish or Christian capitalists and that Jew-baiting served antirevolutionary aims. These workers were on the lookout for the ulterior motives of anti-Semitic demagogues. In fact, Stoecker was frequently embarrassed by the uninhibited anti-Semitism of his followers and often had to quell their outbursts at his own party meetings. It was not until September 19, 1879, after the futility of his

attempt to win away the Social Democratic following had become manifest that he launched his first full-dress anti-Semitic attack, a speech on
"What We Demand of Modern Jewry."*

The impact on the political life of the capital was extraordinary. The
speech gave a new impulse to Stoecker's agitation and established his
party, which up to then had remained weak, as an aggressive force in
Berlin. From 1879 to the mid-eighties the so-called Berlin Movement,
with Stoecker as the most prominent leader, kept the capital in a turmoil.
Its ideology was a hodge-podge of many ingredients, Christian Social,
conservative, orthodox, anti-Semitic, social-reformist, and state-socialist.
The Conservative Central Committee served as its coordinating body,
and artisans, clerks, students, petty officials, small businessmen, and
other members of the *Mittelstand* made up the bulk of its adherents.

The logic of his self-assumed mission drove Stoecker to make anti-
Semitism the central issue. While he had not succeeded in supplanting
the Social Democratic Party or splitting the Social Democratic vote,
the government had decided to take care of this menace in its own
way. In 1878 Social Democracy was outlawed and driven underground.
Political liberalism was next to be attacked. In the fight against "Jewish
liberalism" anti-Semitism was the logical weapon. It may well have been
the fear of being outdone by other agitators that prodded Stoecker on
his anti-Jewish course. "That the battle [against the Jews] was necessary
was to be gathered, too, from the overwhelming interest which it
aroused," Stoecker's friend and biographer Oertzen writes. "Thousands
of newspaper articles, hundreds of pamphlets, innumerable full-sized
books were written to discuss the [Jewish] question and to work out clear
objectives."

Stoecker always conceived of himself as having rekindled the flame of
Christianity in the hearts of his followers, of having built his movement upon the rock of Christian faith, not upon hatred of Jews. His
speeches and writings are replete with protestations that he dearly loved
religious, modest, industrious, and loyal Jews. He wrote to the Kaiser:[15]
"I have declared publicly in all my speeches against Jewry that I do not
attack the Jews but only frivolous, godless, usurious, fraudulent Jewry
which, indeed, is the misfortune of our people." His audience, however,
was obviously more attracted by his anti-Jewish slogans and attacks on
big business than by the Christian content of his speeches. The following table, compiled by his biographer Frank from police records, gives
the varying number of listeners that attended his meetings:[16]

---

* A complete translation appears in Document No. II.

Date	Topic	Number of Listeners
1880		
April 9	The Jewish Question	2,000
April 30	Is the Bible the Truth?	500
September 24	The Jewish Question	2,000
November 19	The Being of God	1,000
December 17	Old and New Testament	700
1881		
January 21	Handicraft Once and Now	2,500
January 28	The Sins of the Bad Press	3,000
February 4	The Jewish Question	3,000
February 11	Compulsory Accident Insurance	3,000

A Protestant opponent of Stoecker's[17] put it aptly when he wrote that audiences cheered Stoecker's anti-Semitic statements and merely tolerated his "Christian interjections, in the belief that he also had to talk church because he was a parson." The extraordinary response to Stoecker's anti-Jewish agitation[18] must be seen in the light of larger events. The years 1878 and 1879 were decisive in the economic and political development of Germany. "In 1870 all Germany was for free trade."[19] Thus the historian Ludwig Bergsträsser sums up the economic doctrine prevailing at the time when the Reich was founded. Prussia had been leading the endeavors to break down trade impediments between the German states and to create legal uniformity adequate to the needs of interstate commerce. Successes in the drive for German economic unification were so many Prussian victories in the fight for "the smaller-Germany-solution," that is, national unification under Prussia's leadership, with the exclusion of Austria.

Prussian conservatives, large-scale producers of exportable grain, were naturally in favor of free trade. "Protective tariffs are a protection against the freedom of the people to buy where it seems most economical and convenient."[20] Such Manchester wisdom had been voiced in 1849 by a *Junker*, the present Chancellor. Germany's industrialization was accompanied by sharp rises in the price of grain and consequently of cultivated land. The inflated prices of the early seventies encouraged agrarian entrepreneurs to take more acreage under cultivation and to invest heavily with borrowed money. Then the market "broke." The story sounds familiar to the American reader. One difference, however, should not be overlooked. The American farmer's outcry against "Wall Street" did not have the anti-Jewish connotation of German agrarian charges against "the powers of the stock exchange."

The drop in grain prices was partly due to the nationwide depression,

and partly to the larger quantities of American and Russian wheat which
were being dumped on the unprotected German market. In Germany,
as in Central and Western Europe generally, the trend had been toward
intensive agriculture ever since the agrarian depression after the
Napoleonic Wars. In the middle of the century scientific and technological advancements had given it new impetus. Rising prices of
agricultural products encouraged capital investment to increase the yield
per acre. From the seventies on this intensive type of producing had to
compete with the extensive farming done on the apparently limitless ex-
panses of free lands overseas. Railway and steamship were now able to
bring the crops of the North American continent to Europe at competitive prices. Germany began to import grain. Hesitatingly at first, and
from the mid-seventies on with growing insistence, the agrarian conservative movement clamored for protection against overseas competition.

In the industrial field a similar development took place. By annexing
Alsace-Lorraine Germany acquired prosperous and technically advanced
industries. The textile industry, for instance, had more than half as many
cotton spindles and almost as many mechanical looms as there were in
the rest of the country.[21] Germany also took possession of huge deposits
of iron ore in Lorraine and potash in Alsace, both of the greatest potential value for the advance of German heavy industry. So convinced was
Germany then of the benefits of free trade that the most-favored-nation
clause had been written into the peace treaty with France. In 1873, in
the process of carrying out its international trade obligations, Germany
abolished the import duties on pig iron, scrap, and shipbuilding material. Those on half-finished iron products and machinery were cut, to
be completely eliminated after a four-year period of grace. The Conservatives were among those who pressed for these measures.[22]

Germany heavy industry had hardly been put on a level of free competition with that of Great Britain, its superior rival in Europe,[23] when the
international business slump drove the British to invade the open German
market. Increased competition at home and from abroad convinced
many a liberal Manchester man that a "national" trade policy had to
replace cosmopolitan free trade. The cries for new tariffs on iron and
steel products went up, mingling with the voices of the agrarians.

Neither the grain producing Junkers nor heavy industry could hope to
get protective tariff legislation passed without mutual support. Although
the agrarians were in favor of low-priced industrial goods and the industrialists wanted food prices kept low, each group was finally persuaded
to compromise. In order to get through their own tariff the agrarians
supported the demands of heavy industry; heavy industry in turn promoted the tariff on agricultural products. In 1878 the brief era of free

trade came to an end with the passage of a new tariff act. It laid the foundation for the political alliance between heavy industry and the big agrarian interests which did much to determine the nation's economic, social, and political structure, and to set the course for her foreign policy.

Economic protectionism was not a peculiarly German development but in no other industrial country did it have such drastic political consequences. The surrender of the free-trade philosophy undermined the prestige of political liberalism, linked as it was with the free-trade parties. Conservatism increased its influence as the authoritarian state enlarged its powers. The pressure of the protectionists on the government did not seriously inconvenience the Chancellor, although he had once been devoted to the principles of economic liberalism. Bismarck never allowed ideological or political commitments to sway him from his one fixed resolve—to strengthen the power of the centralized authoritarian state in every way and by any means. In 1866 he had taken it upon himself to alienate Prussian conservatism by dethroning the king of Hanover, thus violating the sacred rights of dynasties. Again, in a fight that lasted from 1868–72, he had abrogated old administrative Junker privileges in the eastern provinces and humiliated his adversaries by appointing twenty-five new peers to the upper chamber of the Prussian Diet in order to get the reform bill passed. When he became convinced that the particularist interests of the Catholic church threatened the authority of the Reich, he had not hesitated to offend Protestant orthodoxy by having high Catholic dignitaries thrown in jail. Throughout these years political liberalism had stood by the Chancellor, jubilant at every step he took toward greater national unity and the centralization of government. But there remained an area of conflict between the Liberals and Bismarck in which an undeclared war had been going on even during the years of closest cooperation. The basic controversy was over the nature of centralized government, over the question of whether its autocratic or parliamentarian features should prevail.

The one concession to democratic government that had been wrested from Bismarck in 1867, when he negotiated with the National Liberals about the future Reich constitution, was the Reichstag's right to control government expenditures. The greatest hindrance to autocratic rule was that the Chancellor had to have a Reichstag majority to grant him the money he planned to spend on the army. The tragicomic history of German political liberalism might well be written solely in terms of the Liberals' attitude toward the military budget. Friction between the Chancellor and his loyal supporters, the National Liberals, developed as early as 1869 when Bismarck had asked for a loan to build up the navy of the North German Federation. The issue was settled by a compromise. In

1871 the National Liberals, in consideration of the abnormal situation created by the war with France, agreed to wave the Reichstag's budgetary power over army expenditures for a period of four years. In 1874 another decision had to be made. The National Liberals were ready to grant the additional funds which the government then wanted. But Bismarck in addition demanded that parliament should henceforth automatically agree to all army expenditures. These would be calculated on the basis of peacetime army strength and the only right reserved to the Reichstag would have been that of establishing this strength by law. If the National Liberals had accepted this audacious proposal, parliament would have suffered the loss of its most important prerogative. Even the right wing of German liberalism could not readily consent to a measure that would have weakened the Reichstag so irreparably. Instead, another uneasy compromise ensued and the power Bismarck had attempted to wrench from the Reichstag permanently was conceded to him for a period of seven years. The *Septenat* act was passed by a vote of 224 to 146. For reasons of national prestige a large number of Progressives cast their ballots in its favor, the National Liberals voted for it to a man.

The *Septenat* was a victory for Bismarck but the struggle had again revealed the basic flaw in the structure of the Reich; the incompatibility of the principles of authority and majority which manifested itself in every sphere of government and all areas of public life. Any antiauthoritarian expression, in the arts or in politics, in education or in the social sciences, was considered a threat to the regime. The free liberal and socialist press was especially distasteful to the Chancellor and it aroused a passionate hatred in Conservative, Christian Social, and nationalistic circles where it was usually characterized as "Jewish" and its writers as "Jewish *journaille*." It was feared as a source of antiauthoritarian thought, and anything antiauthoritarian was bound to be subversive and unpatriotic.

Yet, when in 1874 and 1876 the Chancellor tried to muzzle the Social Democratic press, the Reichstag refused to pass his bills. In spite of all the difficulties the government put in the way of the young socialist labor movement it grew rapidly. By the end of the seventies the Social Democratic Party had already acquired the status of the most important and dangerous enemy of the Bismarckian state. His determination to get rid of the revolutionary menace was among the Chancellor's foremost reasons for a change in domestic policy. As long as both the left wing of liberalism, the Progress Party, and the moderate wing, the National Liberal Party, refused to back discriminatory legislation, there was no parliamentary majority to enact Bismarck's anti-Socialist program into law. It was imperative to break the resistance of political liberalism.

This was done by means of a political crisis which Bismarck handled masterfully making use of every accumulated aggression, economic discontent, cultural resentment, and political fear that lurked in the German body politic. In 1878 an attempt upon the life of the Kaiser[24] gave him the pretext he needed. When the Chancellor was informed of the news he is said to have responded with the triumphant exclamation: "Now we've got them!" "The Social Democrats, your Highness?" he was questioned. "No," he answered. "The Liberals."[25]

The Chancellor moved quickly and introduced a bill into the Reichstag designed to suppress the Social Democratic Party. The Liberals, he felt sure, could not afford to stand up for civil rights when it was a question of punishing a "party of assassins." But he miscalculated. The bill was defeated, with most National Liberals voting against it. Three weeks later a second attempt was made upon the Kaiser's life. This time the monarch was seriously wounded and popular indignation rose to a feverish pitch. Bismarck immediately dissolved the Reichstag, elected only half a year before, and called for new elections. He was determined to crush the opposition in a patriotic campaign for "king and country." The forces that stood in the Chancellor's way were branded as Germany's enemies, subversive internationalists, friends and protectors of murderers. Parliamentary government itself was attacked and the liberal elements in the civil service intimidated. Bismarck let it be known that he considered it harmful to the country to have so many lawyers, civil servants, and scholars, "men without productive occupations," seated in the Reichstag.

As a result of the campaign "against the red terror," the liberal Reichstag majority formed by Progressives and National Liberals was wiped out in the elections. The number of National Liberal seats, already reduced in 1877 from 152 to 127, shrank to 98; the Progress Party retained only 26 of the 49 seats it had won in 1874. On the other hand, the Conservatives nearly tripled their strength (1874—22 seats, 1878—59 seats) and the Free Conservatives grew by more than fifty per cent (1874 —33 seats; 1878—56 seats). The Catholic Center Party[26] consolidated its earlier gains, demonstrating that the *Kulturkampf* had failed. It elected 91 Reichstag members in 1874, 93 in 1877, and the same number in 1878.[27]

Thoroughly disheartened, the National Liberals decided that resistance was futile. A new and even more oppressive bill against the Social Democrats was introduced, and the National Liberals voted *for*, no longer *against*. On October 21, 1878, their "ayes" ensured the passage of the "law against the pernicious pursuits of the Social Democracy," the notorius *Sozialistengesetz*. The act declared the Social Democratic Party to be illegal, abolished freedom of speech, press, and assembly and gave the police authority to refuse the right of residence to persons who might be considered dangerous to the preservation of law and order.[28] If the National Liberals had hoped to get back into Bismarck's good graces by reversing their position, they must have been bitterly disappointed. They had only given additional proof to their enemies that nationalism and unconditional loyalty to Kaiser and Reich were all that mattered any longer. The harvest was gathered by Conservative-monarchist forces.

Having outlawed the Social Democratic Party, the government proceeded to complete its victory over liberalism. It started a systematic consolidation of the state administration and a reorganization of the civil service, from which liberal elements regarded as unreliable were purged, and of the army which, although enlarged, was carefully protected against any liberal infiltration.[29] It introduced a program of economic and social legislation to which the Conservative and Catholic Center parties lent their support. Ideologically and economically this policy united the forces which wanted a strong "Christian National State" under the authority of church and throne; the National Liberal Party, bulldozed into a numb fear of socialist revolution, was decisively beaten. Its right wing was henceforth ready to ally itself with the ruling powers if and when accepted as partner. The Progressive Party, in the Chancellor's phrase the "seed of Social Democracy," was no longer able to function as a partner in a liberal parliamentary majority.[30]

CHAPTER III

THE STATE AND THE RABBLE-ROUSERS

Anti-Semitism had proved useful in bringing together political Catholicism and Prussian conservatism. It had done a good job in unleashing nationalist instincts. It had helped intimidate vacillating liberals. Anti-Semitic agitators now found, if not open support, at least tacit encouragement from above. Political anti-Semitism could claim to be close to the state authority which accepted it, although not without reservations and embarrassment. It became respectable on the strength of the governmental coloring which it had acquired. As Eugen Richter, the leader of the Progress Party, noted in 1881, "the [anti-Semitic] movement is beginning to attach itself to Prince Bismarck's coat tails, and although he does not want it and occasionally lets his press blame it for excesses, its leaders continue to snuggle up to him and to refer to him, just like noisy children eagerly surrounding their father."[1] In Wilhelm I, Stoecker had a benevolent monarch who knew how to appreciate his chaplain's endeavors for throne, altar, and the national state, although he felt ill at ease about Stoecker's public agitation. Prince Hohenlohe, who was at that time German ambassador in Paris, remarked after a visit to the Kaiser on November 29, 1880: "The Kaiser does not approve of the way Court Chaplain Stoecker is carrying on, but he thinks the matter will run its course harmlessly and considers the noise useful in order to make the Jews a little more modest."[2]

That the Jews be "more modest" had also been the keynote of Stoecker's first open blast more than a year before. It was a warning plainly directed at the liberal press and parties to be more restrained in their criticism of state, government, and orthodoxy. Of course, the Kaiser's concern was less about the impact of Stoecker's agitation upon Jews or Liberals than about the potential danger of mob incitation. In the conversation with the ambassador he gave voice to the intrinsic fear which conservatism experiences in the face of any social agitation, revolutionary or demagogic, of every stirring from below. The Kaiser, who was flattered by Stoecker's adoration and favorably influenced by the chaplain's friends among high Protestant dignitaries and the Prussian aristocracy, only vaguely sensed the menace. Bismarck was fully aware of it. His concern about the aftereffect of Stoecker's social demagogy is shown in the developments that followed Stoecker's attack on Bleichröder.

At a mass meeting held on June 11, 1880, Stoecker, to fend off Social Democratic attacks on the clergy, had thrown Bleichröder's name into the debate. He called the banker a capitalist with "more money than all the clergymen taken together."[3] A week later Bleichröder addressed a letter[4] to the Kaiser in which he complained about the incident and Christian Social agitation in general. The letter is an interesting document of the time, particularly because of the Jewish banker's complete self-identification with the powers of state and throne. Bleichröder stressed the revolutionary hazards in Stoecker's political activities, which he said differed from Social Democratic agitation only in being "more practical and therefore more dangerous." He warned that the final outcome could only be revolution. "Your Majesty," he wrote, "I am not afraid of this ultimate event which will be unavoidable if the agitation is not checked in time. I try to prepare myself for it, hard as it would be for me to leave the fatherland. I know that the high authority of the state would come to my protection in the final and most acute catastrophe. But I think I may assume that the use of force against me to which men are being incited by the speeches of Herr Court Chaplain Stoecker and his collaborators, could not remain isolated, that it would necessarily be only the beginning of horrible and disastrous social revolution."

The Kaiser sent Bleichröder's letter to Bismarck who forwarded it to Robert von Puttkamer,[5] Prussian Minister of Public Worship and Instruction, with the request that he investigate and take appropriate steps against Stoecker. Puttkamer, a close friend of Stoecker's, delayed his report to the Chancellor for several months and finally submitted a draft which Bismarck did not accept. On October 16, 1880, the latter wrote to von Puttkamer:[6]

I cannot entirely agree with Your Excellency's interpretation of the whole affair. In my opinion, the activity of Court Chaplain Stoecker remains serious even if the meetings he organizes should in the future lose their tumultuous character. The tendencies he furthers are in several points identical with those of the other Social Democrats. I take the liberty to call to Your Excellency's attention the speech which Herr Stoecker made the day before yesterday at the general meeting of the *Zentral-Verein für Sozialreform*. In this speech he calls the government's program insufficient and sets economic security for workers in case of unemployment as the goal to be achieved; he demands the standard working day and the progressive income tax. That the latter measure would mean only a relatively very small increase in the present income tax, he should well know; but his listeners do not know it. When he calls for a standard working day he is working toward the ruin of our industry in favor of its competitors in England, Belgium, France, etc.; and when he demands economic security for the workers in case of unemployment, he must be aware that this goal is actually unachievable. He rouses desires that cannot be satisfied.

With reference particularly to the Jewish question, it is an error to assume that the *rich* Jews of our country exert a strong influence upon the press. It may be different in Paris. Not the moneyed Jews but political reformers among the Jews are aggressive in our press and in the parliamentary bodies. Rather the interests of wealthy Jews are tied up with the preservation of our state institutions and cannot dispense with the latter. Jews in the press and in parliament who have little to lose and much to gain, and who join any opposition, can under certain circumstances also make an alliance with Social Democracy, including Stoecker. Herr Stoecker's agitation is not primarily directed against these liberal and discontented Jews. His speeches address themselves to the envy and greed of the have-nots against those who possess.

Bismarck's son, Herbert, likewise informed a high government official[7] that his father objected "much more to the socialistic than to the anti-Semitic" content of Stoecker's agitation, and elaborated: "Stoecker agitates against Bleichröder not because he is a Jew, but because he is rich. Decisive in my evaluation of Stoecker's conduct are the meetings at which he promises the workers mountains of gold at the expense of the well-to-do classes, by means of the progressive income tax he wants introduced. . . . Had Stoecker attacked only the excesses and the hypertrophy of Jewry in press and parliament, Bleichröder would have had no reason to beg for his Majesty's help against his agitation, and one could have let him carry on. The dangerous thing, however, is the communistic-socialist tendency of Stoecker's agitation." Both letters suggested that Stoecker's party be outlawed for violating the anti-Socialist act.

A communication from the Kaiser to Stoecker finally settled the matter. It rebuked the chaplain for not having avoided excesses in his well-intentioned efforts. The Kaiser regretted that Stoecker had "incited rather than calmed greed" by having drawn attention to individual big fortunes and by proposing reforms that went beyond the government's program. The imperial admonition was benevolent and did not dishearten the chaplain.

While action on the Bleichröder incident was still under advisement, a new anti-Jewish campaign was launched. In the fall of 1880 Bernhard Förster, Max Liebermann von Sonnenberg, Ernst Henrici, and other anti-Semitic leaders of the Berlin Movement began collecting signatures for a petition to be submitted to the Reich Chancellor. The Anti-Semites' Petition, as it was called, declared as its aim "the emancipation of the German people from a kind of foreign domination which it is in the long run unable to bear," and it asked the government to curb the civil rights of the Jews. The signers demanded prohibition or, at least, restriction of immigration of foreign Jews; exclusion of Jews from all government jobs; restriction of employment of Jews in the judiciary, especially as judges; exclusion of Jews from teaching positions in primary schools and restriction of employment in higher education; the reestablishment of a special census of the Jewish population. In April, 1881, this petition, signed by about a quarter of a million people, was presented to Bismarck.

In November, 1880, the Progress Party, in order to expose the anti-Semitic movement to public criticism,[8] asked the Prussian government for a statement of its attitude toward attempts to deprive Jewish citizens of their civil rights. This interpellation led to a parliamentary debate that lasted through several sittings. The government's answer was tendered by the vice-president of the Prussian Cabinet. He briefly stated that the equality of all religious denominations was guaranteed by the Constitution, and that the Prussian government had no intention of permitting a change in the legal situation. This answer was characterized by the liberal interpellant Virchow as "correct and cool to the core." The anti-Semites interpreted it as a sign of the government's displeasure at the interpellation and felt rather encouraged to go ahead with their drive for more signatures.

By the end of 1880, anti-Semitic agitation seemed to dominate Berlin's public life. "It was like a breaker of anti-Jewish reaction," Eduard Bernstein writes in his history of the Berlin labor movement.[9] "A whole press sprang up which fed it. Anti-Semitic leaflets and libels against everything Jewish or suspect of Jewish sympathies were spread on a large scale; they advocated social and economic ostracism of the Jews and this ostracism was occasionally also carried out in a most insulting manner. . . .

"With scenes of rowdyism the like of which Berlin had never known before, the New Year of 1881 was rung in, after B. Förster, E. Henrici, Ruppel, Liebermann von Sonnenberg and other speakers had gone to work on an anti-Semitic mass meeting the night before. Organized bands roamed through the Friedrichstadt section, took positions in front of the popular cafés and, after listening to all kinds of insulting speeches, kept yelling: 'Juden raus!' They stopped Jews or Jewish-looking people from entering and provoked brawls, window smashing and other savageries. All this, of course, in the name of defending German idealism against Jewish materialism and protecting honest German workers from Jewish exploitation."

In June, 1881, after the government's compulsory accident insurance bill had been defeated by the liberal and socialist opposition, the Reichstag was dissolved. In the subsequent election campaign political anti-Semitism reached unprecedented heights. Stoecker describes the spirit of the campaign as follows:

It became emphatically clear that after the great military victories the capital of the German Reich could not be permitted to remain in democratic, Jewish, un-German hands. The rich and the poor, the high and the lowly alike participated wholeheartedly in the electioneering. . . . The spoken word of hundreds of popular meetings was augmented by the printed word. The *Reichsbote*[10] which had enthusiastically greeted the first upsurge of the Christian Social cause, had since supported our fight unwaveringly. The *Kreuzzeitung* had remained critical for a short time, but soon joined the ranks of our friends. Thus, really every organization in Berlin that called itself conservative or anti-Progressive, collaborated and worked with enthusiasm. The Conservative Central Committee, the much slandered, much feared C.C.C., took command in the fight for God, Kaiser and Reich.

Stoecker had a leaflet[11] distributed on election eve, in which he said:

For four years I have been in Berlin public life and have been fighting, openly and freely, the supremacy of capital, dishonest speculation, the vile exploitation of labor, big and small usury. I consider the concentration of mobile capital in a few, mostly Jewish, hands an acute danger and one of the main causes of Social Democratic rebellion. However, I have opposed not only the rule of mammon, but also the revolutionary desires of Social Democracy, the impractical and not realizable promises of a socialist people's state; I have emphasized that the social revolution has to be overcome by healthy social reform, built on a Christian foundation. This reform, initiated by the strong hand of the government, is before us as the greatest task of the time. To cooperate with it today is real progress. But the Berlin Progress Party which wants to prevent the reform by all possible means is reactionary. . . . If Berlin wants to stay at the head of the social and national movement, it must part with Progress. . . . Herr Professor Virchow has defended Jewry and has signed an appeal for Russian Jewish usurers. . . .[12] A Progressive proclamation calls him the representative of culture and the candidate of the educated world. I do not want any culture that is not Germanic and Christian. That's why I am fighting against Jewish supremacy.

By now Stoecker had succeeded in rallying not only shopkeepers and artisans but also officers and civil servants, teachers and professionals, the educated strata of the *Mittelstand* which had displayed but little interest in the Conservative Party. Conservative Citizens' Leagues were set up, and the Association of German Students, founded in 1881, quickly gained influence. Academic youth, which had once exhibited liberal and democratic leanings but lapsed into political apathy after 1848, began to shift its allegiance towards the "national" state. The Christian Social auxiliaries of the Conservatives had become a force which could not be lightly dismissed in the battle with liberalism. There were even signs that Bismarck's appraisal of the Christian Social Party had begun to change. He still had no personal liking for Stoecker and never spoke to him. Nevertheless, political expediency now dictated a less hostile attitude towards the movement and his official and private statements during this period indicate that Bismarck behaved accordingly.

In the cabinet meeting of November 14, 1881, the Chancellor declared that he was "only against Progressive Jews and not Conservative Jews or their press."[13] On November 26 he told his Minister of Agriculture that "while he was opposed to anti-Semitic agitation he had done nothing against it because of its courageous stand against the Progressives." Earlier in the year, on April 2, he had stated before the Reichstag that he had nothing in common with the anti-Semitic movement, but in a letter dated October 14, he advised his son Wilhelm that it was highly desirable that Stoecker should be elected.[14] A few days before the election, on November 5, 1881, the Chancellor permitted an inspired newspaper article to quote him as having said privately that "the Jews do all they can to make an anti-Semite out of me."[15] The article moreover reported that the Chancellor fully approved of the brave fight Stoecker and the Berlin Movement were carrying on against the Progress Party; it claimed to know that the Chancellor's initial animosity against Stoecker had given way to sincere admiration. It confidently stated that in the event of a run-off election between the liberal candidate and Stoecker, Bismarck would "unquestionably and openly vote for the latter." After the elections the Chancellor is reported to have said:[16] "At first I was not in favor of this [anti-Semitic] agitation. It was inconvenient to me, and went too far. Now, however, I am glad that the Court Chaplain has been elected. He is an energetic, fearless, and resolute man and he cannot be muzzled." It is indicative of the nature of German politics during this period that while political anti-Semitism tried to draw strength from unfriendly statements about Jews which the almighty Chancellor made at one time or another during his long public life, liberal defense found it necessary to claim him as an authoritative ally against the anti-Semites. The question as to whether Bismarck was actually a friend or enemy of the Jews has been widely discussed in German literature. Every bit of evidence in his official speeches and private conversations, in the letters and memoirs of his friends and enemies has been diligently scrutinized.[17] The argumentation mostly misses the point.

The Chancellor's personal relations with Jews and general attitude toward Jews may easily be shown to have been friendly within the limits of the mores of a wealthy, cosmopolitan Prussian *grandseigneur*. When, commenting on the futility of the second anti-Semitic movement in the early nineties, he told a friend that "it is a fact that the Jews are superior to other elements of the population as far as business transactions are concerned,"[18] he was acknowledging an ability of which he gladly availed himself in Bleichröder but which he was not too eager to have associated with himself. (He possessed extraordinary talents for managing his private business affairs.) When he continued that "this fact and its consequences cannot be changed if one does not like to use methods such as the night of St. Bartholomew in Paris," a measure "which even the most violent anti-Semites would not deem feasible," he spoke as an aristocrat who could not really get excited over a mere matter of business.[19]

The point, however, is not Bismarck's personal likes and dislikes but the motives of his political behavior. It is as wrong to attribute to him the rise of Conservative-clerical anti-Semitism, as some historians have done, as it would be to absolve him of having tolerated and at times encouraged political anti-Semitism as a gratuitous contribution to his fight against the Liberals and Socialists. Bismarck must be considered the first great manipulator of anti-Semitism in modern Germany because of the very fact that he harbored neither racial nor religious prejudices against the Jewish group and that he did not aim at Jews *qua* Jews[20] when he gave comfort to anti-Semitic agitation. His conduct was of symptomatic importance. The powerful and proud statesman did not disdain to align himself and conservatism with anti-Jewish rabble-rousers in times when it was relatively easy to make economic and political compromises and conservative power was not seriously threatened. When later, under the Weimar Republic, the conservatives were engaged in a life-and-death struggle, they did not shy away from an alliance with anti-Semitic murderers.

After 1881 Bismarck's interest in Stoecker waned. In spite of the official and semiofficial encouragement which the Conservative Party received, and in spite of the outlawing of the Social Democratic Party, the elections did not bring the overwhelming victory the anti-Semites had expected. Still, the new Reichstag had a majority that was willing to support the government in its program of financial and social reforms. This was largely due to the crumbling of the National Liberal Party; its parliamentary strength was substantially reduced by an internal struggle which broke the party's unity. A left wing, opposed to the government's new course, seceded and constituted itself as the *Liberale Vereinigung* (Liberal Union). The "Secessionists,"[21] among them Lasker and Bamberger, conquered 47 seats, two more than the National Liberals who from first place in the Reichstag of 1874 had now fallen to fifth.

In Berlin, however, the anti-Semitic movement had reason to rejoice over the outcome of the 1881 elections. In 1878, the Conservatives had obtained 14,000 votes, as against 86,000 Progressive and 56,000 Social Democratic votes, while in 1881 a total of 46,000 Conservative votes were cast as against 89,000 for the Progressives and 30,000 for the Social Democrats. Stoecker was elected; not in Berlin, it is true, but in the orthodox Protestant districts of Siegen and Minden in Westphalia. From 1881 to 1908, with the exception of the 1893–98 legislative period, he represented the Siegen district in the Reichstag.

The years 1881–1884 may be regarded as the period of Stoecker's greatest triumph. The Imperial Message, which carried Bismarck's social reform program before the newly elected Reichstag, was, as it were, taken by the Christian Social leader as a personal victory. He said that the government plan "as a program designed to give the worker security by means of corporations conceived in a Christian spirit, came near to putting into effect Christian Social hopes."[22] The very wording of the message, which emphasized "the ethical foundations of Christian folk life," gratified Stoecker's aspirations. He praised it as the beginning of a new cultural evolution, as one of the highlights in the history of social thought. Spiritual unity between his movement and the rulers of the Reich seemed established.

A gesture of recognition from the highest authority was likewise forthcoming. In the spring of 1882 the Kaiser paid his respects to the Berlin Movement by granting an audience to Stoecker and some of his lieutenants. Stoecker's record of the event reads:

His Majesty the Kaiser agreed to receive delegates of the Berlin Movement on the eve of his birthday, something that had never happened before in the case of a political party. I had the honor to deliver the speech and to read an address. Dr. Cremer, professor Dr. Adolph Wagner and businessman Hertzog[23] were present at the audience and listened to the address. The Kaiser aptly replied that there had been very strange developments during the past year; that both the most autocratic monarch in the world, the Russian Emperor, and the least authoritarian president of a republic, the American Chief of State, had been assassinated; that authority was in terrible danger; and that it was necessary to be fully aware of this.

As long as this unity of interests with the government lasted, it was safe for Stoecker to count on favors from the highest quarters. His standing was somewhat impaired by the international scandal he caused when in 1883 he made two speeches in London which infuriated Bismarck and annoyed the Kaiser.[24] His position was further damaged by a series of events which had an adverse effect on public opinion. In 1884 he instigated a suit for libel against a Berlin newspaper which, in the course of the election campaign, had printed an article under the headline, "Court Chaplain, Reichstag Candidate and Liar." There Stoecker, among other things, was said to have committed perjury and the paper's editor stood trial for libel. The case, the details of which are without general interest today, kept Berlin and all of Germany in suspense for months. Although the defendant at the end incurred a minor penalty, the trial was a political defeat for Stoecker. The accused editor, found guilty, was granted extenuating circumstances as a Jew, i.e., as an adherent of the faith constantly attacked by the plaintiff. The court explicitly stated: "Whoever cherishes his faith and that of his forefathers is bound in the long run to become irritated and indignant when he sees his faith and the legal status of his religion attacked over and over again, particularly when these attacks come from a clergyman."[25] Two outstanding lawyers, one of them a Jew himself, acted as counsel for the defense, visibly enjoying the sympathy of the court. The trial's atmosphere was such that the president of the court repeatedly referred to Stoecker, the plaintiff, as the defendant. Shortly afterwards Stoecker actually became a defendant for having slandered a liberal opponent in his constituency. He was found guilty and fined.

Adverse publicity was plentiful. Stoecker's political enemies made the most of the trials to destroy his prestige. After the trial in which Stoecker had sought to defeat the liberal newspaperman, the chairman of the Progress Party publicly congratulated the defense counsel in a statement which said: "The anti-Semitic movement could not have been characterized more adequately than was done by the court's findings concerning the ethical qualities of the movement's chieftain." The liberal press acclaimed the court decision with the greatest satisfaction; even the *Konservative Korrespondenz*, the semiofficial mouthpiece of the Conservative Party, carried an article unfriendly to Stoecker.

The Imperial Court, which usually remained aloof from the turmoil of public controversy, was finally forced to act in the matter. The Kaiser was painfully reminded that rabble-rousing was incompatible with the office of Court Chaplain which was in an "immediate relation to the Sovereign" and thus made the Chaplain's "political activities . . . reflect upon His Majesty's person."[26] In fact, old Wilhelm I seriously considered to demand that Stoecker tender his resignation as Chaplain to the Imperial Court when the latter was saved by a high-placed admirer, His Imperial Highness Prince Wilhelm, later Emperor Wilhelm II. In a letter dated August 5, 1885—its full contents were never published[27]— the Prince advised his grandfather that the Jews in the Reich, supported by their press, had intentionally contrived the trial to trap Stoecker. Selected newspaper clippings were attached as evidence of the perfidy of the Jewish press. The Prince had to report that the German people were outraged by the Jewish maneuver, that he had been requested to enlighten his grandfather as to the background of the intrigue. The Jews, backed and pushed by the Social Democratic and Progress parties, were out to ruin Stoecker, Prince Wilhelm insisted; it was regrettable that Jewry through its press had gained enough power in the German Reich to venture such an attempt. He had decided to write to the Kaiser, the Prince said, after he had learned that the Jews had influence even at the Imperial Court.

The letter proceeded to extol Stoecker's service to the monarchic cause. The chaplain had his faults, but he had been the mightiest supporter of the Hohenzollern monarchy and its most courageous and aggressive protagonist in the ranks of the people. In Berlin alone, the Prince wrote, Stoecker had taken 60,000 workers away from the Social Democratic and Progress parties. Finally, the letter pointed to Stoecker's efforts in charitable and social work through which he had gained the sympathy of Prince Wilhelm's wife, Auguste Victoria, who joined in the appeal and implored the Kaiser not to deprive her of one of her best fellow workers in the field of practical Christianity. As a result of Prince Wilhelm's intervention the Kaiser merely renewed his warning to Stoecker in the future to conduct his social and political activities in accordance with the requirements of his high office.

Nevertheless, Stoecker's star was declining. The patronage he had enjoyed from above wore off as the course of governmental politics changed once more. At the same time, the leadership of political anti-Semitism passed into the hands of men who were not hindered by considerations which the Court Chaplain had to respect. A new type of anti-Semitism began to spread, unfettered by Christian or conservative tradition and often in open opposition to church doctrine and *Junker* interests. The center of this new movement was no longer Berlin, but the provinces, especially Saxony, Westphalia, and Hesse.

To sum up, Jewish emancipation, a legally recognized improvement of status, was achieved in the drive for German national unification. The first years of the Reich witnessed an unprecedented industrial and financial boom in which Jews took a prominent part. Political and economic leadership was with the liberal parties. The young Reich turned its face toward the modern Western world. Apprehensive of, and lukewarm toward, Bismarck's state were Prussian conservatism and German Catholicism, each for reasons of its own.

Anti-Jewish attacks grew in number and virulence only after the big crash of 1873. Without exception these attacks combined demands for curbing Jewish rights with demands for state intervention in business. Jews and economic liberalism, anti-Semitism and social reform were commonly paired. On a platform of anti-Semitism and antiliberalism three main forces met: members of old *Mittelstand* groups, Prussian orthodox Conservatives, and Catholics. The charges against the Jews were usually on political, economic, and cultural issues. Religious hostility was almost entirely absent. Racial overtones could be heard but the leitmotif was protest against the "Jewish-liberal regime."

Of the three main groups which had recourse to political anti-Semitism in the period surveyed, Catholicism abandoned it rather quickly and found it in the long run inopportune. The Conservative Party continued to avail itself of the political advantages anti-Semitism had to offer. The behavior of both these groups was on the whole politically rational. Ideological developments in the *Mittelstand*, however, are not so easily explained. Judging from what happened in Berlin we may conjecture that between 1870 and 1880 a major political reorientation took place in the formerly radical petty bourgeoisie. It turned against its allies of 1848, the liberal middle class, which thus lost its mass support. The process was probably accelerated by the simultaneous rise of the socialist labor movement; labor's separation from liberalism in turn strengthens the interpretation that the liberal bourgeoisie was no longer regarded as the champion of the small man's democratic aspirations.

Whatever the reasons for this shift in *Mittelstand* loyalties—the shock of the first full-fledged capitalist world depression certainly ranks high among them—its most significant consequence was that from the eighties on conservatism could tap the large reservoir of *Mittelstand* voters. Anti-Semitism and antiliberalism were the ideological bridge over which *Mittelstand* groups traveled into the camp of the former enemy.

PART TWO

Racial Anti-Semitism

CHAPTER IV

STOECKER'S DECLINE (1886–1890)

In the middle of the 1880's, the government of the Reich was bending all its energies toward the realization of two major purposes—the acquisition of colonies and the strengthening of the army. The Catholic Center which had, only a few years previously, been made a partner in the government coalition hesitated to cooperate. To get parliamentary backing Bismarck had to look for a new majority combination. In the meantime, the National Liberal Party, after its sharp decline and the secession of its left wing in 1880, had been reorganized under the leadership of Johannes Miquel and was anxious to get back into the Chancellor's good graces. In the "Heidelberg Declaration" of 1884, the party announced its approval of Bismarck's economic, military, and foreign policy. It promised "relentlessly to fight for the preservation of a strong German armed force and not to shun any sacrifices necessary to secure the independence of the fatherland against all vicissitudes."[1] Not only did the party endorse Bismarck's social and financial reform program, it also fervently expressed itself in favor of continuing the fight against the Social Democratic Party. The signers of the Heidelberg Declaration pledged themselves "to grant to the Reich government the means necessary for the defense against subversive intrigues" and, therefore, "regarded the extension of the *Sozialistengesetz* as urgently required."

Reformed and repentant, the National Liberal Party had become governmental again at the very moment Bismarck needed it most. Together with the two conservative parties (German and Free-Conservative) the National Liberals formed a close political alliance, the *Kartell*, which was to be the parliamentary backbone of the government. It proved its strength in the 1887 elections. The crucial issue over which the Reichstag was dissolved this time was the government's insistence on advance appropriations for the army for another seven years. The Progressives and the Catholic Center Party were willing to grant increased military expenditures for a period of three years only. It was a half-hearted attempt to maintain some vestige of parliamentary control over the military arm, a faint echo of the struggle between

liberalism and Bismarck during the 1862–1866 constitutional conflict.
Again Bismarck won, this time with greater ease. Twenty years earlier it
had taken a victorious war to split the liberal forces. Now the mere
specter of war was enough. General Boulanger had become French
Minister of War, and an anti-German war party was gaining influence
in French politics. German relations with Russia were not auspicious.
Heavily propagandized German colonial aspirations had worked up
strong anti-British feelings in the populace. "The fatherland in danger"
became the election slogan of the government parties. The calling up
of military reservists for winter maneuvers gave an air of stark realism
to the campaign. The "state-conserving parties," the German Conservatives, Free-Conservatives, and National Liberals, won a major victory. With 220 out of 397 Reichstag seats, they held a majority. The
Progressives lost heavily; so did the Social Democrats.[2] The Catholic
Center Party held its own.[3]

The *Kartell* created a difficult situation for Stoecker. It was important
that the new political coalition should not become unnecessarily embarrassing to all concerned. The National Liberals, not so long ago
known as "the party of the Jews," had to make sure that they would
not be exposed to the scorn of the Progressives and Socialists for lining
up with a party that harbored Stoecker. It would be necessary, the
National Liberal leader, Rudolf von Bennigsen, wrote to Miquel, "to get
out of the predicament caused by our opponents' continuing to saddle
us with Stoecker's anti-Semitic demagogy."[4] Discretion and moderation
with regard to anti-Semitism was now imperative in bringing the Conservatives and National Liberals closer together. Stoecker's movement
was an obstacle in the path of the new alliance and measures had to
be taken to clear it away.

In the *Norddeutsche Allgemeine Zeitung*,[5] Bismarck's mouthpiece,
Stoecker was sharply advised to confine the activities of the Christian
Social movement to the realm of Protestant charities. The Conservatives
suddenly grew cautious in nominating their candidates and refrained
from nominating notorious anti-Semites to run in Berlin. These new
tactics prompted the liberal *Frankfurter Zeitung*[6] to comment sarcastically that it was not so much anti-Semitism which distinguished the
followers of Stoecker from the Conservatives as it was the willingness
to avow anti-Semitic beliefs openly, for "the Conservative in Berlin who
is not an anti-Semite must be looked for with a lantern."

Stoecker's close relations with the Conservatives was now a severe
handicap to the Christian Social Party. When first elected to the Prussian Diet in 1879, Stoecker had joined the Conservative group and submitted to its discipline. He soon had become one of the leading spokes-

men for the Conservatives in the Diet, later in the Reichstag. Thus, through its leader, the Christian Social Party became entangled in all the political hazards which grew out of Bismarck's opportunistic dealings with individual parties and party combinations. Stoecker's party shared in the benefits accruing from the Conservatives' support of the government and it likewise suffered all the disadvantages of an opposition whenever the Conservatives lined up against Bismarck. This could go on just as long as the Conservatives did not find the alliance with the anti-Semites an impediment to a more desirable political liaison, and as long as no forces developed within the Christian Social Party itself to make further acceptance of Conservative tutelage unbearable. The first condition had now come to pass. The Conservative-National Liberal alliance spelled doom for the Berlin Movement, the antiliberal, anti-Semitic coalition. Only the *Kreuzzeitung* ultraconservative wing remained opposed to the *Kartell* and favored Conservative cooperation with the Catholic Center. Backed by this right-wing opposition, Stoecker could continue to fight Bismarck's "middle-parties-policy" within the ranks of the Conservatives. The Christian Social Party itself, however, was caught in an impasse: as long as the government relied on the National Liberals, one of the favorite targets of Stoecker's anti-Semitic blasts; as long as the *Kartell* lasted, the Stoecker party could not do anything but consistently oppose the government. But "an opposition party under the leadership of a court chaplain was an impossible idea in Prussia."[7]

Stoecker's position grew still more precarious when be became involved in an intrigue against Bismarck which was led by Alfred von Waldersee, then deputy chief of the general staff and general quartermaster of the army. Bismarck suspected Waldersee of having designs on the chancellorship himself and of trying to acquire influence on Prince Wilhelm who soon was to succeed to the throne. In November, 1887, Waldersee, at the Prince's initiative, invited a group of dignitaries to discuss plans to raise funds for the Berlin City *Mission,* the Protestant charity organization headed by Stoecker. Prince and Princess Wilhelm were present, together with Stoecker and von Puttkamer, Prussian Minister of the Interior (since 1881), as well as other members of the cabinet, the court, and the Conservative Party. Waldersee spoke about the urgency of fighting anarchist tendencies by spiritual as well as material means. The *Mission* should rally all those who were loyal to the king and concerned with cultivating the spirit of patriotism. Prince Wilhelm responded warmly to Waldersee's request that he sponsor a nationwide committee for furthering the cause of the Protestant *Mission.* In his answer he also referred to the spiritual depravity of the Berlin masses and to the forces of destruction which only the Christian social spirit could overcome.

The liberal and the governmental press at once underscored the political implications of the Waldersee meeting. The Waldersee circle was exposed as an ambitious clerical-Conservative clique trying to use the future Kaiser as a front for its own designs. "The same evening a storm broke loose in Berlin and Vienna," Stoecker wrote.[8] "What the Berlin Jews did not have the courage to say, for fear of punishment, the Jews in Vienna did. It was a vicious campaign . . . but not dangerous. What concern was Christian charity work to these strangers, to these enemies of our faith? Their malicious statements deserved to be treated with contempt and this was done.

"Then, all of a sudden a roaring was heard as if of an approaching gale in the mountains. With a wild article, the *Norddeutsche Allgemeine Zeitung* jumped upon the Christian Social movement . . . Now the semi-official paper wrote that the Christian Social Party was denominationally sectarian and not a political party at all; that it carried the dead weight of the Berlin Movement with which the *Kartell* parties ought not to get involved; that nothing but anti-Semitism was the leaven of the Berlin Movement. . . . This article was the signal for a general attack. There could not have been any doubt as to its source of inspiration."

Bismarck later[9] disclaimed authorship of this and the following articles in the *Norddeutsche* for himself as well as for his son. But that he took the Prince Wilhelm-Waldersee-Stoecker intimacy extremely seriously may be seen from his memoirs. The opening chapter of the third volume of Bismarck's *Gedanken und Erinnerungen,* dealing with his relations to Prince Wilhelm, is almost exclusively devoted to the Waldersee meeting and the ensuing correspondence about Stoecker between himself and the Prince. "With cogent reasons, but with all due devotion in form," Bismarck advised the Prince against sponsoring the *Mission.* It was this controversy which led to the first estrangement between the Iron Chancellor and the future monarch.

There was more behind the adamant stand Bismarck took against Stoecker in 1887 than bureaucratic rivalry. True, by striking at Stoecker, Bismarck hoped to eliminate Waldersee as Prince Wilhelm's potential Chancellor. It is a matter of record how he was always jealous and suspicious of possible pretenders to his office, and broke them ruthlessly. But much more was at stake. It was with growing apprehension that the aging statesman watched every new development that threatened the relatively untested structure of the Reich. Could it endure the ever mounting pressure of internal conflict? Would the system of government, not a full-fledged parliamentary regime yet one that permitted such conflicts to come to the surface, withstand the strain? However confident Bismarck was of his own ability to plan successfully for the future of the Reich, his power to carry out his resolutions was not as absolute as it may have appeared.

The Chancellor's position itself had one basic weakness. It depended on his relations to the Kaiser. With his high-handed treatment of political parties, there was not one of them on which Bismarck could fully rely. Neither was he the accepted spokesman of any one social group. The common notion that he acted solely as the agent of his own class, the *Junkers*, is far from the truth. Not even the Prussian army was a reliable instrument in his hand unless he enjoyed the unlimited confidence of the King. Wilhelm I, was, it is true, completely dependent on the Chancellor. And as long as the old Kaiser lived, Bismarck was more or less justified in the belief that, by skillful maneuvering, or, if necessary, by scrapping the constitution, he could succeed in preserving the Reich's undemocratic structure.

But Wilhelm I would not live forever. Once the ambitious young Wilhelm II became Emperor and King, a major conflict between government and Reichstag would be bound to cause a tempest that might wreck the ship of state. The *Kartell*, Bismarck hoped, would be a representative and lasting union of the basic forces upon which the Reich was founded—aristocracy, army and civil service, and moderately liberal, national-minded bourgeoisie. Combined, they ought to be strong enough to check the greatest danger, Social Democracy, and to guide the young Kaiser's steps. The *Kartell* was Bismarck's ultimate design for ruling Germany by constitutional means. When he saw it endangered by Stoecker's opposition faction within the Conservative Party, he struck back with all the power at his command.

"There are times of liberalism," the Chancellor warned the Prince,[10] "and times of reaction, also of tyranny. In such times, to keep one's hands free, it is necessary to avoid the possibility of public opinion identifying Your Highness . . . with a specific political party. This would happen if Your Highness by becoming the high protector of *Innere Mission* established an official relationship with the latter."

Bismarck's authority and the excitement which the Waldersee meeting had aroused throughout the country moved Prince Wilhelm to drop the *Mission*. The Stoecker circle regretfully saw the future Kaiser won over to the Chancellor's *Kartell* policy. "Every personal contact between the Court and the *Mission* and its leader has since been discontinued. Both are now ostracized in certain high circles," Stoecker's devoted biographer complained.[11]

In March, 1888, Wilhelm I died. His ailing son, Friedrich III, upon whose liberal views the Progressives had so heavily banked and who was credited with the statement that "anti-Semitism is the shame of the century,"[12] reigned only three months. He was thoroughly determined to put an end to anti-Semitic agitation and had the Stoecker problem brought up for discussion at the very first meeting of his privy council. With Kaiser and Chancellor in agreement, Stoecker's downfall seemed imminent. But once more political considerations interfered. Bismarck succeeded in preventing the Emperor from simply dismissing the agitator from his ecclesiastic office. The decision—for the third successive time—was that Stoecker should be made to choose unconditionally between his office and political activity.

Bismarck's intervention was not the result of a change of mind. The Chancellor wanted Stoecker eliminated but he did not want the Progressives, his old opponents, who had long been demanding the court chaplain's dismissal, to benefit by a spectacular ouster of the nation's chief liberal-baiter. For Bismarck's purposes it was enough to have Stoecker's hands tied by an ironclad agreement that would keep him out of politics. The decision of the privy council was not delivered to Stoecker before spring of 1889. By that time Wilhelm II had ascended to the throne. Stoecker decided to retain his office and renounce politics.[13] In a formal agreement which he himself drafted after a conversation with a representative of the Imperial Court, he undertook to withdraw from the political scene and to discontinue his activities in the Christian Social Party. The text of the agreement was:

Since His Majesty considers activity in the political life of Berlin, of the kind in which up to now I have been engaged, as incompatible with the office of Court Chaplain, it goes without saying that I give it up while being entrusted by His Majesty with continuing in office. After the experiences I have had, I, myself, have lost for the time being all zest to continue the public fight which I waged against the revolution (*Umsturz*) in the political, social and religious fields. Under the present circumstances to give up entirely the political fight, for myself as well as for the Christian Social Party, is therefore not a hardship but the answer to my wishes. I shall leave this part of my activities to others and arrange my speeches, with regard to topics, content and tone in such a way as not to give His Majesty any cause for objection. When speaking in public I shall deal solely with religious, patriotic and social matters, and with the latter only to the extent that they come within the realm of Christianity, the church and *Innere Mission*. Should I at a later time feel compelled by my conscience to resume the fight for the fatherland or the church, I shall dutifully notify His Majesty and most humbly leave everything else to His Majesty's august decision.

From then on every move Stoecker made was watched. His ecclesiastic superiors refused to give him permission to speak abroad. On several occasions he was reprimanded for having made statements which, in the opinion of the church, violated the spirit of his agreement. But in spite of his difficulties with church and government, his political prospects looked far from hopeless. All he apparently had to do was to bide his time. Had not his warning that the "subversive" forces could not be defeated by the only weapon at the disposal of the "middle parties," the national idea, been amply justified? Indeed, in 1890 the *Kartell* was decisively beaten at the polls. Instead of the former majority, the two Conservative parties and the National Liberals now mustered hardly more than one third of the Reichstag. The Progressives had more than doubled the number of their representatives and the Social Democrats had tripled theirs.[14] The industrial masses had registered their protest against the rising cost of living caused by the government's protectionist policy. In Berlin, the socialist vote had been higher than that of any other party. With the *Sozialisten-Gesetz* now off the statute books,[15] socialist progress threatened to become irresistible.

The new Reichstag of 1890, with a majority of Catholics, Progressives, and Social Democrats opposed to extending the anti-Socialist act, had failed to renew it. The infamous law expired on October 1, 1890. A last attempt of Bismarck's to revive the Conservative-Catholic bloc met with the Kaiser's disapproval. Wilhelm II also rejected the Chancellor's proposal to shelve the Constitution and suppress the socialist movement by force of arms. The young Emperor was confident that it would be possible to win back the industrial masses by putting into effect a comprehensive social insurance program. In March, 1890, he forced Bismarck to resign.

At first moving cautiously, then with increasing boldness, the Court Chaplain broke out of his political retirement. Already in 1889 he had started a newspaper, *Das Volk*, which was to serve as the official organ of the Christian Social Party. Its articles held out the hope for a great revival of the Stoecker party once Bismarck was gone. "[In Germany] the soul of public life is the Chancellor," a *Volk* editor wrote.[16] "He is now 74 years old. A venerable age! After the days of prostration, days of feverish excitement will come again in the nation's life. Such days will face us the moment the Chancellor no longer dominates our public life. Moderate liberalism will then ask for the benefits of the present [*Kartell*] policy. If they are granted, the conditions of the [liberal era of the] 1870's will return. If they are not granted, democratic liberalism will raise its head. With both, Jewry will raise its head. But we, too, must be on hand. We must prepare in advance for the day when we face the Chancellor's successor and build a movement that will merit being invested with the people's yearning. . . . When Court Chaplain Stoecker realizes that the moment for action has come again, he will act and then he will not be concerned with . . . his office but with the movement only."

Now Bismarck was out of the way. The Kaiser had returned to a policy of reconciliation with the industrial masses. Stoecker and his followers jubilantly greeted the dawn of a new era. Shortly after the 1890 elections the Christian Social Party became active again. The Kaiser's declarations about his program of social reform had made the discussion of the "social question" respectable once more. "The hand that had so heavily been weighing upon the development of social reform, presses no longer," wrote the *Kreuzzeitung*.[17] "Overnight, the world has become Christian Social," Stoecker remarked triumphantly. Three days after Bismarck's downfall, he once again was heard in a debate on anti-Semitism in the Prussian Diet. On October 2, 1890, the day after the anti-Socialist law expired, the *Volk* wrote that Bismarck, Stoecker's enemy and the creator of the law (which Stoecker, incidentally, had supported all along) had become a silent man, but that Stoecker "held huge meetings as in the days of the most lively agitation."

Nevertheless, before a month had passed, Stoecker was compelled to request his own retirement from public office, and the Kaiser's permission was promptly granted. As a Prince, Wilhelm II had saved the Chaplain from Bismarck's ire and had given many demonstrations of the high personal esteem in which he held the arch-enemy of liberalism. As Emperor he forced Stoecker to resign without the slightest sign of compunction. A clue for the Kaiser's motives may be found in his memoirs where he refers to Stoecker only once, and this in passing, though in a revealing context. Explaining his attitude to various political parties, Wilhelm makes it a point to emphasize his good relations with the National Liberals and his endeavors to bring them closer to the Conservatives. "I often pointed out that the National Liberals were devoted to the Reich, and thus to the Kaiser, and accordingly should be welcomed as allies of the Conservatives; that I could not and would not govern the Reich without them, and never against them. . . . For this reason, for instance, I removed the Court Chaplain Stoecker—a man who had done excellent social work in his *Mission* activities—because he had delivered a demagogic, incendiary address in South Germany against the liberals there."[18]

The speech referred to had been made by Stoecker at the Congress of the Conservative Party of Baden. Its keynote was the urgency of the fight against socialism and liberalism, and it did not fail to attack the Jews.

So as not to tickle Israel's vanity any more, I shall not say much about the Jewish question. But since others are permitted to speak about everything else and to pull down God and monarchy, throne and altar, wealth and property, why should it not be allowed to point to the danger which Jewry represents? I don't think this is liberal. I for one will speak of this sore until it is healed; for our slogan is, one mansion (*Haus*), one people, one lord![19]

Why did Wilhelm II, who, only a few short years ago, had condoned much more violent and inflammatory attacks against Jews and liberals by Stoecker, consider this brief digression serious enough to warrant a severe reprisal? Tactical considerations had now begun to take precedence over sentimental scruples. Personal ambition as well as political expediency made the Kaiser seek the preservation of the *Kartell* and, if possible, an enlargement of its basis by including elements of the Left. He had to justify Bismarck's dismissal. Nothing would have demonstrated the wisdom of Wilhelm's decision to get rid of the Iron Chancellor more thoroughly than the success of a political coalition ranging from the governmental wing of the German-Conservatives to the Catholic Center with the National Liberals in the middle. The new Kaiser envisaged himself as the autocratic but benevolent ruler of a united nation which he would lead to greater glories. He could no longer afford to have the intensely controversial figure of Stoecker associated with him if he was to succeed in his plan of winning the support of parties that were irreconcilably hostile to the Court Chaplain.

CHAPTER V

THE CAPRIVI ERA (1890–1894)

The Kaiser's "dropping of the pilot" and the appointment of Leo von Caprivi as the new Chancellor indicated to the whole nation that a turning point in the history of Germany had been reached. The future appeared cloudy and uncertain. The country's economic situation in the early 1890's was not such as to warrant much optimism. Industrial activity lagged and German agriculture seemed to be heading towards a crisis. The western hemisphere with its huge agricultural output at lower cost had become a competitor to be reckoned with for a long time to come. The whole structure of rural Germany, built on semifeudal large-scale grain production and intensive diversified peasant farming, was in jeopardy.

The political prospects in domestic and foreign affairs were equally troubled. What to do about, and what to expect from the revolutionary labor movement were questions that preyed on the minds of every government official, burgher and *Junker*. In 1878, when the act against the Social Democratic Party had been passed, the party had polled 437,158 votes. After the eleven-year proscription it emerged with 1,427,323 votes, defiant as ever and threatening to settle accounts for "all the viciousness and infamy, for all the hardship and despair"[1] the act had brought forth. State, church, and property, conservatism and liberalism, had cooperated in depriving socialist labor of elementary democratic rights. None of them could feel at ease in the face of labor's "woe to those upon whom there will descend one day all the hatred and fury that this vile law has bred and stored up." Fear of eventual civil war was exacerbated by the specter of an armed conflict with one or several of the greatest European powers. It was no exaggeration when a socialist writer observed at the time that "with Bismarck the solid feeling of security was gone with which the German middle classes had looked upon Germany's political situation." The lack of confidence in the nation's ability to provide economic, social, and political security for its citizens is apparent from the greater number of Germans who decided, in this period, to seek their fortunes abroad. From less than a quarter of a million in the five-year period 1876–80, the number of emigrants jumped to 857,000 in the following five years and was still close to half a million in 1886–90.[2]

The first years of Wilhelm's reign and Caprivi's chancellorship were marked by a policy of compromise and moderation. The parliamentary situation was not unfavorable to such a course. The Progressives and the now legal Social Democrats, though by no means friendly to Caprivi, opposed him less aggressively than they had Bismarck. The Catholic Center, in return for the administration's abandonment of more *Kulturkampf* measures, supported the government. So did the National Liberals. Even most of the Conservatives went along with it at first.

The new Chancellor was anxious to improve Germany's foreign relations and alleviate European tension. As a demonstration of good will he removed Field Marshall von Waldersee, protagonist of a "preventive war" with France and Russia, from his position as Chief of the General Staff. Another decision of major importance altered the direction of his predecessor's system of foreign alliance. The "reinsurance treaty" with Russia which Bismarck had negotiated in 1887 was up for renewal. The treaty—whose full contents, by the way, were not made known until after World War I[3]—had committed Germany and Russia to "benevolent neutrality" in any war which involved either of the two nations, except in the case of a German attack upon France or a Russian attack upon Austria. Germany furthermore recognized Russian interests in Bulgaria and promised diplomatic and moral assistance should Russia be "compelled" to occupy Constantinople and the straits. Thus Bismarck had hoped to repair relations with Russia, badly damaged in 1878 by the Berlin Congress. Caprivi let the treaty lapse and instead steered towards friendlier relations with Great Britain. In 1890, seeking to allay growing British misgivings about Germany's colonial ambitions, he negotiated an agreement by which Germany yielded the African colony of Zanzibar to Britain, in exchange for the North Sea island of Helgoland.

In domestic affairs, too, the Caprivi administration moved with caution. Rather than wave the mailed fist in the face of the Social Democratic Party, it banked, as did the Kaiser, on appeasing labor by extending the government-operated social insurance system. Backed by a Catholic-Liberal coalition, the Chancellor continued the reorganization of the old Prussian system of local administration, a formidable task, as Bismarck had come to learn. The law of 1891 (*Landgemeindeordnung*) cut further into old *Junker* privileges and granted the rural communities a modicum of self-government.

The direction of the "new course" was most clearly indicated by Caprivi's economic policy. To encourage industry and commerce, and to fortify Germany's leading position in central Europe, he negotiated a number of trade agreements with European nations, with Austria-Hungary and Italy, Germany's allies, in 1891; with Switzerland, Belgium, Serbia, and Rumania in 1892; with Russia in 1894. The agreements were explicitly based on a "moderate tariff policy" and were presented as an alternative to "extreme protectionism." More than any other measures of the Caprivi government, the trade agreements determined the political alignment in parliament. For the first time the Social Democrats voted for a government bill. With Social Democratic support the treaties were approved by the Reichstag against vociferous Conservative opposition.

After an initial attitude of wait-and-see, the Conservatives decided on a counterattack against the new Chancellor. Reorganization of local administration in rural Eastern Germany, stronghold of Prussian landed aristocracy, had been the first government action which conservatism strongly resented. Prussian orthodoxy was further antagonized by the defeat of a school bill which the Conservative Prussian Minister of Worship and Instruction had introduced. The bill would have given the church authority in questions of religious education in the Prussian elementary school system. Public opinion reacted so violently to the Conservative-Catholic bid for control of the schools that the Minister, Robert von Zedlitz-Trützschler, had to resign. Caprivi, in spite of the National Liberal support he enjoyed, had not opposed the clerical bill; now (1892), under pressure, he had to give up his premiership in Prussia which he had held simultaneously with the office of Reich Chancellor. Public controversy over "Christian" versus "liberal" education proved, of course, a magnificent vehicle for Conservative-clerical anti-Semitism. The government came in for harsh criticism for its retreat, for "striking sail before a storm in the ink wells of liberal editors," as Stoecker put it. What was it going to do, he exclaimed, "when a serious revolutionary howl goes up in the country?"[4] The government's foreign trade policy made the simmering Conservative kettle boil over.

Caprivi modified but certainly did not abandon the protectionist policy inaugurated by Bismarck in 1879. The import duty on grains, for instance, was merely reduced from five marks for 100 kilograms to the three-mark rate, which had been in force up to 1887. But between 1891 and 1894—the period in which the trade treaties were signed—the agricultural slump played havoc with grain prices. In 1891 the price of a metric ton (1,000 kilograms) of rye at the port of Danzig was about 208 marks; in 1894 it was down to 110 marks. The repercussions of the agrarian depression, in conjunction with Caprivi's liberalized foreign-trade policy, were so serious and widespread as actually to change the character of the Conservative Party.

As long as Bismarck had ruled, opposition from Conservative ranks originated mainly with the *Kreuzzeitung* faction, the party's aggressive right wing. Bismarck had been able to cope with antigovernment rebellion within the party, not only because of his superior statesmanship but because his name, his entire career, his personal and political life, were sufficient guarantee to Prussian conservatism that he would prevent government by majority no matter what other concessions to liberal and democratic forces he saw fit to make. As long as Bismarck stood at the helm, parliamentary rule would be kept in check; and it was certain that "the mob" would not come to power. Caprivi gave the Conservatives no such feelings of security. A professional soldier, inexperienced in politics, Caprivi, as they saw it, had succumbed to the pressure of liberalism in no time at all. What was more, in pursuing his trade policy he had, for the first time in history, made use of the Social Democrats to win a parliamentary victory over Conservative opposition. This was an augury which could not be overlooked. Was it not the ultimate consequence of the "new course" that the administration would rule without and against aristocracy and orthodoxy, that revolutionary, atheistic Social Democracy and liberal money interests would be the government's allies and eventual masters?

Prior to the Caprivi administration the Conservative Party had been a loosely knit organization, held together by an unwritten code of caste rather than by an active party machine under centralized leadership. There were no locals with paid officials. The work was done in committees of notables, mostly aristocrats. Where landed aristocracy was too weak to run an organization—in the western and southern parts of the country—the party often had no organizational representation at all. After Bismarck's departure, the Conservatives no longer dared remain a government party by definition. No compromise appeared within easy reach; the Caprivi administration was an enemy to be fought and destroyed before its policy led to the destruction of the conservative society and all it stood for. But with the Kaiser and Chancellor in collusion with the forces of liberalism and revolution, even Conservative diehards could not think of having recourse to "direct action," that is, of having the executive branch scrap the constitution and rule with bayonets. The battle had to take place in the arena of parliamentary politics. More than ever before the Conservative Party needed the vote of the little man. A mass movement from the Right and led by the Right, was what the hour demanded. Under these circumstances a man of Stoecker's dynamic magnetism again became an invaluable asset to the Conservatives, and solid Conservative backing offered Stoecker his best chance to make up for the loss of prestige under which he had smarted ever since he was unceremoniously fired by Wilhelm II. "Let them," said Heinrich von Treitschke, who prior to 1890 had opposed Stoecker's agitation, "call him a demagogue. The present franchise compels us to use the kind of oratory which everyone will be able to understand."[5]

The position in the conservative ranks of the extremist group around the *Kreuzzeitung* grew stronger as the party's opposition to the Caprivi administration deepened. Its leader was Wilhelm von Hammerstein, a member of the Prussian Diet since 1876, and of the Reichstag since 1881, who as editor of the *Kreuzzeitung* since 1881 had displayed enough journalistic talent and political ability to make what had been the *Standesblatt* of provincial aristocrats into a powerful political organ. A rabid anti-Semite, Hammerstein had long been Stoecker's friend and protector. These two men were now swept into the leadership of the Conservative Party and scored their first success when the party decided to call a national convention to draft a new program.

The last Conservative Party convention had taken place in 1876. Prussian Conservatives had always shown an aristocratic repugnance towards dragging their affairs in the limelight of a national meeting. They preferred having political negotiations take place *"en petit comité."*[6] Now, again, the old-fashioned, moderate-minded *Junkers* tried to avoid a convention. As late as May, 1892, the Conservative group in the Diet resolved to postpone revision of the party platform, arguing that it would be very difficult to arrive at an adequate formulation of the party's position on the Jewish question. By August, 1892, the Hammerstein-Stoecker group, having mobilized anti-Semitic followers in Stoecker's constituency, succeeded in getting the Westphalian Conservatives to confront the party executives with an ultimatum. Either the national office would call a convention or the provincial organizations would do so, going over the head of party headquarters in Berlin. The leadership promptly yielded. In December, 1892, the convention of the Conservative Party met at the Tivoli hall in Berlin. It was attended by more than a thousand delegates, the nonaristocratic *Mittelstand* element being present in conspicuous numbers. "It was not a party convention in black tails and white gloves but in street clothes. This was the Conservative Party in the era of general and equal suffrage. . . ." Stoecker remarked.[7]

The earlier decision of the Diet moderates to delay revision of the party program because of the "Jewish question" had made it obvious that the discussion would center on political anti-Semitism. For Hammerstein and Stoecker it was of the greatest urgency to commit the party to an openly anti-Semitic platform. The leadership of political anti-Semitism was slipping from Stoecker's hands, threatening to turn anti-Conservative. In 1887 the voters, in the *Kartell* elections, had sent to the

Reichstag the first anti-Semite who not only refused to join the Conservative group but also vehemently spoke against the landed aristocratic exploiters, a man who had made his traditionally Conservative constituency a center of anti-Conservative, anti-Jewish agitation. Furthermore, in 1889 an anti-Semitic convention had met in Bochum, which was by no means under Stoecker's influence; it plainly indicated that the secession of "radical" anti-Semitism from the Conservative Party was in full swing. Reichstag elections in 1890 had brought the radicals further gains; and in a by-election which took place just a fortnight prior to the Tivoli convention, another anti-Conservative anti-Semite had beaten his Conservative opponent in the very heart of *Junker* territory. Stirred up by "radical" anti-Semitism, peasant and *Mittelstand* groups, the only ones from which a mass movement from the Right could draw support, were moving away from conservatism. At the Tivoli convention the Conservatives convinced themselves that they could not afford to be cut off from this new wave of anti-Semitism if they wanted to channel a mass movement into their party. It was a strategy deliberately thought out and accepted; it had nothing whatsoever to do with the Conservatives' like or dislike for Jews. When in November, 1892, against all expectations, more than twice as many votes were cast for the anti-Conservative anti-Semite Ahlwardt as for the Conservative candidate, the *Kreuzzeitung* emphatically called the event to the party's attention: "Anti-Semitism which once in the Berlin Movement was the bridge for crossing over from the Liberal to the Conservative Party,"[8] could again serve Conservative interests if the party took the lead in the battle against Jewry.

For the understanding of later developments it is important to note that the anti-Semitic wave of the early 1890's was not brought into being by Conservative Prussian aristocracy. The latter, however, used it and by using it created something new. The Tivoli convention showed very clearly that the fanatical anti-Semites were not *Junkers*. In the draft of a new party program prepared by the leaders of the moderate party majority there was still a plank which read: "We condemn the excesses of anti-Semitism." After a heated debate, the convention struck it out. The non-*Junker* element was prominent among those who opposed the "moderate" formulation. A lawyer from Westphalia (Klasing) declared: "We are tired of the opportunism which for years has been paralyzing the party's energy! A certain faction in the party has made it its task to strangle the child [anti-Semitism] at birth. . . . The plank is a back door, a bow to Jewry, as it were. It can only blunt the edge of the Conservative program." A high-ranking aristocrat defended the clause on the ground that it was unthinkable to be both Conservative and pro-Ahlwardt. He was noisily interrupted, and another lawyer rebuffed him: "I consider myself to be as good a Conservative as the speaker preceding me, yet in the run-off elections I voted for Ahlwardt. That's all I have to tell you." A non-*Junker* delegate from Saxony coined the phrase that the Conservative Party had to become "demagogic in a good sense." The *Junker* attitude was expressed with characteristic cynicism by Count Otto von Manteuffel, chairman of the Conservative groups in the Diet and Reichstag, and chairman of the Tivoli convention, in a Berlin speech half a year after Tivoli. Said the Count: "We could not avoid the Jewish question unless we wanted to leave to the demagogic anti-Semites the full wind of a movement with which they just would have sailed by us."[9]

The revised program of the Conservative Party, adopted on December 8, 1892, contained among other tenets and demands the following:

State and Church are institutions decreed by God; their cooperation is necessary as a prerequisite of our people's moral health.

We consider the denominational Christian grammar school the basis of public education and the most important safeguard against the growing brutalization of the masses and the advancing disintegration of all social ties.

We fight the multifarious and obtrusive Jewish influence that decomposes our people's life.

We demand Christian authority and Christian teachers for Christian pupils.

We want the monarchy by divine grace (*Monarchie von Gottes Gnaden*) to be left untouched; while we stand for civil liberties legally assured to all, and for the nation's effective participation in its legislation, we fight every attempt at restricting the monarchy in favor of a parliamentary regime.

An irresponsible press which undermines state, church and society must be opposed with energy.

To revere Christianity, monarchy and fatherland; to protect and encourage all honest work; to respect legitimate authority—these are the supreme principles written on the banner of the German Conservative Party.[10]

The economic plank of the program called for protective tariffs for agriculture and industry; "the abolition of the privileges high finance is enjoying"; protection of the *Mittelstand* by the introduction of the license system and the strengthening of guilds and cooperatives. "Honest trade and commerce must be protected by restrictions on, and strict supervision of, peddling and instalment buying, also by the prohibition of itinerant sales exhibits (*Wanderlager*) and roving auctioneering (*Wanderauktionen*)."

A young lieutenant of Stoecker's, who had a hand in the management of the Tivoli convention, later reflected on the events that had taken place. Anti-Semitism, he wrote, "made the greatest gain in prestige it could hope for when it became part of the Conservative Party's program. Previously it had been represented only in various small splinter-parties; now it became the legitimate property of one of the biggest parties, of the party nearest to the throne and holding the most important positions in the state. Anti-Semitism had come close to being accepted at the highest level of social respectability. (*Der Antisemitismus war hart an die Grenze der Hoffähigkeit herangerückt.*)"[11]

At Tivoli the mass movement from the Right was started. It succeeded beyond expectations. However, it was not the ideology of anti-Semitism which made it a political reality. At the time of the convention a little-known agricultural journal in Silesia published an unusual suggestion for remedying the distress of the farmers. The author, a local agriculturist, advised his readers "to do neither more nor less than what the Social Democrats are doing and to take a determined stand against the government."[12] He told them that Caprivi's neglect of agricultural interests could not be changed by appealing and begging. "We must make [the government] feel our power . . . ; we must stop complaining . . . ; we must yell until the whole country hears us; we must yell until it reverberates in the halls of parliament and the offices of ministries; we must yell so that we may be heard even at the steps of the throne!

"But at the same time we also must act lest our yelling dies away without being heeded. We must act by refusing to do any longer what we have always done as a matter of course, namely, making the elections for the government in our districts; we must refuse all honorary functions. . . . We must . . . adopt a policy that suits our interests. . . . For only by pursuing a ruthless and unabashed policy of interests might it perhaps still be possible to save the existence of today's farmers."

The outcry of this Silesian farmer was instantly echoed in all parts of Germany. It started a powerful drive for a political organization of agrarian interests. By February, 1893, the preparatory work had progressed to the point where the Agrarian League (*Bund der Landwirte*) issued invitations for a constituent convention and fashioned a program. The program makers wasted no words on ideological formulations. The first article called for "sufficient tariff protection for German agriculture and its auxiliary industries."[13] The second demanded that the government abstain from negotiating trade agreements which would result in lower duties on agricultural imports "from Russia and other countries"; and that "our relations with America be accordingly adjusted." With the request that the produce exchange be put under strict government supervision the League hung out the anti-Semitic shingle. Finally it straightforwardly declared itself opposed to the existing social insurance system for labor and demanded that it be "revised."

The Conservative convention, guided by Stoecker, had moved cautiously in approaching the problem of industrial labor; the problems of agricultural labor were so bound up with the fundamental interests of the landed aristocracy that Stoecker could not afford to tamper with them. The Tivoli program had confined itself to the statement that the Conservatives had made every effort "to improve the lives of the workers, at considerable cost to the employers." It wanted to remind labor that Bismarck's social insurance legislation had been passed with Conservative support against liberal opposition. Now the Agrarian League threw such cautions to the wind. This did not prevent Stoecker from greeting the League's entrance on the political scene. Its program had hardly been made public when he declared that a sound agricultural economy, comprising large, middle, and small land property, was essential for Prussia's existence. It would in any case be preferable, he said, to have gentlemen of old aristocratic families sit on the eastern estates than to have "Kohn and Itzig" take over by foreclosing on their mortgages and "corrupt the people with their subversive ideas."[14] For the sake of uniting *Junker* and peasant in the fight against liberalism Stoecker was willing to ignore the fact that the League had announced its intention of attacking the social insurance program, the mainstay of Christian Social politics, once solemnly proclaimed in the Imperial Message and greeted by Stoecker as the dawn of a new humanism.

Antiliberal, anti-Semitic, and antilabor, the Agrarian League became the foremost organizer of the mass movement from the Right. Bismarck lent it his prestige, seeing it as an instrument that could prove of service in his feud with Wilhelm II and Caprivi. His son Herbert accepted the League's vice-presidency and its practical leadership was soon in the hands of Conservatives, not all *Junkers*, but all representatives of big agrarian interests. At the end of the century, the League had close to a quarter of a million members. More than half of them resided west of the Elbe river, that is, in regions where up to then Prussian conservatism had been weak. Through their connections with the Agrarian League, the Conservatives extended their influence as far as Bavaria and the Rhineland, and were enabled to transform the Conservative Party itself into a mass party with a solid nationwide organization. At last the Conservatives were able to bridge the political gaps that had existed between *Junker* and peasant, between Prussia, Southern and Western Germany. This union of agrarian interests, even though largely a sham because of the conflicting needs of large-scale and small-scale, extensive and intensive, monocultural and diversified farming, proved a cohesive force of such strength that it lasted as long as parliamentary parties existed in Germany.

One might think that the Conservative Party paid for this increment of power with its political soul. How could it henceforth preach against

"materialistic liberalism" without having the word "tariff" thrown back
into its teeth? How could it convincingly uphold the ideals of the Christian State when in political reality these ideals dissolved into demands
for government protection of big landed interests, with consumer and
taxpayer footing the bill? The truth of the matter is that the Conservative Party was not at all handicapped by its metamorphosis from a
gentlemen's party, ostensibly concerned chiefly with questions of *Weltanschauung*, to a mass organization openly devoted to specific economic
interests. Germany's whole political life was undergoing a similar transition. The material interests of social groups were breaking through the
ideological forms in which they had first presented themselves. The great
national and liberal demands of the middle classes had partly been
realized, partly been silenced. General ideals could no longer carry party
programs; they had lost their power of attraction.

The trend toward socioeconomic homogeneity in political groupings
had been steadily gaining ground since the late seventies. "The old
names remain," Maximilian Harden wrote in 1893,[15] "but in the 1848
sense everything, with few exceptions, has become liberal just as everyone has become conservative in his desire to see the new Reich structure preserved. . . . From now on the party names Conservative, National
Liberal and Progressive may be safely translated as standing for landed
property, industry and money capital, whatever ecclesiastic and pro-
fessorial influences might still exert themselves here and there." Harden
omitted two major forces in this excessively simplified translation of
economics into politics, namely, the Social Democratic Party and the
Catholic Center. But the history of these two parties tends to confirm,
rather than refute, the truth of his statement. The Social Democratic
Party was avowedly a class party, and had, by stressing its class function,
only accelerated the transformation of the bourgeois parties. The Catholic
Center, although founded on a denominational, supra-socioeconomic basis
and therefore, the party best equipped to resist the general trend
toward the reorganization of political life along class lines, was nevertheless seriously shaken by the aggressive proposals of the Agrarian
League. The historian of the Catholic Center Party, Karl Bachem, himself a prominent Catholic Reichstag member, has described the difficulties the Center Party had in holding its rural flock together in the face
of the League's violent agitation against the government's proposed trade
treaties with Russia and Rumania.[16] The Center Party had been prepared to support the government, but the League's campaign had been
so effective that when the treaties were actually placed before the
Reichstag, only some of the Catholic deputies voted affirmatively while

a considerable number voted against them. The Catholic Center Party was in serious danger of a split over an economic issue.

The first major test for the mass movement from the Right came a few months after the Agrarian League's inauguration. Caprivi ran into difficulties on the perennial issue of the reorganization of the army, the peacetime strength of which the administration was anxious to augment. The main argument offered by the government in support of its proposals was the army's inability to take care of the growing number of recruits annually available for training. A political rapprochement between Russia and France furnished the element of national insecurity which always manifested itself in periods of planned military aggrandizement. Progressives, Social Democrats, and Catholics opposed the government's bill although Caprivi had tried to make it more palatable by reducing military service from three to two years. The Chancellor had no choice but either to retreat before parliamentary opposition or to dissolve the Reichstag in the hope that new elections would bring a friendly majority.

He chose the latter alternative despite the fact that the political circumstances were clearly unfavorable for a government victory in the new elections. Rural Germany was in revolt against Caprivi's foreign trade policy. Bismarck, symbol of national and international victories, helped to undermine the Chancellor's prestige with his attacks on the Kaiser's "personal regime." The nationalists were riding high, accusing Caprivi of gambling with the Reich's security by reducing the period of military service. Anti-Semitism was rampant as never before, the "radical" agitators barnstorming through the provinces from Hesse to East Prussia, raging against Jews, *Junkers,* and imperial bureaucracy. The Social Democrats, brimming with confidence, readied themselves to score another spectacular success at the polls.

The outstanding novelty of the 1893 elections was the political combinations in the run-offs. The Agrarian League made endorsement of its platform the condition of its support. In this way it succeeded in pledging not only Conservative but a good many National Liberal candidates as well to an antisocialist and anti-Semitic policy. In electoral districts where the Social Democratic Party was ahead, time and again a united front ranging from anti-Semites to National Liberals worked to defeat the Social Democratic candidate. *Vorwärts,* the Social Democratic newspaper, commented on what "a wonderful illustration of capitalistic culture it was that the Conservative and National Liberal parties had stooped to anti-Semitism."[17] The paper thought it "only logical that the anti-Semites in the bourgeois camp have taken the leadership in the fight against socialism."

The campaign also proved that the anti-Semites, whether organized in the Agrarian League, in Stoecker's Christian Social Party, or in one of the independent groups of racial anti-Semitism, had a far better machine in the countryside and in small towns than the Conservatives. A Christian Social candidate who was elected by the combined vote of anti-Semites and Conservatives remarked afterwards on the division of labor that developed between the two parties: "The Conservative Party carried the expenses for the election campaign and the anti-Semitic party supplied the speakers for agitation in the villages; it could count particularly on the cooperation of eager youth."[18] The same division of labor was to function, a generation later, in the relationship between the German Nationals and the National Socialists.

The outcome of the 1893 elections was explosive. The results showed both the Social Democrats and the anti-Semites to have made the most startling advances. With 1,786,700 votes the Social Democratic Party had almost tripled its strength since 1887, the year of the last election that took place under the anti-Socialist act. Since 1890, it had gained more than 300,000 votes. True, the antiquated and discriminatory definition of electoral districts[19] had robbed it of a proportionate representation in parliament—it won 44 Reichstag seats, whereas the Conservatives, with a million votes, captured 72 seats; the Catholic Center Party, with a million and a half votes, 96; the National Liberals, with a million votes, 53—but the absolute number of ballots cast for the most intransigent opposition party was enough to terrify government, conservatism, and liberalism alike. The success of the anti-Semites, though they still had not received enough votes to rival the major parties, was, nevertheless, spectacular. From 47,000 in 1890 the anti-Semitic vote had jumped to 263,000, raising the number of Reichstag representatives from 5 to 16.[20] For the first time the anti-Semites had a sufficient number of seats in the Reichstag to enable them to act as an independent parliamentary group.[21]

The Progressives suffered the worst loss in the elections. As usual, they had not been able to agree on the merits of the government's case for army reorganization and had entered the elections with two competing factions. A minority group, led by Heinrich Rickert, was in favor of Caprivi's army bill and organized itself as the Progressive Association (Freisinnige Vereinigung). The majority, under the leadership of Eugen Richter, opposed the bill and set itself up as the Progressive People's Party (Freisinnige Volkspartei). Taken together, they obtained a total of 37 seats in the new Reichstag (13 and 24 respectively). Only three years before, they had managed to win 67 seats. The election of 1893 was a defeat from which the Progressives never recovered.[22]

The new Reichstag passed the government's army bill but it was a Pyrrhic victory for Caprivi. His parliamentary majority amounted to a slim 16 votes. Moreover, it was obtained only because the Polish group,[23] whom Caprivi had befriended after Bismarck's policy of oppression, had voted for the government. The situation was little short of grotesque: the German army had been saved by the Polish "enemies of the Reich" whom German nationalism looked at as potential traitors in times of war and uncivilized riffraff in times of peace. The weakness of the administration's position, the increased independence of the Reichstag, and the rapidly developing trend towards a parliamentary regime, were only too plainly apparent.

The Kaiser quickly cooled towards Caprivi. After the 1893 elections one "Chancellor crisis" followed another. Wilhelm II, who had set out with the vision of reigning by the Grace of God over a nation united in devotion to the Hohenzollern dynasty, had grown tired of the endless, unheroic tasks of social conciliation. One domestic objective seemed as far from realization as ever: the industrial masses obstinately refused to be won over to throne and altar. Instead, they became more firmly attached to the Social Democrats who continued to proclaim revolutionary aims. The policy of moderation which the Emperor had been determined to follow now appeared utterly futile and impractical. The break between the Kaiser and Caprivi finally came in 1894, and was caused by the very same problem that had led to Bismarck's dismissal, the menace of the socialist labor movement. The dangers of parliamentary government were highlighted by the sweeping advances which it had permitted the revolutionary party to make. To save the state and society, the "subversive forces" had to be suppressed. This time, however, it was the Kaiser who favored the plan which he had rejected when Bismarck proposed it in 1890. Among those who encouraged him were King Albert of Saxony and King Wilhelm of Württemberg; the Prussian Prime Minister Count Botho von Eulenburg; the Conservatives around von Hammerstein; high-ranking army officers and industrialists; the recently founded, aggressively nationalistic Pan-German League (*Alldeutscher Verband*) and the equally militant Agrarian League—an array of cliques, groups, parties, and individuals who were united in what they hated and feared: parliamentarianism, liberalism, socialism.

A series of Reichstag elections and dissolutions, following each other in quick succession, would, they hoped, demonstrate once and for all the impracticability of the constitutional setup and prepare the nation for a *coup d'état*. The Kaiser played with the idea[24] but had neither the personal stature and authority required for this hazardous enterprise nor the backing of his Chancellor. When he saw his regime faced with the dilemma of a parliamentary majority which he had to keep at arm's length, and an unconstitutional usurpation of power which he did not quite dare attempt, he tried to imitate the strategy of the Iron Chancellor. Bismarck in 1878 had used the plots on Wilhelm I's life to create a political crisis which he could solve by outlawing the Social Democratic Party and switching from Liberal to Conservative-Catholic support. In June, 1894, the assassination of the President of the French Republic, Sadi Carnot, and a series of other anarchistic acts of violence in France, seemed to the Kaiser a suitable occasion for following the precedent. He demanded that energetic measures be taken against the subversive forces in Germany and asked the Prussian Prime Minister Eulenburg, who had demonstrated his skill at the time of the anti-Socialist act, to introduce adequate legislation for the protection of Reich, monarchy, church, and family. Eulenburg suggested that such legislation be enacted first in the Reich, that is, sponsored by Caprivi. But Caprivi, who was not in favor of discriminatory laws of any kind, feared the final outcome of the Kaiser's and Eulenburg's designs.

The Kaiser pressed the issue and undertook to carry the fight to the nation. In September, 1894, in one of his first outbursts of oratorical irresponsibility, of which many were to follow, he called upon his subjects to protect religion, ethics, and order against the parties of sedition. A few weeks later, in another speech, he wrecked Caprivi's policy of fostering friendship towards the Polish minority. Caprivi's enemies exploited the rift between Kaiser and Chancellor. Bismarck hastened to express his approval of the Kaiser's new policy. Eulenburg sent an Agrarian League delegation to the Kaiser to encourage his desire for a strong executive power and repressive legislation. Even the National Liberals felt that they should not be left behind and demanded, at a convention in Frankfurt in September, 1893, that the fight against Socialists and Poles be taken up anew. On the strength of the Kaiser's speeches Eulenburg drafted an antisedition bill of such severity that, if passed and enforced, the existing courts and prisons would not have been sufficient to handle the expected number of violators.[25]

Caprivi still continued to work for a compromise. He wanted the powers of the executive strengthened by more stringent laws against associations, meetings, and the press that were hostile to the state. He was ready to curb, but not to abolish, freedom of speech and assembly.

The time for the Kaiser to choose between Caprivi and Eulenburg came when the Ministers of the German states were summoned to Berlin to consider the antisedition bill. When they warned him that excessively drastic measures might lead to civil war the Kaiser lost heart for proceeding with the Eulenburg plan. The dismissal of both the antagonists,

Caprivi and Eulenburg, now appeared to the Kaiser as the only way out of the untenable situation he himself had helped to create. In October, 1894, with Caprivi's resignation, the utopian phase of Wilhelm II's reign, the dream of the social monarchy, of the benevolent authoritarian state, came to an end. As Caprivi's successor the Kaiser picked Prince Chlodwig zu Hohenlohe-Schillingsfürst, seventy-five years of age. Under Hohenlohe—although not of his making—the policy of repression at home and aggression abroad, in which German imperialism excelled, began to bloom. The conservative reactionary forces of Prussia and the the once liberal industrial bourgeoisie found themselves united in the desire to suppress the labor movement, to curtail democratic rights, to abolish the general franchise as it existed in the Reich, and to put an end to the "sentimental philanthropy" of social reform. The new program was personified in the steel magnate von Stumm-Halberg who belonged to the Kaiser's intimate circle and whose rigid policy of "getting tough" with organized labor caused the chancellorship of Hohenlohe to be labeled "the Stumm era."

CHAPTER VI

THE FIRST WAVE OF RACIAL ANTI-SEMITISM

The analysis of German anti-Semitic literature, movements, and agitators discloses some rather unexpected and puzzling facts. The most implacable enemies of the Jews were urban rather than rural; indifferent, if not hostile, to the church rather than devout Christians, and members of the "educated" rather than the "ignorant" classes. The most virulent kind of anti-Semitism was spread throughout Germany by teachers, students, industrial and commercial employees, petty officials, professional people, and followers of cults of every variety: members of "life reform movements," whole-rye bread dietitians, opponents of vivisection, and "back to nature" builders of body and soul. From these groups, not from the peasants or the land-owning aristocracy or the reactionary clergy, narrow-minded though they might have been, came the fanatical haters of Jews.

To the conservative *Junker* the liberal or radical Jew was a source of annoyance, as the Jewish cattle dealer and middleman was to the peasant; to the one the Jew appeared as a political danger, to the other as an economic evil. But the antagonism of both was circumscribed. The economic function of Jews within the sphere of agriculture had to be accepted as necessary—resentment or no resentment. Cattle, grain, and fertilizers had to be bought and sold, credits negotiated and industrial products brought to the villages. Jews engaged in these fields did not compete with the agrarian producer. They appeared as the agents of the cities, of trading, banking, and industry, but still, for a long time, they were to some extent part of the agrarian community. Friction and animosity undoubtedly developed from the clash of interests between Jewish middlemen and farmers, yet an awareness of common interests and mutual dependency was not entirely lacking.

The urban sector of the old and new *Mittelstand* presented a different picture. Insecurity and instability were the dominant notes of their existence. Taking advantage of easier access to higher education, members of the lower middle classes vigorously pushed their way up into new occupations which had only a limited absorptive capacity. Competition was bitterly intense and the competitors were frequently Jewish. That aspirants from the lower middle classes, unsure of their prospects, were particularly sensitive to this fact is testified to by numerous, recurrent complaints about the disproportionately high ratio of Jewish high school pupils and university students, lawyers, and physicians. The nature of the struggle precluded compromise. Baptism and other symbols of assimilation could not be permitted to establish equality of opportunity in a limited field where the candidacy of every new claimant seemed to impoverish the prospects of all the others. Whatever sacrifices and adjustments Jews might be willing to make, the exigencies of competition were such that many participants felt that no individual merit should enable Jews to gain access to spheres from which it was desirable to eliminate them altogether. The interests of petty bourgeois high school and university graduates, who coveted jobs and positions as teachers, judges, lawyers, journalists, physicians, engineers, administrators, and politicians, were at variance with the old-fashioned notion that religious conversion and political reliability, honesty, and public-mindedness established civil equality.

To gauge the depth of this antagonism it is well to compare it with the attitude of a Treitschke or Stoecker. Treitschke's anti-Semitism was anchored in his nationalism, but this nationalism was still related to some of the traditional values of Western civilization. For him the national state was the most worthy object of an individual's devotion.[1] As a consequence, Treitschke thought that Jews were dangerous because he felt that they remained aloof from the state and the Protestant monarchy. He believed that they were undermining the heroic idealism that had brought about the Reich. The frame of reference of this anti-Semitism was the conflict between the state and the individual, between unity and liberty, authoritarian decision and parliamentary compromise. It held out to Jews the possibility of complete national and social integration if they would but side with the forces of national self-assertion whose passionate advocate Treitschke had become. As he saw it, a good German was assessed by his individual beliefs and conduct; not only was assimilation possible, but it was actually the Jews' foremost duty—and their salvation. The idea of revoking the emancipation law was unacceptable to Treitschke; this, he argued, would constitute "an act of obvious injustice, a break with the fine traditions of our state, which would sharpen rather than mitigate the national conflicts that plague us."[2]

To a lesser degree, Stoecker's position involved similar considerations. Like Treitschke, Stoecker did not want legal emancipation rescinded; instead he favored discrimination as an administrative policy.[3] Bona fide baptism was to assure complete equality between converted Jews and Christians. No racism underlay Stoecker's violent rejection of the "Jewish spirit." He was too deeply committed to the ethical concepts of conservative Protestantism not to be aware of the dangers to state, church, and rule-by-law inherent in the racial philosophy of the extremists. "I have no use for a movement that is merely anti-Jewish and is not also motivated by a deep love of the Gospel," he said in 1881, in an address to German students.[4] However ardent his nationalism, he did not want to render unto Caesar without rendering unto God. "If one makes an idol out of the worldly fatherland, if there is no longer a heavenly fatherland beyond the worldly one, even patriotic thought can become dark; today, in many a mind an idea of fatherland and state prevails which does not serve the light."[5]

Racial anti-Semitism, however, which gained strength in Germany during the last decades of the nineteenth century, was no longer tempered by Christian or conservative considerations. On the contrary, it attacked Christianity hardly less violently than Judaism and often turned against the Conservatives with the battle cry "against *Junkers* and Jews." Some of its extreme spokesmen wanted to eradicate every vestige of "Jewishness" by destroying with it the Christian religion, "child of Jewish religion and Platonism, born out of wedlock," whose reign in the final analysis implied the "*Verjudung* of humanity."[6]

Of course, Christian Social criticism of Jews had fertilized the soil for racial anti-Semitism. Without the "moderate," respectable variety of anti-Semitism preached by the Court Chaplain the inflammatory, "plebeian" agitation of a Henrici would have been unthinkable. Even Stoecker's friend and biographer Oertzen concedes that "the racial and rowdy anti-Semites would hardly have appeared had not Stoecker previously started his fight against Berlin's Jewry."[7] With regard to the Jews' sinister role in the economy and in the cultural life of the nation, there was little difference of opinion between the two schools. One need only look at the authoritative catalogue of Jewish misdeeds which the racial anti-Semite Theodor Fritsch compiled in *Antisemiten-Katechismus*[8] to see the numerous points of agreement between him and Stoecker. Under the heading, "What are the Jews really guilty of"? the following charges were listed:

1. Jews engage in usurious dealings with peasants, artisans, officials and officers.
2. Their sharp business practices lead to the decline of honest trade and make it their prey.
3. They ruin handicraft and cause formerly independent artisans to submit to wage slavery.

4. They force wages and prices down to a level where honest labor can hardly exist any longer and the threat of a bloody revolution constantly grows.

5. They have a monopoly of the press and use it to deceive the people as to the true causes of their misery and to divert discontent toward wrong targets (government, church Junkers, police, officials).

6. They demoralize the people by feeding them sensational and obscene news, degrading our entire culture.

7. They committed fraud on a gigantic scale at the time of the financial crash.

8. They influence legislation through Jewish parliamentarians (Lasker, Bamberger, etc.) and through paid non-Jewish underlings, with the aim of furthering their own designs (fraudulent insolvency, gambling at the stock exchange; freedom of movement).

9. They commercialize all values: offices, titles, prestige, honor, love; causing moral devastation especially among the nation's young womanhood. ("The Jews' low sensuous disposition and their lack of decency make them the most unscrupulous seducers.") They run the white slave trade.

10. They have lured into their nets and bribed many prominent persons; the few men of character who resist are mercilessly slandered in the Jewish press.

11. They dominate even governments through shrewd financial operations, have pull with all cabinets through international contacts so that "no individual state can dare to take steps against the Jews without being set upon by neighboring states."

Stoecker had voiced much the same beliefs about the socioeconomic role of the Jews. Solicitude for the ruined artisan, the underpaid petty official, the indebted army officer, the starving industrial worker, was typical of all anti-Semites. So was the fear of social revolution, the contempt for parliamentary authority, the hatred of the influential liberal press, and the grief about the passing of the old virtues.

But there were also significant innovations in the new bill of particulars. Its last two points were entirely out of line with Christian Social convictions. Never would Stoecker have thought of painting so gloomy a picture of Christian corruptibility, of such low resistance to Jewish temptation on the part of "many prominent persons." Never would he have spoken of the "few men of character" who kept their integrity. The very theme of tragedy and Untergang was repugnant to Stoecker's belief in the basic stability of a conservative Christian world, whose Judaic inheritance he acknowledged. He chided the racial anti-Semites for the nihilistic pessimism which had become the characteristic feature of their Weltanschauung ever since Wilhelm Marr had introduced it in his Sieg des Judentums über das Germanentum. "We do not believe the end of the German spirit to be so near," Stoecker had said in his first public speech against "modern Jewry," and expressed his confidence in a German recovery.

The racists were not reveling in despair merely to make their agitation more effective. They actually suffered from a pervasive lack of the psychological security which comes from belonging to a powerful, cohesively operating social group rather than one in the throes of disintegration. The Christian Social anti-Semites, still close to the old social hierarchy, to the church and the monarchy, found some emotional compensation for the loss of status they had suffered in the friendly proximity of high-ranking Conservatives. No self-respecting Conservative would have even thought, much less publicly stated, that only a "few men of character" were not bought by the Jews, or that all governments were venal. But assurance, the security of "belonging," was exactly what the racists did not have. They had no real ties with the powerful social classes and no loyalties to any of the leading parties. The fury of their total assault was the fury of total frustration and envy. Desperately in need of self-assurance, they only had threadbare and pitiful rationalizations at their disposal to explain their lack of success and standing. How, for instance, were they to account for the fact that the Jews, an inferior race, had contributed so many prominent men to all spheres of public life? Listen to Fritsch: "It is ten times as easy for a Jew to become famous as it is for a German. As soon as a Jew shows as much as a trace of talent, the Jewish press all over the world backs him up and blows his horn in all corners of the earth. Even the most talented German is killed by silence if he does not play the Jews' game."[9] Why—another enigma—were the creative, industrious, more intelligent Aryans taken in by the inferior race? Listen to Ahlwardt:* "The German is fundamentally trusting, his heart is full of loyalty and confidence. The Jew gains this confidence, only to betray it at the proper moment, ruining and pauperizing the German. This abuse of confidence on the part of the Jews is their main weapon."[10] The racial literature of the time is shot through with indications that the anti-Semitic movement suffered from a strong sense of isolation. Its leaders were painfully aware of being "the few men" to whom the *Antisemiten-Katechismus* referred as not having succumbed to the lure of money. The groups from which the agitators recruited the bulk of their followers were most lacking in social cohesion and unity of purpose. Cohesion and purpose became in the anti-Semitic mind the most sinister attributes of Jews, who were accused of considering themselves "a natural aristocracy," of forming "a political, social and business

* For excerpts of Ahlwardt's speech see Document No. VI.

alliance for the purpose of exploiting and subjugating the non-Jewish peoples."

By 1880, when racial anti-Semitism in Germany began to become an organized myth, racial theories had long been current in European thought. They did not originate in Germany[11] nor was Germany the only country where they were taken up by political movements. Racism became an element of nationalism everywhere in Europe. French nationalists, for instance, humiliated by their country's defeat in 1870–71, saw the ultimate reason for France's decline in the pollution of the true Gallic race by "foreigners." In the chauvinistic atmosphere created by the Dreyfuss case, French Jews were designated as the agents of Germany on French soil. "A veritable xenophobia animated the conservative and reactionary ranks in all countries," writes Jacques Barzun[12] in his study of racist ideologies in Europe since the middle of the nineteenth century. Eduard Drumont's *La France Juive* (2 vols., 1885, 1886) is a classic in comparison to which Wilhelm Marr's pamphlet, usually referred to as a landmark in the evolution of racial anti-Semitism, reads like the essay of a Gobineau-inspired amateur. Life in a France ruled according to the ideas of Charles Maurras, in a Germany governed by disciples of Paul de Lagarde, or in an England taken over by the followers of Thomas Carlyle, would be difficult, indeed, for any person of liberal belief—and more so for one of Jewish extraction.

That anti-Semitism was linked with nineteenth-century nationalism is all the more reason for scrutinizing the German variety. What was it that made the latter so uniquely dangerous and eventually so destructive? From where did it draw a strength which it could not acquire in England and France?

The answer must be related to the fact that German anti-Semitism was woven into a sociopolitical struggle, similar to and yet unlike that of the other Western nations. In Germany, the forces that bred and used anti-Semitism were stronger and resistance to them weaker than in England or France. Politically speaking, conservative-clerical France, the France of the anti-Dreyfusards, had been beaten in 1789 and ever since had been engaged in a difficult comeback fight. Its counterpart in Germany had never lost its paramount position in state and society. In England and France, a national ideology had been developed by the middle classes which regarded themselves as the backbone of the modern state. In Germany conservatism took the national ideology away from the middle classes, its erstwhile herald, infused it with conservative-clerical values, and monopolized it to the exclusion of all other groups. By the end of the century Germany had become a leading industrial nation but its astounding industrial transformation was grafted upon a preindustrial political structure. Groups victimized by industrialization saw the villain in "liberalism," in those forces which made for the socioeconomic transformation of the nation but did not have the power or will to account also for its political life. In Germany, anti-Semitism thus found allies it could not have found at all or not in such strength in nations where the industrial revolution was accompanied by one in politics. In France and England the same social groups suffered from the advance of capitalism which in Germany registered their protest through anti-Semitism and antiliberalism. But in these countries they found no semifeudal, semiabsolutistic forces in power with which to align themselves against the upper bourgeoisie. They had to fend for themselves but they also had the opportunity to participate in forming the political will of the nation. In imperial Germany, however, political representation of social groups in the sense of actual influence upon government was in glaring disproportion to their number and weight.[13] This absence of political power was compensated for by enlarged notions of social status. In a society as highly caste-conscious as Germany's this situation was bound to affect even groups which were opposed to political reaction and class rule. Exclusive, not egalitarian, trends were predominant throughout German society; even the labor movement, the political organization of the class lowest in esteem and completely excluded from the business of government, was not free of signs of a caste ideology and caste behavior of its own.

Strong allies of anti-Semitism were matched by weak defenders of the Jews. German liberalism had never won a decisive victory. It proved particularly vulnerable to the pressure of the national ideology which it had permitted conservatism to usurp. In every election where a "national" issue was involved, whether it concerned a larger army and navy, colonies, or internal "sedition," liberalism was defeated if it dared go against the current. Political Catholicism, which in imperial Germany acted as a parliamentary, rather than an authoritarian force, had greater inherent powers of resistance. Nevertheless, after the *Kulturkampf* it did not dare expose itself again to the odium of committing treason against the Reich by following a consistently liberal policy. It steered a cautious course aiming at a parliamentary regime, with general civic and political safeguards as Catholicism's best protection against Protestant autocracy. To this extent political Catholicism, once its militant anti-Jewish period was over, could be counted upon to be "anti-anti-Semitic," though it had no love for either orthodox or atheist Jews. At no time did it prove anxious to associate itself with left-wing liberalism or socialism beyond the exigencies of a particular situation, such as an election. Socialist labor, finally, did not defend the Jews *qua* Jews, although it was on principle opposed to anti-Semitism. But as it rejected the prevailing social order and the national state, it came under attack as a "Jewish protective guard" (*Judenschutztruppe*). The anti-Semitic stereotype was enriched by those features which identify socialism in the eyes of its enemies: revolutionary designs and treacherous internationalism. While socialist labor showed extraordinary strength of conviction and purpose against Conservative-clerical reaction, including anti-Semitism, it lacked initiative against the onslaught of the nationalistic ideology.

After all this has been stated, there remains a quality in German racial nationalism which seems to elude a purely politico-economic interpretation. How is one really to understand a philosophy or religion that, in the nineteenth century, makes "blood" its Holy Grail? That worships "race" as a spiritual ultimate and dreams of a racial community which would at once be egalitarian and elite-bound, brotherly toward its members and merciless toward the world outside?

From its very outset German racism was essentially un-Christian. The study of its literature and cults almost prompts one to look for its roots in pre-Christian German history. The paganism which the Western world later was to discover in the Nazi *Weltanschauung* was not at all identical with the antireligious and anticlerical enlightenment of the seventeenth and eighteenth centuries; it was not motivated by reason and tolerance but by mythologic concepts of race, folkdom, blood, and nature which had all the imponderable force of religious persuasion. There are many elements, however, which link this modern paganism to post- and anti-Enlightenment nineteenth-century German Romanticism.

The realm of nature held a central place in racist thought. It saw individuals and cultures as governed by inexorable laws. All that man could ever hope to achieve was to become more aware of his blood, and thus of his fate, his calling, his duties, to which he had been predestined by nature. This fatalism, impervious to doubt and reason, was embraced by the racial anti-Semites as the highest revelation of science. In the name of science they claimed a paramount place in the natural hierarchic order of the races of mankind. While Christian-conservative rejection of Jews was concerned with the preservation of a society divided by the will of God into the high and the lowly, racial anti-Semitism preached the solidarity of the nation as a racial community and advocated suppression of "the Jew," a lower species of man, as an obligation to nature.[14]

No less characteristic was the fascination which the sphere of sex held for the racial anti-Semites. Notions of "blood pollution" and "purification" preoccupied them intensely. "Thou shalt keep thy blood pure," said the third commandment* of their decalogue.[15] "Consider it a crime to soil the noble Aryan breed of your people by mixing it with Jewish blood. For you must know that Jewish blood is indestructible and determines the Jewishness of body and soul onto the latest generations." Taken up by the racists, Theodor Mommsen's statement that the Jews in Roman antiquity had also been "an effective fermenting agent of cosmopolitism and national decomposition"[16] acquired an entirely new connotation. When the racists talked about "the Jews" causing the decomposition of German society, they were not satisfied with accepting the interpretation which conservative anti-Semitism gave to Mommsen's statement. Stoecker's anti-Semites deplored the social and cultural changes which they attributed to the disintegrating effect of allegedly Jewish intellectual traits and behavior upon a specific culture in a specific society. The racists regarded "decomposition" as a phenomenon unrelated to any historical situation; as a purely physiological process caused by the "well-known sexual inclinations of the Jews." Sexual orgies were visualized against the background of a sinister conspiracy. While the Jews practiced and enjoyed libertinism, they also accomplished their secret racial mission, namely, to ensure the moral and physical degeneration of the host nation.

Modern psychology has paid much attention to the mechanisms that are at play in the projection of repressed individual desires upon suitable objects of the outside world. Historical and sociological circumstances have made the Jews as a group particularly fit to serve as a screen upon which such desires can be projected. One of the psychological springs of anti-Semitism may well be an unconscious revolt against the burdensome restraints of civilization, either religious or secular. Strong sexual repression has frequently been found to be a component of the personality structure of anti-Semites.[17]

In racial anti-Semitism, the merging of psychological and political categories made for an aggressive ideology of nationalism and imperialism. Aryan blood, embodying the secret of the highest creation, was glorified as the only guarantee of national survival in a hostile world, and consequently, as a providential promise of world domination. Hitler's apocalyptic prediction that the nation of purest blood would eventually rule the universe was formulated in the anti-Semitic literature of the 1890's. "The people which first and most thoroughly rids itself of its Jews and thus opens the door to its innate cultural development is predestined to become the bearer of culture and consequently the ruler of the world," Ahlwardt wrote in 1890.[18] Hitler merely paraphrased this statement in *Mein Kampf*: "A state which in the days of

* For the racists' Ten Commandments see Document No. VII.

race poisoning endeavors to cultivate its best racial elements is bound to become some day the master of the world."[19]

Morally, spiritually, and aesthetically, nothing was more offensive to the racists than the characteristics they attributed to the Jews: the so-called unproductivity of the Semitic mind, their alleged propensity for acquiring without creating, for atomizing the organic structure of the state, for despoiling the purity and beauty of the racial body. The term "Jewish" in the racists' vocabulary stood for selfish, individualistic, asocial behavior and it also designated the physical traits of a human subspecies—ugly, mollusc-like, sensuous. Stoecker had felt called upon to raise his voice against Jewish arrogance, materialism, and lack of reverence for the Christian-conservative world. Racial anti-Semitism in addition engraved upon the stereotype the traits of perversion and treachery; more ominous still, it learned how and taught others how to look at the Jews as one of nature's caprices, destined to plague and to test her noblest creation, the Aryan. To the Aryan the very existence of Jews was a reminder that nature was watching to see how her favorite child would pass its test. If its premises were accepted, the racial theory was a closed, logical system of thought. Uncompromising in its conclusions, it was sped along by a hysteric will for action. Prognostics of impending doom, dire warnings that the German nation will be quickly destroyed unless it finds the strength to eject the poison from its blood stream, reverberate endlessly in the racist literature. Immediate action or national obliteration was the fatal alternative offered the German people from Marr's *Sieg des Judentums* and Ahlwardt's *Verzweiflungskampf der arischen Völker* down to Hitler's *Mein Kampf*.

Politically, both Conservative-Protestant and racial anti-Semitism were first organized in Berlin and from there carried outward into the provinces. In contrast to the Conservative-Protestant movement, however, which had found an outstanding leader in Stoecker and unified command in the Christian Social Party, the organizational forms of racial anti-Semitisim offer a picture of great diversity and instability. On the trunk of the racial creed a multitude of circles, groups, and parties sprouted and died repeatedly. It is not necessary to describe them all in detail. Most significant is the fact that in the eighties the anti-Semitic movement had been completely dominated by Stoecker and that in the nineties the racists had wrested the leadership from him. A brief summary of the development that led to this change is necessary.

The idea of a political grouping with no other objectives besides radical anti-Semitism was perhaps first propagandized by Moritz Busch,[20] writer, editor, Bismarck's press attaché in the Foreign Office, and known to be the Chancellor's journalistic handy man. Busch wanted an organization supported by all other parties and devoted solely to the elimination of Jews from public life. This "party *ad hoc*" was to welcome in its ranks everybody, "unitarian or particularist, liberal or conservative, orthodox or rationalist, ultramontane or Protestant" provided the adherents would "not tolerate any longer the full equality of the Semitic elements with the native one" and took the pledge never to vote for a Jew, nor to read a newspaper edited by Jews or friendly to Jews, and to work with all their energies for the exclusion of "Semitic intruders" from the political scene.

Wilhelm Marr's League of Anti-Semites (1879) and Ernst Henrici's Social Reich Party (1880) actually attempted to build a political organization around anti-Semitism as the exclusive principle for political action and the solution of national problems. Neither succeeded as a mass organization[21] and the elections of 1881 showed their hopeless isolation in Berlin where they had tried to get a start in the backwash of the Stoecker agitation. Marr's gloomy outlook on the "cultural and political bankruptcy of the Occident" was confirmed by his failure to receive financial support for a weekly through which he intended "to bring moral pressure to bear upon the Jewish *Fremdherrschaft*" (alien domination) and which would "least of all render homage to Social Democratic utopias."[22] His mission ended when he turned "with revulsion and nausea"[23] *(Ekel zum Erbrechen)* from rowdy anti-Semitism.

The span of Henrici's agitation was also short. It hardly lasted more than three years (1880–1882). But his turbulent appearance on the political scene marked the beginning of "enlightened, progressive" as opposed to "Christian-conservative" anti-Semitism. He was the first agitator who claimed to speak for "all truly liberal citizens." He castigated the liberal parties for their friendliness to Jews and the Conservatives for their "opportunistic" stand on the Jewish question. Not that his own anti-Jewish demands contained anything new. Jews were to be forbidden by law to occupy civil service or army positions or to be elected to legislative bodies; the census of denominations was to be restored; Jewish immigration to be stopped.[24] Besides the usual demands for social reforms, which made up the bulk of the "practical" suggestions in all anti-Semitic platforms, Henrici's party called for a stronger central administration and an active colonial policy. Next to loyalty to the Kaiser and the Reich it placed loyalty to the German people. Like the Social Democratic program, it demanded legislation on standard working hours. Henrici's attempts to find a political approach broad enough to overcome existing political cleavages were as yet awkward and unsure. But the trend was discernible: centralization of governmental power; aggressive foreign policy; reconciliation of the liberal middle classes and labor with the *Kaiserreich* on the basis of a budding imperialism. The concept of the Nation, once liberal and democratic, was fast becoming a bureaucratic and imperialistic one.

Henrici for a while cooperated with ultraconservative Max Liebermann von Sonnenberg, an ex-officer and, like Henrici, an anti-Semite of the racial school. Liebermann saw the salvation of Germany in "the material and ethical rebirth of German folkdom" and in "more practical Christianity." As the best way to put such ideals into practice he suggested doing away with parliamentary government, the source of all corruption, and replacing it temporarily by a dictatorship of the Kaiser, "constitutionally arrived at,"[25] until the political representation of the corporative state was established. The two agitators, however, soon parted company. Liebermann, together with Nietzsche's brother-in-law, Bernhard Förster, tried his hand with an anti-Semitic organization of his own, the German People's Association (*Deutscher Volksverein*), which he aligned with the Conservative Central Committee, the high command of the Berlin Movement. This was not to Henrici's liking. During the 1881 election campaign Henrici attacked the Committee for its dependency on the Conservative Party. The Conservatives, he said, "in truly Jewish fashion" exploited the great national movement of Berlin for narrow party interests and were out to pull themselves up by the coattails of the anti-Semites. It might be said in passing that the charge of exploiting the achievements of the popular movement often recurred in the working alliance of anti-Semites and the Conservatives. Every so often the anti-Semites would feel shortchanged and unfailingly try blackmail by alluding to social cleavages between their own "people's" movement and the privileged upper classes. The classic case occurred in 1932 when Hindenburg's selection of Franz von Papen rather than Hitler as Reich Chancellor temporarily disrupted the cooperation between the Nazis and the German Nationals. Goebbels' attack on Papen's "cabinet of noblemen" culminated in the indignant outcry: "Upon our broad backs they climbed to power."

After the national elections of 1881, the relations between the Conservative Central Committee and the racial anti-Semites of liberal and conservative coloring deteriorated. Henrici's and Liebermann's parties had pulled no weight. In 1883, the Conservative Central Committee, encouraged by the governmental press, dropped the anti-Semitic extremists in the preparation of municipal elections in the Reich capital and organized the various Citizens' Leagues into the "unpolitical" German Citizens' Party with which it unsuccessfully tried to break Berlin's Progressive majority. The Committee itself disintegrated soon afterwards. Some of the most notorious agitators disappeared from Berlin. Bernhard

Förster emigrated to South America. Henrici left for the United States. Liebermann von Sonnenberg, whose *Deutsche Volkszeitung* had to stop publication in 1885, was also on the verge of sailing to the New World, but changed his mind and transferred his activities to the new centers of political anti-Semitism, Westphalia and Saxony. In 1884 and 1885 several new attempts in Berlin to form anti-Semitic parties outside of Stoecker's organization, such as the "Anti-Semitic German-Progressive League," ended in failure. But even if none of the ventures prospered and the modern party which would cut across the lines of Germany's political life failed to emerge, the cumulative efforts were not inconsequential. The radicals succeeded, to some extent, in ridding anti-Semitism of the stigma of bigotry and obscurantism, a severe handicap in the sophisticated climate which prevailed in late nineteenth-century Germany. Henceforth, an anti-Semite no longer was necessarily a conservative, a reactionary, a lackey of the *Junkers*, or a pious churchgoer. He could pose as a liberal, progressive, even as a revolutionary.

In Berlin, racial anti-Semitism was kept in check by its conservative-clerical rival. It gained in the provinces where Stoecker's influence was weak. Organizations of some stability that embraced the racial theory, and thus put themselves outside the Christian Social camp, developed in Saxony, Westphalia, and Hesse. The German Reform Party (*Deutsche Reform Partei*) in Dresden (1880), led by Alexander Pinkert, was in its social composition similar to the Stoecker party, with small businessmen, artisans, shopkeepers, and petty officials making up the bulk of its followers. For the most part, it merely repeated the slogans and demands which the Berlin Movement had made popular. It stood for "social reform" by way of compulsory guilds, easier credit for the *Mittelstand*, higher taxation of mobile capital, and the exclusion of Jews from public administration. Within a few years, the party had watered down its anti-Semitic principles sufficiently to make common cause with the National Liberals in defeating at the polls, in 1884, the Social Democratic candidate, August Bebel; the anti-Semitic candidate who won Bebel's seat enrolled in the Conservative Reichstag group. Outside of Dresden, the party had local branches in a number of cities, including Berlin, but it never was able to build up a nationwide, centralized organization.

Two of its branches, one in Leipzig, under Theodor Fritsch (1884), the other in Kassel, under Otto Boeckel (1886), tried to revive the ailing movement and in 1886 joined the German Anti-Semitic Alliance (*Deutsche Antisemitische Vereinigung*). It stressed its opposition to the Stoecker movement by pledging its members to work for the repeal of the emancipation law and for the passage of special legislation which would treat Jews as aliens. In 1887, Boeckel was elected to the Reichstag. He was the first anti-Semitic deputy who remained independent from the Conservative Party, the founder of an autonomous anti-Semitic Reichstag group, henceforward a permanent feature of the German parliament.

Boeckel was elected in a rural election district, Marburg-Frankenberg-Kirchhain in Hesse, a region notorious for the poverty of its peasant population.[26] The constituency had long been uncontested Conservative territory. Now a youth of 26, a librarian and a student of German folklore, had broken its allegiance. Boeckel had gone from village to village, spreading the slogan, "Peasants! Free yourselves from the Jewish middlemen!" and campaigning for rural credit cooperatives and markets from which the Jews were to be barred. His popularity was extraordinary. "The peasants adored him as their awakener and liberator," Hellmut von Gerlach, Boeckel's opponent in the elections of 1898 and 1903, relates.[27] "From miles away they came to his meetings. Peasant lads on horseback would escort him when he honored a *judenfreie* cattle market with his presence. Garlands were strung across the streets, the mothers held their little children up and told them 'Look at the man, he is our liberator!' For a few years he was truly peasant king of Hesse."

Following in the footsteps of Moritz Busch, Boeckel wanted the Jewish question treated as "a national question which concerns every German regardless of creed and political affiliation."[28] In his opinion the decline of the anti-Semitic movement was entirely due to the fact that it had permitted itself to be taken in tow by the Conservatives. The fight against the Jews, "a tough, old and alien race which cannot be subdued either by baptism or intermarriage," which "thinks differently, feels differently and acts differently," should be above party politics. All good Germans should cooperate in arriving at a solution—in a strictly legal and honorable way, Boeckel insisted—and the beginning of such a solution would have to be recognition by constitutional law of the fact that "in Germany there live two different nations: Germans and Jews; the former are the country's masters; the latter are guests who may enjoy the rights of hospitality but never those of masters." In the parliament the Jewish question should be discussed "over and over again until the German people will learn no longer to regard the repeal of the emancipation law as 'intolerable,' as 'persecution mania' but to view it instead as an imperative requirement for the people's salvation." Boeckel's paper, the *Reichsherold*, coupled hatred of Jews with contempt for the Conservative Party. It campaigned against "that discredited Jewish clique" led by big landowners and political careerists, to whom Stoecker was only a bait for catching the anti-Semitic vote. Boeckel stood for the freedom of the press and for the extension of the general, equal franchise to include Prussia; with the Progressives and Social Democrats, he favored a federal income tax and opposed the growing military budget and the government's endeavors to create state trade monopolies as sources of revenues over which the Reichstag would have no control. He was equally firm in rejecting all clerical designs upon public education.

In the fight for the soul and the vote of the rural population, "democratic" anti-Semitism began to prove superior to anti-Semitic conservatism. Boeckel's anticlerical and anticonservative agitation was a matter of great concern to Stoecker. The latter complained: "In Hesse, Dr. Boeckel has gained such a reputation in towns and villages that clergymen do not dare to oppose him, even though he pursues the wrong kind of anti-Semitism. If they did, they would lose the last bit of influence in their communities. Reason enough for the church to try to familiarize itself with the right way of fighting Jewry and thus to keep in harmony with the folk soul as well as with the duties exacted by its calling as the guide of the people's religious aspirations."[29] The Conservatives and Stoecker had to write Boeckel off as a total loss. They deplored his "Social Democratic" methods of agitation. Boeckel struck back at them by refusing to have any dealings with the *Cohn*servative spokesmen for aristocratic privileges. In 1888, he resigned from the Anti-Semitic Alliance which was too much to the right for his taste. When in 1893 the Agrarian League began to operate, he denounced it as a tool of Conservative reaction.

What made this sudden irruption of a new political force into rural, traditionally conservative territory possible? How could two anti-Semitic movements coexist, whose rivalry at a superficial view was derived solely from different shades of anti-Semitism? Surely, there were considerable cultural and political differences between Western and Eastern Germany. But they can hardly account for the division as the Eastern provinces, too, were successfully invaded under the flag of racial anti-Semitism a few years later. The split in the anti-Jewish camp seems to have grown out of a clash of group interests brought into the open as a result of the deep-seated agricultural depression and the government's tariff and fiscal policy. Put in a nutshell, the essential conflict was between large-scale grain production and small-scale intensive farming. Stoecker was close to grain and feed producers, the *Junkers*, whose economy hinged on high prices for their main crops; to keep prices high they needed protective tariffs and government subsidies. But whoever sided with the *Junkers* antagonized the small peasant who made his living from dairy and animal farming and depended on cheap feed, i.e., low grain prices. This conflict between *Junker* and peasant farming ran through the entire history of the *Kaiserreich* and the Weimar Republic; it engendered peasant organizations outside and in opposition to the Agrarian League, associate of the Conservative Party. It is on the strength of this conflict that Liberals, and after 1918 the Social Democrats, too, tried to break the Conservatives' hold on millions of small farmers, to make them realize how much their own well-being depended on that of the urban industrial masses. The attempts on the whole were not successful, but still the economic conflict persisted and made itself felt in many ways. It influenced the choice of political candidates, the parliamentary line-up in trade and tax legislation, and the growth of the cooperative movement.

To understand the success of Boeckel's racial agitation it must be seen in still another context. When Boeckel embarked upon his political career, the parliamentary scene was dominated by the *Kartell*. Stoecker's hands were tied by the Conservatives' coalition with the National Liberals, and his Christian Social movement was at low ebb. The Conservatives soft-pedaled political anti-Semitism and had little opportunity to cash in on the benefits of anti-Semitic agitation. What was more, by sharing with the National Liberals the responsibility for the government's policy, they exposed themselves to the wrath of the lower middle classes. Thrown back into isolation, the *Mittelstand* rediscovered the Conservative Party to be the tool of *Junker* interests; it now perceived the role of conservative anti-Semitism in its true light as a tactical device used by powerful groups in temporary opposition to the government for the purpose of intimidating the latter and staging a comeback.

Boeckel's anti-Conservative campaign also impelled the right wing of the racial anti-Semites, the groups around Liebermann von Sonnenberg, Theodor Fritsch, Paul Förster, etc., to move away from the Conservatives. In 1889, at the Anti-Semites' Day in Bochum, Boeckel and Liebermann agreed on a platform which contained side by side rather incongruous demands, such as the revocation of the emancipation law and the nationalization of basic industries. Liebermann, propagandist of the corporative state, sworn enemy of the parliamentary system, went so far as to declare his opposition to further legal restrictions on the Social Democratic Party, because he saw in "each parliamentary representative of this [Social Democratic] tendency a living reminder to the government to hasten social reform; but [in] each National Liberal Reichstag member a weight on the scale of *laissez faire* that has brought us already so near the abyss."[30]

Unity, the aim of the Anti-Semites' Day, however, could not be achieved. The "democratic" and "conservative" wings of racial anti-Semitism simply could not fuse. Unable to come to a satisfactory agreement with Boeckel, Liebermann in 1889 founded the German-Social Anti-Semitic Party (*Deutschsoziale Antisemitische Partei*). Boeckel followed suit in 1890 with the Anti-Semitic People's Party (*Antisemitische Volkspartei*). Bochum (Westphalia) and Erfurt (Province of Saxony) were the respective headquarters of the two organizations. In the 1890 electoral campaign, however, the two parties supported each other's candidates. Four of the Boeckel group, and Liebermann as the sole representative of his party, won over their opponents. Altogether about 48,000 votes were cast for anti-Semitic candidates, out of a total vote of more than seven million. The four members elected as candidates of the Anti-Semitic People's Party officially formed in the Reichstag the "anti-Semitic group" (*Antisemiten-Fraktion*) with Boeckel as chairman. Liebermann refused to join.

Election returns[31] for the four districts conquered by the Boeckelites in 1890 reveal interesting details. In one district, several thousand votes cast in the first balloting for the Social Democratic candidate went in the run-off election to the anti-Semite rather than to his National Liberal opponent. In another district, run-off elections gave the anti-Semite nearly the entire National Liberal vote, which assured the defeat of the Progressive contestant. Where Stoecker had failed, the radical anti-Semites appeared fairly successful. Dissatisfied voters were not averse to taking a chance on a new-fangled party of opposition, perhaps even rebellion. Political boundaries had become fluid; loyalties that had belonged to the Conservatives, National Liberals, or Social Democrats were being shifted to the leftist, "democratic" wing of the anti-Semites.

The racists followed up their first major political victory with an intensive campaign. The *Antisemitische Correspondenz*, publication of the German-Social Party, reported in 1890[32] that 3,000 to 4,000 leaflets and other pieces of literature were mailed daily by the Leipzig office "quietly to enlist new friends of the ideas of the anti-Semites." Leipzig, the seat of the German Anti-Semitic Alliance and of the *Hammer* publishing house, both under Theodor Fritsch's management, became a major propaganda center for racial anti-Semitism. In the elections of 1893, the "pure" anti-Semites stunned the nation when their vote jumped from 48,000 to a quarter of a million.

Anti-Semitism as a political force was no longer a reliable ally of the Christian conservative state. It had grown bold, and what it demanded was in open conflict with the material and ideological interests of all the privileged groups, bourgeois or aristocratic. The "valve of anti-Semitic hatred" which alone, Maximilian Harden had said, prevented the anti-capitalist *Mittelstand* from joining forces with Social Democracy,[33] was failing to function for conservatism. Anti-Semitism as a political grouping displayed visible elements of social radicalism which brought it uncomfortably close to sedition. This was most obvious in the agitation of Herman Ahlwardt who for years was a celebrated anti-Semitic rabble-rouser and a very controversial figure among the leaders of the anti-Semitic movement. Ahlwardt was born in 1846 in a small Pomeranian village. The son of an artisan, he received a good education and became a schoolteacher. At the age of 35 he had worked his way up to an appointment as the principal (*Rektor*) of a Berlin public school. His career as educator, however, ended prematurely and the circumstances throw some light on the man and his later "calling."

By the time he was made a school principal Ahlwardt was heavily in debt. It was through no fault of his own, he said, but due to an act of friendship—underwriting a loan for a colleague who failed to meet his obligations. However that may be, the fact is that Ahlwardt never managed to solve his financial problems. Friends and benefactors—they ranged from Stoecker to liberal notables, including Jewish ones—repeatedly came to his rescue but to no avail. Ahlwardt became hopelessly entrapped in a tangle of short-term loans and usurious interest rates. One hundred out of the 250 pages of his first book[34] are devoted to a minute record of the author's dealings with Jewish usurers, a weird example of exhibitory self-humiliation combined with persecution mania. In the course of time Ahlwardt's "negligence" in financial matters reached the point where he began to pocket school collection money for himself. The authorities started proceedings, and in 1890 Ahlwardt was removed from his position. Shortly afterwards, he entered the field of politics with his book *The Aryan Peoples' Battle of Despair Against Jewry*. The German public had by then been accustomed to anti-Jewish writing but nothing had been printed yet to match Ahlwardt's attack in vituperation, irresponsibility, and sheer madness.

The Jewish octopus, as the *Verzweiflungskampf* depicted it, had sunk its arms into every vital sphere of German society. Neither the army nor the government nor any social group was able any more to shake off the monster. Educators, officers, peasants, civil servants, workers, businessmen—all had to pay their tribute. A Jewish conspiracy had been behind the attempts upon the old Kaiser's life in 1878; Jewish bankers had financially enslaved high-placed members of the ruling dynasty; Jews exercised a controlling influence on a number of ministerial departments whose officials they had bribed and corrupted. Jews and their underlings abused, exploited, and undermined the German nation's healthy and stable social relations. All this was put forth with an elaborate apparatus of "evidence." The second part of the *Verzweiflungskampf*, under the heading, "The Oath of a Jew," consisted almost entirely of

private documents, police records, court decisions, and newspaper reports, so arranged as to prove that Bleichröder had commited perjury in
an alimony case and that he owed his liberty only to the protection of
Chancellor Caprivi and other important men in the government.

Such reckless charges against the honor of the courts and the integrity
of public officials were unheard of. They certainly did not go un-
answered. Brought before a court of law, Ahlwardt's "evidence" evaporated and part of the royalties on the *Verzweiflungskampf* consisted of
four months in jail for libel and slander. However, the alleged Bleich-
röder-Caprivi conspiracy aroused enough political excitement to result
in a parliamentary debate. The Conservatives were only too eager to
seize upon it to damage the Chancellor's position.

Hardly had the excitement subsided when Ahlwardt with another "disclosure" of Jewish corruption created a new sensation. In a pamphlet,
Judenflinten[35] (Jewish Rifles), he accused the industrial firm of Ludwig
Löwe of having supplied the government with faulty military rifles. The
inferior quality of these Löwe rifles, Ahlwardt asserted, was more than
just the usual result of Jewish greed, it was a plot hatched out in cooperation with the *Alliance Israélite Universelle* in Paris, in which high
German officials were criminally implicated.

International Jewry did not overlook anything that could contribute to Germany's defeat in the next war, and it finally made a monstrous attempt to put
a rifle in the hands of the German soldier which might be usable in peace
time when subjected to modest wear but which must soon break down under
battle conditions.

This attempt succeeded beyond expectation. Today the army already has
in its possession 425,000 rifles, supplied by the firm of Ludwig Löwe, Isidor
Löwe manager, which in wartime are bound to be almost less dangerous to
the enemy than to those who fire them.

Jewry, the Jewish central board of control (*Centralleitung*) as well as top
men at the Stock Exchange, must have thorough knowledge of this fact
which it took me great efforts to discover.

A first-rate scandal resulted. Twenty editions of the pamphlet were
sold out within a few weeks. The author, "adorned with laurels and
celebrated as the savior of the fatherland is being listened to with roaring applause in a number of popular mass meetings," *Neue Zeit*,[36] the
Social Democratic periodical, sarcastically reported from Berlin. The
pamphlet finally was confiscated by order of the government and
Ahlwardt himself was arrested. But public opinion roused to a well-
organized frenzy clamored for his release and for speedy investigation
of the charges he had made. The scandal broke when nationalist passion
was at its height. In the perennial struggle for the expansion of the

German army a new phase had been reached as the nightmare of a two-front war was conjured up by a Franco-Russian military rapprochement.

An investigation by the War Ministry established Ahlwardt's "disclosure" to have been a figment of his imagination from beginning to end. A statement in the official *Reichsanzeiger*[37] said that Löwe rifles met all requirements; that tests had revealed some technical deficiencies of weapons used by the army, but that such deficiencies did not concern weapons manufactured by the accused firm. In the suit brought by the Ludwig Löwe company Ahlwardt was sentenced to another five months in jail. Meanwhile, however, the condemned slanderer had been elected to the Reichstag, and the Reichstag held that the privilege of parliamentary immunity suspended the sentence.[38]

Ahlwardt was repeatedly exposed in law courts as a reckless, malicious, and dishonest slanderer. Officially documented evidence proved that his "revelations" were fabricated out of whole cloth. Yet, this did not ruin his public career. Quite the contrary. The damning evidence of his lack of integrity only seemed to improve Ahlwardt's political prospects. Apparently, whether successful legal proceedings also worked to discredit an agitator socially and politically depended chiefly on the esteem in which the law was held by the groups that supported him. The same observation applies to the history of those revolutionary movements which on principle rejected the existing law and judiciary as essentially the institutions of hostile class rule. In the early days of European organized labor the imprisonment of radical leaders usually served to cement the beliefs of their followers. Harsh sentences, far from diminishing the popular appeal of the prisoner, frequently made him into a hero and sanctified his name. The Social Democratic Party not only gained a million votes under the anti-Socialist act when party leaders and officers were persecuted; it also acquired extraordinary political cohesion in the course of its twelve-year proscription. In the critical years of the Weimar Republic the National Socialists rejected the laws of the land which they denounced as infamous and mismanaged by the "Jew Republic." In the few cases where the law decided against them they would proudly point to their punishment as a trophy of their national struggle and martyrdom. The situation was, of course, different for men like Stoecker for whom the slightest brush with the law was bound to have unfavorable repercussions. It embarrassed and alienated the groups whose support he wanted. It was unthinkable that throne and altar should be defended by a man whom the courts of the country exposed as a violator of established law and accepted morality. Stoecker's prestige, in fact, was damaged by law suits and trials, in one of which he had made a statement under oath which the court later was to declare "objectively wrong but not deliberately untrue." This was enough to earn him the sobriquet of *Meineidspfaffe* ("the clerical perjurer"), a label that plagued him for the rest of his life. In Stoecker's world, law and order still meant a great deal. By contrast, the fact that two jail sentences failed to damage Ahlwardt's public career indicates a considerable defiance of state and law among the people that backed him.

The full implications of the racists' defiance of the law were not realized at Ahlwardt's time. Social Democracy, a force that challenged existing law as class law, came nearest to understanding the phenomenon. In the socialist literature of the time this problem was repeatedly discussed and analyzed. Franz Mehring, the historian, who as a contributing editor of *Neue Zeit* wrote the most caustic commentaries on the cultural aspects of the Ahlwardt scandals, had an answer of his own to the baffling question as to why it was that "Ahlwardt's accusations were the more furiously acclaimed the more monstrous they were."[39] The anti-Semitic movement, Mehring and his friends said, was the petty bourgeoisie's more or less natural reaction to the pressures and devastations caused by big business. "Berlin is full of people," Mehring wrote, "who as civil servants, teachers, editors, building superintendents, etc., depend on the [capitalist] clique and who with secret moaning and groaning have to endure a miserable tyranny. They become the easy victims of every reckless demagogue who dares publicly slap the clique in the face. The harder these slaps, the more they will be applauded by people whose shoulders are daily rubbed sore by an invisible yoke. . . ."

In Ahlwardt's case, the ranks of the Berlin *Mittelstand*, which Mehring described as the most accessible to anti-Semitism and the least swayed by legal prosecution of the agitators, were augmented by rural groups. Ahlwardt's constituency was the rural Arnswalde-Friedeberg district east of Berlin. In 1892, without an organization, without funds to back him, he defeated the candidate of the all-powerful Conservative Party,[40] repeating the feat which Boeckel before him had accomplished in Western Germany. Ahlwardt's campaign procedures have been described by Hellmut von Gerlach:[41]

"Accompanied by his secretary, he systematically made the rounds of the farms and asked every peasant how many acres of land and how many heads of cattle he had. Then he would turn to his secretary who flashed a gigantic note book and would dictate to him: 'Take it down! Gussow has 12 acres, 5 cows, 4 pigs. Should have 24 acres, 12 cows, 10 pigs.'"

Ahlwardt not only told the peasants that they deserved to have more land and cattle, he also told them where to get it, viz., from the huge possessions of the landed aristocracy. His battle cry "against Jews and

Junkers" pointed at the twofold pressure to which the population was subjected in a semifeudal environment. Small farmers and farm laborers suffered from the inroads of a new economic system as well as from the vestiges of an old one. They paid twice, for too much and too little capitalism. Intimidated by centuries of *Junker* rule, they admired the man who publicly attacked what they dared only privately complain about. To support Ahlwardt was to rebel by proxy. Of the personal qualifications a peasant's candidate required, courage was more important than wisdom; malice and aggressiveness were more acceptable than reason and plausibility. Peasant mistrust of the city in general and of lawyers in particular was proverbial. The outcome of court cases was regarded as a matter of having the better, that is, more expensive counsel. To the peasant mind it was only natural that the powerful and wealthy should have recourse to the courts to ruin the one who spoke against them. That Ahlwardt should be imprisoned for libel was to be expected and not at all dishonorable. He had lost out because he took up their cause against the big shots. The peasants of Brandenburg regarded the sentences as a confirmation of Ahlwardt's honesty and plainspoken sincerity.

The racists attacked established law on two grounds: that it had been degraded and corrupted by the infiltration of Jews into the judiciary; and that it had become ever farther removed from folk thinking and the popular sense of justice. The official administration of justice was experienced as a distant manipulation for sinister purposes. It was "the Jews" who hid behind the intricacies of a complex legal system which the common man could no more understand than he could afford to set it in motion. "If we did away with the Jews, we could also do away with half the laws now on our books," Ahlwardt once exclaimed in the Reichstag.[42] Boeckel said of himself that his conversion to anti-Semitism had received the strongest impulse when he had seen dejected peasants file into court at the heels of "grinning" Jews.[43]

The very impartiality of the law and of law enforcement was taken as evidence of the miscarriage of racial justice. A peculiar example of anti-Semitic argumentation is to be found in the protests of Willi Buch, veteran of racial anti-Semitism, against the attempts of German Jews to defend themselves by law. "The *Zentralverein deutscher Staatsbürger jüdischen Glaubens,*"[44] writes Buch, "took upon itself the task of watching the anti-Semitic newspapers and speakers and bringing them before the public prosecutor, on the strength of the notorious article 166 of the criminal code. For this reason it [the *Zentralverein*] was generally called the 'Denouncers' League.' Unfortunately, the public prosecutor's office was bound by law to follow up all these denunciations and the courts

were forced to pronounce sentences which often were very hard. To
the best of my knowledge, not a single anti-Semite who was at all active
in the interests of Germandom, either through the spoken word or
through writing, got away without paying fines or going to jail."[45] Referring to Fritsch's survey of the court proceedings and verdicts which
were brought against anti-Semitic violators of the law thanks to the
Zentralverein's efforts, Buch explains: "The public had to be told about
the dirty fighting these 'German citizens' resorted to, and how infamously
they behaved."

The wilful naiveté of the sentences is revealing. If the Jews like any
other citizens appealed to the courts for protection, what was base and
infamous about it? Was it not, on the contrary, damning to anti-Semitism
that there was not a single anti-Semitic agitator who did not run foul
of the law at one time or another? Such, indeed, was the reasoning that
inspired the liberal and Jewish "anti-anti" work. The anti-Semites' thinking followed a different logic. If the gaps in Buch's argumentation were
filled in, it would run like this: the Jews take advantage of a law which
is ours, not theirs. When they invoke our law they abuse its highest
principle, that of being impartial towards all. This is a trick as the Jew
can claim equality with the German only by an obvious subterfuge. They
thus force an insoluble dilemma upon us Germans: either we have to
abide in impotence by the law's decisions and see its spirit violated by
the Jews for their benefit, or we have to go on with our just fight and
infringe the letter of the German laws which have been perverted by
the Jews.

The notion that emancipation was a gift of the German people to the
Jews was always behind such reasoning. Civic equality for the Jews
was conceived of as a voluntary, revocable dispensation granted out of
the generosity and mercy of the Germans, but by no means as an ac-
knowledgment of an inalienable right. The ideas of a corporate state
founded on privilege and caste motivated the anti-Semites' relationship
to Jews. The appeal to the principle of equality of all citizens before
the law failed to impress them. "Equality" was just another privilege
the Jews had managed to wangle and which they had no right to insist
upon. As the unemancipated Jews once had depended upon princes and
potentates to save them from the people's wrath, the emancipated Jews
now found protection behind rule-by-law. They had been and remained
Schutzjuden in anti-Semitic eyes.

By publicizing instead of concealing their troubles with the courts,
the racists did their best to associate the terms "law" and "Jews" in the
minds of their followers. The idea that existing law had, in some sinister
fashion, become inextricably involved with the machination of the Jews

contributed to breaking down respect for the law and supplanting its authority with the higher one derived from "folk feeling" and the requirements of "national salvation."[46] A generation later, National Socialism actually swept away the "un-German" system of impartial law along with the functions of the courts, of law enforcement, and legal authority, and replaced it by a new one more suited to the racist philosophy.

CHAPTER VII

THE RATIONALE OF RACIAL ANTI-SEMITISM

The political performances of racial anti-Semitism and the apparent absurdity of the theory misled many of Ahlwardt's contemporaries as to the social nature and direction of the movement. Some were inclined to deny that any specific social and economic problems were involved; they focused attention on the psychology of anti-Semitism, particularly on the emotional gratifications to be gained from any hate movement. An extreme interpretation of this kind, resembling opinions often put forth at present, may be found in the writings of Hermann Bahr.[1] Anti-Semitism, Bahr was convinced, was

not a means to an end. An anti-Semite wants to be an anti-Semite. It is a sensation to be indulged in. To galvanize wilted and ravaged nerves our times ask for artificial stimuli to take the place of the sweet ecstasy once inspired in the masses by faith, now lost, and by ideals, now gone. The rich take to morphium and hashish. Those who cannot afford them become anti-Semites. Anti-Semitism is the morphine of the small people. . . .

Since they cannot attain to the ecstasy of love they seek the ecstasy of hatred. . . . It matters little who it is they hate. The Jew is just convenient. The French first used the Prussians, then the Jews, and recently the bankers but they never really cared whether it was the Prussians, the Jews or the bankers: what they wanted was simply to hate, to enjoy the strong sensations hatred affords. If there were no Jews the anti-Semites would have to invent them. . . .

The anti-Semitic leaders, so far as they are not simply in it for business, are pretenders to power who want to win the favors of the mob. In his own little clique, each tries to become some sort of Nietzschean superman who will hesitate at nothing to enjoy the pleasures of power. They itch to exploit mass drives and greed. . . .

This is my opinion of anti-Semitism and I therefore do not believe that reason will get anywhere. An anti-Semite is what he is out of the yearning for the delirium and intoxication of a passion. He uses any arguments which happen to be at hand. When these are refuted he will look for others. If he does not find any he still will not be converted. He does not want to do without passion. Only a nobler passion can cure him, an ideal, an ethical pathos that will win over the masses. Perhaps for this reason socialism is the only medicine for anti-Semitism.

That socialism was the only cure for anti-Semitism was the fervent belief of the Social Democrats, though for very different reasons. Marxism stressed the lower middle-class character of anti-Semitism as a mass phenomenon. But the Social Democrats let themselves be deceived into expecting the economically ruined *Mittelstand* to join forces with labor, the other great army of the dispossessed. They were right in the observation that the radicalism of anti-Christian, anti-Conservative racism was about to become a menace to state, church, and big property. However, with their analysis based on the assumption that the only possible alternatives were capitalism or socialism, they mistook the anticapitalist aspects of racism as revolutionary in the one and only meaning of the word in the Socialist lexicon. What the world has come to know as fascism did not yet exist in socialist thought.

Finally, there were those who viewed the anti-Jewish movement as nothing but a child of conservative reaction. This view was predominantly held by the liberals. Indeed, anti-Semitism's strong rural following often made it appear a mere adjunct of the agrarian movement.[2]

Racial anti-Semitism, however, originated neither as an ideology nor as a political enterprise in high society. It was not sponsored by the ranking bureaucracy, the army, Protestant church, *Junkers*, government, or big business. This holds true in spite of the fact that racial ideas later gained ground in all nationalist circles. But the teachers and leaders of the racial anti-Semites were certainly not members of the ruling groups.

From the few and scattered biographical references available it would seem that the ideologists and organizers of racial anti-Semitism in the period under discussion had a number of characteristics in common.[3] Most of them came from Lutheran-Protestant families of lower middle-class status, enjoyed above-average schooling, and were neither untalented nor outstanding in any particular field of intellectual or technical endeavor. Many had renounced their original occupation for some new career or other, lived in precarious material circumstances, had tried their fortunes abroad, and had not infrequently had brushes with the law. All of them, with the exception of Boeckel, were ultranationalist.[4]

In every mass movement two types of agitators may be distinguished, the missionary and the racketeer. The preponderance of the one or the other type is relevant for evaluating the movement's dynamic power. In German racism the anti-Semitic fanatics far outweighed the racketeers to whom Jew-baiting was one way of making a living. There was a high proportion of elementary and high school teachers among its leaders (Henrici, Bernhard and Paul Förster, Jungfer, Bruhn, Schwarzschulz, Dühring, Ahlwardt, Holtz, Hentig, etc.) some of whom paid with the loss of their positions for the tenacity of their opinions.[5] As a political career racial anti-Semitism in the *Kaiserreich* had little to offer in terms of spoil. Unlike Stoecker, whose movement was generously subsidized by Conservative friends, the racists were always short of funds and income. Prior to 1906, Reichstag members were not paid either a salary or a per diem allowance. There was little if any remuneration in lecturing. Anti-Semitic mass meetings were usually free of charge and organizers passed the hat around to get reimbursed for their expenses. A semblance of a paying anti-Semitic show was once staged in Berlin. An anti-Semitic schoolteacher, Wilhelm Bruhn, got hold of a mentally deranged aristocrat, one Count Pückler, whom he exhibited in popular meetings for a small admittance fee. The Count threatened to drive all the Jews out of Germany as he had driven them out of his *Junker* domain at the head of a "flail-guard" of peasant boys, and his performance attracted big crowds of entertainment-seekers who enjoyed the megalomaniac's antics. Eventually Pückler was institutionalized. This one celebrated exception where anti-Semitism was offered as commercial *divertissement* only serves to underscore the general rule that German anti-Semitism was taken with deadly seriousness by its partisans.

If racism was predominantly the ideology of urban, educated strata alienated from the Christian church and socially uprooted, how are we to understand the conspicuous inroads which racial anti-Semitism made into rural parts of Eastern and Western Germany? One thing is certain. The peasants who voted for Boeckel and Ahlwardt were not enraptured by notions of race superiority. They were concerned with more sober matters, such as cheaper industrial goods, cheaper government, cheaper credit, feed, and *Schnaps*. Their anti-Semitism telescoped many elements of discontent, and they lumped together as "Jews" a host of foes whom they thus could abuse in violent language without fear of punishment. Disgruntled peasants saw "Jews" everywhere—in Berlin, in the government, in the legislature, in subversive Social Democracy; at the stock exchange, in the press, in the Conservative Party, and even at the Royal and Imperial Courts. The racial agitators' success with the rural population was due in part to the aggressiveness with which they put forth demands for economic remedies, but perhaps even more to the fury and bluster that distinguished their oratory, to the emotional gratifications which their violent invective provided for the rural audience.[6] The most noticeable gains of radical anti-Semitism among peasants and farm hands were made when the agrarian depression was at its worst. They were largely lost again when "the Jews" gave less cause for discontent, an indication that the reactions of the peasants depended on other factors than a permanent body of racial doctrine.

Besides, there is no evidence to show that spontaneous acts of anti-Semitic violence, altogether rare in the history of German anti-Semitism prior to Hitler, were more frequent in the villages, where isolated Jews had the least protection, than they were in the cities. It is even doubtful whether the turbulent propaganda of the anti-Semites caused a general deterioration in the relations between peasants and Jews who lived in the villages. Exactly what did anti-Semitic gains at the polls mean in terms of individual Gentile attitudes toward Jews? Do such gains lend themselves to any other than a political interpretation? The electoral victories of independent anti-Semitic candidates signalled the presence of unchanneled discontent. To vote for them meant to disavow all the existing parties in the field. But this was not at all incompatible with having good business relations and even living on neighborly terms with Jews.

The hard core of Jew-hatred was confined to a small "élite" to whom the racist myth was an all-pervading philosophy of life which regulated their political as well as personal behavior. The nature of the virtues extolled as truly German, the directives of the racial code of honor and conduct, the particular categories of socioeconomic and cultural behavior branded as "Jewish" classify the racists' ideology as eminently static. It culminated in the dream of a noncompetitive society based on private enterprise. Understood as an attempt to reconcile the irreconcilable, the contradictions, the theoretical sterility, the outright insanity of racist thought take on a definite meaning. Here is the key to the racists' most baffling and apparently most ludicrous endeavor, namely, the attempt to transpose all sociological categories into biological concepts, to subject all human processes to one immutable natural law, in short, to dehistorize history.

The ideal of a racial brotherhood grew out of the desire for a community of a special kind. This was to be an exclusive brotherhood, not akin to the Christian concept of universal humanity or to the socialists' vision of human solidarity. The racial myth was born in opposition to both. It had to compete with socialism in filling the void created by the disintegration of the conservative world. Marxism had entered the field with a challenging philosophy of social change that inspired a rapidly growing mass movement and assured its followers of the inevitable triumph of their cause. Socialists welcomed the dynamism of the capitalist system as irrevocably ensuring its historical demise; they saw in the social ravages capitalism brought in its train the objective evidence of the soundness of their analysis.

The racists despised Marxism as a theory and as a movement. Did it not condemn the individual to become extinguished in the herd? They shared the typical middle-class fear of socialism as a cultural nightmare, a soul-killing monster. But they resented likewise the informal and yet most exclusive solidarity of the upper classes, which was entirely out of their reach. The community they were willing to embrace had to exist independently of church, power, and wealth but also outside the poor man's collectivism. It was to be built on timeless, indestructible qualities, the sum total of which was the Aryan blood. One future day, in spite of present adversities, they would rule and reconstruct Germany in the immortal spirit of honor, beauty, friendship, and the regulation of profit. They were destined by fate to prevail in the end against the Jewish forces of mammonism and Marxism.

The ideology of racism, then, was of a dual character. It gave assurance, gratification, and a promise of security to threatened status-conscious social groups. But at the same time its premises led to the most radical conclusions. If the purity of blood was to be the ultimate source of authority in all spheres of the nation's life, legitimate pretenders to leadership did not have to be endowed with material possessions, station, or title. Aristocratic in appearance, the racial theory actually entailed a bid for power put forth by claimants who did not possess and did not rank, have-nots who challenged the position of the haves. Its total rejection of Jews reflected the total disaffection of the individuals and groups who took to the racial myth. Their outlook and program of action may be summarized in one sentence: "Everything will have to be changed." This universality of protest gave racial anti-Semitism an enormous advantage over the doctrines of competitors like Stoecker who, although superior in education, social standing, and oratorical talent to all racial agitators, was limited in his appeal by ideological and organizational ties which bound him to the powers that be.

Unconditional and total in the attack on Jews, racism could not have compromised with ideas and institutions favoring total or conditional acceptance of Jews. Its premises called for radical rejection of the existing social order, and this radicalism accounts for a number of typical fluctuations in the racial movement. In periods of great socioeconomic cohesion, racism in Germany found itself in an isolation so hopeless that every manifestation of the racial credo appeared ridiculous and insane. Only "cranks," secure in paranoia, were able to withstand the immense discrepancy between doctrine and reality. The relatively tiny core of unswerving agitators attests to the liabilities of preaching the anti-Semitic gospel during periods unfavorable to its spread. On the other hand, the radicalism of its onslaught on the established order enabled racial anti-Semitism to become the repository and common denominator of a multitude of opposition currents, often incongruous and at cross purposes with each other. The greater the disorganization within society, the more numerous the elements of discontent attracted by the finality of the racial ideology, by its claim to a total critique of society and dogmatic guidance. This accounts for the upsurge of anti-Semitism in times of economic and national crises and for the manipulative success which organized anti-Semitism was able to achieve in such times of distress and malaise. "The Jews" stood for the causes of many grievances and fired many passions.

As an ideology racism was intransigent. As a political party it had to come to a *modus vivendi* with other parties or be barred from all chances of attaining its program of reform. In practical politics the anti-Semitic Reichstag group found itself mostly on the side of the Conservatives, and this for good reasons. No anti-Semitic movement, whether guided by Christian Social or by racial doctrines, could have expected solid assistance from any of the big political parties save from the Conservatives. Relations between the independently organized anti-Semites and the Conservative Party were and remained crucial.

There were beliefs which made harmonious cooperation between the two possible, the most important of them being chauvinism. Propaganda for Germanic world supremacy was welcomed by nationalists of all shades, including those who ridiculed the racial argument. It was a potent force of mass integration and held no threat to the social order. But anti-Semitism, nationalism's twin brother, also contained the sting of a social critique. Subversiveness of this kind was not to be encouraged, the Conservatives felt, unless a specific situation required that it be used for good purpose.

It seems quite clear today what the circumstances were that made for such situations. Whether conservatism chose to fall back on political anti-Semitism depended above all on whether the Conservatives were friendly or hostile to the government. This in turn was largely determined by their relations with the middle classes and labor. Whenever the Conservative Party was strongly governmental, efforts were made to shake off the anti-Semitic "rabble." Whenever the Conservatives turned against the government, they unfailingly sought to make use of anti-Semitic pressure. From the beginnings of organized anti-Semitism to the last days of the multiple-party system in Germany this elementary strategy remained fundamentally unchanged. Conservatism was utterly cynical about tapping the lower middle-class reservoirs of anti-Jewish hostility.

We have seen how through the use of anti-Semitism the Conservative Party organized the opposition to Bismarck's policy during the liberal era (1875–78); how it put the anti-Semites on the leash during the years of *Kartell*-cooperation (1886–1890); how Caprivi's moderate course was met with new anti-Jewish attacks (1890–1894). We shall soon learn how in 1896 the Conservatives finally parted company with Stoecker, at a time when Christian Social insistence on social reforms sharply clashed with the reactionary course of the Stumm era. The Conservatives' approach to the "Jewish question" was governed by undiluted class interests. Political anti-Semitism was to them an instrument of attack, intimidation, and blackmail. If and when the situation made it appear opportune, ruling Conservative groups were ready to ignore the anti-Christian ideology of racism, its irreverence for monarchy and state bureaucracy, its assault on the law, even its hostility against big property owners.

At the bottom of their strategy was contempt for the lower classes which they were sure of being able to manipulate at will. Arrogance of caste and class prevented the Conservatives from fully realizing the lasting damages such strategy was bound to cause to the state and society on which their own existence depended. In many respects the Conservatives' attitude toward Caprivi and Ahlwardt anticipated their attitude toward Brüning and Hitler. "Rather ten Ahlwardts than one Progressive," the defeated Conservative candidate declared at the Tivoli convention and was jubilantly applauded for his sporting spirit. It tickled the Conservatives to hear Ahlwardt call Crown Prince Friedrich Wilhelm, the later short-lived Emperor Friedrich III, a prisoner in the hands of Jewish usurers. For the aristocrats suspected this scion of the Hohenzollerns of liberal leanings. Caprivi repeatedly and vainly appealed to the Conservatives to be more responsible:[7] "You [anti-Semites] started with agitating against the Jews but you did not stop there. Before long you went further. You searched for everyone with a Jewish father or a Jewish wife. You traced the Jews back to the third and fourth generation. Religious anti-Semitism began to mix with racial anti-Semitism and what resulted was anticapitalist anti-Semitism. This is precisely the danger of your agitation. The trouble is that in the end everything will be topsy-turvy. The circles which you address are often not willing, perhaps also not able, to differentiate. They sense that capital is under attack. Human hatred and hostility are thus directed against capital as such. You will not be able to stop the movement—should it gain momentum—when it reaches Jewish capital. The movement will turn against capital in general."

The racial anti-Semites, on their part, hated Jews of flesh and blood and suspected everyone who tolerated them, the Conservatives not excluded. The latter proved to be untrustworthy, by making common cause politically with the right wing of "Judaized liberalism," by mingling socially with Jews, and even entering into race-polluting marriages with them. It was impossible to rely on aristocratic conservatism for building a just society in which everybody would find a secure livelihood. But neither was it possible to achieve this goal without Conservative support. Feelings of love and hate, hope and distrust pervaded the rebellious *Mittelstand's* attitude to the groups that still represented cherished traditional values but had become contaminated by the Jewish spirit and even by Jewish blood.

The ambivalent emotions of the racists toward the old powers, characteristic also of the Nazi movement, were expressed in periodic cycles of cooperation and opposition. Ahlwardt started out as a Conservative. At the height of his political career he bitterly denounced the Conservatives for having exploited anti-Semitism to further narrow party interests; he railed against *Junkers* and Jews in order to win a Reichstag seat and at his tumultuous mass meetings would demand the breaking up of *Junker* estates. Soon afterwards, however, his antifeudalism subsided again, and his attitude to Prussian aristocracy underwent an astonishing "clarification." The *Junkers* he attacked, it then appeared, were a specific group not at all identical with the feudal caste in the entirety; those whom he had in mind were only the "bastards of corrupt *Junkers* and Jews who held the largest share of the nation's wealth."[8] The shift of attack from *Junkers* to Jews was more than a demagogic device. Ahlwardt had to give assurance to the powers that be that anti-Semitism's social and economic demands in the last analysis actually obtained only in the realm of ideology. His dilemma was the same as that which Hitler later faced; nor was the latter free to choose a different line of conduct. Hitler, too, was confronted by the opposition of landed aristocracy; and when he was compelled to "clarify" his intentions, nothing more ingenious than the Ahlwardt twist occurred to him.[9] But even when "Jews" were substituted for "*Junkers*," the agitator left intact the concept and imagery of the Jew-*Junker* association, and never quite surrendered the threat which the imputed stigma of racial degeneration enabled him to hold over the Conservatives. Whenever he chose to, he could proclaim that the poison of "Judaization" had made the *Junkers*, too, unfit for national leadership.

The racists' charges of *Verjudung* as leveled against ruling groups had some factual basis. Gentile-Jewish intermarriages had increased since the emancipation. In Prussia, marriages between Jews and non-Jews amounted to 10 per cent of all purely Jewish marriages in 1880, and by 1890 the figure had risen to 20 per cent.[10] Ahlwardt had something even more specific in mind when he referred to "the bastards of corrupt *Junkers* and Jews." Frequently, scions of aristocratic families, in reduced financial circumstances, gilded their coat-of-arms by marrying daughters of wealthy middle-class families, Jewish heiresses not excluded. The center of wealth had long shifted from the feudal to the bourgeois world, and such alliances symbolized the high degree of social emancipation which the Jewish upper middle class had actually achieved. Aristocracy's "racial pollution" gave the anti-Semites ammunition and greatly extended the possibilities of political blackmail. In the *Semi-Gotha*,[11] the racists later compiled a register of more than 1,000 names of old aristocratic and recently ennobled families which they claimed to be totally or partly Jewish.

Neither the anti-Semitic movement of the eighties nor of the nineties succeeded in bringing about any changes whatsover in the legal status of the Jewish group. Not a single law was passed that infringed upon the emancipation act of 1869. This in a country in which there was at the time considerable discrimination against Catholics, Socialists, and Poles. The demands of the racial anti-Semites that the Jewish group be put under legal restrictions never had the slightest chance. When, at the first "International Congress of Anti-Semites" at Dresden (1882), Ernst Henrici moved that all Jews be expelled from Germany, no other than Adolf Stoecker assured him that, in a contest as to who should be expelled from Germany, the Jews or the anti-Semites, the decision would most certainly go against the anti-Semites.[12] Stoecker's biographer, Nazi professor Walter Frank, agrees that "the whole anti-Semitic movement which, between 1876 and 1900, had such a wide appeal, did not noticeably change the nature of the Jewish problem one way or the other. The situation in the Prussian-German state continued to be such that by and large Jewry's economic, social and cultural power was left untouched, whereas Jews were, on the whole, excluded from the administrative apparatus."[13]

On the other hand, Germany's political character did undergo drastic changes during the two periods of rampant anti-Semitism. In the eighties, after the Conservative-Protestant outcries against "Judaization" of German culture, morals and government had died down, political power had shifted to the side of the anti-Semitic assailants. When in the nineties the wave of racial anti-Semitism receded, it carried with it the chances of democratic reform. After Caprivi, until Germany's military defeat in World War I, it was impossible to form a parliamentary majority that did not include the Conservatives. From Hohenlohe to Bethmann-Hollweg no chancellor dared govern without them, much less against them. No further attempt was made to rebuild state and society along democratic lines.

If the achievements of political campaigns, in which anti-Jewish pas-

sions are roused, are at all indicative of their genuine aims, then the
conclusion is inescapable that in 1893 as in 1880 the attacks upon the
Jews were tactical measures subordinated to other motives rather than
ends in themselves. The campaigns, as far as their ultimate beneficiaries
were concerned, were essentially manipulative. Powerful conservative
forces and powerless lower middle-class groups entered into a relationship that was mediated by anti-Semitism. But this anti-Semitism meant
something different to both participants.

The manipulative character of Conservative anti-Semitism may have
a bearing on the fact that Jew-baiting in Germany led to few acts of
personal violence and that social discrimination against Jews was slight.
"The Jews," who functioned as Conservative scapegoats, were phantoms
rather than human beings one knew. There were some outbreaks of
group violence. In 1881 the synagogue in the Protestant town of Neu-
Stettin in Pomerania was burned down, and Jewish stores were stoned
and plundered. This was the first fruit of Henrici's agitation. Critical
situations developed in connection with two unsolved murder cases
which anti-Semitic agitation sought to dress up as ritual murder—one
in 1891, in the town of Xanten in the Rhineland; the other in 1900, in
Konitz, a town in Western Prussia. In Xanten, an appeal by the Bishop
of Cologne did much to calm the excitement of the predominantly Catholic population; in Konitz, the Prussian government proclaimed martial
law and sent in troops. The fact that the inhabitants of Konitz were
mostly Poles may not have been the least important reason for the government's strong stand.

It has been said that as a result of the Xanten affair, Jews who had
lived in the surrounding countryside were forced to leave. It is unconvincing, however, to ascribe the cityward trend of German-Jewish migration to anti-Semitic agitation in the countryside.[14] The increase of the
Jewish population in the cities, especially in Berlin, was part and parcel
of the general process of industrial and commercial concentration, accentuated by the occupational structure of the Jewish group. Locally,
discrimination may have played a part in making some Jews move to
places where there was a strong Jewish community and where the individual was less exposed to social and economic animosity. But to
explain the greater attraction of the cities for Jews by pointing to rural
anti-Semitism is about as convincing as it is to make socialist propaganda
responsible for the migration of farm laborers toward the centers of
industry.

If the contention is accepted that the anti-Semitic movements of the
last quarter of the nineteenth century did not lead to a deterioration in the
situation of the Jewish group but entrenched the anti-Jewish manipu-

lators more firmly in power, it would follow that the groups believing in anti-Semitism lost out to those exploiting it. Manipulation, however, implies that conflicts of interest exist and that the relationship between manipulators and manipulated is potentially dynamic. Recent history has shown how the erstwhile manipulated groups turned the tables on the manipulators and subjected them to their own will. The fate of the Jews under the Nazi regime indicated—and was meant to indicate—a real shift of power. First through legal discrimination and later through mass murder the racial anti-Semites announced that they had taken over and would brook no interference.

The years 1875–1895 were the formative period of all German political anti-Semitism. In the economic transformations and political conflicts of these twenty years anti-Semitism was established as a quasi-automatic group reaction as well as a consciously used instrument of power. The conditions of its growth and its inherent explosive forces had become discernible a generation prior to the Nazi ascent to power.

PART THREE

Anti-Semitism and Imperialism
(1895–1914)

CHAPTER VIII

POLITICAL ANTI-SEMITISM ON THE WANE

During the two decades from 1895 to the first World War, when German imperialism was at its height, political anti-Semitism lost its mass appeal.[1] After reaching its high-water mark in the 1893 elections its tide seemed to have spent its force. The anti-Semitic Reichstag group dwindled to 13 in 1898, 11 in 1903, and 7 in 1912. The only success it was able to score in that period was in the 1907 elections. But this victory at the polls seemed to be merely an inconsequential episode. "By 1911," Willi Buch writes, "anti-Semitism with a political party organization had actually ceased to exist."[2] For years Theodor Fritsch, the "hammerer" and last of the old guard of racist agitators, cried alone in the wilderness of indifference towards the Aryan creed. "Henrici, Liebermann von Sonnenberg, Paul Förster, Otto Boeckel, Raab, Zimmermann, Ahlwardt, Karl Paasch—they all gave up, either tiring of the battle or having made their peace," Buch dolefully reminisces.

The anti-Semites' cause seemed indeed hopeless during those twenty years. There were no indices of continuing progress to uphold the morale of the agitators and their followers. The anti-Semitic press was negligible compared with the big "Jewish" papers. Funds were chronically lacking. The very idea of gaining enough support for anti-Jewish legislation appeared preposterous. The campaign to keep Jews out of "German" shops, inns, hotels, and resorts was a failure. Racists who as owners or managers had authority to exclude Jewish customers, were far too few to establish any "restricted" areas. With very rare exceptions—Borkum, a little island and popular summer resort in the North Sea, was one of them—Jews could and did go and travel wherever they pleased. Even less successful were the racists' educational efforts to teach the Aryan German that he should not buy in Jewish stores, consult Jewish physicians or lawyers, read the "Jewish press," or go to see the work of Jewish artists. The available data on the life stories of the anti-Semitic agitators who had gained notoriety during the upsurge of the eighties and nineties, illustrate the disintegration of the once so belligerent and vociferous movement.

Among the apostles of "pure," "radical" anti-Semitism, Ernst Henrici gave up early and withdrew so completely from the political scene that his name was soon all but forgotten. Even standard works on the history of anti-Semitism contain no reference to his further fate. Buch mentions that its erstwhile hero had turned out to be an embarrassment for the anti-Semitic movement. Henrici had gone to the United States from which he returned with a spouse of "mixed blood."[3] Bernhard Förster and his wife Elizabeth Förster-Nietzsche, Friedrich Nietzsche's sister, left Germany in 1886 and founded a *judenreine* colony, *Neu-Germania*, in Paraguay. In 1889 Förster, despairing of the success of his project, committed suicide.[4] Karl Paasch, pamphleteer and contemporary of Henrici and Förster, went to Switzerland where he died, a victim of persecution mania. Otto Boeckel, "peasant king of Hesse," lost his Reichstag seat in 1903, withdrew from political life "completely impoverished, bitter and withdrawn,"[5] and died forgotten in 1923. Hermann Ahlwardt, "*Rektor* of all Germans," fared even worse. Although reelected to the Reichstag in 1898, he found himself in complete isolation[6] and stopped attending parliamentary sessions. By the turn of the century he had practically disappeared from the political scene. After an unsuccessful trip to the United States where he tried to organize the fight against "the Jewish rabble that does not want to work,"[7] he opened a cigar store in Berlin which he soon gave up again. For a while he sold mining stock in the German-speaking parts of Bohemia. In 1907, "having completely turned his back on anti-Semitism,"[8] he approached Theodor Fritsch with a suggestion to take up the fight against the Jesuits and Free-Masons. In 1909 he was sentenced for blackmail.[9] His family was impoverished and sunk to the level of the *Lumpenproletariat*; Ahlwardt himself died in 1914 from injuries he suffered in a traffic accident in Leipzig.

The *Zeitgeist* clearly did not favor anti-Semitism during the years of imperial Germany's rise to the position of a world power. This conjunction of expanding imperialism and waning anti-Semitism appears baffling. Is not imperialism as an ideology and practice inherently aggressive and discriminatory toward the weak, the foreign, the "other" group? Does it not produce, in infinite variations, the same rationalizations for economic greed, political domination, cultural arrogance? And was German imperialism not particularly notorious for its blustering megalomania, its glorification of militarism and chauvinism, its cult of authority, for breeding a type of citizen whom the popular wit designated as "cyclist"—back bent before those above, feet kicking those below?

The argument is sometimes put forth that the anti-Semitic movement went on the rocks because it lacked integrity, leadership, and inner cohesion. Looking back on his anti-Semitic years, von Gerlach comes to the conclusion: "I met few really decent men among anti-Semitic leaders and those whose character was without blemish were so uneducated and ignorant that I, as a young man, was repelled when I had the opportunity of watching them at close range. They were all demagogues, some against their better knowledge, the others for lack of knowledge. The anti-Semites did a better job of curing me of anti-Semitism than the Jews."[10] The same witness remarks on the "horrible intellectual aridity" that he observed in the anti-Semitic camp. Gerlach, in agreement with Wawrzinek[11] and other students of German anti-Semitism, sees the movement's fatal weakness in its lack of political direction and discipline, in the unscrupulousness of its agitation, and finally in the racists' dilemma as to how to define a Jew.[12] Later experiences easily disprove the pertinency of such reasoning. The young Nazi movement was faced with the same difficulties but this did not prevent it from coming to power. And once in power anti-Semitism simply decreed who was a Jew and defined by law the concept of race. The impetus of political anti-Semitism after the middle of the nineties was not checked by dilemmas issuing from the racial myth or the political and personal inadequacies of its leaders. One would rather assume that the importance which such problems acquired is symptomatic of the movement's decay. The reasons for this decay must be sought in new developments in the life of the nation at large.

The fate of the most skillful and influential agitator, Stoecker, provides us with a number of clues as to the nature of these developments and their bearing on the anti-Semitic movement. In 1892–93, at the time of the Tivoli convention and the formation of the Agrarian League, Stoecker had made a strong political comeback and, indeed, seemed to be on the verge of capitalizing on fifteen years of political labor. His prestige in the Conservative Party was at its peak. His hand was visible in every plank of the new party platform. The Hammerstein-Stoecker combination, the ticket of the extreme right wing in the party, was irresistible and swamped whatever progovernment tendencies there still were. Not in many years had the Conservative Party been able to put up such a show of strength and unity.

There had been only one serious clash of opinion which was settled before it could reach the public ear or mar the well-managed harmony of the party. But the incident foreshadowed difficulties to come. The preliminary draft of the Conservatives' new program had stated in unequivocal language their opinion of the Social Democratic Party and of "anarchism" in general. It read:

The followers of Social Democracy and anarchism, whose unpatriotic and revolutionary activities endanger broad strata of our people, are to be designated by law as enemies of state order and accordingly are to be fought with the powers of the state.

Stoecker himself apparently had found no fault with this declaration of war. But opposition arose within his own party which forced his hand. The opposition started with the Christian Social "young guard" (*die Jungen*), leading members of which attended the Tivoli convention. Each of them independently later reported what happened.[13] Upon seeing the draft's anti-Socialist provision they went to Hammerstein and asked him to drop it. Hammerstein is said to have replied: "What do you want? There is no other way out but to provoke the workers and have them shot down." Thereupon they went to see Manteuffel, chairman of the Conservative Party. Gerlach, who was "dead set against all discriminatory legislation," threatened: "Herr Baron, should this passus remain, we will raise the banner of rebellion at the convention. We do not want a new anti-Socialist act, not even in a veiled form." After an unfriendly exchange of arguments Manteuffel gave in and Gerlach reformulated the plank to read:

Those followers of Social Democracy and anarchism whose unpatriotic and revolutionary activities endanger broad strata of our people are to be fought as enemies of state order.

Gerlach's version, supported by Stoecker, was accepted by the convention. Thus the Conservatives were prevented from committing themselves to a policy of forcible repression of socialist labor. But it was not a comforting thought either to Stoecker or the Conservatives that the Christian Social Party harbored elements that had proved unreliable in a crucial test of "national loyalty."

Indeed the conflict between the Christian Social young guard and the Conservatives had been smoldering for some time. In 1889, when Stoecker had chosen to retire from political life rather than lose his office, he had had to leave to his lieutenants a greater share of influence in the Christian Social movement. In the same year he had founded the newspaper *Das Volk* which he hoped to make the popular medium of Christian Social ideas. The paper, however, quickly became the instrument of the left-wing opposition within the party. Among its editors were the leading spirits of the young guard faction. The history of some of these men before and after their cooperation with Stoecker is not without significance. The editor in chief of the Stoecker paper was Heinrich Oberwinder, once a charter member of the Lassallean General Workingmen's Association and later active in the Austrian labor movement. Oberwinder hated the Marxists (who in turn accused him of having become an informer in the service of Prussian Minister von Puttkamer)[14] but thought of himself as a Socialist. A second editor was

Hellmut von Gerlach, scion of a Prussian *Junker* family, who had given up his civil service career to go into politics. Young Gerlach displayed, together with all the "natural" prejudices of his caste,* a strong sense of social justice. He was the first member of the Stoecker party who openly spoke against the anti-Socialist act while it was still in force. At Tivoli he still "jubilantly applauded the speaker who shouted into the hall, 'rather ten Ahlwardts than one Progressive!'" A few years later he had made up his mind that he would rather have "ten Jews than one anti-Semite."[15] He became a courageous citizen in the fight against chauvinism and militarism under the *Kaiserreich*, a "good European" under Weimar, and died in exile a few years after Hitler had come to power. The third of the three editors, Hans Leuss, was an able political publicist who later wrote a noteworthy biography of Wilhelm von Hammerstein. His public life ended after a jail sentence for perjury committed in an "affaire d'honneur." Vestiges of his political development may be found in *Neue Zeit* (1899–1900), the Marxist periodical,[16] whose contributing editor Franz Mehring, impressed by Leuss' "democratic convictions," invited him to write about his prison experiences.

Towering above the three editors of *Das Volk*, however, was the figure of a young minister of orthodox Lutheran extraction whose writings and speeches began to attract the attention of all those concerned with "the social question." He was Friedrich Naumann. Naumann, born in 1860, was the son of a Protestant minister. From 1883–1885 he worked at the *Rauhe Haus* in Horn, birthplace of the Protestant *Innere Mission*. As minister in a poor community of Saxon hosiery workers (1886–1890) he had earned for himself the honorary title of "the small man's parson." During those years he wrote one of his first books, the Catechism for Workers (*Arbeiter-Katechismus*), which attested to his sincere desire to reconcile the ethics of Christianity with those of modern economics. In 1890 he was called to Frankfurt am Main to officiate as minister of the *Innere Mission*. It was the year of Bismarck's dismissal; of the Imperial decrees announcing the government's intentions to proceed with social legislation "for the welfare of the economically weaker groups in the spirit of Christian ethics"; it was also the year in which the anti-Socialist act expired, and in which Stoecker, dismissed from office and therefore politically more independent had founded the Protestant Social Congress (*Evangelisch-Sozialer Congress*). The Congress, among whose members were such outstanding men as the theologian and church historian Adolf Harnack,[17] the economist Adolph Wagner, the historian Hans

---

* See von Gerlach's own explanation of his anti-Semitism in Document No. VIII, a.

Delbrück, the sociologist Max Weber, brought back the spirit of the early *Verein für Sozialpolitik*, the academic organization which almost two decades before had taken it upon itself to awaken government and state to the social dangers of Manchester capitalism.

Naumann came to Frankfurt already convinced that Christian soul-saving among the poor—the primary objective of Protestant charity work—was a hopeless undertaking in the face of modern mass poverty and unhappiness; that the social ills of industrial civilization could no longer be cured by the church's efforts toward the individual's spiritual and material salvation. The remedies for society's ailments, he was convinced, would have to come from political action. Like chaplain Stoecker before him, pastor Naumann had dared to leave the sheltered life of the Protestant clergy to venture forth on the hazardous path of party politics. The first political milieu in which he felt himself at home was the conservatism of the Protestant Social Congress. Naumann's starting point was the same as Stoecker's with whom he shared a passion for politics rooted in the missionary zeal of conservative orthodoxy. Social Democracy, the enemy of state, church, and private property, was for both men the great challenge. Through Naumann "the social question," in the original meaning of the phrase, as the problem of labor's reconciliation with the state, came to the foreground again. He seemed determined to lead Christian socialism back to the point from which it had started and to become, as it were, the reawakened conscience of the movement. The Protestant-clerical tradition, *Mittelstand* politics, and anti-Semitism, until then the primary components of the Stoecker movement, were minimized now by the intensity with which Naumann and his friends struggled for the soul of labor.

Preoccupation with labor and the unqualified support of labor's cause which the Christian Social youth faction had shown in such major disputes as the miners' strike of 1889, began to arouse Conservative misgivings. The conspicuous influence of "romantic idealists" and liberal scholars within Stoecker's organizations was disquieting. "Such one-sidedness as to consider each and every issue of party politics from the point of view of labor's interests is to us [Christian Social] conservatives unbearable. . . ." a loyal Stoecker man of the old school protested.[18] But until 1894, an open conflict between the Christian Social and the Conservative elements could be avoided. Then a crisis broke over the agrarian question. A number of events had drawn the attention of Christian socialism to the problems of the agricultural proletariat. The racial anti-Semites had shown that the rural areas were seething with unrest. The Social Democrats, too, prepared for action. At its first convention after the anti-Socialist act, the Social Democratic Party had resolved to extend its educational and organizational work to the rural areas, and to concentrate particularly on the farm hands in the territories of *Junker* agriculture. If Christian socialism ever could hope to block the advance of Marxism, here was its opportunity. The "agrarian question," which Stoecker had always been careful to sidestep, became prominent among Christian Social concerns.

It would be a misjudgment of the motivations of political movements in general and the traditions of Protestant conservatism in particular if we were to cast doubt on the sincerity of those Conservatives who took their place by the side of the poor and oppressed. There was much conservative disillusionment and indignation at the sight of "the small but mighty party" quickly being swallowed by the Agrarian League, the political pressure group of the big agrarian interests. The fact that the code of the Prussian aristocracy was hardly compatible with the capitalistic spirit that rapidly seized the party of big landowners who had now become modern agricultural entrepreneurs, did not go unnoticed. How little some of the followers of Christian socialism thought of the money-minded descendents of the Teutonic Knights, became public knowledge at the fifth Protestant Social Congress (1894). This meeting, as usual graced by the presence of government and church dignitaries, was devoted to the findings of a survey which members and friends of the Stoecker organization had conducted among agricultural workers. The report was most critical and so was the discussion it provoked. The speakers, among them Max Weber and Paul Göhre, a Protestant minister who since 1891 acted as secretary general of the Congress, unreservedly took the workers' side against the landowners. Weber considered it necessary for the Protestant Workers' Associations which had been formed in the Rhineland and Westphalia to take the lead in the fight of the agricultural workers against the landowners. Naumann and the youth faction wholeheartedly supported him.

Nothing incensed the landowning Prussian nobility more than interference with their way of running their business. *Junker* farming was a peculiar mixture of increasingly modern large-scale agriculture and semifeudal labor relations. Even after Bismarck and Caprivi had taken away some of the *Junker* privileges—before the administrative reforms the *Junkers* had unlimited authority in the administration and enforcement of the law in their districts—the *Junker* considered himself the absolute master in his domain. He still could and did haul refractory domestic employees back to work. He also took it as a traditional prerogative of his caste that his estate should bring him in an income appropriate to the elevated rank he held in the social hierarchy. He could be benevolent, and on occasions even generous, to his humble and obedient hands but he would not stand for any mediation in his dealings with them. The idea of organizing agricultural labor could have only taken root in the minds of socialists and anarchists! It was unthinkable to contrive a political alliance with men who held such views. The Conservatives put pressure on Stoecker to rid the Christian Social movement of elements which, in his own paper *Das Volk*, displayed such a lack of respect for Conservative feelings and received further encouragement from Naumann's own publication, *Die Hilfe*.

Stoecker did not find it easy to give in to Conservative demands which meant parting from so many old friends, able lieutenants, and forceful preachers of "practical Christianity." He took exception to their social radicalism but defended them against the onslaught of reaction which rang in the "Stumm era." On the other hand, he could scarcely see himself continuing his work for the Protestant social monarchy without the support of the Prussian aristocracy. It was to him the highest and most honorable of all estates which, together with the Protestant clergy, had shown the deepest understanding of Christian Social ideas and the Jewish question. As in his earlier conflict between office and politics, he wavered and hoped that the storm would pass.

Relations between the Naumann wing and the Conservatives, however, deteriorated quickly. The new program which the Christian Social Party prepared at this time added fuel to the fire. Since 1878, when Stoecker had drafted the nascent movement's platform, many of its planks had become obsolete and noncontroversial; other vital issues which the old program had not dealt with at all had meanwhile come to the fore. For one, Christian socialism had lost its base in Berlin and had shifted its activities to outlying areas where the original demands for reform legislation in the interest of industrial labor fell flat. The Social Democratic Party, moreover, had made strides no one could have foreseen in 1878, the year when it was outlawed. Finally, the unity of the Christian Social movement and its alliance with conservatism were now imperilled by growing internal opposition. It was time to take stock and chart the future course. In the summer of 1895 Stoecker presented the draft of a new program. He recommended it as presenting a sound middle-of-the-road policy which would give both the right and left wings of the party ample opportunity to line up behind it. But the attempt at compromise did not satisfy either one of the two opponents. Even during the discussion of the draft, high-ranking Conservative friends of Stoecker stalked indignantly out of the convention, among them Count Roon, who saw in one of the draft's provisions—organization of rural workers' associations—unequivocal evidence that the radical element had gained the upper hand in the party.[19] Undismayed, the

Naumann group continued to press for greater independence from the Conservatives. In a personal letter to Stoecker, Naumann warned him not to make any concessions whatsoever. "Give them your little finger—and we are lost. Only when we are completely independent from above can we gain a strong position as a national labor movement beside the international one."[20]

As the breach between Christian socialism and conservatism grew wider a sensational scandal occurred which stunned even so adept a politician as Stoecker. Early in 1895, rumors began to circulate to the effect that, in his private life, Baron Wilhelm von Hammerstein, editor in chief of the *Kreuzzeitung*, Conservative member of Reichstag and Diet, foremost champion of aristocratic-Protestant *Weltanschauung*, did not quite live up to the high principles which he espoused in public. It was hinted, among other things, that he had embezzled some of the funds of his paper. A *Kreuzzeitung* Committee, charged with an investigation, tried to shield him, but in vain. By midsummer the rumors had become more specific. The Baron was said to have appropriated the paper's pension fund of 400,000 marks; to have received huge personal loans from a businessman in turn for which the paper had paid him exorbitant prices for newsprint; the name of a lady involved did not remain a secret. The Conservative Party was now compelled to act. Despite the incriminating evidence Stoecker, who himself had loaned his friend a sizeable sum, refused to believe in the guilt of his old comrade-in-arms and fought within the party's governing body against the motion to expel him. In September it was discovered that Hammerstein had also forged checks adding up to the sum of 200,000 marks. "He has really become a criminal," Stoecker confessed to his wife the day after the *Kreuzzeitung* investigating committee had decided to turn the case over to the public prosecutor's office, "and this is not the only crime he committed. May God have mercy on his soul. The warrant will come any day now. What is he going to do?"

To fill the cup of Stoecker's misfortune, *Vorwärts*, the Berlin Social Democratic daily, chose this time to publish a letter which highlighted the long and intimate cooperation between him and the criminal. The letter had been written by Stoecker in 1888, at the time of the *Kartell* when Bismarck's strategy had succeeded in establishing a parliamentary majority with the Conservatives and the National Liberals arrayed against the Progessives, Catholics, and Social Democrats. The extremist Hammerstein-Stoecker-*Kreuzzeitung* opposition hoped to break out of the isolation to which the *Kartell* combination condemned them, by driving a wedge between Bismarck and Wilhelm II who had just succeeded to the throne. Hammerstein's articles in the *Kreuzzeitung* seemed too

direct to Stoecker who recommended a more subtle approach. "I heard
only yesterday," he advised his friend, "that [the Kaiser] is entirely sold
on the *Kartell*. What one could and should do is in my opinion the following: issues involving basic principles like the Jewish question,
Martineum,[21] Harnack,[22] Reichstag elections in the sixth district[23] which
will certainly end in a fiasco for the anti-Social Democratic forces, must
be presented in the sharpest form—without mentioning Bismarck—so
as to create the impression in the Kaiser's mind that he is not well advised
in these matters and leave it to him to draw his own conclusions with
regard to Bismarck. We should light pyres around the political center,
the *Kartell*, and make them flare up by throwing its present opportunism
into the flames, showing the true situation in the glare of their light. If
the Kaiser realizes that we want to sow discord between him and Bismarck, he will be antagonized. If we feed his discontent in matters
where he is instinctively on our side, we will basically strengthen him
without arousing personal irritation. He recently said: 'I will give the
old man a breathing spell of six months, then I'll take over.' Bismarck
himself has remarked that he will not be able to keep the Kaiser in hand.
Therefore, without making undue concessions, we must nevertheless proceed with caution."[24]

The letter did immeasurable damage to Stoecker. It insulted the
popular image of the Iron Chancellor which nationalist veneration had
enlarged to legendary size. It revived embarrassing memories of the
conflict between the Kaiser and Bismarck which in the interest of
"national unity" would better have been forgotten. Finally, it showed the
sacred realm of Imperial government in the profane light of political
intrigue. "Public opinion" was outraged. The liberal papers commented
on the utter hypocrisy of Stoecker who only recently had taken part in
the ovation which the Conservative Party had rendered the retired
Chancellor. *Kladderadatsch*, the satirical liberal weekly, needled the
Conservatives:

> Den frechen Lügner sehn wir schänden
> Allsonntäglich das Gotteshaus,
> Wir sehn das Sakrament ihn spenden
> Und keiner wirft den Kerl hinaus![25]

Conservative papers could not hide their embarrassment and annoyance.
The party's official *Konservative Korrespondenz* and even such an old
stand-by of Stoecker's as *Der Reichsbote* strongly hinted that the time
had come to part company. The disclosure of the "pyre-letter," of course,
was water in the mills of all those who wanted Stoecker disciplined for
the protection he still gave to the left wing in the Christian Social Party.

The *Kreuzzeitung*, although less agitated by his plotting with Hammerstein, was adamant on this point. As a last warning to Stoecker to halt the dangerous trends in the Christian Social movement, it carried an article in its issue of November 11, 1895, "Court Chaplain Stoecker and the youth faction," which deplored the fact that the esteemed party member Stoecker had not drawn a sharper line between himself and the left wing. "It is his duty to keep in their proper place the spirits he has conjured up, or to break with them as he did with Ahlwardt." While Stoecker still hesitated to make the step, the governing body of the Conservative Party forced a decision. On December 2, 1895, he was invited to appear before the party's ruling "Committee of Eleven" of which Stoecker himself was a member. Officially his relation to the Christian Social paper, *Das Volk*, was to be clarified; he had still not satisfactorily renounced the paper's anti-Conservative line nor fired its left-wing editors. But as he himself later wrote, the controversy about the paper was only "the side track upon which the whole matter has been shunted."[26] The real issue at stake was the policy towards industrial and agricultural labor. The Conservatives had decided that they could no longer tolerate the social-reformist tendencies which they had hitherto allowed and used in the fight against "Jewish liberalism" and Social Democracy. A motion was put before the "Committee of Eleven" which read:

The strong opinion within the Conservative Party which lately has taken exception to the attitude of former Court Chaplain Stoecker—particularly with regard to the Christian Social Party—makes it appear desirable for tactical reasons that Herr Stoecker give up his mandate as a member of the Party's Executive Committee.[27]

It took several sittings before a decision was reached. Stoecker gave repeated assurances that he would do everything in his power to change the editorial staff and policy of *Das Volk*. He promised to break all relations with the paper as long as its political line alienated his Conservative friends. In the meeting of February 11, 1896, he was pressed for a final answer: Would he publicly disavow the Christian Social paper? This he declined to do on the ground that his opponents would seize upon it as proof that he had retreated before reaction. It was the end. Stoecker resigned from the Committee and severed his relations with the Conservative Party. In an overflowing mass meeting, a few days later, he rendered his own account of the conflict, ending his speech with a declaration of principles:

"I read in the papers that the Conservatives now will move towards the Right, Stoecker towards the Left. No, gentlemen, that will never happen. We will move even more towards the Right. We intend to hold on to the old conservative foundations of Christianity, monarchy and patriotism, and to build social relations upon them."[28] For the benefit of his Conservative friends who had abandoned the cause of Christian Social reform he added: "No political movement can have favorable prospects which undertakes to tackle the problem of labor by force but leaves intact our Jewish system of economics (*Judenwirtschaft*), this rule of mammonism."

Thus one phase in Stoecker's two-front war had come to an end—an end he had not wanted. The second task, cutting his ties with the left wing of Christian socialism, found him better prepared. In his dealings with the youth group at the party convention at Frankfurt which he convoked for the end of February (1896), he showed none of the emotional strain that had characterized his negotiations with the Conservatives. The convention resolved that the reorganized Christian Social Party considered it impossible to cooperate politically with the "younger wing" of the movement, "in spite of certain points of agreement." With the same determination Stoecker now solved the problem of the editorial policy of *Das Volk*. Oberwinder and Gerlach were fired. Dietrich von Oertzen, until then editor of the *Konservative Monatsschrift*, took over. Stoecker instructed him "to be more Conservative than the Conservatives." The purged Christian Social Party adopted the new program at the 1896 convention at the Wartburg, shrine of German Lutheranism. The program showed vestiges of the young guard's influence in so far as it called for a government policy in favor of agrarian property that was "economically sound," discouraged mammoth land holdings, and emphasized the need for settling rural workers on the land; it asked for legal recognition of a workers' trade association (*Berufsvereine*) which eventually should grow into compulsory cooperatives (*obligatorische Genossenschaften*). It was the old ideal of the corporative state in which labor as a *Stand* should have its well-defined rights and obligations.

The show of activity and optimism which the reformed party put up could not conceal the fact that it had suffered a death blow. In the 1898 Reichstag elections not a single Christian Social candidate was successful. Stoecker himself barely regained the seat he had lost in 1893 and had to make a tremendous effort to do so. Even the friendly press comments on the occasion of the twentieth anniversary of the Christian Social Party (January 4, 1898) read like so many obituaries. "What Stoecker in the ten years from 1878 to 1887 accomplished with his brilliant, tireless and never-failing eloquence is above all praise and can never be appreciated too much by those who are convinced of the importance which the church and Christianity have for German life. It is with deep sorrow only that one realizes that the power of this movement has been broken," the *Reichsbote* editorialized.[29] In the narrow confines of Protestant trade-unionism, Christian Social ideas continued to exert some influence but as an aggressive political force the Stoecker movement had ceased to exist.

A few months after his break with the Conservatives Stoecker wrote to a friend: "There is no authority any more in the Berlin Movement. If monarchic movements are suppressed, democratic ones inevitably come to the fore. This is what happened with the anti-Semites and it is happening now with the Christian Socials. Those who govern don't mind it at all."[30] There was more than personal bitterness in Stoecker's cryptic remark that those who govern did not at all mind seeing his forces dislodged and supplanted. He seemed to realize that his work of twenty years had been destroyed because his objectives had become obsolete. Indeed, the ruling powers did not hesitate to tell him so. Stoecker had hardly been forced to withdraw from the Conservative Party when the Kaiser publicly opined:

Stoecker has ended as I predicted years ago. Politicians of the cloth are monstrosities (*ein Unding*). He who is a Christian is also social; the Christian Social idea is nonsensical and leads to arrogance and intolerance, both totally opposed to Christianity. The gentlemen of the cloth (*die Herren Pastoren*) should busy themselves with the souls of their flock and cultivate Christian love but they should keep out of politics which is none of their business in any case.[31]

The new convictions of Wilhelm II had ripened quickly during the struggles of the last two years, and the Protestant Church was not slow to adjust itself to the changed views of its *summus episcopus*. Up to 1894 its dignitaries, together with the representatives of the government, had officially participated in the annual conventions of Stoecker's Protestant Social Congress. From then on the Congress was boycotted by the government and the Protestant authorities followed suit. In a decree of December 16, 1895, the Superior Council of the Protestant Church (*Oberkirchenrat*) issued a sharp warning to those ministers who had heedlessly made themselves the "champions of a single group" (i.e., labor). It reminded them that the task of the clergy was to take care of spiritual needs, "to impress upon the conscience of the well-to-do classes that wealth, education and status are given into their trust to be administered for the welfare of their fellow-men; on the other hand to convince the classes who endure the burdens of life that their welfare and contentment are dependent upon their trusting submission (*gläubige Einfügung*) to God's world order and government, upon industrious, honest labor and thrift as well as upon conscientious care for the growing generation; but that envy of, and greed for, the property of their neighbors are against God's commandment."[32] God, the Superior Church Council's decree summed up, had not meant the Church to be the arbiter of worldly matters.

The hierarchy of the Protestant Church had not always preached political abstinence. By its decree of 1879 it had put the seal of approval on the government's repressive measures against godless Social Democracy. It had raised no objection to Christian Social agitation when the Imperial Message of 1881 had inaugurated Bismarck's social legislation. In 1890, when the young Kaiser had demonstratively turned his back on Bismarck's policy and had steered a course towards a reconciliation with labor, Protestantism had admonished the clergy to take an active part in this attempt, to go to workers' meetings and speak up for Christian ideals. Now, as Stoecker's biographer Frank put it, "the Protestant Church's Superior Council gave the Stumm era its ecclesiastic blessing."

More baffling and grievous than the rebuke of the temperamental Kaiser and the "shameless and dishonorable" submission of the Protestant State Church—Stoecker used these adjectives in a letter to his wife—was to him the behavior of so many of his old friends among the Conservatives. The Conservative Party not only dropped him without a qualm, it also seemed bent on destroying his personal reputation. The chairman of the Berlin party organization, Colonel von Krause, disclosed the background of the Conservatives' controversies with Stoecker in a pamphlet[33] which insinuated that Stoecker had displayed an appalling lack of integrity, had engaged in double-dealing, and had carefully shut his reverend eyes to the immoral life of his friend von Hammerstein. In the opinion of Stoecker's remaining friends, the "Jewish liberal press" could not have done a better job.

The vigor with which the Conservative Party shook off the Stoecker-Hammerstein command indicated the outcome of a struggle that had been taking place within the party for new leadership and reorientation. It may not be necessary to go all the way with Franz Mehring who in the *Neue Zeit*[34] interpreted Hammerstein's downfall as the result of a Conservative intrigue. But the Social Democratic weekly touched upon a crucial point when it drew attention to developments within conservatism which had a great, perhaps a decisive, bearing on the party's decision to oust the leaders most intimately associated with anti-Semitism. Anti-Semitism as such was not the issue at all. The underlying problems were economic and political.

CHAPTER IX

NEW DIRECTIONS AND NEW TARGETS

The years from the middle of the nineties to the turn of the century are known in German history as "the Stumm era." The rise to political prominence of a big businessman, the steel manufacturer Carl Ferdinand von Stumm-Halberg, symbolized the new trends in Germany's political life.

Stumm was born (1836) into a prosperous middle-class family of the Saar region and continued in the tradition of his father, a pioneer in iron and steel production. At the age of thirty, after having taken command of the family's industrial enterprises, he joined Bismarck in his fight with the Prussian parliament. Stumm's home territory, the Saar, situated between France and the Rhenish Palatinate, had a liberal tradition. Like the Palatinate, it had strongly supported the 1848 revolution and had throughout the following years of reaction regularly sent two well-known liberals to the Diet, Rudolf Virchow and Franz Duncker. Before then, Bismarck's political opponents had never lost an election and at times had won as much as eighty per cent of the total vote. Stumm tried to conquer the district for Bismarck.

The main source of the Saar's industrial wealth was, and has remained to this day, coal. The Prussian State had taken the coal mines in possession and management when it had annexed the territory in 1815. Bismarck now threatened to sell the mines to France unless the Prussian parliament would grant him the funds which he wanted for army reorganization. Stumm seconded the Chancellor's blackmail. If the government were forced to sell the mines in order to finance its military program, he argued—and what alternative was there in the face of liberal opposition but selling or letting the army disintegrate—France's economic, cultural, and political hegemony over the region would be assured. Patriotic duty as well as material interests, therefore, called for the election of men on whom Bismarck could depend. "The Saar must remain German." Utilizing this slogan Stumm ran in the 1866 election for the Prussian Diet. He was defeated. The border region, although extremely sensitive to the dangers which threatened from Louis Napoleon's regime, nevertheless elected all Liberal candidates again. But the campaign had won Stumm

Bismarck's friendship. A year later, in the elections for the Constituent Reichstag of the North-German Federation, Stumm was victorious. Bismarck's successful war against Austria, the surrender of the National Liberals, and the prospect of national unification had begun to tell. The government, incidentally, helped Stumm along by rearranging the Saar's constituencies.[1] In the same year he was also elected to the Prussian Diet.

In the legislative bodies Stumm joined the Free-Conservatives who in support of Bismarck's Reich policy had just seceded from the Conservative Party. The centers of their strength were Upper Silesia and the Rhineland, both border regions, both highly industrialized and predominantly Catholic.[2] Whereas the Conservatives were the party of Prussian landed nobility, the Free-Conservatives might be characterized as the party of German aristocratic industrialism. They did not look back toward Prussia's feudal past but forward to national unity, industrial expansion, and world politics under a centralized government which should not be dependent on parliamentarianism. "The Fatherland above the party, national interest above everything else," declared the Free-Conservatives in their platform of 1867. They also stated that they were against "pseudo-constitutionalism" and the "out-lived but still influential doctrine of the separation of powers."

Stumm, only 31 years old, was one of the youngest members of the Free-Conservative group. In a short time he made his way up into the leadership. His great personal wealth was not the only reason for his political success. Wealth was nothing extraordinary in a party which counted among its members the Prince of Pless, the Duke of Ratibor, the Duke of Ujest, and other notables of fabulous possessions. Stumm's prestige must be partly credited to the determination with which he pursued his aims—aims that happened to be also those of strong social forces. His philosophy was all of one piece: society in its entirety rested on the authority derived from private capital. The power of the state was necessary to back private capital whenever the authority of private capital was unable to assert itself. The propertied groups and the state belonged together; the welfare of the groups without property was given into their common trust. Stumm was not an anti-Semite. The Jewish group, being propertied, belonged to the "state-preserving" forces that had to protect themselves and the Reich against the onslaught of "anarchy and revolution." Next to his own political party, the National Liberals were his most loyal supporters. In 1871, at the beginning of the Kulturkampf, he was elected to the Reichstag with the assistance of the National Liberal Party against the candidate of the Catholic Center. (The Socialists had, as yet, not put up a candidate in his district.) In

1874 the Free-Conservatives and National Liberals of the Saar entered into a formal coalition as "the parties loyal to the Reich" and succeeded again in electing him against the Catholic candidate. But by 1877 the situation had changed and the Socialists had begun to organize the Saar workers. Stumm immediately set up in the Saar the "Employers' Committee to Combat Social Democracy," with the following drastic program:

1. No workers shall be tolerated in the plants who directly or indirectly participates in Social Democratic agitation; specifically those who
   a. read and distribute Social Democratic newspapers;
   b. attend Social Democratic meetings or join Social Democratic associations;
   c. frequent saloons which permit Social Democratic meetings and subscribe to newspapers of a Social Democratic character.
2. Workers who are dismissed in accordance with this decision shall not be employed in any other plant.

The blacklisting of Social Democratic workers and trade unionists was complete since the government-owned mines and railroads joined the Employers' Committee. Thus, even before Bismarck was able to have the anti-Socialist law enacted in the Reich, his friend Stumm had made his own *Sozialistengesetz* for his industrial empire and was carrying it out with utmost severity. His example was followed in 1878 by heavy industry throughout Western Germany. So sensitive was he to anything resembling socialist criticism that in 1880 he put the Progressive newspaper *Neunkirchener Tageblatt* on the Employers' index for publishing a poem on the fate of an old unemployed worker. The state-operated mines and railroads concurred in the banning of the paper but the Progressives took up the issue in the Diet and forced the Prussian Minister to repeal the decision. Rather than yield Stumm withdrew from the "Employers' Committee to Combat Social Democracy." Twenty-four hours after the Prussian government had lifted the ban on the paper in the state-owned enterprises, he posted a letter at the gate of his steel-works in Neunkirchen which said:

. . . The Committee's base has been destroyed; I consider its further existence impossible and have already resigned from it. In view of the new situation I regard it as futile . . . to carry on the fight against socialist and other tendencies hostile to the Reich. I am, therefore, determined to retire from political life. . . . Subscription to the *Neunkirchener Tageblatt* remains prohibited as before. . . .[3]

Stumm's voluntary political retirement did not last long. In 1882 he was appointed a lifelong member of the Herrenhaus, Prussia's upper chamber. "You wanted to leave us," Kaiser Wilhelm I told him on the occasion, "but I roped you in again." In 1888 Kaiser Friedrich III, on Bismarck's suggestion, made him a baron. A year later he was reelected in the Reichstag where he immediately came to the support of Bismarck in the latter's attempt to enact a new anti-Socialist bill.

The Kaiser's conflict with Bismarck put Stumm in a difficult situation. He had been the Chancellor's loyal agent in the fight against Catholicism and Social Democracy; he had supported Bismarck's program of protectionism and railroad nationalization. When Bismarck was forced to resign in 1890, Stumm assured him of his lasting devotion. But he felt it impossible to join the retired Chancellor's *fronde* against the Kaiser. In 1892, after Bismarck's open attacks upon Wilhelm II and Caprivi, Stumm wrote Caprivi: "As things are at present I am resolved to give up all contacts with Friedrichsruh [Bismarck's estate] and do not question for a moment that my place is with your Excellency and His Majesty's government."[4] In the same year the Kaiser visited Stumm in the Saar; His Majesty was greatly impressed by the social services which the Stumm management provided for workers and employees, and he expressed his approval publicly.

Stumm's solution of the social question was simple enough: the workers' own organizations must be utterly suppressed. The individual worker must prove himself loyal to the management, industrious, skilled, thrifty, patriotic, and religious; his welfare and advancement should depend only on his possession of these attributes. Stumm's business empire was run in strict accordance with these principles. An industrial enterprise that wants to prosper must be set up along military not parliamentary lines, he liked to say. He personally determined the wages of each of his workers. Military discipline during working hours was taken for granted. But Stumm even claimed the right to control the private activities of his workers and employees. "If I were really prevented from keeping an eye on my workers and their conduct outside the plant, and not allowed to set them straight, I would not head my business for another day because I would be unable to fulfill the moral duties which my conscience dictates to me before God and my fellow men." A worker in any of the Stumm enterprises was not permitted to marry without Stumm's personal consent. The management's approval was only given to bridegrooms who had passed their twenty-fourth year and had saved enough money to set up a household of their own. The bride had to be presented to Stumm for his judgment on her abilities as a *Hausfrau*. Children had to go to church regularly. No literature which Stumm considered harmful was permitted in the homes of his workers. The ban included, of course, all Social Democratic and trade-union publications but was, at times, even extended to Catholic and liberal newspapers. In return for good behavior, Stumm's workers and employees could count on well-run social services, such as health, life, disability, widow, and orphan insurances, savings banks, company-owned apartments, bonuses to offset the high cost of living, trade schools for the sons, and sewing courses for the daughters. On Sundays, Stumm's private parks were opened to the families of the workers, and military bands were provided for entertainment after church. All who worked under him and with him in the "honorable trade of the hammer-mill" were to feel like members of one big family. Stumm's business had gradually evolved into a number of monopolies. In 1886 Stumm organized the German Rail Cartel (*Deutsche Schienengemeinschaft*) and the Sleeper Cartel (*Deutsche Schwellengemeinschaft*); in 1894 he combined the heavy industry of the Saar (*Gebr. Stumm, Gebr. Röchling, Völklingen, Burbacher Hütte*) into the South German Girder Association (*Süddeutscher Trägerverband*). The plants of his friend Friedrich Krupp in Essen and his own *Dillinger Hütte* produced most of the armor for the growing German fleet.

The complete victory of the state over organized labor was Stumm's foremost objective in domestic affairs. The man who held paternalistic slavery to be the ideal form of society and had actually established it in his own private realm derided socialism for proposing to establish "a big prison with a common rabbit cage attached to it [for sexual promiscuity]."[5] Even during Caprivi's last years in office Stumm had tried to convince the Kaiser that moderation towards Social Democracy would only be construed as a sign of the government's weakness and that Bismarck's plan of 1890 was the only way out. Wilhelm von Kardorff, organizer of the Central Association of German Industrialists (*Zentralverband Deutscher Industrieller*, 1876) and a leading spirit of the Free-Conservative Party ever since its inception, could in the summer of 1893 privately inform Bismarck that Stumm "was confident he holds a secure grip on His Majesty and would procure a complete change of mind toward the Social Democrats."[6] After a formal reconciliation between the Kaiser and Bismarck had been brought about, Stumm renewed his friendship with the ex-Chancellor who, though in retirement, remained a political power of the first order and to whom all plans for a *coup d'état* must be traced. Backed by Bismarck, Stumm urged Caprivi to initiate new legislation against "sedition" and when, after Caprivi's resignation, the government's sedition bill (*Umsturzvorlage*) came before the Reichstag it was Stumm who espoused it in one of the most provocative speeches the parliament had ever heard. His only regret was that the bill did not go far enough. If he had his way, he told the Social Democrats in the House, the law would be short and simple:

1. The Social Democrats, including the anarchists, are deprived of the right to elect and to be elected;

2. All agitators will be deported or interned. Executive orders will take care of the details.[7]

His main desire to destroy every vestige of labor's political power made Stumm a remorseless foe of every idea or trend that carried with it some kind of recognition of labor's demands. Christian socialism was one of them. From 1895 to 1898 Stoecker, Naumann, and the *Katheder*-Socialists had no opponent as violent as this blunt representative of big industry.[8] He thundered against everyone who in his opinion "gave comfort to sedition and anarchy."[9] In this line of attack heavy industry was not alone. Labor had become the all-important target of the *Junkers* too. The Conservative party, dominated by agrarian interests, did not remain unaffected by the progress of capitalist economy. Industry, banking, trade invited the agricultural entrepreneur to participate in their activities. The *Junker* was offered a chance to become a modern capitalist, but his ability to avail himself of the opportunity depended on such objective conditions as the size and location of his property, the local supply of labor, his access to credit, etc. The varying degrees to which the *Junkers* could meet the prerequisites of capitalistic agriculture made for group differentiations and divisions unknown within the old caste.

The modern type of aristocratic agrarian employed the cheapest labor he could get. It came from Catholic Poland. Polish farm hands moved into the areas depopulated by the German exodus to the industrial centers. As a result, the position of the Protestant village parson changed. His traditional function of mediating between the *Junker* and his hands became less important as capitalistic contractual relations replaced feudal personal ones. But it was now all the more important that the union organizer should not occupy the role which the parson had been compelled to relinquish.

Hammerstein and Stoecker had their most loyal supporters among those who were least capable of adjusting their production to modern requirements—the "cabbage-*Junkers*" in the remotest provinces of the East. This group could afford to have sympathies for the industrial masses. They could cling all the more proudly to their traditional virtues and reject "Jewish capitalism" with contemptuous finality because the temptations of capitalism were not addressed to them. In this respect the "cabbage-*Junkers*" were in the same situation as the *Mittelstand*. The dimensions which "the Jewish question" took on in the ideologies of both groups attested to a common economic fate: they were both cut off from the mainstream of capitalism. With due allowance for the exceptions which generalizations of this kind require, one might say that the opposition against the Stoecker-Hammerstein forces within the Conservative Party came chiefly from the ranks of the more modern agrarian producers. The organization of the Agrarian League in 1893 had favored their rise within the party. They were "moderate" with regard to anti-Semitism for the same reason that made them adamant in their opposition to social reform. They dealt with realities such as higher tariffs on grain, lower taxes for agriculture, and revision of protective labor legislation. Their leaders were practical men whose outlook did not basically differ from that of the captains of industry. *Realpolitik*, rather than ideologies, counted with the League; it looked for friends in many political groups and worked out electoral agreements with Liberal as well as Conservative candidates, provided they endorsed its economic program. It helped elect many a National Liberal who was hard pressed by his Social Democratic opponent; and many a National Liberal voter preferred the League's candidate to a Socialist without caring about the former's anti-Semitism. The trend was all for treating anti-Semitism as a "private" affair which should not be mixed up in politics.

By organizing the fight for agrarian interests solely on an economic class basis, the Agrarian League tended to dismiss as irrelevant a host of concepts that were part of the old conservative culture, among them the quasi-instinctual abhorrence of "Jewish liberalism." The decision to come down to earth and to change conservative strategy was not arrived at arbitrarily. It had gradually taken shape as a possibility and finally imposed itself as a necessary step by virtue of events over which the Conservatives had no control. The inroads of capitalism into agriculture abroad and at home was one important factor in the change. The beginning of a sustained period of general prosperity had a marked effect as did the rise of organized labor as the most powerful political opposition. The fear of the revolutionary movement was also a cogent reason for political liberalism to forego its claims to power and accept the Reich as Bismarck had created it. As the Liberals became more "reasonable" and the Conservatives more "modern," opportunities for mutual understanding multiplied. On "patriotic" issues such as loyalty to the Kaiser and the state and the fight against the Social Democratic "scum without a fatherland," the cooperation of Liberals and Conservatives became well-nigh complete. The "Jewish question," which Stoecker and Ahlwardt had tried to put in the forefront of politics, was no longer relevant to the major conflicts between the propertied groups. Anti-Semitism as a political issue took on a tinge of provincialism. The enlightened member of the ruling groups did not display his feelings of superiority in public and he undoubtedly counted some Jews among his best friends.

Stoecker was right. "Those who govern were not at all displeased" by the fact that Christian socialism had lost its appeal. The fronts had utterly changed. Industrial and agrarian interests alike stood against Christian socialism, the vehicle of clerical anti-Semitism, because it had become a hindrance rather than an aid in fighting socialist labor. The phalanx against Social Democracy reached from the Kaiser and Bismarck to the left wing of political liberalism under Eugen Richter. Anti-Semitism from above could not be allowed to disturb this solid front.

But though united against Marxist labor, the partners could not agree upon a course of action. The political mess which Hohenlohe inherited was highlighted by the fate of the government's sedition bill. Caprivi had warned against reenacting discriminatory legislation. Hohenlohe, too, had no heart for it. The Conservatives and the National Liberals supported the bill but they alone were a minority in the Reichstag. The government tried to win the Catholic Center Party but the Catholic Center made its approval dependent on an extension of the original bill to include restrictions of the freedom of teaching. The revised bill created a storm of public protest. In May, 1895, it was rejected by the Reichstag. The whole "sedition campaign" had ended in a most embarrassing defeat of the government, the conservative *Preussische Jahrbücher* wrote. It had put the Social Democrats in an "incredibly favorable position to fight and win shoulder-to-shoulder with educated Germans (*mit der gesamten deutschen Bildung*)."[10] The lesson was lost on the Kaiser and his entourage. "We still have the fire brigade for ordinary occasions and shrapnel as the last resort," Wilhelm II openly wired his Chancellor.[11] Stumm, Waldersee, and the Prussian Minister of the Interior, Köller, pressed the monarch to take action against the Social Democrats, at least in Prussia, but Hohenlohe refused to go along. The Kaiser, who did not dare to change his Chancellor again, vented his rage in incendiary oratory against "the rabble who do not deserve to be called Germans." He had become utterly disgusted with the constitutional system. "My Reichstag," he wrote in 1895 to the Czar, "behaves as badly as possible; it swings back and forth between the Socialists who are driven on by the Jews, and the ultramontane Catholics; as far as I can see, the whole pack of both parties will soon be ripe for hanging."[12] He spent the next years waiting and working for the opportunity to send the "bunch of monkeys" in parliament to the devil. In 1897, when the longshoremen of the Hamburg port went on strike and again when the Reichstag refused to furnish the means for expanding the navy, the Kaiser made new threats of a *coup d'état*. As always, in such times of acute frustration he looked to Stumm and Waldersee for encouragement and swore to fire his uncooperative Chancellor.

But the *Staatsstreich* never came off. Even the government's endeavors to curtail the labor movement by legislation met with but little success. The "lex Arons" was passed by the Diet in 1898. It made it impossible for a Socialist to teach at any Prussian university. But the attempt to enact in Prussia the so-called "little anti-Socialist act" (1897) was defeated by the common opposition of all major parties against the two Conservative groups. So was the government's "penitentiary bill" (*Zuchthausvorlage*), directly inspired by the Kaiser and designed to break the labor unions by "protecting nonstriking workers against union terror," (1899). The Catholic Center, aware of the resistance of Catholic labor unions to the bill, refused to vote for it. It was a sharp defeat for Stumm who had vehemently espoused the bill throughout the summer of 1899. With this failure a period came to an end which was characterized by the constant temptation to break the political deadlock by using violence against the organizations of socialist labor. The personal weakness of the nation's ruler contributed largely to the government's vacillation but the indecision was, in the final analysis, the expression of a confused power situation which made it next to impossible to take the calculated risk.

Another solution, less radical but also less dangerous, had to be found to weaken the "state-destroying" forces. The first attempt in this direction was made in the 1898 Reichstag election when under Free-Conservative leadership a policy of "national concentration" (*Sammlungspolitik*) was launched.[13] *Sammlung* and *Weltpolitik* with the aim of territorial aggrandizement were the great aims and promises by which the imperial government hoped to control the political situation at home. When Chancellor Hohenlohe resigned in 1900, Germany's political affairs were as chaotic as ever. Hohenlohe's successor, Prince Bülow, realized that the time for unconstitutional adventures had passed and that the badly impaired relations between the government and the Reichstag had to be mended. The *Kartell* parties had proved too weak to give the government a parliamentary majority. Bülow, therefore, decided to take in the Catholic Center which, after most *Kulturkampf* legislation had been rescinded, was eager to gain influence as a government party. This coalition was kept together by substantial economic concessions. In 1902 a new tariff law was enacted, raising the import duties on grain and meat and making Germany's food prices the highest in Europe. A new series of trade agreements, based on the new tariff, was ratified in 1905. It was the government's gift to the export industries. The construction of a bigger navy amounted to another subsidy of heavy industry. The material conditions for *Sammlung* and *Weltpolitik* were brought about by Germany's socioeconomic development from the middle of the nineties to 1914. The national wealth, after 1896, kept increasing at a rate, first of five, and later of ten billion marks annually. The greatest progress was made in heavy industry, in terms of both capital investment and output (coal, iron, steel, and electrical power); in tonnage and quality the merchant marine improved rapidly; foreign trade expanded; the development of railroads and waterways kept pace. In a number of technological skills and processes such as the extraction of dyestuffs and the production of optical instruments, German industry was leading the world. In 1910, one fifth of the total German population lived in cities of more than 100,-000 inhabitants. In relation to the size of the population more Germans were engaged in industry than Englishmen or Americans. From less than 50 million in 1890, the total population figure rose to 67.8 million in 1914.

From such improvements in the nation's material life it would seem obvious that group tensions would decrease sharply; the decline of political anti-Semitism might appear to confirm the observation. But the concurrence of a business boom and an anti-Semitic ebb is in fact no more self-explanatory than the earlier concurrence of an economic depression with the rise of anti-Jewish movements. What is more, business prosperity did not include forces that would eventually cure the basic ills of imperial Germany. It only permitted the deflection of the tensions generated in the Reich's anomalous political structure. It made possible a temporary compromise between the ruling groups as well as the integration of the *Mittelstand*. The "little man" who had crowded the meeting halls and had wildly cheered the vicious harangues against Jews, Liberals, Social Democrats, even against Conservatives and the high imperial bureaucracy, found in the long period of economic prosperity opportunities to adjust his material needs to the forms of industrial society. In the course of this adjustment he could not help rearranging his stock of ideological goods. He, too, became more "tolerant." The workings of this process of integration are particularly visible in the case of an occupational group whose members were predestined, as it were, to be anti-Semitic. They were the salaried commercial employees, a subgroup of the "white-collar workers."

Economically, the salaried employees at the end of the nineteenth century had become modern wage earners who depended on selling their specific skills and were hardly less subject to the vicissitudes of the market economy than the manual workers. Socially, and in their own consciousness, nevertheless, they ranked higher than the industrial wage earners. Their political performance makes sense only if it is seen as dictated by considerations of status, by the fear of being identified with the lowest strata of the German caste society. The overt expression of this status-consciousness was anti-Semitism and anti-Marxism.

The salaried commercial employees displayed all the characteristic *Mittelstand* traits. Their outlook, conduct, and attire were patterned after petty bourgeois rather than proletarian values and symbols. Thrift, "*Kultur,*" Sunday church service, patriotism, the hat as against the worker's cap, were their marks of social distinction.[14] The conservative disposition of the commercial employees, so blatantly at variance with that of the industrial workers, was rooted in the social traditions of the group which had largely developed from strata of the "old" *Mittelstand.*[15] Their special working and living conditions enhanced their caste-consciousness. They were, for the most part, employed in middle-size stores in middle-size towns which involved personal relations to bosses and customers, and furthered the illusory but stubborn hope of some day achieving the independence of owners and masters as had the journeymen in medieval guilds. With this goal ahead, low salaries and interminable working hours were bearable.

The introduction of cheaper and more efficient methods of merchandising, however, played havoc with the commercial employees' dreams of independence. The rise of the department store, the one-price store, the consumers' cooperative, and the chain-store system tended to cut down the clientele of the old-fashioned store and also affected the status of the salaried employee by emphasizing his subordinate role in the distributive setup. Poorly paid, quickly replaceable, caught in a dreary and limited system of promotion, the salaried employee could not forever shut out the realization that identification with the boss or management was not the answer to his problems. He had to defend his existence by building an organization, as the industrial workers had done. But it had to be an organization which drew a sharp line between him and the rest of labor.

In 1893[16] the first modest attempt in this direction was made when a group of thirty commercial employees in Hamburg joined and set up the German Federation of Salaried Commercial Employees (*Deutscher Handlungsgehilfen Verband*). The name was chosen to keep the organization free of the internationalists associated with the socialist trade unions. To underline its loyalties even more sharply, the Federation two years later enlarged the adjective "German" in its name to "German National." The implication of the term "national" was not "nationwide," as the American reader might assume, but nationalist. Originally meant to designate "the people" who wanted national unity against the feudal powers which resisted it, the very concept of "the nation" had begun to change after Bismarck had succeeded in breaking the power of liberalism. Once democratic and inclusive, "national" now stood for the exclusive principles of an élite. It excluded the Social Democrats. It cast a shadow of suspicion on the national loyalty of minority groups, be it Alsatians or Poles because they spoke another tongue, or German Catho-

lics because of their church's ties with Rome, or the Jewish group because of its international trade contacts.[17]

The Federation's élite philosophy was succinctly formulated by one of
its leaders: "A community (*Gemeinschaft*) which wants to fight against
all the depressing drabness of its social situation (*die ganze Dumpfheit
der Standeslage*) and against all the brutal force of the Social Democrats, needs a clear criterion for the selection of its members, not unlike
an aptitude test. [The Federation] therefore decided to accept only
comrades-in-arms sharing in a common fate (*Schicksalsgenossen*), that
is, only salaried commercial employees, and furthermore only those who
would remain comrades-in-arms for the rest of their life, that is, only
men. To be able to expose the organization to the hardest tests of loyalty
in times of need, they decided to accept only blood brothers and to keep
away the agents of decomposition, the Jews."[18] This exclusiveness,
sharply contrasting with the principles of trade unionism, did not impede the Federation's growth. Although closed to all women employees,
to all non-German Gentiles, to Jews, and barring from admission even
those salaried employees who were not skilled commercial clerks, the
organization soon gained in membership and prestige. In 1896 it found
a capable agitator and organizer in the anti-Semite Wilhelm Schack
whom it elected to the 1907 Reichstag.[19] In 1911 it had over 100,000
members, comprising approximately one-fourth of all the organized
private salaried employees.

This extraordinary success was certainly favored by economic trends.
Between 1895 and 1907 the number of independent entrepreneurs in
industry and commerce decreased by 2.5 per cent; the number of salaried
employees, however, rose as much as 160 per cent.[20] The figures high-
light the radical change in the employee's traditional position. Future
economic independence was ruled out. Socially, the employee's status was
degraded by the sheer number of jobholders whose employment depended on the flourishing of the despised streamlined, impersonal, "Jewish" commercial establishments. But this does not quite answer the
question as to why a growing awareness of the employees' situation
should not have induced the Federation to make common cause with
the labor movement.

The answer does not seem to lie in strictly economic factors but in
Germany's peculiar sociopolitical structure. Amidst unprecedented industrial, technological, and scientific advances, Germany had retained
whole blocks of the precapitalist social structure, its institutions and
thoughts. The German National Federation of Salaried Commercial Employees was one of the organizations which perpetuated the ideals of
the corporate state, preference for a hierarchic order, authoritarianism,

anti-Semitism, and general xenophobia. Its growth indicates that its social philosophy fitted concepts prevailing in a large segment of the population.[21] The Federation's members saw in their women colleagues, as in all women working outside the family, evidence of the destruction which industrial society had wrought upon the only tolerable human order. Man's authority and independence, shattered by large-scale industrialism, should at least be able to assert themselves in his relations to wife and children.

Despite the *Mittelstand* ideology, which dominated the Federation to such a degree that it rejected the strike as "a proletarian weapon of class war," the organization was nevertheless compelled to assume the genuine functions of a union. Much as it stressed the necessity for harmonious relations with management, it was not a company union. Employers could join but had no vote. Financially, too, it maintained strict independence. It had to occupy itself with questions of wages and hours and was soon drawn into the struggle for social legislation. It campaigned energetically for closing stores and offices on Sundays (*Sonntagsruhe*), supported old-age and disability insurance, and came out for state mediation in industrial conflicts. And though it always strove for objectives particularly important to its own members, these objectives forced it to operate rationally within the framework of German capitalism. The chief attraction of the Federation turned out to be its protective power as a union and its political influence as a pressure group. Anti-Semitism and anti-Marxism remained articles of faith but they could not dominate its practical efforts in the interests of its members. "Unfortunately, the Federation later lost itself entirely in trade union thinking. Its new president Beckly [Schack's successor] was from the racial (*völkisch*) point of view a complete failure," complains Willi Buch.[22] To be effective as a pressure group, the Federation had to cooperate with political parties which were eager to get its backing. Like the Agrarian League, it was anxious not to be forced into a position of total dependence on the Conservatives. It used them for its ends but it also sought to reach an understanding with the National Liberal and other parties. Last but not least it exerted a strong influence on the fate of politically organized anti-Semitism.

During the years of prosperity the two occupational organizations, the Agrarian League and the Federation of Commercial Employees, well managed, solidly financed, and going about their business in a rational way, proved to be far superior to the parties which had nothing to sell but anti-Semitism. The anti-Semitic parties became financially dependent on them and were accordingly treated. The anti-Semite W. Giese, member of Liebermann's German Social Reform Party, wrote accusingly in 1901:

"It is well known that our leaders and the various party branches unsparingly assisted in organizing the German National Federation of Salaried Commercial Employees. Today a good many of our local party organizations are languishing because their members have been drawn into the Federation. . . . How the party is carried by the Federation I want to show by still another illustration: the Hanseatic Printing and Publishing House which is the home of [the anti-Semitic paper] *Deutsche Wacht*, lives essentially on the income it derives from printing the [Federation's official publication] *Handelswacht* and the numerous blanks which the Federation needs."[23] Giese's problem was essentially the same as that of the revolutionary socialist in his relations to the trade union movement. The party embodying the pure doctrine must be protected against the temptations of "economic philistinism." Revolutionary Marxism was affected in the same way as was counterrevolutionary anti-Semitism by the economic adjustments which the prospering nation made possible for both labor and the *Mittelstand*.

Viewed as a whole this process of *Mittelstand* adjustment appears to have been highly dialectic. It demanded an occupational organization which was facilitated at the outset by specific group ideologies. The more successful the organization was, however, the more readily it relegated the ideology to the background. Anti-Semitism in the Agrarian League and the Employees' Federation became less rather than more pronounced as the two organizations became more successful in defending economic group interests. The ideologies, however, did not die in the process. They came to the surface again when the possibilities of social compromise became more difficult or appeared exhausted. Then, however, the existence of strong organizations became a factor making for a crisis rather than a denouement.

National unity and world politics found enthusiastic support in another *Mittelstand* group, the nationalistic intelligentsia. Imperialism was the ideology which fitted this group to perfection. Up to the sixties, the intellectual *Mittelstand* had played a part in Germany's political life similar in nature to that of the liberal middle classes in France and England. In view of the weakness of the German middle class it had devolved upon the intellectuals to liberalize the old state, to work for national unification, and to transform the subject into the citizen. Professors of history and law had been leaders in the National Assembly of 1848. "These academic and intellectual auxiliaries of the middle class"[24] turned away from a bourgeoisie that gave up its own position. Since Puttkamer had reorganized the civil service in the eighties, administrative careers were closed to nonconservative candidates. "Prussia's liberal civil servants quickly disappeared. If the middle class wanted to participate in official patronage it had to sever itself from political liberalism. The huge losses of the National Liberals and Progressives between 1878 and 1893 are a good index of the feudalization of Germany's capitalist society."[25]

Officials of middle-class origin vied with their aristocratic colleagues in devotion to Kaiser and Reich. The younger generation especially outdid itself in proving its patriotism by adopting the mores of conservatism. The world of business and the democratic notions of equal rights for all were equally distasteful to the civil service caste, which, incorruptible and "nonpolitical," was a pillar of the authoritarian state. The only political creed considered proper for this solid portion of the *Mittelstand*, with its life-long tenure of office and unwavering devotion to the state, was that of nationalism and *Weltpolitik*, which, as Max Weber has said, was the dogma that had to be believed in by any one group who wished to become socially acceptable to the ruling groups. Political careers, such as the Western nations provided for those who wanted to participate in the governing of their countries, were discouraged in the "Prussian civil service state" whose head insisted that "the cabinet of the Prussian King should not be and cannot be a cabinet of parties but must stand above them in complete independence."[26] Identification with the nationalist state gave the civil servant social status and life-long economic security.[27]

German university professors and teachers were wont to think of themselves as the educators of the nation in behalf of the state, although they themselves could not rise to the positions of greatest political influence or social esteem.[28] These positions were monopolized by a small aristocratic clique. Through *Weltpolitik* the intellectual groups saw a chance to take their place alongside of the traditional military and civil service aristocracy. A far-flung empire would require an expanded personnel. Positions invested with the authority of the state would be created in greater numbers than the élite could possibly fill. The academic *Mittelstand* youth were determined to take advantage of the opportunities that appeared in the making and were anxious to qualify as candidates by being above the slightest suspicion of disloyalty to the nationalist cause.

In the Pan-German League the ideology of *Mittelstand* imperialism found its ultimate embodiment. Ten years after its inception the League numbered somewhat more than 20,000 members, one-third of which belonged to the academic professions. Professors, teachers, artists, writers, and government officials together made up half of its membership[29] and supplied its leaders. The controversy about the Zanzibar agreement be-

tween Caprivi and the British government gave the League its initial
impetus. It launched a vehement attack on the Chancellor for having
exchanged "the three kingdoms of Zanzibar, Witu and Uganda" for
Helgoland, "a washtub." Carl Peters, founder of the "Society for German Colonization" and one of Germany's first African Conquistadors,
was one of the founding fathers; another was Alfred Hugenberg, later
a director of the Krupp works in Essen. The university professor Ernst
Hasse whose energetic support of the 1893 army bill enabled him to
receive a National Liberal Reichstag seat, became the League's first
president. Under his rule, the League still acted with caution in carrying
out its role as the whip of the Greater Germany movement. The leadership did not want liberals and officials to be frightened away from the
fledgling movement by the idea that they would be aligning themselves
with an organization that could be deemed in opposition to the government.

The League set itself the task of influencing public opinion, "by
creating an independent center, rooted in the middle classes, for all
the national aspirations of our people." With fanatic ardor, tinged with
desperation—for, ever since Marr's agitation, German nationalistic sects
had felt that if their warnings were not heeded the nation was doomed
—the association set out on its mission of educating the German people
in a common patriotic belief.[30] The preamble to its program of 1893
read: "The Pan-German League fights for the cultivation of German
national values all over the world; for the preservation of German culture in Europe and overseas; and for the establishment of closer ties
among all people of Germanic stock."[31] The revised program of 1903
stated the League's purpose as "the furthering of the German national
belief, particularly the awakening and cultivating of the feeling of the
racial and cultural solidarity of all German groups." It called "for an
energetic policy in the interests of Germany everywhere in the world,
and particularly for continuing the German movement for colonies and
leading it towards practical results."[32]

Lebensraum in Central Europe and overseas; a strong navy to conquer
and protect a colonial empire; political domination rather than economic
penetration—these were the goals of the League which it justified by
the claim to the racial superiority of the German people. In 1897, Ernst
Hasse, a moderate Pan-German compared to his successors, wrote "Our
future lies in our blood."[33] The racist anthropologists Otto Ammon and
Ludwig Wilser provided a scientific rationale for the League's imperialism. The League itself became an active member of the Gobineau Society which the Pan-German Professor Ludwig Schemann had founded
in 1894. Houston Stewart Chamberlain, whose book The Foundations of

the Nineteenth Century appeared in 1899, was a member and shining light of the *Alldeutschen*. The racist argument in Pan-German propaganda gained, rather than decreased, in importance over the years. The social roots of its philosophy were at times revealed with pathetic innocence. Professor Ludwig Kuhlenbeck, in a speech on "race and folkdom" before the League's convention of 1905, demanded legislative measures for the protection of the *Mittelstand* because a sound *Mittelstand* was in his opinion "the true reservoir of the racial substance."[34]

It could be taken for granted that the League, adopting as it had a racist philosophy, would assume an open anti-Semitic position. It did not do so in the early days of its organization. A motion to exclude Jews was defeated largely through the opposition of Carl Peters. Some local branches, Berlin, for instance, barred Jews from membership, but officially the League declared itself to be "neutral" with regard to Jewish membership. While it favored the enactment of laws prohibiting the immigration of Eastern European Jews into Germany, its arguments for this position were those of conservative, rather than racist, anti-Semitism. The constant influx of Eastern Jews, so the argument ran, would create obstacles to the process of "Germanizing our Jewish residents (*die Eindeutschung des bei uns ansässigen Judentums*)."[35] It was a consideration to which many German Jews were not unresponsive.

The initially "unofficial" anti-Semitism of the League became official when in 1908 the lawyer Heinrich Class succeeded Professor Hasse. After some hesitation Class had decided to take over the League's leadership only when he felt assured that he could achieve three objectives. "I had to succeed," he wrote in his autobiography, "in getting the League securely in hand, that is, to become its unchallenged leader; to impose acceptance of the *völkische* conception of the world and the state slowly but surely and, finally, to increase greatly the League's capacity for doing political work."[36] Class goes on to evaluate the degree of success he had in carrying out his program. "I may say that after 1909, at the latest, I had the reins completely in my hands and I also received cooperation in dealing with problems which had up to then been neglected. Above all, I must mention here the changed attitude toward the *Jewish question*, which finally led to the officially accepted stand that Jews and kin of Jews (*Juden und Jüdisch-Versippte*) could not be members of the League. This change was not brought without resistance but we fought it through to complete victory with tenacity and patience. Most closely related to this was the fact that much more attention was given to the race question and everything connected with it."

The fact that the new leader of the League was unambiguously racist in his pronouncements and unequivocally opposed to the government, had the widest significance. The main recruiting ground for the League was the National Liberal Party, the party of the "educated" and "national-minded" middle class. The developments within the League underscored the transformation of National Liberalism as a political force: it had once stood for national unification under a liberalized regime and had since become an agency of imperialism and a supporter of racial discrimination. This evolution had taken place within a single generation. Class himself points out that the older people in his group rejected anti-Semitism and racism and that his own anti-Semitism[37] brought him into conflict with his parents. They were old-fashioned liberals who swore by the principles of equal rights for all citizens. "We younger ones were advanced; we were national without reservation; we did not want to hear anything about tolerance if it protected the enemies of society and state; we rejected humanitarianism of the liberal type because our own people had to pay for it."[38] In the League, too, he wrote "the older gentlemen were not anti-Semitic even though they would occasionally use a strong expression against the Jews. They were particularly ignorant of the wealth of literature on the question. Moreover, they did not take at all to the race question as it came to the fore through Schemann's translation of Gobineau's *Essai sur l'inégalité des races humaines* and later through Chamberlain's *Grundlagen des Neunzehnten Jahrhunderts.* To my mind, it would have been entirely impossible during Hasse's lifetime to make the Pan-German League the vehicle of *völkische* politics, as it was developed from findings based on the racist doctrine. We younger ones, therefore, had to be patient and happy that, in view of the origin of the League, [we were able] to make of it the most militant brotherhood of warriors, the standard-bearers of the 'national opposition.' "[39]

When Class took over he did not have to be cautious any more lest the educated *Mittelstand* be alienated by a "national opposition" to the government, by criticizing it for lacking in zeal, courage, and the will to create the greater Reich to which Germany was entitled by virtue of her industrial, scientific, and cultural achievements. The nation had by then tasted some of the sweet fruits of *Weltpolitik*. The military thrusts into the South Sea, East Asia, Asia Minor, and East Africa had whetted the nation's appetite for empire. Almost all parties, from the Conservatives and anti-Semites to the Progressives and Catholics, had been won over for the naval policy. It was no longer the task of the Pan-German League to agitate for the ideology of *Weltpolitik* but to drive the government into more foreign adventures, even at the risk of war. As the government's "national opposition," it conducted a ruthless campaign against members of the imperial bureaucracy whom it suspected of liberal, that is, moderate inclinations. At first it warred against Bülow and the secretary of state, von Kiderlen-Wächter; later against Chancellor Bethmann-Hollweg whose resignation during World War I was largely due to the Pan-German accusation that he had tried to conclude a peace of compromise (*Verzichtfrieden*).[40]

How much power and influence on the government's policies the League actually had is a much-debated question.[41] Numerically, it was a small organization. Even at its peak, in World War I, it did not have more than 30–40,000 members. Its importance, however, was out of all proportion to its size. The contradictory opinions of historians, political publicists, and statesmen about so recent a phenomenon in Germany's political life may be due to two factors; to Germany's opaque, irrational structure of power in general and the League's strategy and tactics in particular. The Pan-Germans concentrated on working through personal channels rather than public agitation. They looked for adherents mainly in the groups of the intellectual *Mittelstand*, and the higher officialdom. Its official publication, the *Alldeutsche Blätter*, was an inconspicuous sheet, printed on poor paper, and with a very limited circulation. The big press hardly took notice of it. But its content was disseminated through many channels and through many channels important information came back to the League. "Locals and agents sent in their reports from all parts of the world. Members of the League sat in the parliament and committees as high up as the Federal Council; its personal contacts reached to the courts as well as to the leaders of science and business; confidential information was obtained from departments of the government and administration; through [German] Balts and German-Austrians the League extended its contacts into the Foreign Committee of the [Russian] Duma and the court of Archduke Franz Ferdinand, the successor to the throne. Thus the Pan-Germans felt entitled to their own opinions on foreign affairs. . . ."[42]

The value of such strategic positions was enormously enhanced in the twilight surrounding the decisions of the government. The Reichstag had no competence in foreign affairs. The imperial bureaucracy let the parliament and the people know only what it wanted to be known. "The worst of it," writes Karl Bachem, the historian of the Catholic Center Party, in defense of the party's support of the government's imperialistic ambitions, "was that the Reichstag hardly had any knowledge of events in the field of foreign policies and was never sufficiently informed as to the actual state of affairs. The Reichstag never was able to get the necessary data."[43] There was no political "public opinion" in the Kaiser's Germany that was based on free access to the facts, on intelligent information. If the Reichstag remained in the shadows, the public at large was left totally in the dark. When, after the downfall of the *Kaiserreich,* the Republic opened the archives, a bewildered people learned for the first time about such crucial incidents as the repeated offers of the British government to come to an understanding with Germany in regard to a naval and colonial policy.

After Bismarck no chancellor ever again succeeded in holding together the contending powers within the nation. The government itself disintegrated into more or less autonomous departments and bureaus. Army and navy, states within the state, made policies of their own, against each other as well as against the chancellor. Once parliament was relegated to a subordinate role the actual struggle for political leadership was transferred to the secrecy of private chambers. The intrigue in permanence became the *modus vivendi* of the high imperial bureaucrat. It was all-important to have the ear of the Kaiser who, unable to master the situation, relied on his "intuition" and improvised from one blunder to the next. The "Huns" speech, the Krüger telegram, the *Daily Telegraph* interview were only a few of the typical fruits of the Emperor's political talents.

Since the sources and motives of political information were obscure, the press acquired an exaggerated importance. The memoirs of German statesmen and politicians are studded with reference to this or that newspaper article.[44] The significance they attributed to them would be incomprehensible in the setting of a democratic government. The political utterances of individual publicists were given such a weight because of the authors' real or alleged "connections" in government circles. Bismarck had introduced the technique of planting articles in friendly or critical newspapers, often with the purpose of using them as a springboard for statements in the Reichstag. In his hands, the device was used chiefly against the parties and the parliament. When, under his successors, the governmental machinery disintegrated, the device became a weapon of intrigue for high government officials. In the absence of genuine public opinion in matters of foreign policy, a synthetic one had to be manufactured for the home use of high-ranking individuals in the government. By means of planted articles they produced the show of popular support necessary to impress the Kaiser and maintain their position. Only in this atmosphere was it possible for a publication like Harden's *Zukunft* to make the highest dignitaries of the Reich tremble: one never knew who it was that spoke through Harden. And in this twilight, too, the propaganda of the Pan-German League took on awesome dimensions.

In the ultimate analysis, however, neither the impotence of the Reichstag nor the people's ignorance of the issues of foreign affairs can wholly account for the momentum of Germany's imperialism. The irresistible

power of the nationalist ideology which swept along the liberal as well
as the conservative groups, the anti-Semites, Catholics and Progressives,
was the result of a compromise between conflicting social forces. The
national ideology united the old powers of the Prussian-German state
with the powers of modern big business in a partnership that had its
attractions for both sides. It left the archaic structure of power intact,
permitted rapid military and economic expansion, and hitched the *Mittelstand* to the undemocratic state. Moreover, it successfully isolated the
one great and still growing danger to the Reich, socialist labor.

The remnants of the old Christian reform movement, too, seemed to
have no other alternative any more but to choose between imperialism
and Social Democracy. Some of Stoecker's former friends and co-workers
made the jump into the labor movement. Pastor Paul Göhre, secretary
general of Stoecker's Protestant Social Congress, left the organization and
joined Friederich Naumann's National Social Association (*National-
sozialer Verein*). In 1899 he parted company with Naumann and joined
the Social Democratic Party. In 1903 another friend of Naumann's, the
Protestant theologian Max Maurenbrecher, known for his iconoclastic
history of the Hohenzollern (*Die Hohenzollern-Legende,* 1905–1906) did
likewise. Naumann himself chose a different road. He hoped to unite imperialism and Social Democracy. His National Social Association set out
to win the support of socialist labor for the national state,[45] an endeavor
which made his adversaries on the Left say of the National Socials that
they wanted to sing the *Marseillaise* to the tune of the *Wacht am Rhein*.
In the election of 1903, the complete failure of the attempt became obvious. The National Social Association dissolved and Naumann joined the
Progressive Party in which he fought for closer collaboration with the
Social Democrats. He dreamed of extending the political basis of German
imperialism to include the whole nation, "from Bassermann to Bebel,"
from the National Liberals to the Social Democrats. He was an eloquent
spokesman for territorial expansion, naval and army supremacy, and the
"social monarchy"; the theoretician and propagandist of a modern type
of imperialism that would not be carried on any longer by the ruling
classes alone, but would incorporate the industrial masses of the nation.
In World War I, Naumann's "democratic" imperialism achieved its max-
imum realization.[46]

What, then, were the interrelations between imperialism and anti-
Semitism in the last two decades of the Reich? The "Marxist danger"
had almost wholly displaced the "Jewish danger." Consequently, none
of the major parties or the government found the attack on German
Jewish citizens useful any longer. Liberalism had ceased to be a threat
to the regime, and one must add, anti-Semitism had ceased to be a threat

to liberalism. In such contests as the 1907 Reichstag elections and the 1909 municipal election in Berlin, anti-Semitic candidates were supported by liberals not because they were anti-Jewish but in order to defeat the Social Democrats.

To a lesser or greater extent, there always was an anti-Semitic component in the ideology of imperialism, particularly so, of course, in racial imperialism. But the chief targets were outside Germany. The "inferior race" was not yet clearly defined. "Rowdy" anti-Semitism had given way to "scientific" anti-Semitism, which remained as yet the ideology of a rather esoteric cult of intellectual and artistic endeavor. The cultural anti-Semitism inherent in the conservative authoritarian society did not exclude the fact that some Jews—the pride of many German Jews—could have access to the Imperial court and enjoy the Kaiser's personal acquaintance.

The German sociologist Franz Oppenheimer once called anti-Semitism "the face of aggressive chauvinistic nationalism turned inward toward the nation itself (*das nach innen gewandte Gesicht des aggressiven chauvinistischen Nationalismus*).[47] During the period of successful imperialism the face was turned outward, toward the British, French, Slavs, Chinese, Africans. When the march towards a place in the sun was stopped, anti-Semitism, the "twin-brother of extreme German nationalism"[48] made the defeated nation itself the new battleground and redefined the enemy.[49]

PART FOUR

Socialist Labor and Anti-Semitism
(1863–1914)

CHAPTER X

THE SOCIALIST VIEWPOINT

In theory and practice socialist labor was opposed to anti-Semitism. The Socialists never wavered in their stand against all attempts to deprive Jews of their civil rights. They treated with contempt the anti-Semitic agitators and the groups behind them. They never gave in to the temptation—considerable at times—to gain followers by making concessions to anti-Jewish prejudice. From the rise of the socialist labor movement in the 1860's to the time of its defeat by National Socialism, the statements of the labor leaders, the resolutions carried in party conventions, the methods of coping with the situations created by political anti-Semitism, testify to its unswerving opposition to any kind of discrimination against Jews.

On the other hand, socialist labor was indifferent, if not actually hostile, toward all efforts to preserve and revitalize autonomous Jewish religious, cultural, or national traditions. Marxism, its guiding philosophy, had as little use for the Jewish religion as it did for the Christian. Eager to have the processes of industrial society do their work of obliterating cultural differences, socialist labor could see no more than an obsolete religious heritage in the beliefs of orthodox Jewry and had even less sympathy for conscious attempts to revive the Jewish nation.

Little attention has been paid in nonsocialist literature to the work of enlightenment and education which German socialism carried on among its followers. The Socialists, on the other hand, have done little in the way of critically reevaluating this work. On the whole they still refuse to acknowledge weaknesses which have by now become obvious, and cling steadfastly to a dogmatism that even the Nazi catastrophe has not shaken. Their chronic underestimation of anti-Semitism which they continue to view as a mere byproduct of the class struggle, is symptomatic of such dogmatic thinking.

The Socialists' evaluation of both the "Jewish question" and anti-Semitism was part of their general appraisal of the class society. When Germany began her late rise as a modern industrial nation, she retained the essential structure of a caste society. The middle classes represented the liberal forces of industrialism but ranked below the topmost level of the social hierarchy. The lowest ranking group, the workers, had at first supported the Liberals in the struggle for constitutional rights. But they had asked in return that the Liberals join them in a program of democratic reforms in which the abolition of the discriminatory class franchise figured prominently. The Liberals refused to commit themselves with regard to the workers' demand for general, equal, direct, and secret suffrage. They were lukewarm about the question of the freedom of the press, and unwilling to accept the workers' associations into their own political organization, the *Nationalverein* (founded in 1859). They had likewise turned down, in the name of laissez-faire philosophy, the workers' demands for social reforms. The fruitless negotiations between the nascent workers' associations and the liberal parties finally convinced the workers that the middle class could not be trusted as an ally in the fight for basic democratic rights.

The first efforts of labor to break away from the tutelage of middle-class liberalism and to create an independent political organization of its own[1] were made during the years of the constitutional conflict in Prussia when crown and parliament were deadlocked in a struggle over constitutional rights. After Prussia's victorious wars against Denmark and Austria the liberal opposition crumbled. Democracy had suffered another defeat, hardly less severe than the one inflicted on it in 1848. The antagonism between labor and the middle classes remained characteristic of their relations throughout the history of imperial Germany. The workers never forgave the parties of the bourgeoisie for their betrayal of democracy. They despised them and rarely missed an opportunity to discredit them for the equivocal role they had played and were destined to continue playing in the involved political drama of modern Germany. Before Germany's national unification in Bismarck's *Kaiserreich*, the Liberals were indeed in a difficult position. Their two great political aims were unity and liberty. But unity under Prussia's leadership—there was, short of a nationwide revolutionary upheaval, no other power capable of bringing it about—required the sacrifice of basic democratic rights. The middle classes preferred to make the necessary concessions rather than risk the dangers of a social revolution which might not have stopped at the destruction of a system of conservative rule. Fearing the necessary though dangerous alliance with labor, the middle classes relinquished their claims to political leadership at a time when they had become strong enough to overthrow the old powers. It was the price Germany paid for being "late" on the European scene.[2]

Disappointed and antagonized by the Liberals, the workers turned to a revolutionary philosophy, which assigned to their own class a mission no other was capable of undertaking. The task ahead was no longer that of replacing one system of domination by a more "progressive" one, the substitution of enlightened bourgeois rule for that of the old reactionary powers, but the elimination of both. Socialism held out the vision of a classless society in which the exploitation of man by man would no longer form the basis of human relations.

The man to whom a number of workers' associations first turned for political leadership was a brilliant scholar, orator, and pamphleteer whose democratic radicalism and struggle for labor's independent role had made him "the only man in all Germany who could help";[3] and he was Jewish. At the height of the constitutional conflict, Ferdinand Lassalle[4] had vainly tried to stiffen the Liberals' backbone for a showdown between parliament and crown. Disgusted by the Liberals' indecision in fighting the people's battle, he had addressed himself to the workers as the power to which the cause of freedom would have to be entrusted. When, in 1863, a workers' committee was charged with the preparation of a general labor convention, it solicited his counsel on the strategy to be followed. His reply became the credo of the first German labor party, the *Allgemeine Deutsche Arbeiterverein* (General German Workingmen's Association).

In his *Offenes Antwortschreiben* (Public Answer), Lassalle stated that the Liberal Party had betrayed the cause of true democracy. The workers could no longer rely on it. They would have to form an independent party. "Organize yourselves in a general German workingmen's association," he advised them, "with the purpose of a legal and peaceful but untiring and relentless agitation for the introduction of a general and direct franchise in all German states." To alleviate the poverty and insecurity of the workers, Lassalle recommended that industrial cooperatives be organized with the help of government credit. These cooperatives were to function eventually in all spheres of industrial life and should enable the workers to compete successfully with private enterprise. Universal suffrage and the reorganization of capitalistic production on the basis of government-sponsored workers' associations should be the two immediate goals of German labor. "This is the banner you must raise. This is the sign under which you will triumph!"[5]

Such a program was bound to bring the Lassalleans into sharp conflict with the liberal middle classes as well as with the followers of Marx, who at that time had not yet severed their political ties with the Liberals or built a party of their own. The middle classes, the champions of free enterprise, were naturally hostile to the idea of workers' industrial cooperatives, and the more so, as the government's part in their establishment would have enormously strengthened the powers of the conservative state. Nor did they view Lassalle's political demands with much favor. The French experience, the caesarism by plebiscite of Napoleon III, had made them realize that they might not necessarily benefit by a more democratic suffrage. The fact is, as we know today, that Bismarck felt sure he could turn general franchise into a weapon against the Liberals and parliamentary rule. He hoped to consolidate the position of the monarchy by winning the vote of groups which, like those in France, were losing confidence in liberal leadership.

It was with growing apprehension that Marx and Engels in London and their followers in Germany watched the course which the first socialist workers' party was taking under Lassalle's leadership. There had been clashes before between Marx and Lassalle over questions of economic theory and political strategy, particularly concerning the position a revolutionary movement should take in the fight for German or Prussian national unification. Now Lassalle's program and tactics seemed to Marx and his friends an outright betrayal of the workers' cause. The Marxists, too, were enemies of the Liberals, yet their conception of the conditions under which in Germany the fight for political and social emancipation had to be carried on, did not exclude tactical agreements with the Liberals in the fight against Prussian reaction. Their conviction that the bourgeoisie had shed its revolutionary character and was only too eager to compromise with the old powers did not prevent them from seeing the greater danger to labor's cause in these old powers.[6] From London, where they lived in exile, Marx and Engels untiringly warned the workers against all shades of "royal Prussian governmental socialism," one of which they saw in Lassalle's agitation.

The anomalies of Germany's development could not have been better illustrated than by the reaction which the Lassallean movement evoked in various quarters. Protestant and Catholic conservatism hopefully expected to see it come into a head-on collision with the forces of Manchester liberalism over questions of social reform. Thus the conservative spokesmen of social reform, the Catholic bishop Ketteler of Mainz and the Protestant Franz Aimé Huber, as well as the leading theoretician of state socialism, Karl Rodbertus von Jagetzow, entered into friendly relations with Lassalle. Bismarck shrewdly calculated the services he might obtain from him[7] and sought his personal acquaintance. The liberal bourgeoisie, however, fought the new party tooth and nail.

These peculiar political alignments are responsible for some of the odd manifestations of anti-Semitism that took place. The groups which traditionally harbored and exploited anti-Jewish sentiments made remarkably little of the fact that Lassalle was a Jew, and an "eastern Jew" at that, whose father, a silk merchant of Breslau, still spelled his name Lassal and whose grandfather had been the rabbi Braun of Lozlau in Silesia. The *Historisch-Politische Blätter für das Katholische Deutschland*,[8] one of the oldest Catholic reviews which ten years later, at the time of the *Kulturkampf*, took the initiative in the Catholics' attack upon the Jews, referred to Lassalle as a "scholar" and "a really remarkable man," without even mentioning that he was Jewish. Yet in the same volume of the review, a furiously anti-Semitic outburst may be found, entitled "Viennese Cabinet Pieces: Jews Without End," which berated the Austrian and Hungarian Jews for their alleged arrogance, crookedness, and crimes. Apparently, in Lassalle's case, there was little incentive for injecting anti-Semitism into the political struggle. The Liberals, the immediate targets of his attack, could not do it. They were committed to the fight for the political emancipation of the Jews. Conservatism, hopeful of finding an ally in the young labor movement, had no interest in doing it. However, political anti-Semitism was resorted to, at least occasionally, and those who used it were, oddly enough, high-ranking and devoted leaders of Lassalle's own party.

The situation illustrates the complexity of political anti-Semitism. Here was a movement headed by a Jew who was enthusiastically acclaimed by the workers. But some of his personal friends and admirers evidently did not consider it a reflection on him when they attacked their opponents in an unmistakably anti-Semitic fashion. One of Lassalle's disciples, Johann Baptist von Schweitzer, who after Lassalle's death (1864) became his successor in the General Workingmen's Association, dedicated a novel[9] to him in which he depicted the liberal bourgeoisie in the most unflattering colors. To leave no doubt as to whom he had in mind when he ridiculed the Liberals and their propensity for ringing but empty speeches, their declamatory protests and resolutions, and their political cowardice and social hypocrisy, he bestowed Jewish names on a good many of the representatives of liberalism in the novel.

Schweitzer's biographer Gustav Mayer[10] observed that the anti-Semitism that cropped up in the Lassallean party was directed against two opponents: the liberal bourgeoisie and the nascent rival organization of the Marxists. In the last analysis, it was generated from the party's antagonism to the liberal bourgeoisie. Historically and politically, the fate of the Jewish group was so intimately linked to that of the liberal middle classes that an identity of interests between the two was taken for granted. The wing of socialist labor, which saw a hope of obtaining political and social emancipation through an alliance with the authority of the conservative state, was responsive to anti-Semitism and included into its anti-Semitic attacks all forces that sided with the liberal bourgeoisie. Cooperation with the Liberals, even if it was only with the radical wing of liberalism, made the Marxists *Judenknechte* (the Jews'

lackeys) in the eyes of a good many Lassalleans. In this group alignment
it did not matter that among the theoreticians and leaders of most political parties were some men of Jewish descent. As a rule, whenever
an anti-Semitic note was sounded in the political controversies of the
Lassalleans against the Marxist *Eisenachers*[11] we may be sure to find
questions of strategy involved bearing on the role of the Liberals. Such
is the case, for example, in Schweitzer's efforts to exploit the hesitations
that still existed within the newly founded Marxist Social Democratic
Worker's Party as to its further relations with the left wing of liberalism. Whenever the issue came up, Schweitzer would lambast the
rival organization as dominated behind the scene by "capitalists like
Löb Sonnemann"[12] and Hasselmann, editor of the Lassallean paper
Socialdemokrat, would editorially whip the "little Jew boys" (*Juden-
jüngelchen*), that is, the socialist leaders who believed in tactical cooperation with the liberal democrats against Prussianism.

Schweitzer's contempt for liberal indecision, tinged as it was with anti-
Semitism, went together with an outspoken reverence for political daring, power, and force. He was an admirer of Napoleon III (to whom
Marx and Engels referred only in the most derogatory and drastic terms)
and of the conservative die-hards. "Call the followers of the *Kreuzzeitung* party obscurantists, reactionaries, enemies of the people, whatever you please, but nevertheless, hats off! They are men!"[13] This reverence was not confined to words. When in 1867 the Constituent Reichstag was elected, for the first time since 1848 on the basis of equal, secret,
and general manhood suffrage, Schweitzer ran in the district of Elberfeld-
Barmen against Bismarck, candidate of the Conservatives, and against
the Liberal Max von Forckenbeck, President of the Prussian Diet. The
result of the first balloting was 6,525 votes for Bismarck, 6,123 for
Forckenbeck, and 4,668 for Schweitzer, which meant that a run-off election had to take place for Bismarck and Forckenbeck in which the socialist vote would decide the outcome. It went almost entirely to Bismarck. In his address to the socialist workers of the region Schweitzer
afterwards told them: "The issue at this election was to decide between
the Prussian Prime Minister and the President of the Prussian Diet.
Through your votes Count v. Bismarck won. Could it be, workers, that
your decision was an homage rendered not to the candidate of the Conservative Party but to the Minister who on his own initiative returned
to you a popular right [universal suffrage] which the liberal opposition
had so steadfastly forgotten to demand?"[14]

It should not be overlooked that toward the middle of the nineteenth
century ideologies similar to that of the Lassalleans were gaining ground
in other European countries. In France, for instance, the attacks of

Proudhon's followers upon French finance capital had a marked anti-Jewish slant. Common to the Lassalleans and Proudhonians was also the total rejection of Marxism and it might not be entirely erroneous to attribute this hostility to the fact that the Marxists prophesied nothing but failure for every movement which aimed at supplanting capitalist production by economic experiments of the kind Proudhon and Lassalle suggested. By ridiculing all attempts to replace the complex market economy of capitalism through conscious cooperation in some areas of the economic system; by emphasizing the objective role of the bourgeoisie as the most developed agent of capital, the Marxists seemed to make themselves the allies of a class which prospered best the more it destroyed the old texture of society and whose new wealth was symbolized by the rise of Jewish fortunes.

In the fight for theoretical and political leadership of the socialist movement the Marxists won over the Lassalleans. As a consequence, the Social Democratic Party adopted a different attitude toward both the Jews and the anti-Semites. As early as 1844, Marx had expressed his views "on the Jewish question" in an essay of the same title, published in the young Hegelian review *Deutsch-Französische Jahrbücher*. The essay was meant as a contribution to the discussion then current in the materialistic wing of the Hegelian school on the individual's relation to state, society, and religion; on the conditions of religious, political, and human emancipation in general and their specific application to the Jews.[15]

Bruno Bauer, a member of this school which had broken with the Christian-Conservative interpretation of Hegel's philosophy, had taken issue with the "mendacious situation" in which the Jews were being held by the "Christian-Germanic state." He had found that the Jews, while being repressed, ill-treated, and despised, nevertheless were also favored and protected in the interests of the monarchy and the nation's economic development. Although deprived of political rights, they had, in Bauer's judgment, begun to subject the ruling classes to their own rule and were levying a heavy tribute on the common people. Bauer was aroused by this "hypocritical" state of affairs which the Christian state, as well as the Jews, was perpetuating. He had written that the state, by its religious nature, could not emancipate the Jews politically as long as they held on to their religious belief. Both, Christians and Jews, would have to forego religion in order to be free.

In his critical answer to Bauer, Marx presented the problem of human emancipation as one transcending its political or religious forms. Bauer had questioned the right of the Jews to demand political emancipation as long as they held on to their religious distinction. Marx challenged the state's right to demand that for the sake of political emancipation, Jews or Christians should relinquish religion. He pointed out that in a fully developed modern state, such as America, religious emancipation coexisted with political emancipation. For what else was political emancipation of the Jew or the Christian, of the religious individual in general, but the emancipation of the state from Judaism, Christianity, and from religion in general? Human emancipation, however, was inconceivable in the framework of bourgeois society. Religious and political emancipation of the Jews, therefore, would not solve the Jewish question as the question of the individual's emancipation in the sphere of society. The material basis of Jewish existence would remain the same regardless of religious and political emancipation. The "every-day Jew," not Bauer's "Sabbath-Jew" was the subject of Marx's analysis. Even if freed from religious and political fetters and accepted on a basis of equality, would the Jews give up their "secular cult," *Schacher* (huckstering), or their "profane God," money? They would as little as bourgeois society as a whole, motivated as it was by *Schacher* and money. "The emancipation from *Schacher* and money, that is, from practical, real Judaism would be the self-emancipation of our time. An organization of society that would eliminate the conditions that make for *Schacher*, and thereby the possibility of *Schacher*, would eliminate the Jew. His religious consciousness would dissolve like a stale vapor in the oxygen (*Lebensluft*) of society. On the other hand, if the Jew recognizes the futility of his practical existence and strives to put an end to it, he will work . . . toward human emancipation in general and turn against the most poignant practical expression of human self-alienation."[16]

This essay, although relatively little known until it was republished in Marx's posthumous works,[17] was regarded as the model for the revolutionary treatment of the problem. It assured the Social Democratic Party's leaders that a solution of the Jewish problem was as little possible in bourgeois society as the emancipation of women or the working class, and just as certain to be fulfilled under socialism. In 1891, on the occasion of the Buschhoff ritual murder trial, Franz Mehring pointed to the prophetic truth contained in Marx's early analysis. Commenting on the nature of the fight that was raging between the opponents and defenders of the Jews, on the "repulsive features" of a "decaying capitalism" as Mehring saw them revealed in this trial, he referred to *Zur Judenfrage* and drew the following conclusions:

"Today, a single look at the anti-philo-Semitic war enables one to grasp all the depth of these sentences. From this secure bulwark of knowledge one may watch with a calm smile how the furious fighters in both camps storm against and beat each other. A pity each blow that misses, or rather, not a pity. After all, it hits capitalist society. But how firm can the support be upon which this society is resting, a society that can endure only in a state of agony which is bound to end sooner or later."[18]

The characterization of the Jewish group which Marx's essay gives is so evidently unfair and so much in the traditional language of anti-Semitism that it has exposed Marx to the charge of anti-Jewish prejudice. Even when generous allowance is made for the stylistic mannerisms then fashionable among the Hegelians and in which the young Marx indulged with the utmost sophistication; and when one discounts the critic's legitimate device of borrowing his adversary's language only better to destroy his argument, there remains a feeling of consternation at the distorted and unflattering image of the Jews that emerges from the pages of *Zur Judenfrage*. On the face of it, it would seem justified to suspect Marx of an indifference toward the Jewish group bordering on contempt. The charge of anti-Semitism, however, is meaningless in Marx's case because it presupposes a position which he could never have accepted. For Marx, an enemy of the Jews could only be someone who betrayed the struggle for a social order in which "the essence of Jewishness, the drive for profit," would no longer be "the principle upon which contemporary civilization is built," who forgot that "the social emancipation of the Jews is the emancipation of society from Jewishness."[19] But one may well ponder the influence which *Zur Judenfrage* had outside the philosophical milieu for which it was primarily written. When Marx had described the Jews as a group whose social function was reduced to money-making pure and simple, he had attacked the problem at its deepest social root. The Jewish question was the question of man under capitalism. Outside this context, however, the Jews of *Zur Judenfrage* appeared as a parasitic, clannish, asocial, and alien group, held together by a reactionary religion, the agents of money, hated by the people and at once protected and despised by the powers-that-be.[20]

One might venture to say that the Social Democratic Party, as a Marxist party, would have taken the same stand on the "Jewish question" if *Zur Judenfrage* had never been written. A few basic economic and political concepts developed by Marx would have been sufficient to guide the Social Democratic Party in its theoretical and practical treatment of anti-Semitism. Foremost among the "natural laws" which Marx had found governing capitalist economy was the law of capitalist accumulation. As bourgeois society evolved, the more plainly its basic antagonism would be revealed: an ever-diminishing number of owners of the chief means of production would confront an ever-growing proletariat. Capital and labor were the two essential classes of modern society and its dynamics would work inexorably toward the elimination of all intermediary classes. Unable to withstand the technological and financial superiority of large-scale enterprises, hitherto independent forms of business would eventually be forced out of existence. The small merchant and manufacturer, the peasant and artisan of today, was the proletarian of tomorrow. This large army of workers who had nothing to sell but their labor power would have to band together for individual survival. Trained and disciplined by the very processes of modern industry, they would grow in strength and boldness and finally establish themselves as the nation. They were destined to be the class that would abolish the class society with its coercive power, the state, and found in its place the association of free individuals.

This skeleton of revolutionary theory is quite adequate for an understanding of the official Social Democratic position toward the Jews and the anti-Semites. The Social Democrats saw no reason for singling out the Jewish group, either for attack or protection. Jews would share the fate of the socioeconomic classes to which they happened to belong. The revolutionary workers would abolish capital regardless of its religious denomination. In matters of human relations they would be guided by the declaration of the First International which had stated that "this International Association and all societies and individuals adhering to it will acknowledge truth, justice, and morality as the bases of their conduct towards each other and towards all men without regard to color, creed or nationality."[21]

The class theory also governed the Social Democrats' appraisal of anti-Semitism. They were certain that the economic and psychological conditions necessary for anti-Semitism to flourish were to be found mainly in those intermediary classes which modern capitalism had thrown into a "prolonged but hopeless agony." To quote from one of many authoritative pronouncements:

Anti-Semitism stems from the resentment of certain middle-class groups which find themselves oppressed by the development of capitalism and which are destined to perish economically as a result of these trends. These groups, however, misinterpret their own situation and therefore do not fight against the capitalist system but against such surface phenomena which seem to hurt them most in the competitive struggle: namely Jewish exploiters.[22]

The coincidence of economic depressions and rising waves of anti-Semitism seemed to offer substantiation for the socialist thesis that anti-Semitism was the reaction of victimized groups which had been victimized twice: by the objective processes of capitalist economy and by their own illusions as to the causes of their plight. In the eyes of the anti-Semitic population, the Socialists never tired of explaining, the Jews stood for economic forces inherent in capitalism. One had to expect, therefore, that times of acute economic and social disorganization would produce increased hatred and resentment which the endangered groups were anxious to direct against a visible, tangible, and not altogether implausible enemy. The Marxists were the first to emphasize the socio-economic roots of modern anti-Semitism. They warned their followers not to belittle it as a mere product of demagogic agitation, not to ignore the social reality behind the manipulative aspects of anti-Semitic movements. "One cannot pass over phenomena which find a response among the masses," Bebel told the delegates to the Social Democratic Party convention in 1893, admonishing them not to repeat the stupidity of their own opponents who for a long time had regarded the socialist movement as nothing but an artificial bubble. "It is necessary to analyze the causes and, having found these causes, one must look out for the means with which to remedy the ills that have produced these phenomena."

A movement which considered itself in possession of the most advanced social science did not question for a moment that the causes of anti-Semitism as a historical, sociological, and sociopsychological phenomenon could be scientifically established. Nor had the Socialists any doubts as to the remedial measures which would do away with the underlying ills. They had little hope that anti-Semitism as a false social consciousness of the *Mittelstand* could be eradicated as long as the status of these groups permitted and even required them to hold on to illusions about their position and fate in modern society. As petty bourgeois, they would be largely inaccessible to rational arguments. But capitalism would not permit them to remain petty bourgeois. Sooner or later their fate would lead them to accept the workers' revolutionary outlook in which anti-Semitism had no place. It was different with prejudices which workers might harbor. The Social Democrats believed it to be not only possible but imperative for them to eradicate these vestiges of bourgeois confusion. An anti-Semitic worker could not be counted on to be a reliable revolutionary. His prejudice was proof that he had not yet transformed himself from "a primitive man, thoughtlessly persisting in traditional ways of reasoning and feeling, into a thinking revolutionary."[23] In 1893, at the height of racial anti-Semitism, Eduard Bernstein had formulated it similarly:

The strength of anti-Semitism is rooted in confusion and self-deception as to the nature of these [social] evils. . . . Among the masses of the people anti-Semitism will find followers only among those who have not yet been enlightened by Social Democracy and where—as in the case of small farmers, artisans and small businessmen—a falsely conceived self-interest blurs their view.[24]

Enlightening those who, while suffering under capitalist exploitation, believed themselves exploited by the Jews, was part of the task of revolutionary education and a prerequisite of socialist victory. The task called for a satisfactory explanation of a phenomenon that had puzzled men for a long time, and, incidentally, continues to puzzle them. Why did anti-Semitism become the "natural" outlet for resentment which the objective processes of capitalism engendered in specific groups?

The socialists took it for granted that the Jewish group had retained distinct features which set it apart from non-Jews. They likewise took it for granted that such distinctions were relevant to the problem of anti-Semitism. Above all, they considered the Jewish group vulnerable on account of its exposed economic functions. To specific strata of the population, particularly in periods of economic disturbance, Jews appeared conspicuously in the role of exploiters. This economic antagonism, although basic, was accentuated beyond proportion by cultural differences and traditional prejudice.

The nature of the relations between Jews and non-Jews occupies a prominent place in the Socialists' theory on the causes of anti-Semitism. Without the economic role of Jews in modern society and the concrete experience with Jews as representatives of modern forms of exploitation and competition, anti-Semitism as a mass phenomenon appeared unthinkable. The Jewish cattle and grain dealer and money-lender were essential figures of the rural economy; as such they accounted in socialist eyes for essential features of agrarian anti-Semitism. The same was held to be true for the relations of Jews with conservative urban groups. The inroads of anti-Semitism into the civil service had to be ascribed to "the loan sharks who more often than not are Jews";[25] the traditional anti-Semitism of the landed aristocracy was perpetuated by the fear of losing their indebted estates to Jewish creditors. August Bebel, Wilhelm Liebknecht, Karl Kautsky, Heinrich Cunow, Franz Mehring, Eduard Bernstein, Heinrich Braun—these and other spokesmen of Social Democracy—considered it a crucial fact that Jews could be discerned as the active agents of an economic order characterized by its opacity and the anonymity of the forms of exploitation. The immediate stimulus to which all groups who were susceptible to anti-Semitism or were actually anti-Semitic reacted was, in socialist opinion, the presence of Jews, be it as middlemen, moneylenders, real estate "butchers," builders of banking empires, railroad speculators, owners of department stores and large newspapers, or as "numerous and efficient individuals"[26] in the highly competitive professions and arts.

However, the causal connection which the Socialists saw between the occupational structure of the Jewish group and popular anti-Semitism did not, in their opinion, warrant the conclusion that the Jewish group should make deliberate efforts toward changing this structure to lessen group tensions. The Socialists were content to leave the job of "normalizing" and "adjusting" the economic pattern of Jewish group existence to capitalism which would irresistibly break up the religious community of medieval Jewry and disperse the Jews, this time for good, among all social groups. Developments in that direction were in full progress at the end of the nineteenth century, not the least as the result of Eastern European anti-Semitism which accelerated the exodus of Jewish artisans, storekeepers, and peddlers, throwing them into the sweatshops of England and America. The laws of the class struggle would henceforth govern the fate of the Jews and destroy their supra-economic solidarity by integrating them in the conflicting classes of modern society. Through participation, on opposite sides, in the class conflicts of our times, the Jews would eventually cease to exist as a group. This was the course which, in orthodox Marxist opinion, capitalism was compelling Jewish assimilation to run.

In their analysis of the real or imaginary differences of the Jewish group, the Socialists, half a century ago, had already begun to take notice of the psychological and sociological aspects of anti-Semitism which are today in the foreground of scientific interest. Critically distinguishing genuine from spurious cultural or ethnic differences between Germans and Jews, they took care not to discard the latter as irrelevant but to search for the psychological value they might have in the mental and emotional world of the anti-Semites. Perhaps the only genuine sociological difference which the Socialists admitted was the entirely urban character of the Jewish group. Kautsky regarded this point as crucial. He attributed most anti-Jewish prejudice to it, and regarded the notion of Jewish racial characteristics as developed from this sociological factor.

"The Jew has become the urban dweller *comme il faut*. In him we find accumulated and developed to the extreme all the qualities, good and bad, which distinguish the city dweller. Compared to him the Christian is a mere peasant, even the Christian in the city; for he, too, is as a rule the direct or indirect descendant of peasants. What appears to us as the unbridgeable race antagonism between the 'Aryan' and the 'Semite' is in reality nothing but the antagonism between the peasant and the city dweller carried to the extreme. The difference in character between the 'Aryan' and the 'Semite' originates much more from their way of life as it has developed through the centuries, than from specific racial qualities. It is the unvaryingly urban life which has given to this Semitic mountain people (*Bergvolk*) what today are called specific Jewish characteristics."[27] The anti-Semite, according to this concept, would find typically Jewish the alertness of mind, quickness of motion, facility of language, nervous restlessness, muscular atrophy, and lack of physical prowess which the peasant, half suspiciously, half contemptuously, observes as characteristic of urban man. "There are rural districts," Kautsky wrote, "where the peasant uses the terms 'city man' and 'Jew' as synonyms, where all the arguments are brought forth against the man from the city which the anti-Semite marshals against the Jew."

The Jews' age-long status of social outcasts from which they had only recently emerged, added an important psychological element, Kautsky thought. With regard to Jews, the peasants' always present ambivalence toward the man in the city—let us remember that "peasant" stands here for Christian, whether rural or urban dweller—this mixture of suspicion and awe, envy and disapproval, inferiority and superiority, invited rationalization along racial lines. The Christian could explain Jewish success to his own satisfaction by the inborn, despicable character traits of a different race and thus remove the sting of individual defeat. Since, according to this analysis, Christian feelings of inferiority toward Jews were rooted in the antagonism of urban and rural civilization there was no reason to believe that they would disappear in bourgeois society. The relative backwardness of the agrarian community was, in Marxist opinion, an inevitable feature of capitalist economy. Social and cultural differences would, therefore, continue to be rationalized by way of racial myths. Consistent with their concepts of social development, the Socialists would never take issue with Jews for being more alert, resourceful, and eager in business, profession, or study than their Christian competitors. On the contrary, they defended Jews against such charges. While acknowledging economic rivalry and envy as prime movers of Christian hostility, they never regarded Christian complaints as justifiable. The Jews acted according to the rules and in the interest of capitalist economy, and in this frame of reference their success as capitalists was entirely legitimate.[28] Anti-Semitism which indulged in lamentations about Jewish unfairness in business reflected only the economic backwardness of the complainants.

The experience of Russian anti-Semitism forced the German Socialists to refine their basic concept of anti-Semitism as anticapitalism. It seemed impossible to explain the animosity and violence against poor artisans, shopkeepers, and proletarians in terms of economic envy, rivalry, or exploitation. The Jewish question in Eastern Europe was obviously so different that it required a different theoretical treatment. When under the shock of the pogrom of Kischineff (Easter, 1903) the editors of a Social Democratic paper of Russian Poland and Lithuania asked Kautsky as the editor of the *Neue Zeit* to express his opinion on the massacre, Kausky admitted in his answer that the current socialist explanation of Western anti-Semitism would not do justice to the situation in Russia.[29] In Eastern Europe, Jews were not primarily capitalists and intellectuals, but belonged to all urban classes, including artisans and proletarians, "among them the poorest of the poor. What could arouse popular fury against these?"

In Kautsky's formulation of the question one of the obvious answers was anticipated and dismissed as not entirely satisfactory. He did not ask "who" but "what" could have set the Russian population against the Jews. It was true that the pogroms were part of the diversionist strategy of Czarist reaction, but that was not the whole answer. In Russia, the rigid seclusion of the orthodox Jewish community, distinct by religion, customs, language, and physical appearance, was in Kautsky's opinion an essential factor of Christian-Jewish tension. Under the conditions of ignorance and brutalization which characterized the cultural and political life of the masses in Czarist Russia, the authorities found it easy to deflect mass hostility upon the "strangers." Kautsky did not believe that living together would necessarily make for better relations between different groups. The nature of the group and individual relations seemed decisive to him. "People who live under primitive, tradition-bound conditions, separated from the rest of the world, look at themselves as the measure of everything human. Their institutions, their way of thought, even their language, appear to them as natural, everything different is against nature and abominable. Such men easily view the alien with suspicion if not hostility even where no conflicts of interest exist. The aliens are considered as something inhuman and cruelties are committed against them which could never be committed against members of their own group."

The Socialists were convinced that without the existence of genuine group distinctions and ensuing group antagonisms, anti-Semitic manipulation could never be as successful as it proved to be at times. Political, manipulated anti-Semitism presupposed spontaneous, latent anti-Semitism. They would have ridiculed "enlightenment" of the kind that the scapegoat was today the Jews and might tomorrow be "the men who wear striped ties." Hatred of Jews, although irrational, did not settle upon them accidentally as long as the Jewish group offered an inviting target. Beside the weight and inertia of traditional prejudice, this isolation of the Jewish group was being perpetuated by two main factors, one of them a responsibility of the Jews themselves, the other due to wilful hostility. Most Marxists put it up to the Jews not to obstruct the economic and cultural tendencies that worked toward the eventual dissolution of the Jewish group by absorbing the Jews as individuals in the modern groups of society. Everything should be done to further this process of assimilation. All efforts to preserve the Jewish group would facilitate the perpetuation of anti-Semitism.[30]

The Marxists were sure that anti-Semitism had become part of the modern class struggle and that the interests of Jewish emancipation were inextricably linked to those of the greatest emancipatory movement of modern times. Revolutionary classes, Kautsky wrote, had always shown understanding for the Jews' struggle toward freedom and equality. Nor had the community of interest between Jewish emancipation and revolutionary aspirations escaped the forces of reaction and oppression. By keeping the Jewish group in isolation, these forces could use it as the lightning rod to deflect threatening social storms. The Jews would be playing into the hands of their enemies were they themselves not willing to give up the exclusiveness of their group,[31] the cause of alienation and the indispensable condition of manipulated anti-Semitism.

The Social Democrats were not the only ones who believed that the manipulative strength of anti-Semitism rested in the distinctiveness of the Jewish group which made it particularly suited to serve as a lightning rod. For this reason the Liberals, too, stressed the desirability of Jewish assimilation. There was also agreement between Socialists and Liberals that the forces which benefited by hatred of Jews, and at times organized it, were the forces of social and political reaction, whether in Czarist Russia where "maltreating, pillaging and massacring Jews is the only popular movement permitted,"[32] or in imperial Germany where anti-Semitism was "a form of opposition that the government sanctions, the only opposition in which state and government officials may indulge."[33] But the agreement of liberal and socialist opinion as to the role of organized hatred of the Jews was and could be only partial. Liberalism saw in anti-Semitism a survival of medieval ignorance and a tool of reaction, its occurrence and persistence confined to social areas not yet sufficiently opened up by modern society; capitalism's progress would reduce popular anti-Semitism as well as diminish the chances of using it for the benefit of antiliberal interests.

The Socialists were inclined to perceive anti-Semitism as deeply embedded in the irrationality of the class society which offered practically unlimited opportunities for its manipulation. It is true, the liberal interpretation of anti-Semitism also runs through socialist literature and we will see how it gained ground and finally predominance in the course of the political transformation of the Social Democratic Party. During the nineteenth century, however, there were basic differences in the socialist and liberal evaluation of the ultimate function of political anti-Semitism. They became particularly evident in situations where anti-Jewish movements could not be traced to Conservative-clerical reaction, as in the case of racial anti-Semitism. The anti-authoritarian, anticonservative element in Boeckel's and Ahlwardt's agitation could not be ignored. This new kind of anti-Jewish hostility was evidently not linked with the interests of the old ruling groups. What, then, did it express? Who tried to benefit by it? For whom did the agitators speak? The Liberals' concept of anti-Semitism as tied to the powers of the past made it difficult to find a satisfactory explanation for a movement which claimed to speak for the small people and professed a "liberal" creed. To combat this "plebeian" rebellion, liberalism had to fall back on time-honored generalities. It spoke of "mass insanity," of man's "destructive impulses," of a manifestation of "human irrationality," as though the phenomenon were unrelated to a concrete socioeconomic situation. Consequently, it seemed necessary to resign oneself to such outbursts of the human soul and hope that they would pass as mysteriously as they had come, or resort to fervent appeals to the treasured symbols of civilization.

The Social Democrats scorned the liberal defense as evasive, futile, and basically dishonest. They treated with derision the Liberals' usual appeal to lofty ideas, their eagerness to solicit sympathetic statements from prominent citizens and, if possible, from the authorities, their preaching of the gospel of human brotherhood. "The psychology of man," Kautsky wrote, "remains completely untouched by pious statements and exhortation. In so far as it can be changed at all and is not kept by inborn characteristics on immutable tracks, it is dominated by the meaning of his life for him. He who wants to change the world of men must give a new content to their lives. When the hostility against the Jews is deeply rooted in traditional reactions, it cannot be overcome by enlightening people but only by giving a new meaning to their lives."[34] Liberalism could not provide this new meaning, the Social Democrats were certain, because it could not admit its own responsibility for the socioeconomic and cultural changes which had deprived man's life of its former meaning. Reluctant to look for the springs of group hatred in the conflicts of contemporary, not feudal, society, the liberals were forced to obscure the problem of anti-Semitism rather than contribute to its solution.

At the height of Ahlwardt's agitation the writer Hermann Bahr asked Theodor Mommsen for a statement on anti-Semitism that would be "conspicuous, helpful and purifying."[35] The liberal historian had once before taken up the good fight in his dispute with Treitschke.[36] This time,

Mommsen's disgust with the anti-Semites was as great as his despair of effective intervention. "You are mistaken," he told Bahr, "if you believe that I could achieve anything in this matter. You are mistaken if you assume that anything at all could be achieved by reason. In years past I thought so myself and kept protesting against the monstrous infamy that is anti-Semitism. But it is useless, completely useless. Whatever I or anybody else could tell you are in the last analysis reasons, logical and ethical arguments to which no anti-Semite will listen. They listen only to their own hatred and envy, to the meanest instincts. Nothing else counts for them. They are deaf to reason, right and morals. One cannot influence them. What is there really to tell someone who follows the *Rektor* of all Germans [Ahlwardt]? Such a man is hopeless. There is no protection against the mob, be it the mob of the streets or of the parlors. *Canaille* remains *canaille*. It is a horrible epidemic, like cholera—one neither can explain nor cure it. One must patiently wait until the poison has consumed itself and lost its virulence."[37]

The leading Social Democratic daily, *Vorwärts*, fairly jumped at Mommsen when the interview was published[38] and attacked the historian for not recognizing anti-Semitism as the reaction of perishing social groups to the pressure of big business. That a liberal spokesman like Mommsen had nothing else to contribute to an understanding of anti-Semitism but some strong terms was "rather disappointing for a scholar of world repute."

Even more outspoken on occasion was the attitude of the *Neue Zeit*, the theoretical socialist weekly. After the ritual murder trial at Xanten (1891–1892) a group of well-known Liberals took up a public collection for the acquitted defendant Buschhoff. The gesture was fiercely attacked by Franz Mehring. "That the Buschhoff trial could take place in Germany was—of course—the shame of the century." Mehring wrote,[39] "but how it came about that it could take place should finally also have come to the awareness of the century. It is asinine fanaticism to believe in Jewish ritual murders but it takes a fanaticism just as asinine to assume that the belief in such murders can be eradicated by an inexhaustible flood of invectives or even by recommending it to the fatherly care of the police and the attorney general. . . .

"We have the same feeling of compassion for the unfortunate man as for every victim of infamous persecution and gladly pay our repects to those who, after Buschhoff's moral restitution, also want to help him get out of financial ruin. But for one thing we must ask in all modesty: no humbug, no publicity at the expense of human misery!"

Fighting anti-Semitism meant changing the socioeconomic conditions which bred it. This, however, in socialist opinion, was the line at which all capital, be it liberal or Jewish, would stop. What the progressive bourgeoisie wanted was "capitalism *sans phrase*," exploitation without protest, be it socialist or anti-Jewish. Jewish capital, the Socialists felt, was so closely interwoven with non-Jewish capital, that it was very secure despite the anti-Semitic agitation. Besides, Jewish capital was not at all discriminating in its search for profitable investments. Bebel wrote of the "embarrassing and disgusting" impression it made to see how despite the pogroms in Russia Jewish high finance in Central and Western Europe was always ready to keep the instigators and supporters of these savageries in power. He thought it well put when a satirical weekly made a Jewish financier exclaim: "If the Russian government has my poor Jewish brethren butchered, I shall demand one per cent more interest on my next Russian loan."[40]

What then, the Social Democrats asked, was the real purpose of the fight for and against the Jews that kept the upholders of private property so busy? The emergence of the Stoecker movement, with its outspoken aim of undermining the Socialist organization, and the suppression of the Social Democratic Party requested by Bismarck and granted by a subservient Reichstag, did not, in the minds of the Socialists, simply coincide; they had to be seen as interrelated developments.[41] The concurrence of the two events had a deep and lasting effect upon the Socialists' evaluation of anti-Semitism and liberalism. The eagerness with which so many Liberals had participated in destroying one of the pillars of democracy, freedom of speech and assembly, their tacit approval of the three-class franchise in Prussia, deprived liberalism in the eyes of the Socialists of any right to make itself the defender of the civil rights of the Jews. The sharpest Social Democratic attacks on liberal "philo-Semitism" were made in protest against the callousness which economic liberalism exhibited toward the human desolation that accompanied the rise of large-scale industry; against the indifference of the liberal press in cases where the rights and dignity of individuals were violated who happened to be socialist workers, an indifference in provocative contrast to the zeal with which the same press came to the aid of Jewish victims of injustice. The core of the Social Democratic argument against liberal defense and enlightenment was that the liberal concept of justice was that of class justice and that their philosophy made them insensitive to the point of being stupid about the most obvious causes of such expressions of social discontent as anti-Semitism. The Liberals' "philo-Semitism" was in the judgment of the Marxists the reverse side of the Conservatives' "anti-Semitism," a division of labor within the ruling classes which served in the last analysis to defend the existing order against socialism. The philo-anti-Semitic "sham battle" was staged for the mutual benefit of the contestant forces and a Socialist should want no part of it.

CHAPTER XI

MARXISM IN ACTION

Twice in the history of the Social Democratic Party before World War I, German political life was dominated by anti-Semitic agitation to such a degree that the party had to turn its full attention to it. The two periods are characterized by the names of Stoecker and Ahlwardt.

The Stoecker movement was for the Social Democratic Party a matter of life and death. The Social Democrats evaluated it as part of a conservative scheme to take advantage of the anti-Socialist act and emasculate the Social Democratic Party by transforming it into a "state-socialist" auxiliary against liberalism.[1] As one of the first answers to Stoecker's agitation, the party appealed to the workers to leave the Protestant Church. The campaign was led by the impetuous Most and, although not effective if measured by the number of workers who formally severed their relation with the church, it was a matter of great concern to the authorities.[2]

A few days after the anti-Semitic riots that took place on New Year's eve of 1880 in Berlin, the Social Democrats called a mass meeting to clarify "the position of the workers on the Jewish question." Whether out of apprehension that the anti-Semites would try to break up the meeting or as a gesture of class consciousness, the announcement stated that only those would be admitted who could identify themselves as genuine wage earners. The success of the meeting went beyond all their expectations. A capacity crowd cheered the speakers who lashed out against the "lying, conniving anti-Semites," and enthusiastically seconded a resolution the most important part of which read:

Considering that the sense of justice and democratic spirit of the unprejudiced German wage earners—a great number of whom are at present also suffering under the pressure of discriminatory laws—. . . . must resist any curtailment of the civic equality constitutionally guaranteed to the Jews, this public and general workers' meeting. . . . carries the following resolution:

1. We warn all urban and rural workers of Germany against the maneuvers of certain self-styled friends of the people. We warn them not to let themselves be induced to participate in that movement and be abused as tools for

aims which consciously or unconsciously are directed against the interests of the people;

2. We likewise warn the workers to stay away from this movement which is no concern of theirs. We ask all German wage earners in country and city to give their vote in future Reichstag elections—in so far as the present discriminatory law does not make it necessary to abstain from voting altogether —only to those candidates who have committed themselves to vote against all new discriminatory legislation, and to work towards repealing that which is now in force.[3]

The success of the January meeting was repeated in a series of similar demonstrations. The workers would often take the counteroffensive and appear in number at anti-Semitic gatherings where they took over the chair and turned the meeting into a demonstration for the outlawed Social Democratic Party. The anti-Semites reciprocated. With the party greatly hampered by the Act, the unions had begun to occupy themselves with questions of social reform. The anti-Semites took advantage of the opportunity to go on record as favoring reform and frequently spoke in union meetings where their demands for protective labor laws, a standard work day, minimum wages, "prohibition of cut-throat competition," found much acclaim. A conservative guild ideology was still strong in the unions and the anti-Semites' ideal of a closed society, of a regulated corporative community, carried weight. The government encouraged the anti-Semites' attempts to drive a wedge between the unions and the party. But the unions, too, spurned Jew-baiting. The workers' hatred of the government was such as to discredit any anti-Semite who tried to sell them the government by peddling Christian Social reform.[4]

In the tumultuous elections of 1881, the Social Democrats set a decisive example of noncooperation with the anti-Semites. It had become clear after the first balloting that the Progressives, Bismarck's *bête noire*, would not suffer the defeat for which the elections had been engineered. Stoecker, Adolph Wagner, and other prominent men of the Christian Social movement approached the Berlin Social Democrats with an offer to support them in the run-off elections and to oppose the continuation of the anti-Socialist act, provided Bebel, Liebknecht, and Hasenclever as spokesmen of the Social Democratic Party would recognize Bismarck's social legislation as being in the interests of the workers, and would in the future cooperate with the parties of "social reform," that is, the Stoecker movement. So as to leave no doubt that the offer had the government's blessing, the semi-official *Norddeutsche Allgemeine Zeitung*[5] elaborated on the theme that the real beneficiaries of the anti-Socialist act had been the Progressives who had found political support in the ranks of the workers, economically their arch-enemies. It hinted that the government would be ready to drop the Act once it had succeeded in materializing "the healthy core of socialist ideas" and in "satisfying the workers' just demands" by way of social reform legislation. The Social Democratic leaders gave an unambiguous answer. Bebel and Liebknecht publicly declared themselves to have replied

> that we rejected all electoral horse trading and vote buying; that we prefer 3,000 honestly gained votes to 30,000 bought ones; that we were not in a position to regard the government's economic policies, inaugurated by the anti-Socialist law and including such measures as higher indirect taxes and tariffs on essential commodities, increased military expenses, the law regulating the right and duties of trade associations (*Innungsgesetz*) and the like, as taken in the interests of the workers;
>
> that we never refused . . . seriously to consider the government's reform bills, to try to change them according to our wishes and to accept them if they would conform to our point of view; but that we had to refuse to work together with parties which are reactionary and therefore hostile to labor.[6]

The Social Democratic Party remained deaf to all the other overtures made by Stoecker and Bismarck to bring it into an alliance against the Progressives, although little love was lost between Socialists and Progressives. The firmness of the Socialists was the more remarkable as the immediate interests of the workers and the *Mittelstand* exerted a strong pull toward governmental protection and thereby toward a common front against the parties of free enterprise. Stoecker's meetings were crowded with people who felt little if any animosity toward labor and the Socialists. Union with such a powerful anticapitalist opposition might have proved tempting to a less principled movement than Social Democracy. It is entirely to the credit of the Marxists[*] that the party insisted on a clear separation from the various kinds of socialistic ideologies which usually were tinged with, if not built on, anti-Semitism. The position was won in the fight against the philosophy of the anti-Semitic anarchist Eugen Dühring, then a strong influence in the party, and against the corporative ideas of the anti-Semitic *Katheder*-Socialist Adolph Wagner. The confusion that existed may be gathered from the fact that a publication as close to the Social Democratic Party as the *Jahrbuch für Sozialwissenschaft* could interpret the activities of Stoecker as another sign of the irresistible progress of socialist ideas.[7]

So determined was the Social Democratic Party even in the heyday of the Berlin Movement not to make any concessions to the anti-Semitic climate of the Reich capital that in the municipal election of 1883 it nominated a Jewish candidate to run concurrently in two election districts.

[*] see Friederich Engels' letter, Document No. IX.

What was more, this Jewish candidate, Paul Singer, was not a little tailor or grocer but a very successful garment manufacturer. The workers understood the militant gesture. In his acceptance speech Singer declared himself honored by the fact that the workers, by nominating him, had given a demonstration of their attitude toward anti-Semitism. "The meaning of my candidacy goes far beyond me as a person; it is the assurance that the workers will also in the future uphold the principle of equality for all, that they will not ask who the man is but what kind of a man he is."[8]

The speech was greeted with enthusiasm and Singer was elected on the first ballot with a majority over the combined votes of his opponents. A year later, he was elected to the Reichstag and in 1885 became chairman of the Social Democratic Reichstag group. In 1886, under a clause of the anti-Socialist act, he was expelled from Berlin. But the more he attracted the ire of the government and of the anti-Semites, the more the socialist workers seemed to adore him. They made his forced departure the occasion of a demonstration against Bismarck and his brother-in-law, the Prussian Minister of the Interior, Puttkamer. Singer's farewell message to the Socialists was illegally printed and 20,000 copies were distributed in Berlin without the police being able to make a single arrest. In the *"Kartell"* elections of 1887, Singer was reelected to the Reichstag with the highest vote cast for any candidate in Berlin.

During the Reichstag elections of 1884, the outlawed Social Democratic Party made one of the few exceptions to its rule of abstaining altogether from voting in districts where its candidates were hopelessly outnumbered rather than supporting the candidates of other parties. In the run-off elections, Stoecker faced the Progressive Virchow in a Berlin district. Although a decision had been made to keep strictly neutral in the fight between the anti-Semites and the Progressives, the party leaders expressed their wish to see Stoecker defeated. Bebel, Liebknecht, Auer, and Singer made it publicly known that, in spite of the Social Democrats' differences with the Progressives, the election of Stoecker should be prevented. The Progressive Party was thus able to distribute a leaflet[9] which carried the following excerpts from statements by socialist leaders:

Liebknecht writes:
"I deem it the duty of the party comrades to vote for Virchow. Stoecker's election in Berlin would be our shame."

Auer writes:
"I hate the Progressives as much as anyone but I have declared. . . . that, if I would have to vote, I would cast my vote for the Progressive."

Bebel writes:
"It is right to say that both parties are our enemies; but it goes with-

out saying that one chooses the lesser of two evils. It is not for the Social Democrats to vote for Virchow, but against Stoecker."

Hasenclever writes:

"I am strictly for not voting but do not hesitate to declare that it is the duty of those Social Democratic voters who want to make use of their right of suffrage to vote against Stoecker."

Stoecker was defeated and the failure of his campaign was a symbol of his party's decline in Berlin. By 1885, the Berlin Movement had lost its impetus. The Social Democratic Party, however, had more than doubled its vote in Berlin between the elections of 1881 and 1884, and, although outlawed, gained more followers than the coddled conservative and anti-Semitic forces together. Its claim to have been most responsible for holding the anti-Semitic movement of the 1880's in check is certainly not without justification.

The heroic period of the Social Democratic Party, the years of the anti-Socialist act, appears in retrospect also as the period of its most militant stand against political anti-Semitism. Not that the Socialists later changed their basic attitude towards it. They continued to judge it as politically reactionary, sociologically a *Mittelstand* phenomenon, psychologically a manifestation of economic anxiety and displaced aggression. But at no other time did the Socialists find themselves in such an unproblematic, clear-cut position towards organized hatred of Jews. Opposition to Stoecker's agitation was action in self-defense. A refusal to cooperate with the government-controlled social reform program was a declaration of war against clerical-Conservative authoritarianism, the mortal enemy of the Social Democrats. Smarting themselves under the pressure of repressive legislation, they were most sensitive to the danger of further political reaction which the attack on the civil rights of the Jews heralded. Jewish political emancipation and universal suffrage had been too closely linked in time and consequence not to be widely taken as the common fruits of democracy.

The reaction of the Socialists to the wave of radical, that is, racial anti-Semitism in the early 1890's differed perceptibly from their reaction to the Stoecker movement ten years before. The spontaneous hostility which the Social Democratic Party had then displayed gave way to an almost contemplative attitude of wait-and-see, critical, to be sure, but with a strong element of hopeful speculation.

It will not take one far amiss to see one of the chief reasons for this change in the objective characteristics which distinguished the racial movement from its conservative counterpart. Racial anti-Semitism was ideologically and politically a more complex phenomenon. As a political movement, it lacked significant features which had made the nature of

Stoecker's party so obvious. Racial, radical, rowdy anti-Semitism had neither the respectable leadership nor the stamp of tacit approval from the highest quarters which the Christian Social Party had enjoyed. The political objectives of the Berlin Movement were precise and limited. Walter Frank has summed them up as "the last large-scale attempt on the part of the Conservative-clerical powers of Prussia to wrest political hegemony in the Reich capital from the forces of modern democracy, namely, the leading stratum of the liberal middle classes, moneyed Jewry, and the Social Democrats in the background slowly rising to eminence at the polls."[10] But what, concretely, was the goal of racial anti-Semitism? Its political performance was marked by utter lack of direction. It seemed to strike blindly in all directions, against Social Democrats and Conservatives, Liberals and Catholics. The diffuse aggression of its followers, their inability for coordinated and sustained political action made them behave, in a favored phrase of the Socialists, like "petty bourgeois gone beserk."

Moreover, as the character of political anti-Semitism had changed, so had the general political constellation. The fight against Social Democracy was no longer being led by the Old Conservatives, Stoecker's sponsors. Their place was gradually being taken by captains and spokesmen of modern industry and finance, adhering to the philosophy of free enterprise plus cartels, anti-unionism plus tariffs. "We vehemently struck back at the whole Stoecker business and all it stood for as long as it was in power," Mehring wrote in 1896. "But when small *Junker*dom and its allied clergydom (*Pfaffentum*) were shelved in favor of Stumm and consorts, that is, in favor of far more dangerous enemies of the masses, we preferred to give battle to the more dangerous enemy instead of chasing in blind fury after poor thieves on the cross (*arme Schächer*). . . ."[11]

Much as this new political situation may have influenced the Social Democrats' changed attitude toward the second wave of anti-Semitism, it was perhaps not the decisive factor. There were developments within the party itself which indirectly but powerfully influenced the party's position. At the bottom of them was the dilemma as to the future course of Social Democratic action which had been raised by the lapse of the anti-Socialist act in 1890. The Social Democratic Party had not only survived twelve years of a tough tug of war with the government; it had during the time of its suppression greatly gained in political prestige and organizational strength. In Paul Singer's words, the anti-Socialist act had held the Socialists together like an iron ring. Intransigeant Marxism had apparently won against the combined forces of government and reaction. It had also proved to be right against the tendencies for compromise which had shown themselves in the party ever since it had been outlawed and which had been steadfastly resisted as the ideologies of defeatism by the radical leaders.[12] Official Social Democratic Party historiography has understandably concentrated on the inspiring aspects of the "heroic years" of 1878–1890, the party's first and last experience with illegality in imperial Germany. But the historical truth is somewhat more complex. There was great apprehension as to whether the organization could maintain itself indefinitely against the government's endless acts of blackmailing, bribing, confiscating, arresting, expelling, and jailing. Continued resistance might eventually force the party to become a conspiratorial organization, with all the dangers such a step involved.[13] The party's defiance of the government might be alienating important groups which a less intransigent policy might win over. These problems had been anxiously discussed by the leading Social Democrats throughout the period when the anti-Socialist act was in force. Despite the party's courageous and intelligent fight against governmental oppression, it was not certain at all that it could withstand a second major conflict. Despite the Social Democrats' claim to have forced the government to retreat in the face of the party's impressive successes at elections, it was not unknown that it had suited Bismarck to prevent the extension of the repressive act in 1889 because he wanted an open showdown with radical labor. None of the Social Democratic leaders shared the optimism of Friedrich Engels who, in 1892, wrote Bebel that the party would easily (*spielend*) survive another *Sozialisten-Gesetz*.

After Marx's death in 1883, Engels untiringly worked to preserve the theoretical and political heritage of the revolutionary philosophy. He took a prominent part in discussions within the Social Democratic Party. Although not officially a member, he was, in Bebel's word, its head. Engels' articles and letters of the period from 1878, the year the anti-Socialist bill was passed, to his death in 1895, give witness of an unfailing faith in the inevitability of the socialist revolution in Germany and in the nearness of its hour. In 1880, he assured Bebel "that all the historical forces are bound to work for us, that nothing, absolutely nothing can happen from which we will not benefit."[14] He refused to rule out the possibility that the abortive bourgeois revolution of 1848 might still come off. The forces of modern industry, he felt, could not resign themselves to the place the Hohenzollern monarchy had assigned to them. Potentially they still were revolutionary vis-à-vis the monarchy, the army, the bureaucracy, and the semifeudal "cabbage-*Junkers*." When Bebel, in 1886, conveyed to him his doubts about such an appraisal of the German middle classes, Engels wrote back: "You cannot possibly have a lower opinion of the German bourgeoisie than I do. But the question is whether the historical circumstances will not force it against its will to become active again. . . . A stagnation such as exists today in political Germany—truly the second *Kaiserreich*—can only be temporary and exceptional; big industry cannot let the industrialists' cowardice dictate its laws; the economic processes constantly reproduce the collisions, accentuate them and will not forever suffer the domination of the semi-feudal *Junkers* with their feudal aspirations." After the Social Democratic victory in the Reichstag elections of 1884, Engels triumphantly wrote Kautsky: "The *Sozialisten-Gesetz* stands condemned. State and bourgeoisie have exposed themselves to deadly ridicule." The startling success in the elections of 1890 made him write to Wilhelm Liebknecht that "three years hence we can have the agricultural laborers and with them we will have the élite troops (*Kernregimenter*) of the Prussian army." In 1891, he predicted "a radical turn of events" to take place around 1898. A major disorganization of the world market would lead to a European war and create the opportunity for a socialist revolution.

Since time was, in Engels' opinion, working for the Social Democrats even under the heavy hand of a semi-absolutistic regime, and since the requirements of modern capitalism excluded a lasting compromise between the old and the new social classes, the Socialists should be careful not to furnish the government with a pretext for setting up an open military dictatorship.[15] An untimely proletarian bid for power would throw the middle classes back into the arms of conservative reaction. However, if labor's alliance with the forces of bourgeois liberalism was, in Engels' opinion, necessary to overthrow the old powers, it could only be a temporary partnership. To assure the victory of socialism, the Social Democratic Party had to remain a revolutionary organization, the organization of the industrial and agricultural workers. On this point Engels was adamant. Lost elections, occasional unpopularity, temporary setbacks of all kinds were unavoidable for a revolutionary party but also irrelevant to the destiny of a party which represented the most advanced class of society.[16] Maintaining the revolutionary character of the Social Democratic Party necessitated abandoning all efforts to placate groups which, although suffering under the impact of modern industry and finance, represented the ideological and material interests of private ownership. Since it was objectively impossible to turn back, even to slow down, the wheel of capitalism under which outdated property relations were crushed, it would be meretricious or demagogic to promise archaic classes their economic salvation. After the impending victory,[17] socialism would help them towards reintegration in the new society.

Engels' friends in the Social Democratic Party, the radicals, accepted his analysis but drew very different conclusions from it. Of all the party leaders, Bebel remained closest to Engels. He sided with him in 1891, against the party majority, when Engels predicted that a new crash was to be expected within a few years.[18] But while for Engels the economic breakdown was the opportunity for revolutionary action, it became for Bebel a reason for abstaining from such action: the impending economic debacle would make political action superfluous. Whereas for Engels the prospect of a brief period of economic stability implied the obligation to prepare for a following revolutionary situation, it meant for Bebel the opportunity to preserve the unity of the party against the "revisionists"[19] on the Right and the ultraradical firebrands on the Left. Capitalism would fall by the weight of its own contradictions! Modern industry was in itself revolutionary! The transformation which the revolutionary theory underwent in the further history of the Social Democratic Party had begun. The radical phrase was henceforth to go together with a growing belief in economic determinism which relied on the "blind forces" of capitalism as a substitute for political action. In the discussion of the agrarian question, which the Social Democrats considered the crux of the anti-Semitic movement of the nineties, this paralyzing combination of radical phraseology and economic determinism dominated the party.

The national economy of Germany was developed as a system of free enterprise and competition to a lesser extent than that of other Western nations. Early and powerful state intervention made it an eminently political economy with its own dynamics. To apply the categories of free market economy to the analysis of this political economy was to open the way to grave errors of judgment. Marx had relied on British empirical data when he formulated the abstract laws of capitalist economy. England, the more advanced nation, would show Germany what was in store for her. Marx's German disciples revelled in conclusions by analogy. In the course of Britain's rise to industrial and commercial hegemony, independent peasant farming had been severely reduced. This fact supplied a powerful argument in Social Democratic discussions on the future of German agriculture, and on the fate of the "intermediary" classes. In 1891, flushed with the "victory over Bismarck and the bourgeoisie," the Social Democratic Party had drafted a new program which confidently started from the premise that "the economic development of bourgeois society leads inevitably (mit Naturnotwendigkeit) to the ruin of small enterprise" and which explicitly included the peasants among the "perishing intermediary groups." The main reason why the Social Democrats could not let the alleged economic funeral of these groups pass in silence was the disturbing fact that the anti-Semitic movement, not the revolutionary party, was their political beneficiary. For the first time, a serious competitor appeared on the scene who seemed able to prevent the future proletarians and potential Social Democrats from joining the revolutionary movement. Radical anti-Semitism, making rapid headway in the rural districts, forced the party to devote its attention to the agrarian problem.[20]

There was no difference of opinion in the Social Democratic Party as to the cause of rising anti-Semitism: The agricultural depression made the rural population listen to the anticapitalistic demagogy of the Jew-baiters. Nor was there any disagreement within the party as to the fate of radical anti-Semitism—in the long run: the "awakened" groups would abandon it and find their way to the only genuinely anticapitalistic party. On this point, radicals like Bebel and Kautsky saw eye to eye with revisionists like Bernstein and Heinrich Braun.[21] The controversial question was how the "awakened" would become Social Democrats. Once this question was seriously raised, the issue of anti-Semitism was drawn into the conflict between the radical and the revisionist wings of the party. For two reasons, if not for others, despite considerable reluctance to tackle it, the issue could not be evaded any longer. One was the political competition of radical anti-Semitism; the other was the fight to preserve the ideological and organizational unity of the party.

There were indications of an increasing demand within the party to extend its influence from the cities to the villages. The advance of radical anti-Semitism blocked Social Democratic progress; local party organizations which felt the pressure of Boeckel's and Ahlwardt's agitation began to be alarmed. In 1890, at the party convention in Halle, the delegate from Marburg (Hesse) complained:

> We in Hesse, too, are convinced that something must be done if we do not want to fall back before Boeckel's agitation.[22]

And the same delegate brought forward a motion which read:

> The comrades of Marburg move that in consideration of the gain the anti-Semitic movement is making in ever-wider circles and of the objectionable methods the anti-Semites are using, particularly in their fight against the Social Democrats, the party give some support to its comrades in Marburg so that a vigorous counteragitation can be developed at the source of the anti-Semitic agitation.

The motion was not discussed but put on the agenda of next year's convention. A more serious development took place in Southern Germany, the stronghold of revisionism. In Bavaria Georg von Vollmar, in the years of the anti-Socialist act one of the most uncompromising leaders, insisted now on a realistic policy toward the small landowners. The party, he claimed, could not expect to make friends in the villages as long as it resigned itself to telling the peasants that their ruin was sealed under capitalism. Vollmar's demand for a program of "peasant protection" was part of a general attack upon the party's orthodoxy. Vollmar recommended a strategy of "prudent negotiations" by which the party could gradually move towards power.

The "agrarian question" was from then on a most controversial issue in Socialist theory and praxis, bitterly fought over in the party literature and on policy-making levels. It imposed itself upon other European socialist parties, too, but in no country was it so closely related to the problem of political anti-Semitism as in Germany. The Social Democrats could not take up one without taking up the other. For a while, they stalled. The annual convention of 1891 did not deal with the Hessian delegate's motion of the previous year, and in 1892, the two topics which were taken off the convention's agenda "for lack of time" were "the economic depression and its consequences" and "anti-Semitism and the Social Democracy."[23] The convention of 1893 finally decided to deal with the latter, but not without considerable dissenting opinion. A Berlin delegate, for instance, moved against it because the anti-Semitic movement, he argued, contained revolutionary elements and the Social Democratic Party had no reason for putting itself in strict opposition to all anti-Semitic parties. The resolution was defeated, largely through Bebel who insisted on a clarification of the party's position.

The party's hesitancy to take a stand can certainly not be attributed to covert sympathies for anti-Semitism. It reflected the notion that the anti-Semitic movement was against its will an auxiliary of socialism, at least a large reservoir of future Social Democratic votes. Moreover, the party had not yet come to a decision as to the policy it wanted to pursue towards the ruined and embittered rural population. At the same convention at which the great debate on anti-Semitism took place, a resolution was passed to deal with the agrarian question. Anti-Semitism and the agrarian question, anti-Semitism and Social Democratic *Mittelstand* policy in general involved inseparable problems and demanded joint treatment.

For Marxists of all shades the cause-effect relation between economic and ideological phenomena was obvious. Changes in the economic situation provided the stimuli which acted on the ideology; to change the ideology required tackling the socioeconomic reality on which it fed. This agreement on the causes only made it more difficult to agree on a line of action in the fight against the Ahlwardts and Boeckels. Peasants and small businessmen had become anti-Semitic because they feared to lose their property. The practical fight against peasant anti-Semitism required the sponsorship of legislation in the interests of the small producer, a program aimed at the protection of his property. But such reform policy would have run counter to the orthodox theory, to basic tenets of Marxist economics. What was more, it would have meant abandoning the proletarian character of the party and with it the conception of the proletarian revolution as the radicals understood it.

The interdependence of the issues was clearly realized. When, under the leadership of Jean Jaurès in France and Georg von Vollmar and Eduard David in Germany, the reformists were seriously threatening to push the socialist parties towards a policy of lower middle-class protection, Engels attacked them in the *Neue Zeit*.[24]

We have in the party no use for the peasant who expects us to perpetuate his small property (*Parzelleneigentum*), nor for the small artisan who wants to remain an independent owner. These people belong to the anti-Semites, let them go there. . . .

The revisionists wanted a program of legislative aid to harassed groups outside of labor. The radicals claimed that the economic decline of these groups was inevitable, that without a social revolution there was no way to cure the ills capitalism had created and was constantly recreating. Bebel in his speech on anti-Semitism at the Cologne convention of 1893 said bluntly: "What makes the position of the Social Democratic Party towards the peasants, the artisans, and small business people so difficult is the fact that as honest men the Social Democrats have to say: we have no way of saving you within the existing framework of society."[25]

The debate on the agrarian question at the national convention of 1896 ended with the rejection of the reform program which a special committee had submitted. Kautsky, the scholarly theoretician and spokesman of the radical group, won the majority of the delegates for his motion not to accept the committee's suggestions (although Bebel and Liebknecht had taken part in formulating them) because they promised to consolidate peasant property, to give additional power to the state, and thereby make labor's class struggle more difficult.

"The proletarian character of the Social Democratic Party has to be kept intact!" The radical argument remained victorious in the nineties. The position to be taken on political anti-Semitism was mapped out accordingly. It had to fit the requirements of the radicals' fight for a "revolutionary" party, for the preservation of the orthodox doctrine, and for cautious maneuvering to avoid another test of force with the state. The official interpretation of anti-Semitism declared that the anti-Jewish movement was a furious reaction mistakenly directed against one capitalist group instead of the capitalist order as a whole; essentially anticapitalistic and therefore potentially revolutionary; an immature form of rebellion, futile and evanescent like the groups that indulged in it; the death rattle of moribund classes. Thus interpreted, anti-Semitism became in itself an important part of the evidence which the radical wing brought forth to secure its position against the pressures of revisionism. The statements of Social Democratic leaders have to be interpreted in this light; their emphasis on certain features of radical anti-Semitism and indifference toward others was governed by the necessities of a grand strategy which had little, if anything, to do with the Jews, but a great deal with the future of the party. Justification for noninterference was provided by resolutions of the kind adopted at the Cologne Convention:

The Social Democratic Party fights anti-Semitism as a movement which is directed against the natural development of society but which, in spite of its reactionary character, and against its will, is bound to become revolutionary. This must happen because the urban and rural petty bourgeois groups which are being aroused by the anti-Semitic leaders against the Jewish capitalists will finally understand that their enemy is not only the Jewish capitalist but the capitalist class itself and that only the success of socialism can liberate them from their distress.[26]

The hope for quick proletarianization of the lower middle classes and speedy socialist victory was the compensation for the passivity recommended by the radical leaders. Indifference to the fate of the Jews was easily maintained by the conviction that they were not actually in danger and that the anti-Semitic movement was bound to fizzle out without doing any real damage. Bebel believed its peak had already been passed in 1893, and the *Vorwärts*[27] found that "with the victories of June 15 [1893, the date of the Reichstag elections in which the anti-Semites had made their spectacular gains] the anti-Semitic movement had reached its climax," and that the elections for the Diets of Saxony and Prussia had already shown "a decisive decline."

The anti-Semitic agitators, themselves, seemed bent on proving that "it must happen"—that in their groping for political orientation the declassed groups would be driven towards the Social Democratic Party. At the height of their careers, Ahlwardt and Boeckel often used a terminology patterned after that of the Social Democrats. The *Vorwärts* took pleasure in commenting on it with an air of irony and condescension.[28] Toward the end of 1894, Ahlwardt presented a platform for a new nationwide anti-Semitic organization. It provided for "the transfer into collective property of large-scale enterprises in industry and agriculture, with indemnity for the owners if not Jewish."[29] Criticized for the "socialism" he advocated, Ahlwardt defended the proposed measure by stating that the hopes of the anti-Semitic movement rested with the workers, and that "whoever wants to win over the masses must offer more than the Social Democrats. If anti-Semitism fails to tear the workers away from the Social Democracy, it will be doomed because the *Mittelstand* by itself is already too weak and exhausted to lead the anti-Semitic movement to victory."

Earlier in the year, Boeckel had published an article in his paper, the *Reichsherold*, in which he had apparently given up the whole racial theory. "The money-greedy big capitalist," Boeckel had written, "no matter whether Jew or non-Jew, is the strangler of our people whom he deprives of the opportunity to work. The accumulation of great wealth must lead to impoverishment and an economic breakdown." The *Vorwärts*, in an article entitled "Anti-Semitism, the seed of Social Democracy," called this "plain language" and concluded that "Herr Boeckel's followers, once they have reached this point, are bound to be led eventually into the camp of Social Democracy."[30] At the height of Ahlwardt's agitation Bebel summed up the Social Democratic attitude by saying: "It's all right with us if the members of the ruling classes wage war against each other, if all confidence is shattered and a revulsion against this whole order sets in. We calmly watch and wait."[31]

CHAPTER XII

THE CASE OF FRANZ MEHRING

At the time of the Ahlwardt scandals, the Berlin correspondent of the *Neue Zeit* contributed more to the discussion of political anti-Semitism than any other Social Democratic writer. His name was Franz Mehring. No Marxist journalist or historian made "the repulsive spectacle of anti-Semitism" so often the point of departure for a criticism of capitalist society as he did. No other writer so consistently combined his attacks on anti-Semitism with sarcastic comments on "philo-Semitism." The spirit of Mehring's writings on the subject often reminds one of the young Marx. But in his reaction to the "Jewish question" there are also mingled sentiments much akin to conservative antipathy to the ideals of *laissez faire*. Mehring's case history offers an excellent opportunity of studying how cultural and political aversion to the new society, with which Jews were prominently associated, was affected by the revolutionary theory.

As a student Mehring had become attracted by the teachings of Lassalle in whom he admired an "ingenious and original mind."[1] Convinced of the necessity for radical social reforms and repelled by Manchesterism, he had embraced socialist thought as the "ideal dream of the world-redeeming union between the highest forms of science and the elementary force of the working classes."

When in 1875 both socialist parties merged, with Marxists winning out over Lassalleans, Mehring turned away from the labor movement; he even began to attack the young Social Democratic Party. The Marxist concept of an irreconcilable conflict within society seems to have disturbed him most. The same "fanatic credo of unbridgeable class differences"[2] he had previously found in Treitschke's attack on socialism. The workers, Mehring hoped, would read Schmoller's rebuttal of Treitschke and would "find reassurance in the thought that there were in the upper classes still men of brain and heart who energetically stood up against the brutal doctrines of Manchesterism."[3] Mehring was repelled not only by the Marxist doctrines but by the means through which they were conveyed to the workers. He loathed the mediocrity of the minor party leaders, their lack of respect for the historical heritage, their cocksure dogmatism. They were to him "like pebbles on the seashore licked flat and smooth by the endless beating of the waves of phraseological clap-trap."[4] He began to fear that, after the Marxists had conquered the party, the envisaged union of science and labor would remain a dream; neither would the cultural heritage, threatened by capitalism, be safe in the hands of the Socialists.

The incident which caused his first sharp clash with the Social Demo-crats, characteristically enough, grew out of an attack he had made on the liberal *Frankfurter Zeitung*. In 1876 he had criticized the newspaper for having encouraged the wild speculations of the early seventies, whereupon the Social Democratic leaders Most and Liebknecht declared him to be a tool of reaction. It was for Mehring a sign of corruption that the Social Democrats should feel it necessary to come to the defense of the liberal paper because Bebel and Liebknecht had once politically collaborated with its owner Leopold Sonnemann. In his opinion, a pro-fessedly democratic organ deserved to be mercilessly criticized for hav-ing compromised the cause of democracy in the interest of capitalism.[5]

It was still in a spirit of *noblesse oblige*, of conservative ethics, that Mehring in the early eighties denounced the irresponsible demagogy of Stoecker and his Christian Social Party. In its approach, Mehring's masterful pamphlet *Herr Hofprediger Stoecker der Sozialpolitiker*[6] re-minds one of the essays which Maximilian Harden devoted to the Berlin Movement and its leading spirit.* Both men, incidentally, knew each other well; the Gentile and the Jew were men of aristocratic tastes who were dismayed by the vulgarity of the big press, the dilution of moral tradition, the transformation of society into a hunting ground for in-dividual gunners all of which seemed to have taken place under the aegis of liberalism. But the disgust with these trends eventually drove the two men in opposite directions. It was perhaps only a matter of individual psychology that the Jew went over to Bismarck and became a spokesman of unbridled German imperialism in World War I, while the Gentile joined the left wing of the revolutionary movement and acted in the same period as a spokesman of the most radical opposition to imperialism and war. But it does not seem accidental that both chose political worlds which held liberal capitalism and its commercialized cul-ture in utter contempt.

In 1886, Mehring accepted the editorship of the *Berliner Volkszeitung*, a popular democratic daily, to which Harden contributed too. Under his stewardship the *Volkszeitung* became the only paper in the capital which dared to attack Bismarck where he was most sensitive: it pro-tested against the government's treatment of the outlawed Social Demo-

* For excerpts of Mehring's writings on Stoecker, see Document No. X.

cratic Party. The government retaliated by frequently confiscating the paper; Mehring himself barely missed being jailed for violation of the anti-Socialist act. We have the testimony of leading Social Democrats that "at the time when Social Democracy was lying prostrate, bleeding from a thousand wounds, when all its liberal friends had backed away from it . . . Mehring turned to it again and forcefully defended its case."[7]

For Mehring never hesitated to challenge the powerful and wealthy when he believed that they were abusing their privileges. As long as he had not yet become convinced that justice was institutionally violated in the class society, he took up the struggle against the individual perpetrators of injustice. One of his experiences put an end to his efforts on the *Berliner Volkszeitung* and drove him further along the road to radical socialism. Apprehensive of the "capitalistic degeneration" which he observed particularly in the newspapers with mass circulation, anxious lest the press should "from a lever of cultural progress" become "a tool of mental obfuscation (*geistige Verdummung*), moral disintegration and social oppression," he attacked in his paper the fashionable novelist and playwright Paul Lindau. As theater critic of the *Berliner Tageblatt* Lindau, of Jewish descent, was the day's authority in the literary and artistic world of Berlin.[8] The millionaire Emil Cohn, co-owner of the *Berliner Tageblatt*, thereupon bought the *Berliner Volkszeitung* and, together with the Progressive Diet member Hermes who was on the *Volkszeitung's* board of directors, brought about Mehring's resignation by a series of provocations.[9] The editor in chief had shown too much independence. Mehring declined a scientific position which the university professors Gustav Schmoller and Lujo Brentano—with Adolph Wagner the leaders of the *Kathedersozialisten*—offered him, and devoted himself from then on to the revolutionary cause. In 1891 he became a staff member of the *Neue Zeit*. Together with Rosa Luxemburg and Paul Lensch he also joined the editorial board of the *Leipziger Volkszeitung*, one of the largest Social Democratic dailies. Within a few years he had made himself the party's most prolific and aggressive polemicist.

In retrospect, Mehring said of the road he traveled that the decisive turn came when he was forced to abandon as illusory his hope for social reforms, "when instead of protective labor legislation we received protective tariffs, instead of trade unionism, police repression of the working classes."[10] The disillusionment over the failure of those in power to act in good faith gradually evolved into the trenchant irony about their activities that characterized most of his later works. Throughout his journalistic and historical writing appears a strain which may easily be taken as anti-Jewish. The "philo-Semites" against whom Mehring lashed out were leaders of the liberal parties which, while pretending to defend the rights of a minority, had themselves deserted the cause of human justice and become partners in exploitation. "In considering the brutalities which anti-Semitism, with words rather than with deeds, commits against the Jews, one should not overlook the brutalities which philo-Semitism, with deeds rather than with words, is committing against everyone, be he Jew or Turk, Christian or pagan, who opposes capitalism."[11] "With words rather than with deeds"—"with deeds rather than with words"—this juxtaposition of the anti-Semitic and the liberal-capitalistic modes of procedure expressed Mehring's appraisal of the two evils. Anti-Semitism was uncouth, noisy, unable to bring about a social change and even to hit its immediate target; economic liberalism was smooth, smug, pontifical, and utterly efficient in the arts of exploitation and corruption. The contest between a coarse, poor, befuddled fanatic like Ahlwardt and the powers of state and finance, supported by the big press, appeared too grotesquely uneven to be judged as anything else but a welcome opportunity for the liberal allies of the Jews to obscure the real social issues. Just this, in the opinion of Mehring and other radical Social Democrats, was the function of philo-Semitism which was "not a bit better than anti-Semitism. If the latter asserts that it fights capitalism by persecuting the Jews, the former asserts that it protects the Jews by defending capitalism with every means."

The rapid growth of reactionary influence in the liberal parties, a hysterical but powerless anti-Semitic movement, the political and economic security of the Jews, and the concerted attack upon the Socialists—these were the features of the German scene in the 1890's which determined Mehring's stand. It was not the antics of anti-Semitic agitators nor the passions of their ignorant followers that constituted for Mehring "the shame of the century" but the solid front of material interests against the underprivileged classes. That wealthy and influential Jews, who were part of this front, would appeal to justice and demand protection when attacked as Jews was an irrational but powerful irritant to men like Mehring. At the bottom of this irritation was perhaps the image of the *Schutzjude* who enjoys double privileges: he has the gratification of wealth *and* a claim to protection, above and beyond the general solidarity of the wealthy, that flows from his otherness. When such an appeal for justice for the Jews was made by the "philo-Semites," Mehring suspected it of ulterior motives: liberalism used the plea for the rights of the Jews to share as equals in the opportunities of capitalist society to defend this society. Mehring's bitter attacks upon "philo-Semitism" were made against what he considered a device of class strategy. "This morning," he would write,[12] "capitalist 'notables,' men so famous in political life as Messrs. Mosse, Davidsohn, Levysohn, Mommsen, Virchow, Barth and others, have published an appeal for a collection for Buschhoff.[13] A most sonorous appeal, to be sure, but did it not occur to a single one of the subscribers that more than one of them would only have to sacrifice an infinitesimal part of his own mammon to help good Buschhoff once and for all. . . . Or is the purpose of it all merely to have another chance of putting for the thousandth time that beautiful phrase of the 'shame of the century' in 'notable' form before the public?"

When the liberals spoke of freedom and equality, Mehring heard the voice of class bigotry. It incensed him all the more as he would not grant the liberals and the Jews the privilege of caste stupidity and caste callousness which he was willing to concede to the Conservative-clerical world. Liberals and Jews knew better! He often castigated Jewish individuals who as bankers, industrialists, newspaper-owners, parliamentarians, or writers practiced in perfect equality with their Christian colleagues the robust philosophy of "St. Manchester," and he never failed to point out the genuine grievances that were expressed in the anti-Semitic agitation. It would be easy to compile from his writings a syllabus of aggressive anti-Jewish formulations.[14] We are even inclined to believe that the tenor of his critical analyses of liberalism and anti-Semitism was disquieting to other Social Democrats. Eduard Bernstein's warning against the use of the catchword of philo-Semitism[15] may well have been written for Mehring's benefit even if Bernstein addressed it particularly to "the comrades of Jewish descent who, just because they themselves are of Jewish origin, consider it their special obligation to protect the party against all suspicion of favoring Jewish interests."

Was Mehring, then, an anti-Semite? To raise the question is to answer it. He keenly sensed "the limitless quantity of social-political tinder" which the anti-Jewish agitation threatened to fire into "a conflagration which all the fire extinguishers of state and society would not be able to control";[16] he was deeply concerned with anti-Semitism as "a historical symptom of persisting social affliction."[17] *Weltanschauung*, not the accident of birth, differentiated his friends from his enemies. Among his intimate collaborators were many Jewish revolutionaries and scholars. Political loyalty and personal friendship united him with Rosa Luxemburg, the Polish Jewess, who took her death from the hands of anti-Semitic counterrevolutionaries in the crucial days of January, 1919. Mehring died two weeks later, at the age of 73, to the last devoted to the cause of the socialist society in which the issue of attacking or defending Jews would be as ludicrous to everyone as it was, in the class society, only to the Socialist.

Nor can it be said of Mehring that his assault upon the liberal parties' "philo-Semitism" tended to bring socialist labor into a shady alliance with the old powers of Prussia.[18] The liberal threat to the conservative state was no longer sufficient to make the Conservatives seek an alliance with the Socialists. The Social Democratic Party had become the only danger to the big industrial and agrarian interests and to the political structure of the Reich. Mehring's criticism was made in the spirit of defiance, of "splendid isolation." No one could be trusted who was not unconditionally on the side of revolutionary labor. The purity of the Marxist doctrine had to be upheld; the party had to be protected against the spirit of compromise that had led to the downfall of liberalism.

One might ask, however, what the effect of Mehring's acid comments on "philo-Semitism" was on the younger generation of Social Democrats who had personally neither experienced anti-Semitic movements nor discriminatory laws nor the common fight for democratic goals. Mehring's contempt for liberal defense against anti-Semitism must have confirmed this generation in the belief that the fate of the Jewish group was of no concern to Socialists, that, as a matter of fact, there was no Jewish group which as such could once more become the target of organized violence.

CHAPTER XIII

THE SOCIAL DEMOCRATIC PARTY IN THE ERA OF IMPERIALISM (1895–1914)

Instead of the economic decay which the Social Democrats saw heralded by the anti-Semitic movement of the early nineties, there began, in the middle of the decade, the most spectacular phase of Germany's industrial development. It lasted, with two brief interruptions, until the eve of World War I. During this period the Social Democratic Party itself underwent a transformation from a revolutionary movement to a legal reform party. It made the change without surrendering its professed revolutionary aspirations. Within one organization, Marxist orthodoxy and revisionism managed to achieve a *modus vivendi*.

The process can hardly be sketched without some arbitrariness.[1] Its significance for our topic will be illustrated in the following chapter by an account of the party's reaction to three phenomena with which it had to deal after the turn of the century: German imperialism, Russian anti-Semitism, and socialist Zionism.

In the Reichstag elections of 1903, three million votes were cast for the Social Democrats. One out of every four German voters had expressed his preference for the party most outspokenly opposed to the government. The tremendous success seemed to justify the radical leadership and was a convincing argument against the revisionists who pressed for cashing in on the popular mandate by fuller participation in state affairs.[2] The party convention of Dresden (1903) "most determinedly disapproved of the revisionist designs to change our tactics, tested and crowned with victory, by substituting a policy of adjustment to the existing order for the conquest of political power and the defeat of our enemies."[3] "The revisionist fog has been blown away," Rosa Luxemburg jubilantly commented, "and before the hateful eyes of the bourgeoisie the steep, sharp rock of the proletarian bastion juts out in its old inaccessibility, in its old harshness. A yawning abyss separates it again from the bourgeois world."[4]

Rapid industrialization favored the radicals because it provided for a growing pool of industrial workers from which the party could recruit new members and followers and thus preserve its proletarian character.

The same process weakened the revisionist claim that the party could not afford to declare itself indifferent to the fate of the peasants and the urban lower middle class. Industrialization expanded the inner market for agricultural commodities, relieved the pressure of agrarian over-production, and, together with the aggressive protectionist agitation of the Agrarian League, helped to redirect the rebellious peasants toward conservatism. By 1895 the worst of the agrarian depression seemed to be over and radical anti-Semitism was on the wane. It had become less urgent to deal with the political implications of both. While the "inter-mediary classes" obviously did not disappear as quickly as the radicals kept insisting they would,[5] their survival was no boon for the case of the revisionists. It became very questionable whether these classes could be viewed any longer as potential allies of the socialist workers.

Intensive industrialization not only favored the growth of the Social Democratic organization but facilitated a compromise between the party's left and right wings. So long as such objective criteria as electoral victories, membership increases, and the rapid concentration of indus-trial and financial wealth supported the theory of a quasi-automatic evo-lution toward the day when labor would "take over," it did not matter too much how the party acted, as long as it remained "revolutionary." The Social Democratic leaders seemed justified in the belief that the revolutionary prospects would not suffer if the party confined itself to those legal methods of agitation which the government could not deny it. The radicals' desire for legality was, of course, wholeheartedly shared by the moderates who saw in the party's growing stature proof of the progress which Social Democracy could make under the constitutional government. In the early nineties, on the occasion of Bismarck's dismis-sal, and again at the time of the Kaiser's conflict with Caprivi when the air was thick with rumors of an impending *coup d'état,* the leaders of Social Democracy had agreed that the conditions of constitutional legal-ity were preferable to a hazardous existence under a military dicta-torship.

In the opening era of German imperialism, the incongruity between the principles of social revolution and social reform led towards a divi-sion of labor within the party rather than a factional split. The leader-ship continued to talk in revolutionary terms, but did not refuse to abide by the requirements of political expediency. The emphasis on automatic socioeconomic developments permitted the party to hang on to a revo-lutionary ideology and, at the same time, to perform its daily tasks ac-cording to the rules of constitutional government and parliamentary routine. A new type of party functionary developed—efficient, expert, bureaucratic, and dignified. The observation which the old Liberal Ludwig Bamberger made at the end of his long political career was as sarcastic as it was true. "Anyone who knew the Reichstag at the time when such beasts as Hasselmann, Most and their consorts were raging in its chambers, can scarcely recognize their successors in the deputies who, as reporters or chairmen of commissions cooperate in a friendly and *gemütliche* fashion with their colleagues to make small changes, for better or worse, in the bourgeois world. . . . Certainly, they have not abjured their belief in the wickedness and untenableness of present-day society but they have become too intelligent to believe any longer that the German state can be overthrown on the barricades and that, even if this were possible, barricades would really do away with [private] property."[6]

Meanwhile the enemies of socialist labor did not "calmly watch and wait" for the "inevitable" victory of socialism. They went on the offensive, politically by such measures as staging nationalistic elections; economically, by putting pressure on the trade unions. At the turn of the century, German business itself had become tightly organized. By 1906, over 500 cartels had come into existence for the purpose of "rational" market exploitation. These were complemented by powerful business associations and by the employers' associations (*Arbeitgeber-Verbände*) which comprised about two-thirds of the employers and were prepared to render each other mutual assistance in case of labor trouble.

Against this strong, disciplined, and cohesive combine, the trade unions, by 1906, could muster all-told about one-third of Germany's workers, belonging, moreover, to unions of widely different political and religious orientations. The Social Democratic organizations, while numerically the strongest, did not have unquestioned authority in problems of labor strategy. The superiority of organized capital over organized labor was impressively demonstrated in a number of clashes in which the unions were worsted. The defeats of the Saxon textile workers in 1903 and of the Ruhr miners in 1905 were the most telling. The 7,500 striking textile workers, backed by the Social Democratic Party and other unions, held out for five months. But the strike was finally lost and the workers had to return to the mills without winning a single demand. The party and the unions had not been strong enough to stand up against the resources of capital and the authority of the state. The Ruhr miners' strike of 1905 ended with an even greater defeat for labor. It started against the advice of the unions and within a few days swept from the Ruhr to Silesia and Saxony and even beyond the German borders. In Belgium and Bohemia miners expressed their solidarity with their German colleagues by a number of wildcat strikes. 270,000 German miners, more than 80 per cent of the total industry, left the pits. Less than half of them were organized, and they again were split into four different unions. Within a few weeks, the strike funds were exhausted. It was impossible for other unions or the party to finance a struggle of such proportions. The strike had to be called off; the miners returned to work thoroughly defeated and resenting the union leadership hardly less than the operators.

The party saw in this show of power and intransigency the united employers' answer to the Social Democratic electoral triumph of two years ago. It could not ignore the implications of the defeat. What were the benefits of its political progress? Additional seats in the Reichstag represented no genuine increment of power in a state where the parliament was not the seat of authority. "The area is growing," Kautsky wrote, "in which we either have to content ourselves with what we have achieved or go on to new methods of fighting."[7] The party's alternatives seemed to be either to break with legal methods and reorganize itself for a fight by every means, such as the Russian revolutionary movements were carrying on against the Czarist regime; or to follow Eduard Bernstein's advice and to have the courage to show itself for what it was, a legal parliamentary party that should not pretend to a radicalism which it had neither the intention nor power to apply. If they accepted the latter alternative, the Social Democrats would have been compelled to abjure revolutionary phraseology and to concentrate, in alliance with other groups, on democratizing the state. The radical leadership chose neither alternative.

The Russian revolution of 1904-05 brought the conflict within the Social Democratic Party to a head. Stirred by the Russian events, a strong wing in the party, particularly in the North-German districts, demanded "new methods of fighting." But the union leaders and the gradualists in the party were less impressed by the Russian revolution than by the defeated strikes and the power of German industrialists. "We need peace to go ahead," one of their spokesmen declared. He expressed the desire of most union leaders. At the party convention at Jena (1905) the struggle was to have been decided. Actually the decision had been made a few weeks before, at the trade union convention in Cologne. The convention turned down a number of radical motions, foremost among them a motion to discuss labor's attitude toward the general strike as a political weapon. Most union leaders had definitely chosen to be content with what had been achieved and still could be achieved by legal methods. They had become anxious to free themselves from the radical philosophy of the party majority and threatened to cut their organizations loose from it. Confronted with this situation, the Jena convention agreed on two formulas which saved party unity and face. It carried a resolution which endorsed the mass strike as a legitimate weapon of labor—provided the fundamental rights of suffrage and coalition were attacked. And even in such a case, the decision to call a general strike was made dependent on the further growth of the party and on more thorough mass indoctrination. It was the radicals' admission that the workers were not ready, and would not be ready for an indefinite time to come, to follow the call.[8]

There remained only the legal road to power, or, in more realistic terms, the hope of whittling down the limitations which unrepresentative government imposed on parliament. Such a road required, on the part of Social Democracy, the willingness to make political alliances and concessions. Besides, it presupposed the existence of allies. There were some, but they were not powerful. After the South-German states Bavaria, Württemberg, and Baden had liberalized their constitutions in 1904 and had granted direct, secret, general, and equal male suffrage, the Social Democrats in these states gained key positions in the respective parliaments. In Baden the Social Democratic deputies even voted for the state budget, a flagrant violation of the party's general dictum not to give such a vote of confidence to capitalistic governments.[9]

The example set by the Southern Social Democrats, however, was not repeated in the Reich, not only because of the greater strength of the radical leadership. There was no political force left with which the party could have aligned itself without giving up every vestige of its tradition, principles, and outlook.[10] The Reichstag elections of 1907—the "Hottentots' elections"—made it abundantly clear that liberal resistance to the hysteria of chauvinism and imperialism had broken down. The Social Democratic Party, against which the fury of nationalistic passions had been directed, lost half of its parliamentary representation.[11] With 43 instead of the 82 seats which it had won in 1903, it would only have been a second-rate partner in a majority group, even if it should now have desired to enter into a coalition. The parliamentary majority actually was formed by the Progressives, National Liberals, Conservatives, and anti-Semites. The Social Democrats were successfully isolated.

The lost strikes of the previous years had demonstrated the strength and maneuverability of organized management to be superior to that of the unions; the lost elections of 1907 gave notice that through chauvinism and imperialism the party's enemies commanded greater masses of voters than Marxism could hope to reach. Within the possibilities of constitutional action, the party could not expose itself to nationalistic wrath without the risk of being reduced to a negligible quantity even in terms of parliamentary power. It did not fail to heed the warning. In 1907, at the International Socialist Congress at Stuttgart, the French socialist leader Jean Jaurès moved for common socialist action, including a general strike, in the case of a European war. Bebel rejected the proposal on the ground that the German Social Democracy could not let itself be forced into a position which might become fatal "even for the existence of the party."[12] Kautsky came to his aid. "In no other country is Social Democracy confronted with a government so utterly soaked in militarism as in Germany; in no other country has militarism so infested the whole capitalist society, including that part of the proletariat that is still steeped in a bourgeois ideology. Under such conditions, our agitation against militarism cannot simply follow a line of conduct which is possible only in totally different situations."[13]

Concern for the fate of the party had become the ultimate criterion in questions of peace and war. The organization should not be exposed to police terror; the nationalist emotions of potential Social Democratic voters were not to be unnecessarily offended. In the same year (1907) the authority of Bebel was used to remove the stigma of *Vaterlandslosigkeit* from the party. At the national convention at Essen, dissatisfaction and protest had been voiced against the speech a Social Democratic representative, Gustav Noske, had made in the Reichstag.[14] He had declared that, in case of a war of aggression, the Social Democratic Party would fight for the country with the same loyalty and devotion as the bourgeois parties. The minister of war had taken notice of the declaration with satisfaction. Kurt Eisner saw in Noske's statement an "aftereffect of our defeat," "a concession to the general mood of depression caused by our setback in the elections."[15] Bebel, however, supported Noske in a speech that actually committed the party to a policy of national defense. He reminded Noske's critics that he himself had declared in the Reichstag: "If we really should have to defend the fatherland, we shall do it because it is the country on the soil of which we live, the language of which we speak, the customs of which we follow; we shall do it because we want to make this country of ours a model of perfection and beauty the like of which shall nowhere be found in the world. We defend this fatherland not for you [capitalists] but against you. And that's why we might have to defend it against attack." When in 1913 a special tax bill (*Wehrbeitrag*) was submitted to cover the cost of military reorganization, the Social Democrats found reasons to vote for it. On August 4, 1914, they granted, practically without dissension, the credits which the government asked for financing the war.

Nothing could be more superficial than to interpret this development of the Social Democratic Party as a conscious betrayal of its humanitarian ideals. As a legal mass party, it did not dare to ignore "public opinion" and "popular demands" which were nursed and manipulated by the

ideologists and profiteers of Pan-Germanism. The bigger and more bureaucratic the party became and the more it concentrated on its growth
and perpetuation, the less inclined it was to alienate the "intermediary
classes" and "that part of the proletariat that was still steeped in a bourgeois ideology." Of this bourgeois ideology, nationalism and imperialism
had become the main pillars. In order not to be frustrated by isolation,
the party had to clarify its relation to the nation. It identified itself with
the state not as this state was dedicated to nationalistic, militaristic, and
imperialistic aims, but to the extent that it permitted the growth of a
progressive, exemplary, and well-organized labor movement. Bebel's
promise that this movement would some day refashion Germany into a
model society was made in good faith.

Social Democratic pride in the achievements of German labor, and
also of German science, industry, and culture grew as the party's revolutionary and anti-capitalist spirit faded. When Germany became one of
the leading nations of Europe and German Social Democracy one of
the leading forces of the Socialist International, the Social Democrats
turned their attention to the dangers from without which threatened the
cause of German labor, and of freedom and progress generally. Czarist
autocracy and Pan-Slavism appeared as the greatest menace. The party's
sympathies with the Russian revolution of 1904-1905 were genuine but
it did not see in the Russian uprising a model of the proletarian struggle
for power. It interpreted it rather as an attempt to do away with an
antiquated, cruel, paralyzing regime and to create in its place the political and social conditions under which a modern labor movement such
as Germany's would be able to develop. The brutality with which the
government put down the revolution, and the white terror and pogroms
that followed in its wake, were not taken as an object lesson by the German Socialists. They felt, like most Western Europeans, that terroristic
anti-Semitism was inconceivable anywhere but in the barbarous world
of Czarist reaction. Pogroms belonged to the dark Middle Ages which
in Russia extended into the present but which had definitely become past
history in Germany. The Social Democrats shared this conviction with
the Liberals and with most Conservatives. In Germany, not even a professional anti-Semite would have dared any longer to instigate physical
violence against Jews. The worst mob demonstrations in the eighties and
nineties had not approximated anything like a Russian pogrom. Meanwhile ten years had passed which had extinguished even these memories.
The use of physical violence against the Jews was only possible among
"backward," "uncivilized," "ignorant" masses, spurred on by ruthless ty-
rants.

In Bebel's writings this transformation of the Social Democratic theory of anti-Semitism is particularly manifest. In 1893 he had stated that Social Democracy could be quite satisfied with watching the outcome of the anti-philo-Semitic controversy. He then had seen the revolutionary movement as the ultimate beneficiary of this struggle among the ruling groups. In 1906 he wrote:

Anti-Semitism in its ugliest and most abhorrent form has shown itself in Russia since the great revolutionary movement has started there. All the horror, brutality and barbarism in which the Christian Middle Ages excelled, holy Russia has reproduced on a greater scale. And just as in the Middle Ages authorities and clergy not infrequently favored the anti-Semitic persecutions, so today in Russia police and high-ranking military officials . . . take command over them and organize the conspiracy by arming the rabble and leading it through their agents. . . . The Russian government favors anti-Semitism because it is anxious to divert the hatred of the masses from its own foul and corrupt system of government and from the representatives of this system, the corrupt civil service. . . . And since the Jews in Russia, intellectuals and proletarians, participated in extraordinary number in the revolutionary movement, the Russian government had an additional reason for having hatred of Jews incited by its agents and for provoking massacres and butcheries the like of which have happened so far only under oriental despotisms. . . . Anti-Semitism which by its very nature can appeal only to the basest drives and instincts of a backward stratum of society, expresses the moral depravity of the groups that accept it. *It is comforting* [to know] *that in Germany it will never have a chance to exert a decisive influence upon the life of state and society.*[16]

The closing sentence, preposterous as it sounds today, expressed the conviction of the German people at large. That Bebel and all the other Social Democrats shared in it shows the degree to which the "revolutionary" party identified itself with the nation, but it also demonstrates that political anti-Semitism in Germany at that time had shed every semblance of actual or potential violence. Like the Social Democratic Party, anti-Semitism had become domesticated. The successors of Boeckel and Ahlwardt were so tame and respectable that even the Progressives, not to speak of the National Liberals, helped them to win elections against the Social Democrats. In the Reichstag, the anti-Semitic deputies cooperated so closely with the Conservatives that they almost lost their identity.

Social Democratic publications, too, scarcely dealt with German anti-Semitism any longer. Between 1903 and 1908, a single article, "Changing Anti-Semitism," appeared in *Neue Zeit*[17] in which Philipp Scheidemann rehashed old Social Democratic notions of anti-Semitism as the transitory ideology of groups which so far had remained politically indifferent. "However severely one may judge anti-Semitism, it must be credited

with one achievement: it has succeeded in awakening the political interest of strata of the population which no other party had been able to set
in motion. In the cities, it has mobilized the petty-bourgeois simpleton;
in the country it has often cured the small peasantry of the notion that
'mylord' knew everything and was anxious to see everything turn out
for the best." The objective of Scheidemann's article was to show the
transformation of the anti-Semitic movement from an anticonservative
rebellion to an appendage of conservatism. This did not prevent him
from ending with the hollow formula:

"That the anti-Semitic groups are still able to exist at all proves how
politically backward the German urban and rural *Mittelstand* still is.
But, after all, the anti-Semitic demagogy has made them politically aware
and they cannot help being driven to a clear decision. They must either
become reactionary *sans phrase*, that is conservative, or recognize the
complete miserableness of anti-Semitism and turn their vision ahead;
that means learning to think politically and becoming Social Democrats."

Within the next five years, from 1908 to 1912, the theme was taken
up only twice by the *Neue Zeit*—both articles dealing with anti-Semitism
in Russia. Anti-Semitism in Germany no longer presented any serious
problems. The danger zone appeared confined to the reactionary, backward, autocratic East, to the state against which even the old Bebel offered to "shoulder a rifle."[18]

The situation in Germany and Russia was as different with regard to
political anti-Semitism as it was with regard to the "Jewish question."
Masses of Jewish workers, artisans, and small tradespeople fled from
Eastern Europe. The process of their assimilation encountered far greater
difficulties than that of the German Jews. In the discussion as to how
the problems of the uprooted Eastern Jews could be solved, a clear-cut
split developed in the Social Democratic Party.

The official party theoreticians insisted on treating this question, too,
as inseparable from the revolutionary class struggle and rejected Zionism,* including labor Zionism, as a diversion from socialism's general
fight for freedom.[19] "Zionism offers an impractical utopia," Kautsky
wrote,[20] but he was equally pessimistic as to the future possibilities of
assimilation in a bourgeois world. "Liberalism is no longer able and
hardly wants any longer to do what until now it has neglected to do.
Its power to accomplish it and its popular backing are continually
dwindling. Where it has not yet already achieved the full emancipation
of the Jews, not only their political but social equality, it will not do so
in the future. . . . The only remaining force that can radically change

* See Document No. XI, for a Marxist review of Theodor Herzl's *The Jewish
State*.

what exists and must do away with all political and social inequality, in order to free itself, is the proletariat. The victorious proletariat alone can give Jewry full emancipation, and Jewry, in so far as it is not clinging to capitalism, is interested in its victory."

But Zionism nevertheless had obtained a following among Jewish Socialists, and quite logically, mainly among those who belonged to the right wing of the Social Democratic Party. The revisionists who were not under the spell of the myth of an inevitable proletarian revolution were unwilling to leave the urgent problems of Eastern Jewry's assimilation to a remote millenium. The *Sozialistische Monatshefte*[21] proved to be a periodical in which socialist labor Zionism made itself effectively heard.

It does not fall within the scope of this study to follow the involved history of labor Zionism. The arguments it put forth in defense of its case were forcefully presented in an article by Maxim Anin, "Is assimilation of the Jews possible?"[22] Anin took issue with the Austrian Socialist leader Otto Bauer who had again recently endorsed Jewish assimilation in his book on the national question.[23] Bauer had written that as long as the Jewish workers, by "the inflection of their language, their gestures, their apparel, their customs, irritated the Christian class comrade, the foreman and the manufacturer, the old economic conflict between the peasant and the Jewish merchant continued to live on in the form of an instinctive dislike. . . ." He had called the Jewish worker's cultural assimilation the condition of his freedom of movement. "Then only will he be able to turn to every place and every trade where the blind working of the capitalist forces may happen to create more jobs; then only will his special Jewish misery disappear and will he be left with nothing but the common proletarian misery which he will fight and conquer in the common battle, shoulder to shoulder with his Aryan colleagues."

Anin questioned the realism of such reasoning. Assimilation, regarded by Bauer and most Socialists as inevitable and desirable, was in Anin's opinion a vastly different problem for middle-class Jews and the Jewish proletariat. Even if incompletely assimilated, members of the Jewish middle classes in Western Europe and Russia could get a foothold in the economic life of the nation, due to the impersonal character of capitalist exploitation. Once economically settled, these Jews were able to absorb the culture and education of their environment and prepare for further assimilation. Not so the Jewish worker for whom personal assimilation, as Anin agreed with Bauer, was almost a prerequisite of his being able to enter into industry. Apart from the difficulties of individual conformism, the Jewish worker had to contend with the anti-Semitism of manufacturers who were under no pressure to employ him since they could rely upon a steady flow of cheap labor from the countryside. Even the Jewish manufacturer, in Anin's opinion, was rarely of any help, either because of his own desire to be assimilated or because of the pressure of competition that made him follow the labor practices of his non-Jewish colleagues. For these reasons Anin doubted whether the assimilation of the great majority of the Jewish people, particularly the large Eastern Jewish proletariat, was any longer possible and he even predicted a deterioration of the situation with the further growth of capitalism. Most Socialists, he thought, had failed to face the complexity of the Jewish question and to deal satisfactorily with the problem of national self-determination for the Jews.

The contributions of the revisionist monthly often revealed a greater sensitivity to ominous cultural and political trends than the robustly optimistic articles of the *Neue Zeit*.[24] Orthodox Marxism was frequently slow and even unwilling to take notice of symptoms whose significance seemed to run counter to the concepts and expectations of "scientific" socialism, an observation not confined to Germany. A rigorous adherence to revolutionary class strategy made Jules Guesde advise the French workers to abstain from meddling in the Dreyfus affair. Socialist workers, in Guesde's opinion, should choose *"ni l'un ni l'autre,"* neither side, in a fight that shook the French nation from top to bottom but which Guesde considered an internal conflict of the ruling classes. Jean Jaurès, not an orthodox Marxist and often attacked for his "opportunism," did not hesitate to throw himself into the campaign for Dreyfus. Guesde's original aloofness to the political and moral issues involved—he changed his stand in the course of the affair—was rooted in the orthodox conviction that revolutionary labor had to reject the values of the old *and* the new ruling classes, and that neither bourgeois liberalism nor clerical conservatism were the legitimate spokesmen for human justice in the "sham battle" for and against the Jews.[25]

The revisionists' greater political realism, however, also made them more susceptible to the nationalistic and imperialistic ideas of the times. Once Marxist orthodoxy was cast aside, labor's interests appeared tied to the interests of the nation's ruling groups. If the goal was no longer revolution but higher wages, labor would have a stake in the benefits accruing from industrial expansion beyond the nation's frontiers and from direct political conquests. The ideology of "social imperialism" was carried into the Social Democratic movement by a subgroup of the revisionist wing. Its guiding spirit was Joseph Bloch, the Jewish editor of the *Sozialistische Monatshefte*, and other Jews (Cohen-Reuss, Kaliski, Georg Bernhard) were prominent members.

On the balance sheet of the success and failure of socialist indoctrination, it will first of all have to be noted that the revolutionary ideology with its insights, beliefs, and shibboleths tended to eliminate or de-emotionalize important spheres in which suspicion of the Jewish group was traditionally harbored. Religion is a case in point. By being indifferent, if not consciously opposed, to all religious creeds as so many varieties of superstition, the Socialists were free to neglect a source of group hatred the importance of which is generally recognized.

Moreover, a reorientation took place with regard to economic notions that had sustained the stereotype of the Jews as an asocial group, amassing wealth at the expense of honest work. Marxist economics taught labor that the original capitalist exploitation took place in the sphere of production, not of circulation. Surplus value, according to this theory, was created in the mines, factories, and on the farms where workers without their own means of production were forced to sell their labor power and to create more value than they received in wages. The middleman, traditionally personified by the Jew, was not the original exploiter. He shared in the spoils as did all owners of capital, according to the size of his capital and not the special function he had in the economic process. While the notion of the Jews as a capitalist group was certainly dominant also among the workers, the socialist workers could not be persuaded to impute to a small subgroup the exploitative nature of the economic system at large.[26] Anti-Semitic efforts to this effect were resented as insults to a worker's intelligence. It is illuminating to read how Social Democratic audiences reacted to the arguments of anti-Semitic agitators. Their response ran through a range of emotions, from scornful laughter to outright fury at what they considered obvious attempts to hoodwink them. A Social Democratic worker was proud of his knowledge of Marxist theory and refused to be taken in by the sleight-of-hand economics of Jew-baiters who tried to enlighten him on the difference between Gentile and Jewish capital. To be convinced by such legerdemain was to him definitely a sign of cultural and political backwardness.

Furthermore, Marxist theory, in contrast to racial theories, conceived of social differences and conflicts in the framework of history. Its severe judgment of capitalism referred to institutions, not individuals. The individual capitalist, too, had to obey the laws of competitive economy. He was not free in his decisions. As man, the social foe was redeemable. No Marxist had as yet thought of the "liquidation" of a social class in terms of physical extermination of its members.

Resistance to political anti-Semitism was part of socialist labor's opposition to capitalist society. Immunization against hatred of Jews went together with a fervent belief in the emancipatory mission of the working classes, with the conviction that the revolutionary movement fought for the future of mankind. Commonly experienced hardships, defeats, and victories were meaningful with regard to the task ahead which was no less than a total transformation of society. The struggle toward this goal gave the Socialists spiritual, moral, and emotional gratifications unknown to the nonbeliever and created a comradeship which no political party in modern times had yet been able to build. The more defiantly and uncompromisingly the socialist doctrine faced the powers that be and the greater the pressure on the labor movement, the more it was permeated by the feeling of solidarity. Within this realm, socioeconomic and ethnic distinctions between individual Socialists became wholly irrelevant.

The official socialist literature of the time and the memoirs or recollections of Socialists, Jews and non-Jews, radicals and moderates* at home or in exile, bear out the statement of Robert Michels that ever since Bebel's and Liebknecht's determined stand against the flood of anti-Semitism in the 1890's, "German Social Democracy had become once and for all immune against the poison of race hatred" and "had, with a good conscience, borne the odium of being called, by ignorant enemies, a party of Jews and Jew-lovers."[27]

Indeed, quite a number of Jews were attracted to the party[28] despite the economic and cultural barrier of class. The Jewish Social Democrats were mostly intellectuals, businessmen, and salaried employees, with hardly any manual workers among them. The reasons that prompted middle-class Jews to expose themselves to additional hostility by joining the Social Democrats must have been strong. Material considerations, as a rule, cannot have entered into their decision. To be known as a voter, member, or even active supporter of the Social Democratic Party was in imperial Germany no boon to anyone's career, and less so to a Jew's. Besides, Jewish intellectuals who joined and worked for the revolutionary party often jeopardized their social relations and damaged their standing in the Jewish community, particularly in small towns. Apparently in the world of socialist labor individual Jews could experience the equality which German society denied to the Jewish group.

As regards the workers' attitude toward Jews who joined the socialist movement, it was important that their personal motives could not be impugned by traditional anti-Semitic accusations. The stereotype of the Jews as clannish and greedy was shattered by the concrete experience of the socialist workers. Some Jews were evidently not interested in material gains; nor was the Jewish group held together by any cabbalistic

* See Eduard Bernstein's article on "Jews and German Social Democracy," Document No. XII.

bonds. Jews acted and reacted as individuals. The acceptance and
"assimilation" of middle-class elements in a working-class movement of
such developed cultural specificity as Germany's were greatly facilitated
by the pride and gratitude which were evoked in the ranks of labor when
men who had gained wealth or fame in the bourgeois world joined their
cause, thus bearing witness to its moral superiority. The unfamiliar traits
and personal peculiarities of such "strangers" in the Social Democratic Party were often the object of good-natured gibes but it testi-
fies to the workers' instinct for personal integrity that their most popular
leaders never "spoke down" to them or made concessions in matters of
personal taste or the general conduct of life. The biographies of Lassalle,
Marx, Engels, Paul Singer, Paul Levi, and other outstanding socialist
leaders offer many opportunities of studying the effect which the personal characteristics of these individuals of middle-class background had
upon the workers. In most cases, such characteristics seemed to have
enhanced rather than detracted from the prestige of the leaders.

Moreover, the Social Democratic Party, itself the voice of the socially
underprivileged and the politically ostracized, was not unaware of the
psychological effects discrimination had on the Jewish group. "Slavery
demoralizes," Wilhelm Liebknecht said at the Social Democratic Party
convention of 1893, "but it also purifies the soul of the strong and
creates idealists and rebels. Thus we find that their humiliating situation
has cultivated in stronger and nobler Jewish individuals a sense of freedom and justice and fostered a revolutionary spirit. There is, in proportion to their numbers, a far greater stock of idealism among Jews than
among non-Jews."[29] There were occasions when the Social Democratic
workers made it a point of honor to demonstrate their feelings of devotion and solidarity with leaders who were attacked twice, for being
Socialists and being Jews. The exiled writer and art critic, Max Osborn,
himself a German Jew, published, in 1944, an account of such a
demonstration.[30]

Osborn's story brings back the years of the Berlin Movement and the
fight of the Social Democratic Party against the anti-Semites. Paul
Singer had spoken at a workers' meeting and the audience was giving
him an ovation when, in Osborn's words, "the thing happened which I
want to tell about: From the uppermost tiers of the hall, a voice, infinitely tender, suddenly was heard: 'Jew-Paul! Jew-Paul!' [*Judenpaule!*,
Judenpaule!]. The workers pricked up their ears; 'Bravo Jew-Paul! Long
live Jew-Paul!' the voice once more was heard. Like a fire it swept
through the hall. A few took it up. Then more. Then whole rows. And
soon it swelled to a storm. The phrase was born completely out of the
idiom of Berlin labor. At other occasions, it would simply have been a

way of addressing a colleague of Jewish faith, with a playful characterization of his difference, without a trace of unfriendliness. Here, too, the epithet was meant without any mischief; it was nothing but an expression of great intimacy. Everyone understood this. Hundreds, thousands kept repeating: 'Jew-Paul! Jew-Paul!' The cry roared around the imposing figure of the celebrated man, who was still standing at the speaker's desk, and who, at first taken aback and speechless, then touched to the quick, acknowledged the strange ovation. The workers would not calm down. They swarmed over the platform and carried Singer down into the hall and from there triumphantly out of the building into the streets. . . . Such a thing once happened in Germany. True, almost two generations have since passed."[31]

The struggle for labor's emancipation made Social Democracy a powerful cultural force. By influencing the thoughts and actions of millions, the revolutionary idea became a prime factor in German life. It gave hope, optimism, dignity, and self-respect where submission to the state and identification with society would have produced fear, hatred, arrogance, and cruelty—the emotions always present where anti-Semitism thrives. But the very strength of the revolutionary idea also made for weaknesses and limitations. When it imparted to labor the consciousness of a noble and unique mission, it also isolated labor in the national community and made it insensitive to the needs and aspirations of other groups. This was particularly true for the relationship of Social Democracy to the *Mittelstand*. Without the quasi-religious belief in labor's revolutionary destiny, its consistent errors of political and psychological judgment would have been impossible.

The categories the Social Democrats applied in their analysis of anti-Semitism were crude and led to self-deception. That the anti-Semites belonged to "politically backward" and "economically moribund" groups revealed as little about the nature of their backwardness as about the reactions to be expected from them.[32] Anti-Semitism was not only a reaction to economic suffering. Peasants, artisans, shopkeepers, students and professors, officers and civil servants were not equally affected by the trends toward large-scale enterprise and by business slumps. Nor could one seriously expect them to surrender and join a working-class movement. The prospect of being declassed was particularly frightening to groups which were so conscious of their status. They developed undemocratic ideologies in order to defend it. They did not want to be equal and egalitarian, either socially or politically. They were opposed to a parliamentary regime of the Western type because it would have redistributed power, accelerated social mobility, and eventually done away with the estate society (*Standesgesellschaft*) on which their cultural existence depended. They were estate-conscious, not class-conscious, and the growing contrast between the conditions of their material life and the social privileges of their station made them only more so. They could be impoverished, but they refused to be pro-letarianized.

The Social Democratic interpretation of anti-Semitism as a phase in the political awakening of these groups that would be followed by more rational behavior—by joining the Social Democrats, for instance—strikes us today as incredibly naive. That the two main variants of Marxism, the radical and the revisionist school, harbored such illusions until well into the twentieth century, must partly be explained by the simple fact that historical experience had not yet disproved them. Our knowledge is richer because of Hitler.[33] But it was not only for lack of histori-cal experience that the Social Democrats failed to understand the true nature of anti-Semitism. Social Democracy was a child of the nineteenth century, imbued with the belief in man's rationality and in the progress of society which was based on the growth of science, knowledge, and technological application, and therefore could not be halted. Probably no Social Democrat took Marx's alternative of "socialism or barbarism" for more than a felicitous phrase. As a dialectic materialist, he knew that ideologies were the false reflections of the social reality in the minds of men; as a rationalistic materialist he was convinced that sooner or later all social classes which capitalism oppressed and deprived would become aware of the real causes of their situation. Sooner or later, that is, according to their relation to the means of production. The pro-letariat whose vision was unobscured by property interests was neces-sarily most conscious of being at once the victim and the final execu-tioner of class society. Other groups would follow. Anti-Semitism, although abominable, was an expression of radical anticapitalist protest, was part of man's groping efforts for a rational social order. Reason some-times seemed to use strange agents and vehicles but its march was irresistible. Such was the essence of Social Democratic thought.

By upholding the belief in the revolutionary mission of the party, the radicals succeeded in mobilizing immense intellectual and emotional energies. The organizational achievements would hardly have been pos-sible without the revolutionary ideology that inspired thousands of de-voted and disciplined party workers. Had the party represented the demands and aspirations not only of the wage earners, but of the artisans, peasants, petty officials, salaried employees, and small businessmen—in other words, had it become a people's party—it would perhaps have clogged the source of its strength, the industrial worker's resentment against a society which treated him with benevolence when he resigned himself to his humble station, and *en canaille* when he insisted on his rights. The elements of fanaticism, chiliasm, and myth in the socialist movement, the absolute devotion which it commanded, characterized all radical movements in Germany and appear typical of nations which have never experienced the rational processes of the fully developed bourgeois society.

Finally, the situation of the Jewish group itself was such that it did not seem to call for the Socialists' special attention. Economically, a "Jewish question" did not exist and had not existed in Germany. Politically, the emancipation law of 1869 was secure; only fools could hope to have it repealed. Socially and culturally, most Jews seemed to feel sufficiently at home in the bourgeois world. What, then, was there left of the "Jewish question" after the anti-Semitic shouting of the 1880's and 1890's had died down? The thwarting of the careers of a few Jews was not enough to get excited about in a nation that practiced mass discrimination against the underprivileged. Could a worker's son, as did that of a Jew, go to the schools of higher learning? Was not Bleichröder's vote in Prussia equal to that of several thousand poor people? Part and parcel of the middle classes, the Jews seemed safely settled in German society. The Social Democrats realized as little as the Jews themselves that the decline of political anti-Semitism after the turn of the century was due to the rise of a more comprehensive ideology, imperialism, by which anti-Semitism was rendered innocuous and yet preserved. The groups that a decade or so before had hailed Ahlwardt, had neither economically perished nor joined Social Democracy nor made peace with "Jewish capitalism." But they identified themselves now with a rising nation in arms; they participated in the psychological and material benefits that could be derived from world power, world politics, industrial and financial expansion, and military supremacy. After the imperialistic period had ended in disaster and the dream of national harmony by world exploitation had come to a humiliating end, anti-Semitism emerged intact, stronger, and more vicious than ever.

NOTES AND REFERENCES

INTRODUCTION

1. The term *"Mittelstand"* is difficult to translate because of the peculiarities of Germany's social structure. *"Mittelstand"* means more than an income group comparable to "lower middle class." It contains concepts of status and caste. German conservatism regarded as a *Stand* a group defined by equality of social status and occupation, of approximately equal property and income, and possessing rights not enjoyed by others. The last-mentioned criterion is essential. The landed aristocracy, the officer corps, the clergy, but also the artisan, the small merchant, and petty official felt entitled to certain privileges by virtue of *Stand.*

   English and American studies on Germany's social structure sometimes use the term "middle classes" to correspond to *"Mittelstand."* Throughout this study the term "middle class" (sometimes "bourgeoisie" or "middle classes") is used to designate the social groups which, in Germany as in other modern nations, represented the interests of industry, trade, and banking, and which on the basis of wealth, knowledge, and education challenged the supremacy of the old ruling forces. The same terminological consistency is not applied with regard to the term *"Mittelstand"*; where the emphasis is on the economic characteristics of *Mittelstand* groups, the term "lower middle classes" is sometimes substituted.

2. Fichte, Johann Gottlieb: *Der Geschlossne Handelsstaat* (Tübingen, 1800), p. 286. "They enjoy the cunning of acquisition more than they do the security of possession. It is they who clamor incessantly for freedom of trade and commerce, freedom from supervision and police, freedom from all order and ethics."

3. Lamprecht, Karl: *Deutsche Geschichte*, 12 vols. (Berlin, 1920–1922), vol. X, p. 481.

4. Valentin, Veit: *Geschichte der Deutschen Revolution von 1848–1849*, 2 vols. (Berlin, 1930), vol. I, pp. 344–5, 397.

CHAPTER I

1. The four Jewish members of the 1848 National Assembly were Riesser (Hamburg), Veit (Berlin), Kuranda (Vienna), and Hartmann (Vienna). In the debate on the draft of a constitution Riesser defeated a motion to put the Jewish group under special legislation.
2. Dubnow, Simon: *Die Neueste Geschichte des Jüdischen Volkes.* 3 vols. (Jerusalem, 1938), vol. III, pp. 345–6.
3. Max Wirth's *Geschichte der Handelskrisen* (Frankfurt am Main, 1874) gives a vivid picture of the *Gründung* period.
4. The *Fortschrittspartei* (Progress Party, in English sometimes called Radical Liberals or Progressists) was organized in 1861 by the left wing of the old Liberal Party and by well-known democratic leaders of 1848. It struggled for complete democratic government, reduction of militarism, and free trade. Its fight against the proposed reorganization of the army and increase of military expenses was so popular that within six months it had become the strongest party in the lower chamber of the Prussian Diet. During the Constitutional Conflict (1862–1866) it refused to support the budget increases and war loans requested by the government, but was defied by Bismarck and gave in with a consequent loss of prestige to the party and to the idea of parliamentary government in general. After Prussia's successful war with Austria in 1866 the right wing of the party supported Bismarck's foreign and military policy, seceded and established itself in the Prussian Diet as the National Party. In the Constituent Reichstag of the North German Federation the group was joined by liberals from Prussia's newly acquired provinces who supported national unification under Bismarck's leadership. The new party which thus emerged called itself National Liberal. Its leader was the Hanoverian Rudolf von Bennigsen. In domestic affairs the National Liberals reserved the right to be a "loyal opposition."
5. The depression lasted until 1879; it was followed by a weak recovery. Cf. Sartorius von Walterhausen, August: *Zeittafeln zur Wirtschaftsgeschichte* (Halberstadt, 1927), p. 62; Also Spiethoff, Arthur: *"Krisen," Handwörterbuch der Staatswissenschaften,* vol. 6, 4th ed. (Jena, 1925), pp. 53 ff.
6. The Conservative Party had been founded in 1848, to organize the counter-revolution. It was Prussian, monarchical, agrarian, and originally exclusively aristocratic. Until well after Bismarck's unification of Germany the Conservatives had little taste for a Reich in which they were to share power with a rising middle class.

In the course of the party's history, it went through a number of schisms which reflected the difficulties of adjustment which the party of a semi-feudal aristocracy experienced in a rapidly changing capitalist environment. The relations of the various wings and factions of the Conservatives in the two chambers of the Prussian Diet as well as in the Reichstag are confusing. Unfortunately, the advice of Eugen Richter, the liberal opponent of the Conservatives, that all conservative varieties be considered as "essentially one and the same," does not do justice to the intricacies of the political situation. (Cf. Richter, Eugen: *Politisches ABC Buch,* 8th ed., Berlin, 1896, p. 275.)

In 1866, when the National Liberals split from the Progress Party, the Conservatives, too, broke ranks. A moderate group, known in the Prussian Diet as the Free-Conservatives, in the Reichstag as *Reichspartei,* seceded. Like the National Liberals the Free-Conservatives were the Chancellor's loyal supporters in all questions of national and foreign policy.

The Old Conservatives mentioned in the text consisted of the party's right wing, or to be exact, of the right wing of the Conservative group in the Prussian Diet. Their mouthpiece was the *Kreuzzeitung.* The schism between the Old Conservatives and the New Conservatives lasted from 1872 to 1879 and was caused by the refusal of the *Kreuzzeitung* faction to support Bismarck in his fight against the Catholics.

After the Old Conservatives had been almost wiped out in the election of 1874, they constituted themselves anew in the German Conservative Party (1876).

For the purpose of this study it did not seem necessary to tax the reader's memory with all these developments. Unless otherwise specified, the term "the Conservatives" in the text refers to right-wing Conservatives.

7. The Catholic Center Party, named not for political but technical reasons—its members were seated in the center of the Reichstag hall—was organized in 1870–71, after an earlier Catholic party in Prussia had been practically destroyed during the Constitutional Conflict. The Center had its main strength in Bavaria, the Rhineland, and Upper Silesia, predominantly Catholic territories. In the first two decades of its existence, the party was strongly under the influence of a conservative-aristocratic wing. After the death of its outstanding leader Ludwig Windthorst (1891), the party made greater concessions to nationalism. The Catholic Center Party had important auxiliaries in the Catholic People's Association (*Volksverein für das katholische Deutschland*) and in the Christian trade unions. Under the latter's influence the party somewhat changed its strictly denominational character, though the clerical element remained overwhelmingly strong.

8. Marr, W[ilhelm]: *Der Sieg des Judentums über das Germanentum. Vom nicht confessionellen Standpunkt aus betrachtet. Vae Victis!,* 6th ed. (Bern, 1879).

Legends have grown up around Marr's origin, spread by his critics rather than his friends. Dubnow (*Op. cit.,* vol. III, p. 430) reports that he was "the son of an actor ostracized, because of dishonorable conduct, by a group of radical journalists with whom he used to meet." Elbogen (*A*

Century of Jewish Life, Philadelphia, 1945, p. 703) calls Marr "a descendant of Jews." The *Universal Jewish Encyclopedia* (New York, 1939, vol. I, "Antisemitism," pp. 341 ff.) mentions that Marr was "said to have been a converted Jew." Other sources still give him a Jewish mother, etc. Marr is also credited with having coined the term, anti-Semitism. (Cf. "Antisemitismus," *Encyclopedia Judaica,* Berlin, 1928; and "Antisemitism," *Universal Jewish Encyclopedia.*) According to Baron (*A Social and Religious History of the Jews,* vol. II, p. 287) Marr or Ernest Renan may have been the author of the new term.

9. Marr states that it was as early as 1863 that he became "aroused by the consequences of Jewish emancipation," an event that was to happen six years later. The contradiction results from the fact that, in Marr's opinion, the emancipation of the Jews took place during the revolution of 1848 and was not undone during the restoration.

10. Marr, W[ilhelm]: *Der Judenspiegel* (Hamburg, 1863).

11. Marr, W.: *Der Sieg des Judentums, loc. cit.,* p. 39.

12. For the significance of the recurring theme of doom in modern agitation see Leo Lowenthal's and Norbert Guterman's study of American fascist agitators, *Prophets of Deceit* (New York, 1949).

13. In a later pamphlet, *Vom jüdischen Kriegsschauplatz* (3rd ed., Bern, 1879, p. 46), Marr wrote that he was mistaken in believing that Russia might support Germany in her fight against Jewry. "Social 'nihilism' is even more rampant in Russia than here. . . . It goes without saying that a revolution in Russia will also open Russian legislation to Israel."

14. Marr, W.: *Der Sieg des Judentums, loc. cit.* p. 43.

15. In *Vom jüdischen Kriegsschauplatz* p. 27, Marr returns to his basic complaint.

16. *Ibid.,* p. 29.

17. Marr, W.: *Der Sieg des Judentums, loc. cit.,* p. 32.

18. Marr, W.: *Vom jüdischen Kriegsschauplatz, loc. cit.* p. 29.

19. Otto Glagau, a talented political publicist, is said to have lost his property in *Gründer* speculations. Besides the series of articles in the *Gartenlaube* (republished as a book in 1878 under the same title and widely read), he wrote a critique of National Liberalism, *Der Bankerott des Nationalliberalismus und die "Reaktion,"* which expresses the same cultural and moral aversion to the new era of capitalism as is to be found in the writings of the Catholic publicist Constantin Frantz. (Cf. the latter's *Die Religion des Nationalliberalismus,* Leipzig, 1872; and *Der Nationalliberalismus und die Judenherrschaft,* Munich, 1874.) From 1880–1889 Glagau edited the anti-liberal, anti-Semitic magazine, *Der Kulturkämpfer,* catering to the taste of the educated *Mittelstand.* Among its contributors were high-ranking officials and influential politicians.

20. *Der Bankerott des Nationalliberalismus und die "Reaktion",* 3rd ed. (Berlin, 1878), p. 20.

21. *Ibid.,* pp. 16 ff.

22. *Ibid.,* p. 71.

23. Cf. Frank, Walter: *Hofprediger Adolf Stoecker und die Christlichsoziale Bewegung*, 2nd ed., (Hamburg, 1935), p. 77.

The concept, of course, did not originate with German anti-Semites. It originally developed from Catholic economic philosophy, is inherent in the economic theory of German romanticism, was worked out elaborately by Proudhon and taken over by German Proudhonians. In *The Communist Manifesto* Marx derides it as the ideological cornerstone of both "aristocratic" and "true" socialism.

24. The historical and economic aspects of this problem are excellently dealt with by Beard, Miriam: "Anti-Semitism—Product of Economic Myths," in Graeber, Isaque, and Britt, Steuart Henderson: *Jews in a Gentile World* (New York, 1942), pp. 262 ff.

25. Hitler, Adolf: *Mein Kampf* (Stackpole, New York, 1939), pp. 210 ff.

26. The name of the paper was actually the *Neue Preussische Zeitung*. It was generally called *Kreuzzeitung* because of the cross it carried on its front page. The *Kreuzzeitung* was founded in 1848, two weeks after the revolutionaries had stormed the Berlin *Zeughaus* (arsenal). Its board of directors was composed exclusively of members of the leading Prussian nobility. Wagener, its first editor in chief, told in his memoirs how the Berlin population greeted the new paper: "The copies were violently snatched from the carriers' hands, torn to pieces and thrown into the gutter; the distributors did not dare to receive copies unless wrapped in covers; the number of vulgar and repulsive letters [we received] was legion; they threatened to destroy our presses, to loot and to kill. On three occasions we thought it best to send our wife and child away to Potsdam and to prepare for an energetic defense." (*Erlebtes*, Berlin, 1884, p. 16.)

Heinrich Graetz, the Jewish historian, passed the following judgment on the *Kreuzzeitung*: "The mouthpiece of this [Conservative] party makes the cross its symbol but neither love nor humbleness nor truth is its device." (*Volkstümliche Geschichte der Juden*, 3 vols., Vienna and Berlin, 9th ed., vol. III, p. 637.)

27. *Kreuzzeitung* (1875, nos. 148 to 152). These anonymous articles gained notoriety under the name of "the era articles." Their author was Dr. F. Perrot, a reserve officer and publicist. See Bismarck, Otto von: *Gedanken und Erinnerungen* (complete ed., Stuttgart and Berlin, 1928), p. 454.

The articles led to an interesting demonstration. Bismarck, on February 9, 1876, sharply attacked the *Kreuzzeitung* in the Reichstag and declared that "everyone who subscribes to the paper indirectly participates in the campaign of lies and slanders which it conducts." As a result, several hundred prominent Conservatives immediately announced in the *Kreuzzeitung* the renewal of their subscriptions.

28. *Germania's* anti-Semitic articles appeared in nos. 174, 185, 189, 190, 201, 203, and 228, all in 1875.

29. Bismarck in his speech before the Prussian Diet (1847) had said:

"I am not an enemy of the Jews and I forgive them if they should be my enemies. Sometimes I even love them. And I do not grudge them any rights except the one to hold, in a Christian state, an office vested with authority. . . .

"In the territories ruled by the edict of 1812, the Jews, as far as I remember, are not denied any right but one: to hold government positions. This right they now claim for themselves; they demand the right to become state officials, generals, cabinet members, and even Ministers of Public Worship and Instruction. I admit that I am full of prejudices; I have sucked them in, so to speak, with the mother milk and I do not succeed in talking them away; if I should imagine having before me, as a representative of the King's Sacred Majesty, a Jew whom I would have to obey, I must confess that I would feel deeply depressed and humiliated, that the feeling of pride and honor would leave me with which I now endeavor to discharge my duties towards the state."

30. The term *Kulturkampf* is attributed to the eminent pathologist, Rudolph Virchow, who in support of Bismarck had called the Prussian government's fight against the Catholic Church a "fight for culture." Virchow was one of the founders and leaders of the Progress Party and took an active part in the Liberals' defense of the Jewish group.

31. Wawrzinek, Kurt: *Die Entstehung der Deutschen Antisemitenparteien (1873–1890)* (Berlin, 1927), p. 13, remarks dryly, in his carefully documented study, that *Germania* was too cautious to demand legal measures against the Jewish group. The Catholics were just experiencing the benefits of anti-minority laws.

32. Cf. Meyer, Rudolph: *Politische Gründer und die Korruption in Deutschland* (Leipzig, 1877); Gehlsen, Joachim: *Aus Dem Reiche Bismarcks* (Berlin, 1894); and anonymous: *Das Kleine Buch vom Grossen Bismarck* (Bern, 1877 and 1894). Gehlsen was also editor of the *Deutsche Eisenbahnzeitung*, later *Deutsche Reichsglocke*, of which Bismarck wrote: "The Kaiser never refused me his grace and assistance in state affairs; this did, however, not hinder him from reading the *Reichsglocke* daily. Thirteen copies of this sheet which lived solely by slandering me circulated in the Royal House Ministry for our and other courts, and it had its contributors not only among the Catholic, but also among the Protestant aristocracy." Bismarck: *Op. cit.*, p. 460.

Meyer's book ends on this note:

"We know now definitely that with Prince Bismarck a change for the better is impossible. His oldest friends, friends of his youth and best years, have warned and implored him in vain, have tried to separate him from people who breathe the plague and whom only his strong arm saves from the public prosecutor. He let the period of grace go by unused.

"We know that, had after 1871 the country's government been entrusted to other hands, had honest simple men sat in the King's council, not one of the horrible *Gründungen* would today exist which disgrace the stocklist of Berlin's stock exchange. We know that no *Kulturkampf* would rend the German nation, nor anxiety dwell in palaces and huts. As long as Prince Bismarck remains its all-powerful idol, the German nation will be sacrificed for the sake of the Reich, the Reich for the sake of the Chancellor and the Chancellor—is owned by the Jews and the *Gründer*. For our political course, therefore, one way only remains open: Elimination of the present system and its carrier."

For an understanding of the cultural and social roots of German conservative anti-Semitism Rudolph (later Rudolf) Meyer's writings offer unparalleled opportunities. He was a devoted disciple of Rodbertus' "conservative socialism." As early as 1874 he published an informed and friendly study of the German socialist labor movement, *Der Emanzipationskampf des Vierten Standes* (Berlin). A second volume (Berlin, 1875) dealt with the labor movement in Europe and America. An adherent of the Christian corporative state under a social monarchy, Meyer despises liberalism which he identifies with parliamentarianism and *laissez-faire*. "Each nation, and particularly the German, wants to be governed but it wants a good government. The wild beasts in the jungle are Manchester men. They will not tolerate a king above them. The jungle law of free competition rules supreme. 'The big beast eats the little game.' " (*Emanzipationskampf*, vol. II, p. 786.)

Meyer admonishes the Hohenzollern to be aware of their social duties and not to forget that "they ought to be strong guardians and protectors of the poor and exploited against the rich and exploiters." (*Ibid.*) Parliamentary rule, in his opinion, is nothing but "an impudent attempt of a numerically insignificant but wealthy and aggressive minority to break the Royal power and to establish itself as the mighty ruler of the state in order to extend and consolidate its own social and economic domination." (*Ibid.*)

Meyer's book *Politische Gründer und die Korruption in Deutschland* aroused Bismarck's wrath and the author had to flee Germany in order to escape a jail sentence. In exile he entertained friendly relations with many socialist leaders. Friedrich Engels in London recommended his anti-*Gründer* book to August Bebel. (Cf. Bebel: *Aus meinem Leben,* 3 vols., Stuttgart, 1919, vol. III, p. 80.) Franz Mehring calls the same book a "fulminating treatise, overflowing with bitter truth," by which Meyer "led an energetic attack against the system of capitalistic corruption from which Bismarck did not want to stay away. . . ." (Mehring: *Geschichte der deutschen Sozialdemokratie,* 4 vols., Stuttgart 1921, vol. IV, p. 130.)

In the period of 1891–95 the Social Democratic periodical, *Neue Zeit,* published numerous articles by Meyer, most of them critical reviews of the government's agricultural policies. In those years Meyer was to a degree the agrarian expert of the Marxist periodical.

According to Mehring (*Op. cit.,* pp. 130 ff.) Meyer was directly responsible for interesting a number of Protestant clergymen in the social reform movement, among them Rudolf Todt and Adolf Stoecker! However, neither Todt nor Meyer wanted any part in Stoecker's work which Meyer considered a "miscarriage" of Christian socialism.

33. *Deutsche Eisenbahnzeitung,* February 17, 1876. The anonymous author was most likely Rudolf Meyer.

34. The leading theoretician of Prussian Protestant conservatism was Friedrich Julius Stahl, a baptized Jew, whose philosophy of the state held divine revelation to be the origin of monarchy, state and law. As a member of the first chamber of the Prussian parliament, Stahl became the leader of the Conservatives.

35. Frantz, Constantin: *Der Nationalliberalismus und die Judenherrschaft, loc. cit.,* p. 22.

36. *Schlesische Volkszeitung* (October 2, 1875). See Wawrzinek: *Op. cit.,* p. 14.

37. Wawrzinek: *Op. cit.,* p. 12.

38. Liberal historians, Jewish and non-Jewish, treat the violent flare-up of Catholic political anti-Semitism in the mid-1870's as an unfortunate episode in an otherwise harmonious relationship, the *faux pas* of an irritated group which was quickly corrected. Elbogen, for instance, states that later "the Catholic party of the Center gained certain successes in church politics and dropped the campaign against the Jews on the ground that Catholics, being themselves a religious minority, should not countenance religious hatred." (Elbogen, Ismar: *Op. cit.,* p. 143.)

Catholic rediscovery of Christian tolerance was directly related to the position of Catholicism in the Reich. After 1879 the Catholic Center Party gained a strategic position in the Reichstag. The only major party which was not predominantly based on a single social group, it was in a position to join the Right or the Left in political coalitions, without having to fear that its followers would desert it. Bismarck liquidated the *Kulturkampf,* in return for which the Catholics gave him conditional parliamentary support. The National Liberal era was then over, and with it disappeared some of the strongest inducements which anti-Semitism had had to offer to political Catholicism.

Catholic hostility toward "Jewish liberalism," however, remained strong for years to come. In 1881, when "the Anti-Semites' Petition" was introduced, two of the three Catholic Center deputies who spoke in the debate expressed their sympathy with the anti-Semitic point of view. Julius Bachem, a prominent figure in Catholic politics, repeated the charges of the *Germania* articles of 1875, and Peter Reichensperger, a charter member of the Catholic Center Party, complimented Stoecker on his courage in daring "to have touched the wasp-nest." August Reichensperger, the brother of Peter, relates in his memoirs that most Catholic parliamentarians were eager at that time to participate in the anti-Semitic campaign. Writes Reichensperger:

"The most notable parliamentary event was the great debate on the Jewish question *(die grosse Judendebatte)* of November 20 and 22 [1880]. It was brought about by [the Liberal Albert] Hänel's interpellation. [In the name of the Progress Party, Hänel's had asked the Minister what position the Prussian government was preparing to take on the Anti-Semites' Petition]. Within the Catholic Center group the discussion of the Jewish question had led to very agitated discussions between Windthorst, who was rather friendly toward the Jews, and the great majority of the group which was raring to join the attack (*die scharf losgezogen wissen wollte*). . . . Windthorst stood almost completely alone in his opinion that the Catholic Center should be as neutral as possible. . . . The debate before the House was a defeat for Jewry and the Progress Party whose phrases turned always against them as *Kulturkämpfer*. The anti-Semitic agitation has greatly increased since." (Pastor, Ludwig: *August Reichensperger 1808–1895*, 2 vols., Freiburg, 1899, vol. II, p. 191.)

Again in the early nineties, when political Catholicism undertook the organization of Catholic peasants, it did not refrain from injecting anti-Semitic propaganda into the campaigns.

Catholic decisions to use or abstain from political anti-Semitism were as little governed by Christian principles as were those of the Protestant Conservatives. Political, not religious or ethical considerations were the primary determinants of Catholic-Jewish relations. These certainly were not unfriendly in the further course of German history but that was due to factors other than belief in the brotherhood of man.

For a satisfactory explanation of the tolerant attitude which political Catholicism later took toward the Jewish group it is not sufficient to point out that, as a minority group, the Catholics themselves shied from discriminatory treatment of another minority. General conclusions of this kind find little support in historical fact. In this case, the concept of "minority," as applied to two groups of which one comprised about 30 per cent of the total population, the other about 1 per cent, is apt to conceal essential differences in the situation of the respective groups.

More enlightenment might be gained by studying the relations between German Catholics and Jews as influenced by their respective group experiences. The Catholics, for instance, slowly gained access to the government machinery while Jews did not. Industrial expansion in Catholic regions— Rhineland, Silesia—took care of other Catholic grievances. The rise of a Catholic trade union movement, comprising hundreds of thousands of industrial and white-collar workers, established Catholic influence in a sphere of power where the Jewish group's weakness was glaring. Germany's close political relations to predominantly Catholic neighbor states (Austria, Hungary, Italy) also tended to strengthen the German Catholic group.

CHAPTER II

1. *"Kathedersozialismus"* was a school of economic and social thought that gained great influence in academic circles during the last decades of the nineteenth century. The term was coined by an opponent, the National Liberal publicist Heinrich Bernhard Oppenheim. Far from being Socialists of a Marxist coloration, the members of the group belonged to all kinds of political creeds but had in common their rejection of the economic and social philosophy of Manchester liberalism. Their academic organization was the *Verein für Sozialpolitik,* founded in 1873, which attracted a galaxy of names: Gneist, Roscher, Schmoller, Nasse, Brentano, Knapp, Conrad, etc. The leading *Kathedersozialist* of the eighties was Adolph Wagner, eminent economist at the University of Berlin, a life-long friend of Adolf Stoecker, vice-president of the anti-Semitic Christian Social Party, later also president of Stoecker's Protestant Social Congress.

   Problems of rural usury were among the early interests of the *Verein für Sozialpolitik.* It repeatedly conducted surveys in this field and its reports stressed the association of Jews with this particular scourge of the peasantry. It would, however, not be justified to classify all *Kathedersozialisten* as anti-Semitic.

2. One of the most obviously anti-Semitic reform programs was that of Judge C. Wilmanns: *Die "Goldene" Internationale und die Notwendigkeit einer sozialen Reformpartei* (Berlin, 1876). Wilmanns advocated the eradication of all the advantages enjoyed by "money capital" to the detriment of landowners, artisans, and small industrialists; this should be done through new legislation in the field of taxation, tariffs, banking, and railroad building. Wilmanns urged particularly a new land law to replace Roman law which he regarded as "a city and a slave law" that could only be disastrous to a free peasantry. His views on the necessity of a "new concept of law, adequate to the needs and the character of the German people," were expounded anew by Nazi philosophers.

3. Quoted from Oertzen, Dietrich von: *Adolf Stoecker. Lebensbild und Zeitgeschichte* (Volksausgabe, Schwerin, 1912), pp. 2-3.

   The literature on Stoecker, written by friends and enemies, is extensive. Among the Stoecker biographies, Walter Frank's *Hofprediger Adolf Stoecker und die Christlichsoziale Bewegung* deserves special mention. It is a highly informative book, in spite of its obvious anti-Jewish bias. The book, incidentally, has a history of its own. In the preface to the second edition (1935)—the first appeared during the Weimar Republic (1928)—Frank writes:

"I did not 'improve' upon the book except for minor formal changes. As it appeared first, with all its shortcomings which no one knows better than I, it had to appear. This was necessary not only because it marked a stage in the development of my personal work but above all because it was that document with which the Hitler revolution broke through into German historiography." (p. 10.)

Frank also relates that he took the unpublished manuscript of his book to Hitler in Munich—apparently to get the Führer's blessing. It paid. Professor Frank had a permanent academic position in the Third Reich, specializing in research on "the Jewish question."

4. When Prussia went to war with France in 1870, Stoecker declared he felt like "crying and at the same time shouting with joy that Barbarossa's old dream finally has come true." He proclaimed: "God cannot and will not leave us. It is the spirit of 1813 that is now stirring!" *(Neue Evangelische Kirchenzeitung,* August 3, 1870.)

This is not far off from Hitler's reaction to the outbreak of World War I: "I am not ashamed to say even now that I fell on my knees, overcome by a storm of enthusiasm, and thanked Heaven out of an overflowing heart that it had granted me the good fortune to live in this age." Hitler, Adolf: *Mein Kampf* (Stackpole, New York, 1939), p. 163.

5. Gerlach, Hellmut von: *Von Rechts nach Links* (Zürich, 1937), p. 103.

6. *Neue Evangelische Kirchenzeitung* (September 4, 1869).

7. *Neue Evangelische Kirchenzeitung* (March 14, 1874).

8. The letter was not published by Stoecker until 1907, two years before his death.

9. Stoecker, Adolf: *Christlich-Sozial, Reden und Aufsätze* (Bielefeld and Leipzig, 1885), p. XIII. In due time Grüneberg sold genuine and faked information about Stoecker and his movement to the highest bidders. He became a source of great embarrassment to the Christian Social Party. Stoecker had him prosecuted for embezzlement, at the same time praying in his political meetings for the swindler's soul. Cf. Bernstein, Eduard: *Geschichte der Berliner Arbeiterbewegung,* 3 vols. (Berlin, 1907–1910), vol. I, p. 393; vol. II, pp. 96 ff.

10. In 1880 Johann Most was expelled from the Social Democratic Party for anarchist views. He had come under the influence of the anti-Semitic philosophic anarchist Eugen Dühring whose ideas, at the end of the seventies, caused enough confusion among Social Democrats to make Friedrich Engels write his famous *Anti-Dühring.*

J. Most left Germany for England where he continued his political work, exhausting himself in bitter opposition to the leaders of the Social Democrats. In England he served a prison term for "subversive activities" and emigrated to the United States where he became a leading figure in the anarchist movement. For more than two decades he edited *Freiheit* in New York. He died in New York City in 1906.

11. The speech was reprinted in full in Stoecker's *Christlich-Sozial, loc. cit.,* pp. 3 ff.

12. "The three-class-franchise" (*Drei-Klassen-Wahlrecht*), as it was properly called, was incorporated into Prussia's constitution of 1850, at the height of the political reaction against the revolution of 1848; it held against all attempts to have it replaced by a more democratic electoral system until the revolution of 1918 swept it away.

The Prussian franchise act prescribed an indirect electoral procedure. The voters first cast their ballots for electors (*Wahlmänner*) who in turn elected the members of the Diet's lower chamber. Each electoral district was divided into three "classes" of voters; the amount of direct state taxes paid by the individual voter determined his voting "class." A class, therefore, could be composed of any number of taxpayers, from one millionaire to thousands of less affluent voters. Each class elected the same number of electors.

The inequities of this electoral system were increased rather than diminished when in 1893 it was decided that the amount of municipal and district taxes, as well as the direct state taxes, were to determine the class to which an individual belonged. The result was that, for instance, in the Prussian elections of 1893 the total of 5,980,538 voters was divided into

class I, comprising	210,759 persons =	3.52 per cent
class II, "	722,633 "	12.06 per cent
class III, "	5,056,146 "	84.42 per cent

(Cf. Arons, Leo: *Die Preussischen Landtagswahlen*, Berlin, 1898, p. 8.)

In each electoral district an average of 10 voters made up the first class, 37 voters the second, and 207 voters the third class. A member of the first class thus had more than twenty times the "voting power" of a member of the third class. The same law applied to communal elections.

The growing wealth of the middle classes permitted them to enjoy the privileges of the three-class-franchise, originally designed to benefit the landed aristocracy. This was not the least of the reasons why the electoral system remained intact for almost seven decades. The liberal parties showed little zeal in fighting for the revision of a franchise which gave the propertied classes a prominent political position in Prussia, the predominant state of the Reich.

13. Stoecker, speech of April 1, 1881, at Stuttgart.

14. "Mass movement from the Right" (*Massenbewegung von Rechts*) is a concept for which the author is indebted to George Fuchs.

15. The letter, dated September 23, 1880, was made public by Stoecker in his book *Dreizehn Jahre Hofprediger und Politiker* (Berlin, 1895).

16. Frank, W.: *Op. cit.*, p. 126.

17. Cassel, Paulus: *Die Antisemiten und die Evangelische Kirche* (Berlin, 1881), p. 40.

18. How deeply public opinion was stirred by the fight against and for the Jewish group may be gathered by a glance at the political and cultural literature of the period. Wawrzinek's study alone has a bibliography of

over 500 books, pamphlets, and articles referring to the anti-Semitic controversies of 1873–90.

In Frank's biography of Stoecker a contemporary's report on the political scene in the Reich capital at the time of the Berlin movement is reproduced. The Berlin correspondent of *Christliche Monatsschrift* (Christian Monthly), published at Barmen, wrote to his paper in 1885:

"Only he who has not seen Berlin for ten years and has suddenly returned can measure the change that has taken place. When he enters a small modest restaurant he will be amazed to find the *Reichsbote* [the conservative paper friendly to Stoecker] not only on display but also avidly read by the small artisan and working man. He would have to make sure that he was not dreaming when he remembered the times these circles would have thrown out the reactionary paper, and its reader on top of it. He would be dumbfounded at the sight of the newspaperwoman carrying the [anti-Semitic] *Deutsches Tageblatt* three or four flights up in the backyard building. Does up there, under the roof, the [liberal] *Volkszeitung* rule no longer? Whence the new intruder? Well, it is all Stoecker's work that has caused the change. The stranger who did not see Berlin for ten years notices how, suddenly, towards evening the crowds are getting thicker in the streets. He lets himself be carried by the current and arrives at a Conservative election meeting. All strata are represented, from the working man up to the officer in civilian attire and to the cabinet member who does not quite succeed in hiding behind a column high up in the balcony. A lively whisper can be heard in the audience which awaits the speaker. All of a sudden, there is silence, the audience holds its breath only to become tumultuously noisy again. Court Chaplain Stoecker has entered the hall and a thunderous *Hoch* from thousands of throats, a *Hoch* that will not end, greets the most popular man in Berlin, a court chaplain! The stranger thinks of former times; the memory of that Conservative meeting which he attended ten years ago comes to his mind. He has still retained the flavor of its sick-room atmosphere. That meeting was more dignified but it was small and arthritic. Who brought about this miracle?"

Cf. also Ludwig Bamberger's secret diaries, edited by Ernst Feder under the title, *Bismarcks grosses Spiel* (Frankfurt, 1932). Returning to Berlin in 1883, after an absence of several months which he had spent abroad, Bamberger was nauseated by Berlin's political climate.

"Directly upon my return I twice overheard vulgar expressions against Jews. Not that they were made for my benefit; my ear just happened to catch them. Once, they were even workers who made them. After having been back for some time, one regains his thick skin. I say one should not leave and let the bad smell escape once the nose is full of it. The moment one airs oneself [abroad] one must go through it all over again" (p. 270).

19. Bergsträsser, L[udwig]: *Geschichte der Politischen Parteien in Deutschland* (Mannheim, Berlin, Leipzig, 1932), p. 85.
20. Bismarck in his speeches before the Prussian Diet, October 18, and 19,

1849. Quoted from Nitzsche, Max: "Die Anfänge der agrarischen Bewegung in Deutschland," *Patrial Jahrbuch der 'Hilfe' 1905* (Berlin), p. 187.

21. Cf. Stolper, Gustav: *German Economy 1870–1940* (New York, 1940), p. 34.

22. In 1873 a Conservative still could declare in the Reichstag that "next to bread and meat free iron is most essential." In the same year several hundred agrarian associations joined in a monster demonstration to protest against continuing the tariff on pig iron. Cf. Nitzsche, Max: *Op. cit.*, p. 200.

23. In 1871 the output of German pig iron was 1,564,000 tons compared to a British production of 6–7,000,000 tons. Stolper: *Op. cit.*, p. 26.

24. The first unsuccessful attempt at assassination was made by Hödel, who for a short time had been a member of Stoecker's Christian Social Workers' Party.

25. Ziekursch, Johannes: *Das Zeitalter Bismarcks* (Frankfurt am Main, 1930), pp. 322 ff. Also Riemann, Robert: *Schwarzrotgold* (Leipzig, 1921), pp. 154 ff.

26. From that date down to the Nazi period the Catholic Center Party, together with its offshoot, the Bavarian People's Party, which was founded in 1920, remained numerically stable. Before World War I it never had less than 90 Reichstag seats. In the terror election of March 5, 1933, its following again proved loyal and elected 92 Center members to the last Reichstag of the Weimar Republic.

27. For the causes of minor discrepancies in the electoral statistics see notes 20 and 21, Chapter V.

28. The general right to hold meetings for Reichstag elections, however, was not impaired by the *Sozialistengesetz*, nor were Social Democratic candidates forbidden to run for election. The anti-Socialist law originally was to expire on March 31, 1881, but was extended four times. Each time, the government made the extension a test case of party loyalties, and the National Liberals fell into line. The phenomenal rise of the outlawed Social Democratic Party and Bismarck's resignation created conditions which brought an end to the law in 1890.

29. For a penetrating analysis of these developments see Kehr, Eckart: "Das soziale System der Reaktion in Preussen unter dem Ministerium Puttkamer," *Die Gesellschaft* (Berlin, 1929), 6. Jahrgang, no. 9.

30. The epithet, *Vorfrucht der Sozialdemokratie*, was first used by Bismarck to characterize the role of the Progress Party. Cf. Bebel: *Aus meinem Leben, loc cit.*, vol. III, p. 12. Later Caprivi took it up in his criticism of the anti-Semitic movement.

CHAPTER III

1. Eugen Richter in a speech before the Reichstag, January 12, 1881.
2. *Denkwürdigkeiten des Fürsten Chlodwig zu Hohenlohe-Schillingsfürst*, ed. by Friedrich Curtius, 2 vols. (Stuttgart and Leipzig, 1906–1907), vol. II, p. 307.
3. Stoecker later reported the incident as follows: "I spoke about Lassalle. Social Democrats in the audience loudly objected. They slandered the Christian Church and clergy for not having done anything for labor. The Jewish tendency was unmistakable. Thereupon I told them they should not ask for help only from us but also from the Jews, from Herr Bleichröder, for instance, who had more money than all clergymen taken together." (Quoted from Oertzen: *Op. cit.*, pp. 158–9.)
4. The original letter was in the archives of the *Kaiserliches Geheime Zivilkabinett*. The quotation is from Frank, W.: *Op. cit.*, p. 86.
5. Conservative Robert von Puttkamer (1828–1900) became in 1879 the successor of the liberal Prussian Minister of Public Worship and Instruction, Falk. From 1881 to 1888 he was Minister of the Interior and, as such, in charge of the Prussian police during most of the years of the anti-Socialist act. To socialist labor he became the symbol of Prussian reaction and police chicanery. The liberal Friedrich III dismissed him.
6. Frank, W.: *Op. cit.*, pp. 304 ff., reproduces the entire letter from a copy of the original in the archives of the *Evangelische Oberkirchenrat*.
7. Letter to Geheimrat Tiedemann of November 21, 1880, quoted by Frank, W.: *Op. cit.*, p. 305.
8. Richter: *Op. cit.*, p. 14.
9. Bernstein, Eduard: *Geschichte der Berliner Arbeiterbewegung*, *loc. cit.*, vol. II, p. 59.
10. The *Reichsbote* was a conservative, orthodox Protestant paper, of similar political complexion as the *Kreuzzeitung*; it supported Stoecker from the beginning of his political career.
11. The leaflet is reprinted in Stoecker's *Christlich-Sozial*, *loc. cit.*, pp. 404 ff.
12. Virchow ran against Stoecker in a Berlin district; he had joined in a public protest against the Russian pogroms of 1881.
13. Lucius von Ballhausen, Robert: *Bismarck Erinnerungen*, 4th–6th ed. (Stuttgart and Berlin, 1921), p. 216.
14. Windelband, Wolfgang: *Bismarcks Briefe an seinen Sohn Wilhelm* (Berlin, 1922), p. 26. An election speech Count Wilhelm von Bismarck had made before a Conservative gathering in Berlin had aroused a controversy in the press. The Chancellor warned his son to be more careful in his public

utterances. "If you speak you will have to support Stoecker because his opponent is a Progressive; but identification with Stoecker is not agreeable to the government and no one will ever believe you to talk anything but government language. It is highly desirable that Stoecker be elected, first of all to avoid election of the enemy, and besides because he is an extraordinary, militant, useful comrade-in-arms. As soon, however, as we support him, we endorse in the public mind everything he and all other anti-Semites have said in the past, and this is something to which I cannot lend my name."

15. Cf. Frank, W.: *Op. cit.*, p. 110.
16. Busch, Moritz: *Bismarck. Some Secret Pages of His History*, 3 vols. (London, 1898), vol. III, p. 16. On Busch see Chapter VI, p. 84.
17. In Otto Jöhlinger's book, *Bismarck und die Juden* (Berlin, 1921), a conscientious collection of such statements may be found. Jöhlinger's treatment of the problem, however, is on the whole apologetic and unpolitical.
18. Quoted from Jöhlinger: *Op. cit.*, p. 185.
19. Parenthetically, Jewish superior abilities were most readily recognized in fields of economic, professional, and artistic endeavors which were not rated highly in authoritarian conservative society. In imperial Germany the businessman ranked lower than the aristocratic landowner, the military and clergy, the academician and civil servant, that is, all restricted, typically "un-Jewish" occupations. The stigma of inferior occupation was only set in high relief by conceding superior aptness for it.

    F. R. Bienenfeld (*The Germans and the Jews*, New York, 1939) treats the significance of occupational status at length. He sees the low esteem in which certain professions were held in Germany as a major reason for Jewish success in journalism, trade, banking, theaters, free professions, and political life (excluding the top levels). He believes that the decline of these professions after World War I, in turn, was disastrous for the Jewish group, that German Jews had lost both fortune and position before they became victims of Hitler's laws.

20. For a correct, though necessarily simplified, analysis of Bismarck's attitude see Parkes, James: *An Enemy of the People—Antisemitism* (New York, 1946), pp. 5 ff.
21. In 1884 the Secessionists joined the Progress Party to form a new liberal organization, the *Freisinnige* Party.
22. Stoecker, Adolf: *Christlich-Sozial, loc. cit.*, pp. L–LI.
23. Rudolf Hertzog, owner of a Berlin department store, was one of the financial backers of German anti-Semitism. He had generously supported the Berlin Movement in the elections and had become known by his huge garden parties where free food and beverages, patriotic songs and anti-Semitic speeches were combined to keep the guests in high spirits.
24. Invited to participate in a Luther festival, Stoecker had gone to London where he addressed two public meetings on the social reform movement and his Christian Social Party. Liberal London was incensed. Public opin-

ion prevailed upon the Lord Mayor to revoke Stoecker's permission to speak at Mansion House. The meetings had to be held elsewhere. German Social Democrats, exiles from the anti-Socialist law, turned up in huge numbers. Bedlam ensued. Stoecker had to leave the hall by a back door.

The *Socialdemocrat* wrote of these meetings: "Our comrades had come, not to take part in a discussion, but to manifest their unmistakable hate and contempt for Herr Stoecker, and through him for Bismarck, his protector, and for the ruling classes of Germany, and in this way to answer the muzzling of our comrades in Germany." (See Frank: *Op. cit.*, p. 119.) The paper compared Luther and Stoecker; it called the former the spokesman of rising absolutism and the latter the eulogist of dying absolutism. Upon his return to Berlin Stoecker gave a detailed and highly colored description of his London experience in a speech reprinted in *Christlich-Sozial*, pp. 233 ff.

25. Quoted from Frank, W.: *Op. cit.*, p. 134.

26. *Akten des Kaiserlichen Zivilkabinetts*, quoted from Frank W.: *Op. cit.*, p. 143.

27. The handwritten four-page letter was kept in the Prussian Crown Archives. Frank was given permission to reveal its content but was not authorized to quote the document.

CHAPTER IV

1. "Heidelberger Erklärung" of March 23, 1884. Salomon, Felix: *Die deutschen Parteiprogramme* (Leipzig and Berlin, 1912), 2nd ed., vol. II, p. 35.
2. The Progressives held 59 Reichstag seats in 1881 and 67 in 1884; in 1887 only 32 Progressives were elected. From 12 seats in 1881 and 24 in 1884, the Social Democrats were down to 11 seats in 1884.
3. The Catholic Center Party showed again that it was capable of holding its following even in opposition to the government. Its 98 seats in the Reichstag were only one less than the number captured by the National Liberals, who had scored the greatest success at the polls. But the Center Party, advised by the Pope, did not choose to urge a struggle against the army bill. Its representatives abstained from voting. Rome did not wish the process of Bismarck's reconciliation with Catholicism to be disturbed. In 1887 Leo XIII told the cardinals that the *Kulturkampf* had at last come to an end. A year later, when young Kaiser Wilhelm II called for an active colonial policy for the sake of "Christian civilization" and the "abolition of slavery," the Catholic Center Party, again guided by the Pope, reversed its stand on the colonial question.

   The Catholic Center's wavering course vis-à-vis the forces of nationalism and imperialism was of singular importance in German parliamentary history, and has not yet been fully explored. The dropping of the Liberals in 1879, Caprivi's middle-of-the-road policy, the *"Bülow-Block"* of 1907, and the "Black-Blue-Bloc" of 1909—these developments depended on the Catholic Center's relations with the government. Whether, after 1890, growing Catholic cooperation with the ruling groups did not influence the Social Democratic Party to remain in opposition and isolation is another aspect of the problem.
4. Quoted from Oncken, Hermann: *Rudolf von Bennigsen*, 2 vols. (Stuttgart and Leipzig, 1910), vol. II, p. 531.
5. September 23, 1885.
6. September 17, 1885.
7. Oertzen: *Op. cit.*, p. 288.
8. Quoted from Oertzen: *Op. cit.*, p. 264.
9. Bismarck, Otto von: *Op. cit.*, p. 585.
10. *Ibid.*, p. 595.
11. Oertzen: *Op. cit.*, p. 267.
12. *Antisemiten-Spiegel* (Danzig, 1892), pp. 154 ff.
13. Stoecker gives the following explanation:

"I naturally did not leave any doubt that I would, of necessity, relinquish my office if faced with this alternative. But I submitted that this alternative did not really touch the crux of the matter; that my agitation was not the case in point but that the *Kartell* was; that His Majesty was apparently of the opinion that if I gave up the fight against the *Kartell*, this combination could assert itself in Berlin. I submitted that as it was, in any case, impossible for me to work successfully for the good of the monarchy against the Royal will I would not be averse to giving up the party's fight in Berlin and letting the *Kartell* policy show what it was able to achieve. I was certain that the *Kartell* could not win and that this would end with a defeat of the government. . . . These, however, were not the only considerations that made me leave for a while the political arena of the capital. There also were considerations of a higher kind. I myself felt that a heavy burden would be put on our public life if it should come to pass that the Kaiser showed his displeasure with me and my efforts and by implication with all our friends in the Reich. Thus strong and effective forces which a determined political course could not have done without, would be paralyzed. Subsequent years proved how much my concern was justified. In Germany a successful propaganda fight against the revolution is impossible without the wholehearted cooperation of the Christian Social and strictly Conservative groups, which now are brushed aside." (Quoted from Oertzen: *Op. cit.*, p. 285.)

14. In 1890 the National Liberals were reduced from 99 Reichstag seats to 42; the German Conservatives from 80 to 73; the Free-Conservatives from 41 to 21. The Progressives climbed from 32 to 67 seats; the Social Democrats from 11 to 35; the Catholic Center, with 106 Reichstag members, led all other parties.

15. Bismarck demanded an even more oppressive law against the Social Democratic movement, this time to be permanent. The National Liberals were willing to vote for a permanent but less discriminatory bill which the Conservatives rejected as too lenient. Bismarck had a hand in preventing an agreement between National Liberals and Conservatives. Historians today are inclined to interpret his failure to negotiate between the two parties as a maneuver designed to convince the young Kaiser that the only course left open was the *coup d'état*. (See, for instance, Delbrück, Hans: *Weltgeschichte*, Berlin, 1931, 2nd ed., pp. 617 ff.)

16. Leuss, Hans, May 1, 1889. (Frank, Walter: *Op. cit.*, p. 204.)

17. *Kreuzzeitung*, March 19, 1890.

18. Wilhelm II: *Ereignisse und Gestalten 1878–1918* (Leipzig and Berlin, 1922), p. 26.

19. The Nazis transposed Stoecker's religious-monarchic slogan into the totalitarian "one Reich, one people, one leader." In both variations, the exclusion of "others," meaning Jews, is the basic texture.

CHAPTER V

1. Auer, Ignaz: *Nach zehn Jahren. Material und Glossen zur Geschichte des Sozialistengesetzes* (Nürnberg, 1913), p. 10.
2. German emigration to overseas countries:

| | Total of Emigrants | |
	to all overseas countries	to U. S. A.
1871–1875	394,814	360,563
1876–1880	231,154	193,303
1881–1885	857,287	797,019
1886–1890	485,136	440,120
1891–1895	402,567	371,506
1896–1900	127,308	107,424
1901–1905	146,640	134,862
1906–1910	133,105	119,711
1911–1914	78,881	61,344

(Computed from: *Der Grosse Brockhaus*, 15th ed., vol. II, Leipzig, 1929, article: "Auswanderung," p. 140.)

The rates of emigration are related to the two long business cycles in the *Kaiserreich*. During the first twenty-five years, 2,370,958 Germans went overseas, but only 485,934 left during the twenty following years. The bulk of the emigrants came from the densely populated South and Southwest, that is, from territories where peasant small holdings prevailed. In this way America resettled many of the people whom its high productivity had uprooted.

3. In retirement Bismarck published a summary of the reinsurance treaty's contents in the newspaper *Hamburger Nachrichten* of October 24, 1896.
4. Stoecker quoted by Frank, Walter: *Op. cit.*, p. 230.
5. Treitschke, Heinrich von: Election speech for the anti-Semitic candidate Dr. Irmer, February 14, 1890. Quoted by Oertzen, *Op. cit.*, pp. 300 ff.
6. Gerlach, Hellmut von: *Erinnerungen eines Junkers* (Berlin, 1926), p. 84.
7. Speech of February 28, 1893. Quoted by Frank: *Op. cit.*, pp. 232 ff.
8. *Kreuzzeitung*, November 29, 1892. See Frank: Ibid.
9. *Ibid.*
10. Salomon, Felix: *Op. cit.*, vol. II, p. 71 ff.

11. Gerlach, Hellmut von: "Vom deutschen Antisemitismus," *Patria! Jahrbuch der 'Hilfe' 1904* (Berlin), p. 154.

12. Croner, Johannes: *Die Geschichte der agrarischen Bewegung in Deutschland* (Berlin, 1909), pp. 131 ff. Cf. also Ziekursch, Johannes: *Politische Geschichte des Neuen Deutschen Kaiserreiches—Das Zeitalter Wilhelm II* Frankfurt am Main, 1930), p. 59.

13. Salomon, Felix: *Op cit.*, vol. II, p. 75.

14. Stoecker's speech of February 28, 1893. (Frank: *Op. cit.*, p. 235.)

15. Harden, Maximilian: *"Fürst Bismarck und der Antisemitismus,"* *Die Zukunft* (Berlin, April 29, 1893), p. 198.

16. Bachem, Karl: *Vorgeschichte, Geschichte und Politik der deutschen Zentrumspartei*, 9 vols. (Köln, 1927–1932), vol. V, pp. 272, 352.

17. "Stichwahlen," *Vorwärts*, Berlin, June 26, 1893.

18. From the unpublished memoirs of the Christian Social Reichstag member Professor Huepeden; made accessible to, and quoted by, Frank, Walter: *Op. cit.*, p. 237.

19. The *Kaiserreich* was subdivided into 397 constituencies (*Wahlkreise*), drawn up on the basis of the census of 1864. Each constituency elected one member to the Reichstag. Population shifts from rural to urban regions called for adjustment of the original boundaries of electoral districts but no such revisions were made under the *Kaiserreich*. Thus, in industrial centers it took many more votes to elect a candidate than in the agrarian provinces, depopulated by the exodus into the cities. "Electoral district geometry" worked against the Social Democratic Party and for the Conservatives, the chief reason for its not being corrected.

20. There are hardly two reference works which give identical figures on electoral votes or strength of party representation in the Reichstag. The differences, mostly insignificant, result sometimes from the fact that candidates who had campaigned for one party, joined, when elected, the Reichstag group of the big party nearest to it in character and aims. Thus, candidates elected on an anti-Semitic platform would often join the Conservative Reichstag group. This happened especially in 1893. A number of candidates who had campained as anti-Semites tied up with the Conservatives. They preferred, as von Gerlach put it, "to find an abode in the larger Conservative mansion which they regarded as more solid after all." (Gerlach, Hellmut von: "Vom deutschen Antisemitismus," *loc. cit.*, p. 154.)

The strength of the anti-Semitic vote was therefore greater than the number of votes cast for members of the anti-Semitic Reichstag group would indicate. Theodor Fritsch, analyzing the 1893 elections in detail, mentions the anti-Semitic candidates who tied up with the Conservatives: "Baron von Langen (Stralsund-Rügen), von Dallwitz (Ost-Priegnitz), Rother (Ohlau-Nimptsch-Strehlen), von Weideck (Cottbus), von Herder (Marienberg-Zschoppen), Sachsse (Nossen-Döbeln), Jakobskötter (Erfurt) —all in complete agreement with the German-Social program and jointly elected by German-Socials [anti-Semites] and Conservatives." On the basis of these and similar post election shifts Fritsch estimates the anti-Semitic vote as high as 400,000, instead of the 263,000 cast for candidates who remained in the anti-Semitic Reichstag group. (Fritsch, Theodor: "Kurze Geschichte der antisemitischen Bewegung," *Antisemiten-Katechismus*, 25th ed., Leipzig, 1893, pp. 345 ff.)

21. A party had to have at least 15 Reichstag members to be recognized as an independent group (*Fraktion*). Only such a group was entitled to being represented in committees and to submit bills; an individual deputy could not propose legislation. It was a parliamentary custom for the established party *Fraktionen* to act as "host" to minor groups or individual representatives, the *Wilde* (Mavericks) if they did not succeed in forming their own *Fraktion*. The "guests" (*Hospitanten*) were sometimes counted as belonging to the "host" party. This, too, accounts for discrepancies in parliament and election statistics (see Note 20).

22. The rapid decline of liberalism caused the Progressive member of the Reichstag, Theodor Barth, to write in 1905: "It sounds like a fairy-tale of olden times if one hears today that in 1874 there were 182 National Liberals in the Prussian Diet and 155 in the Reichstag. With the members of the Progress Party, which then had 72 seats in the Prussian Diet and 49 in the Reichstag, liberalism altogether commanded a solid majority thirty years ago in the Prussian as well as in the Reich parliament." (Barth, Theodor: "Der Politiker Heinrich Rickert," *Patria!*, Berlin, 1905, pp. 1 ff.)

23. The Polish Party (*Polenpartei*) sent a representation to the Reichstag varying in strength between 13 (1887) and 20 (1907) members. It was the political organization of the Polish population in Germany's "Ostmark," the eastern provinces where the German and Polish element met. Coinciding with his *Kulturkampf* against German Catholicism, Bismarck pursued an aggressive anti-Polish policy; first culturally, by making the German language obligatory in the public school system and eliminating the influence of the Polish-speaking Catholic clergy in school matters; later economically, by providing government funds for buying up Polish-owned estates and settling them with German peasants. The Polish-speaking population, however, stood its ground well.

Caprivi's attempt to establish friendlier relations with the Polish group was sabotaged by Bismarck and Wilhelm II. In 1894 the *Deutscher Ostmarkenverein* was founded; ultranationalistic, it endeavored to influence Reich policy toward the eastern provinces in Bismarck's spirit. In 1914 it had over 50,000 members. After World War I it became one of the recruiting stations for Nazism.

24. Hellmut von Gerlach was present at a meeting of leading members of the Conservative Party whom Hammerstein toward the end of 1894 had called together in order to get their approval of an imminent conspiracy against the constitution. The relevant passages of Gerlach's report (*Von Rechts nach Links, loc. cit.*, pp. 134 ff.), read:

Hammerstein. . . . immediately told us: "I have just come from Count Eulenburg [then Prussian Prime Minister]. He has been offered the chancellorship. He is ready to accept it provided that all Conservatives support him in his plan to have the *Bundesrat* at once declare the general franchise invalid." This was the *coup d'état*, this was the occasion for giving the order to shoot the workers down which Hammerstein had wanted in 1892!

First everyone was silent under the impact of the monstrous disclosure. Then, Stoecker took the floor in order to express his scarcely veiled agreement: he had always been in favor of substituting a corporative arrangement for the right of democratic suffrage. The others nodded agreement. Then I let loose. . . .

It was clear that Wilhelm II stood behind the whole treacherous plan. Eulenburg would never have dared flirt with the idea of a *coup d'état* had he not made sure beforehand that he had the imperial blessing.

Eulenburg and Hammerstein dropped the plan when faced with disagreement even among the Conservative leaders. But the threat of the *Staatsstreich*, of an open violation of the constitution, of an army rebellion, reappeared at all major political crises, haunted the democratic opposition, and induced it to make ever-increasing concessions to nationalism and militarism.

25. Cf. Ziekursch, Johannes: *Op cit.*, p. 74.

CHAPTER VI

1. Treitschke's political development epitomized the trend of German political liberalism. Anti-Bismarckian in the constitutional conflict of the 1860's, Treitschke was won over, like so many Liberals with whom he joined in the National Liberty Party, by the success of Bismarck's military solution of the Prussian-German national question.

   Of the extensive literature on Treitschke two studies are particularly relevant for our problem. For the sociological implications of Treitschke's anti-Semitism see Rosenberg, Arthur: "Treitschke und die Juden. Zur Soziologie der deutschen akademischen Reaktion," *Die Gesellschaft* (Berlin, 1930), vol. II, pp. 78 ff. A psychological interpretation of the Saxonian Treitschke's Prussia-cult is given in Wolfgang Hallgarten's study on *"'Fremde' als Schöpfer völkischer Lehren"* (*" 'Aliens' as creators of racial doctrines"*). (Unpublished manuscript in the possession of the Institute of Social Research, New York.)

2. Treitschke, Heinrich von: "Ein Wort über unser Judentum," *Preussische Jahrbücher*, vols. 44 and 45, 1879, Separatabdruck, 3rd ed. (Berlin, 1880), p. 4.

3. On occasion, however, Stoecker did side with the racial anti-Semites who wanted the emancipation law revoked. How ill-at-ease he was in their company became apparent at the time of the "Anti-Semites' Petition." Liberal opponents in parliament questioned Stoecker as to whether he had signed the petition. He first denied it and, then, when shown his name among the signers, went into an excited "explanation" which convinced no one and damaged his reputation.

4. Speech of March 4, 1881, *Christlich Sozial, loc. cit.*, p. 113.

5. Speech of December 3, 1880, *op. cit.*, p. 106.

6. Marr, Wilhelm: *Streifzüge eines philosophischen Touristen* (Berlin, 1876); quoted from *Antisemiten-Spiegel, loc. cit.*, p. 188.

7. Oertzen, Dietrich von: *Op. cit.*, pp. 153 ff.

> After it had become clear that "Jew-baiting" could arouse tumultuous applause at every popular meeting, a multitude of "wild" orators appeared overnight who, without having any of Stoecker's moral pathos, were only interested in getting applause and entertaining the audience with jokes. Stoecker always was anxious to keep these elements out of the Christian Social Party. But they remained an embarrassment since each election campaign brought together and mixed up all the groups of the right.

Oertzen found comfort in the thought that a just fight had to be waged even at the risk of its lofty motives being misunderstood and perverted.

As little as Luther could refrain from bringing about the reformation because the Christian freedom he had in mind was taken by ignorant people to mean the freedom of the flesh, so little could Stoecker refrain from attacking the immense power of evil personified in modern Jewry, just because unscrupulous agitators could appropriate the effective element of agitation inherent in "Jew-baiting" and were able to use it without moral considerations to stir up popular passion.

Christian-conservative efforts to stake off the boundary lines of "legitimate" hatred of Jews and to decide on what was right and wrong in anti-Semitic agitation sometimes appear as plain insanity. A Protestant clergyman of the Stoecker school, reviewing a long list of anti-Semitic leaflets published by the racial school, wrote indignantly:

To reject are Nos. 1, 4–5, 13, 15, 17–20, 24, 28, 30, No. 32, especially 24. A conservative and Christian Social believer in the Bible cannot recommend literature of this kind. Nobility and the clergy may smile in the security of a good conscience when they are insinuatingly depicted as being anti-Semitic for selfish interests (as in No. 4); it might still be tolerated that the bad books of atheist anti-Semites are recommended (as in No. 5 and others) for very few will buy them; but that heathen religions are exalted at the expense of the Revelation of the Old Testament (Nos. 28, 30, 32); that the tales of the Old Testament are treated as legend; that Abraham (with all Samaritans) is declared the servant of the devil (Nos. 20, 34); that the privileged position of the Jewish people, explicitly termed as undeserved in the Bible, is called "Jewish arrogance in the Bible" even before the rejection of Christ (No. 1); . . . that Schopenhauer's judgment on the "miserable Jew religion," as revealed in the Genesis and in all historical books of the Old Testament is approvingly quoted (No. 17)—all this must arouse the indignation of every Christian.

The incensed Protestant clergyman then recommends as "excellent," and "for their special popularity," the remaining anti-Semitic leaflets. (Quoted from *Antisemiten-Spiegel*, pp. 142–3.)

8. Fritsch, Theodor: *Antisemiten-Katechismus* (Leipzig, 1893), pp. 11–17.
9. *Ibid.*, p. 27.
10. Ahlwardt, Hermann: Reichstag speech of February 27, 1895.
11. J. Arthur de Gobineau's *Essai sur l'inégalité des races humaines,* 4 vols. (Paris, 1853–1855) is generally considered the first and most representative attempt at a racial philosophy of history.
12. Barzun, Jacques: *Race—A Study in Modern Superstition* (New York, 1937), p. 201.
13. Veblen, Thorstein: *Imperial Germany and the Industrial Revolution* (New York, 1918); Michels, Robert: *Probleme der Sozialphilosophie* (Leipzig, Berlin, 1914); Kehr, Eckart: *Schlachtflottenbau und Parteipolitik* (Berlin,

1930); Rosenberg, Arthur: *Die Entstehung der Deutschen Republik* (Berlin, 1930) are a few of the many studies of German society which stress its basic anomaly: industrialism without a ruling middle class.

14. "Eternal nature takes implacable revenge for violation of her commandments. Thus I believe I am acting today in the spirit of the Almighty Creator: by resisting the Jew I am fighting for the Lord's work." Hitler, Adolf: *Op. cit.*, p. 74.

15. Fritsch, Theodor: *Op. cit.*, pp. 358 ff. The formulation of the "Ten German Commandments" with the deliberate imitation of scriptural language was in itself a provocative blasphemy, designed to discredit Christian doctrine as having its origin in Judaism.

16. Mommsen, Theodor: *Römische Geschichte*, 3 vols., 6th ed., (Berlin, 1875), vol. III, p. 550.

17. This, of course, may vary according to countries as well as social groups. In a study on Anti-Semitism Within American Labor, which the Institute of Social Research made during the war years, the charge of debauchery was relatively rare in the long list of alleged Jewish individual and social misdemeanors. On the whole, allusions to Jewish lewdness play a much smaller part in American anti-Semitic literature than they did in the writings of German anti-Semites. In America, Negroes rather than Jews seem to be the objects of unconscious sex envy.

18. Ahlwardt, Hermann: *Der Verzweiflungskampf der Arischen Völker mit dem Judentum* (Berlin, 1890), p. 230.

19. Hitler, Adolf: *Op. cit.* (author's translation from the German edition of 1936), p. 782.

20. In his articles in the periodical, *Grenzboten*, 1880, which Busch republished as a pamphlet under the title *Israel und die Gojim*. See Wawrzinek, Kurt: *Op. cit.*, p. 30.

21. Marr claimed that in the first year of its existence the League had attracted 6,000 members, a figure called "most unlikely" by Wawrzinek. (*Op. cit.*, p. 33.)

22. Marr, Wilhelm: *Der Sieg des Judentums über das Germanentum* (Bern, 1879), back cover.

23. According to *Encyclopedia Judaica*, article "Antisemitismus" (Berlin 1928).

24. German anti-Semites pointed to the Chinese Exclusion Law, which the Congress of the United States passed in 1882, as an example of sound racial policy. They cited the act in support of the demand that the German borders be closed to Jews. The freest commonwealth had demonstrated, Henrici wrote, that rights and liberties could stand being curtailed if the common interest so required. (Wawrzinek, Kurt: *Op. cit.*, p. 44.)

25. *Neue Deutsche Volkszeitung*, no. 64, 1883.

26. Boeckel's main support came from *Oberhessen*, a section notorious for the poverty of its soil, lack of industry and cultural facilities. Jews living in those parts made a living as cattle-dealers, innkeepers, mortgagers, and middlemen. Judging by the low esteem in which they were held by other German Jews, they shared in the cultural backwardness of their environment.

27. Gerlach, Hellmut von: *Von Rechts nach Links*, loc. cit., pp. 170–171.

28. Boeckel, Otto: *Die Juden—die Könige unserer Zeit* (Berlin, 8th ed., 1887), p. 3. The title of this 15-page pamphlet seems to have been inspired by the French monarchist, A. Toussenel, who in 1845 had written: "Les juifs, rois de l'epoque." Total circulation of Boeckel's pamphlet allegedly reached 1,500,000 copies. (Cf. Introduction to enlarged pamphlet of the same title, Berlin, 1901.)

29. Quoted from Frank, Walter: *Op. cit.*, p. 229.

30. *Antisemitische Korrespondenz*, no. 69, December 8, 1889.

31. Breakdown of figures from *Antisemiten-Spiegel*, pp. 29-30.

32. July 27, 1890. Cf. *Antisemiten-Spiegel*, p. 27.

33. Harden, Maximilian: "Fürst Bismarck und der Antisemitismus," *Die Zukunft*, April 29, 1893, p. 200.

34. Ahlwardt, Hermann: *Der Verzweiflungskampf der Arischen Völker mit dem Judentum*, loc. cit., pp. 64–164.

35. Ahlwardt, Hermann: *Judenflinten*, 5th ed. (Dresden, 1892).

36. *Neue Zeit*, 1891–92, no. 34, p. 228.

37. Under the dateline of May 29, 1892, signed by the Minister of War.

38. The affair of Ahlwardt's "Jewish Rifles" might remind the reader of the investigation of the Garsson combine by a Congressional Committee. Attempts were made to inject into the American investigation the charge that the firm had delivered defective shells causing the death of American soldiers; but the Committee's findings quickly silenced the accusers and the whole issue hardly created a ripple on the surface of public opinion.

39. Mehring, Franz: "Berliner Geschichten," *Neue Zeit*, 1891–92, no. 34, p. 229.

40. In the first balloting Ahlwardt obtained twice as many votes as were cast for the Conservative candidate. The Conservative Party then withdrew its man and threw its support to Ahlwardt in the run-off elections.

41. Gerlach, Hellmut von: *Von Rechts nach Links*, loc. cit., pp. 113–114.

42. *Reichstag* speech of February 27, 1895.

43. Boeckel, Otto: *Op. cit.*, p. 6.

44. The *Centralverein deutscher Staatsbürger jüdischen Glaubens* was founded in 1893 in Berlin to defend the civil and social rights of German Jews regardless of the members' religious or political affiliation. Opposed to Zionism, the *Centralverein* was devoted to a policy of national assimilation of German Jews. Its "Legal Department" (*Rechts-Kommission*) had the task of bringing suit against anti-Semitic violators of the law.

45. Buch, Willi: *50 Jahre antisemitische Bewegung. Beiträge zu ihrer Geschichte* (Munich, 1937), p. 49.

46. In present-day American anti-Semitic agitation a similar attempt may be observed. The Jews, so the agitators claim, are the ones who constantly talk about democracy because they can hide behind and abuse the safeguards of democratic government. The Jews are "the parasites of democracy." The goal, of course, is to compromise and pervert the very idea of democracy by making it appear as a Jewish sanctuary.

CHAPTER VII

1. Bahr, Hermann: *Der Antisemitismus. Ein Internationales Interview* (Berlin, 1894), pp. 2 ff. Writer, editor, literary and art critic, Hermann Bahr, born in Linz (Austria) in 1863, was in his youth a Socialist. In 1886 he wrote in answer to Albert Schäffle's *Die Aussichtslosigkeit der Sozialdemokratie* (1885) a pamphlet, *Die Einsichtslosigkeit des Herrn Schäffle.* Later he moved away from socialism, first towards idealistic anarchism, finally to Catholicism. In 1912 he announced his conversion to the Catholic faith.

2. The notion that political anti-Semitism of the eighties and nineties was the product of the agrarian movement was expressed with particular conviction by a group of writers contributing to Friedrich Naumann's yearbooks *Patria.* Cf. Max Nitzche's analysis of "Die Anfänge der agrarischen Bewegung in Deutschland," *Patria!* (Berlin, 1905).

3. From 1887 on, when Otto Boeckel won a Reichstag seat as the first anti-Semitic candidate, until World War I approximately 70 men were elected to the Reichstag as candidates of overtly anti-Semitic parties, the Conservatives not included. (The number cannot be accurately determined because of changes in party affiliations after the elections.) All Reichstag members were requested to give some autobiographical information to be recorded in the official Reichstag reference books. On the basis of this information (*Reichstagshandbücher* for the legislative periods of 1887, 1890, 1893, 1898, 1903, 1907, 1912–1918), which is neither complete nor too specific, a few general observations may be made.

   Of the anti-Semitic members who professed a religious denomination, all but two were of the Protestant faith. One of these two was a dissident Catholic (*Alt-Katholik*), the other is listed as a Mennonite. Professing Catholics, it can be seen, were conspicuously absent. In terms of social background, three major social groups were not or hardly represented. None of the members came from the ranks of industrial labor. With the exception of two, Liebermann von Sonnenberg and Count Ludwig von Reventlow, the aristocracy was ostensibly missing. Of these two aristocrats one (Reventlow) was a lawyer who had once been a *Rittergutsbesitzer,* the other (Liebermann) a debt-ridden ex-officer. Although the group comprised men who declared themselves to be merchants and sons of merchants, not one of them came from, or represented, big industry, trade, and finance. Next to small industrial and agricultural entrepreneurs, artisans, and small merchants, the group counted among its members teachers, lawyers, civil servants, and employees.

The group's educational level was above average. Of the 43 men for whom educational data are available, 19 had a university background and only 13 did not have more formal education than high school; the remainder had gone to college or its educational equivalent in special art schools, trade schools, etc. The proportion of men with an academic background and holding public office increased somewhat in later years.

A sizeable number of the anti-Semitic Reichstag group did not follow their original training and profession, even if allowance is made for changes resulting from their parliamentary activities. Seven switched to positions in municipal government, thirteen became writers and editors.

As to racist agitators in general, non-Jewish defense literature rightly emphasized their bad records as citizens, their collisions with the law, their lack of Christian devotion and social respectability. Many of them were men of "personal improbity and mental aberrations." (Baron, Salo W.: A Social and Religious History of the Jews, 3 vols., New York, 1937, vol. II, p. 296.)

4. The lives of many German anti-Semites offer material for the study of nationalism as an ideology of frustration. Recently, a report on the mood of German students contained a striking illustration. A Heidelberg student was quoted as saying "first, that most of the students are still nationalistic, and second, that ninety per cent of them would leave Germany if they had a chance to emigrate." (Anne O'Hare McCormick: "Abroad," New York Times, January 27, 1947.)

The commentator missed the point when she concluded that "the two statements are not exactly consistent" and suggested that this should be attributed to the prevailing confusion.

5. Dr. Jungfer, Dr. Bernhard Förster, and Dr. Henrici were fired for their agitation by Berlin's liberal Lord Mayor Max von Forckenbeck who initiated a "Counter-Declaration" to fight the Anti-Semites' Petition.

6. The defense literature of the period interchangeably uses the three terms —racial, radical, and rowdy anti-Semitism—to distinguish it from Christian Social anti-Semitism.

7. Caprivi's speech of December 7, 1893. Stenographischer Reichstagsbericht of same date.

8. Quoted from Vorwärts, December 22, 1894.

9. The Nazi program of 1920 called for "the enactment of a law to expropriate land without indemnity in the interest of the common welfare." Such land was to be found primarily in the eastern provinces, and the German "land reform movement" had been traditionally anti-Junker. To counteract the unfavorable reaction of big agrarian interests, the Nazis "explained":

"In the light of the mendacious interpretations to which our enemies subject the Program of the N.S.D.A.P. the following statement is necessary: Since the N.S.D.A.P. recognizes the principle of private property, it is self-evident that the phrase, 'expropriate without indemnity' can refer only to the establishment of legal provisions for the expropriation, if necessary, of land not lawfully acquired [by its present owners] or not managed in the interests of the commonweal. This, therefore, is directed primarily against Jewish land-speculating companies." (The Nazi statement appeared in the conservative *Deutsche Zeitung* of April 13, 1928.)

10. Dubnow, Simon: *Op. cit.*, vol. III, p. 447.

11. The full title of the "Semi-Gotha" is *Weimarer historisch-genealogisches Taschenbuch des gesamten Adels jehudäischen Ursprungs.* (Weimar historico-genealogical pocket reference book of all nobility of Jehudaic origin.) In title and make-up the *Semi-Gotha* imitated the *Gothaische Genealogische Taschenbücher*, the Who's Who of European aristocracy. The first edition (Weimar, 1912) was confiscated but in 1913 the confiscation was revoked with the result that the remaining copies sold at a premium. A second edition of 1,009 pages was published in Munich in 1913.

As a document of the racial mind the following advertisement in the second edition deserves quotation. It appeared under the sign of the swastika:

"We have an opening for a co-editor qualified in every respect; of upright character, conversant with genealogy, race history, and the Gotha; conscientious, careful, of military punctuality, reliability and correctness; circumspect, interested and energetic, with firm, clear and small handwriting and precise style; reserve officer preferred; first trial period, then life position."

12. Oertzen: *Op. cit.*, p. 197.

13. Frank, Walter: *Op. cit.*, p. 240.

14. Elbogen, Ismar: *Op. cit.*, p. 165, writes: "The principal sufferers from these activities were the middle-class Jews in the towns and villages. They were unable to maintain their position and were forced to migrate to the larger cities where they surrendered their economic independence and swelled the ranks of the proletariat."

Such an interpretation ignores the other relevant causes of the trend toward urbanization which was neither typically German nor confined to Jews. To state that the German Jews who went to the larger cities "swelled the ranks of the proletariat," is apt to create an entirely wrong impression. In contrast to the United States, Germany had practically no Jewish working class. As a rule, Jews who went to the cities continued to remain outside the proletariat.

CHAPTER VIII

1. The historian Ismar Elbogen (*A Century of Jewish Life, loc. cit.*, p. 166) writes about the years:

   "The feverish heat of political passion cooled gradually. The German people turned to fortifying its position in world politics, and the Jewish problem retired into the background."

   Hellmut von Gerlach calls the year 1893 the "parliamentary zenith" of German anti-Semitism, "just as 1880 had been its spiritual one. From then on it rapidly went downhill." ("Vom deutschen Antisemitismus," *loc. cit.*, pp. 154–155.) Dubnow's chapter on "Anti-Semitism in Germany" ends by mentioning the ritual murder affair at Konitz (1900). (*Op. cit.*, III, p. 445.) All reference and historical works on German anti-Semitism devote less space to the period of 1896–1914 than to the preceding twenty years.

   This is true also for such representative periodicals as *Preussische Jahrbücher; Historisch-politische Blätter für das katholische Deutschland; Protestantische Kirchenzeitung für das evangelische Deutschland; Neue Zeit.*

2. Buch, Willi: *Op. cit.*, p. 59.
3. *Ibid.*, p. 53.
4. Cf. "Antisemitismus," *Encyclopedia Judaica* (Berlin, 1928).
5. Buch, Willi: *Op. cit.*, p. 22. The passage referring to Boeckel's later life reads:

   The loss of his Reichstag seat was especially hard for Dr. Boeckel, since the Reichstag of 1903, for the first time in the history of German parliamentarism, paid the deputies a salary. And Dr. Boeckel, in dire economic straights because of unfortunate family affairs as well as the decline of the anti-Semitic movement had to give up the hope of thus earning a modest livelihood. . . . Although Dr. Boeckel had made noteworthy contributions in the field of folklore and folk songs, the press ignored his books. Finally he withdrew from political life, entirely impoverished, bitter, and shy. In Michendorf in the March [of Brandenburg] he owned a modest little house where he lived like a recluse with an old housekeeper. In 1910–12 he tried once more to become active and organized some courses in public speaking. However, this too failed. During these years in Berlin, when one chanced to meet him, it was hard to recognize in this shabbily dressed old man, who often was dirty and without a collar, the once keen librarian of Marburg, the man of the rapier-sharp tongue and pen. It must be gratefully acknowledged that the Agrarian League had set aside a small grant for him, despite

the fact that Boeckel often disagreed politically with the League.
[Boeckel had in fact attacked the Agrarian League as a tool of
Junker reaction.]

The peasants of Michendorf considered Boeckel a queer old man.
I had a pathetic experience. A group of Berlin *Jungdeutsche* [Young-
Germans, an anti-Semitic youth organization] which had been hiking
through Michendorf, remembered the old leader. We took up positions on the dark village street in front of his house and sang
Schenkendorf's lied of faith (*Treuelied*). He thanked us from a
window. But he refused even the request of myself, who had gained
my first journalistic honors under his tutelage . . . to spend an
hour with us. In the village inn we later struck up a conversation
with the peasants: "The doctor, well, he is a funny bird. Once in
a while he makes a speech here in the veterans' league. For a
Taler. But he does not take the money himself. It must be sent
to him by money order."

We meditated in silence. A man before whom all the Jewry of
the Reich had once trembled, who had been a thorn in the side
of the comfortable gentlemen in parliament, to whom the national
movement in general was so heavily indebted, had to humiliate
himself before the villagers of the March.

6. The anti-Semitic parties had shaken off Ahlwardt at the very beginning
of his political career. As early as November 28, 1891, Boeckel as chairman of the Anti-Semitic People's Party, and Liebermann von Sonnenberg
as chairman of the German Social Anti-Semitic Party, published the following statement:

> Upon several inquiries by party comrades the undersigned feel
> obliged to state that they cannot take any responsibility for the
> behavior and the public agitation of Herr *Rektor* Ahlwardt and that
> *Rektor* Ahlwardt does not belong to any of the two party organiza-
> tions.

The 1893 edition of Fritsch's *Antisemiten-Katechismus* devoted several
pages (pp. 341–344) to an unfriendly appraisal of Ahlwardt's role in the
anti-Semitic movement and accused him of recklessness and megalomania.

7. Cf. "Hermann Ahlwardt," *Yevreyskaya Entzyklopediya* (St. Petersburg),
vol. 2., p. 123.
8. Buch, Willi: *Op. cit.*, p. 16.
9. According to *Encyclopedia Judaica* (Berlin, 1928), pp. 1022 ff.
10. Gerlach, Hellmut von: *Von Rechts nach Links, loc. cit.*, p. 114.
11. Wawrzinek, Kurt: *Op. cit.*, p. 46.
12. "Liebermann von Sonnenberg, Zimmerman, Dr. Boeckel, Paul Förster,
Ahlwardt, Köhler, etc., were really as many parties in their own rights.
The one was pro-*Mittelstand*, the other a friend of labor, a third an aristocrat, the next a democrat. The one called for a fight against the Jews and
Junkers, the other supported the big agrarians, rain or shine. The Reichstag group split over each vote. It did not introduce a single bill of
importance, especially in the field that had been the basis of their

agitation: the Jewish question. It soon became obvious within the group that it could not present an anti-Jewish bill because it could not agree upon the concept of 'Jew.' They all concurred in one thing:

> 'Was er glaubt ist einerlei;
> In der Rasse liegt die Schweinerei.'

. . . . But how to define by law the concept of race? . . . . Since the question could not be solved as to who was a Jew, they [anti-Semites] continued to attack the Jews but could not legislate against them." (Gerlach: *Op. cit.*, pp. 112 ff.)

13. Cf. Oberwinder, Heinrich: "Das Stoeckerblatt," *Die Zukunft* (June 25, 1896); Leuss, Hans: *Wilhelm Freiherr von Hammerstein* (Berlin, 1905), pp. 108 ff.; Gerlach, Hellmut von: *Von Rechts nach Links, loc. cit.*, pp. 133 ff.

14. See Mehring, Franz: *Geschichte der deutschen Sozialdemokratie, loc. cit.*, vol. IV, pp. 301 ff.

15. Gerlach, Hellmut von: *Von Rechts nach Links, loc. cit.*, p. 118.

16. Leuss, Hans: "Das Verbrechen als sozial-pathologische Erscheinung," *Neue Zeit* (1899–1900), vol. XVIII, No. i, pp. 213 ff. "Disziplin in Strafanstalten," *Neue Zeit*, vol. XVIII, No. i. pp. 783 ff; 820 ff.

17. Adolf Harnack (ennobled in 1914), professor of ecclesiastic history at the Berlin University; from 1905–21 director of the Prussian State Library; from 1910 President of the *Kaiser-Wilhelm-Gesellschaft zur Förderung der Wissenschaften*; an eminent scholar and prolific writer. From 1903–1912, Harnack was President of the Protestant Social Congress.

18. Weber, Ludwig: "Stoecker und Naumann," *Die Zukunft*, 1895, vol. XI, p. 418.

19. Roon's statement in *Kreuzzeitung* of January 31, 1896. Cf. Frank, W.: *Op. cit.*, pp. 251 ff.

20. From Naumann's letters in Stoecker's estate; quoted by Frank: *Ibid.*

21. The *Martineum* was a private Protestant school in Schleswig-Holstein which the Prussian Ministry of Worship and Instruction refused to recognize as a *Gymnasium*.

22. Harnack (see Note 17) was attacked by conservative Protestant orthodoxy for the liberal philosophy of his works on church history. Stoecker himself wrote an anonymous article against him in the *Kreuzzeitung* (August 22, 1888).

23. The Social Democrat Hasenclever, elected in the sixth Berlin district in 1887, had become incurably ill. In order to capture the district in the necessary by-election, Bismarck's mouthpiece, the *Norddeutsche Allgemeine Zeitung*, had suggested a coalition of all anti-Social Democratic forces. But the Progressives as well as the anti-Semites balked. Stoecker's pessimism as to the outcome of the by-election proved justified. The Social Democrats retained the district by a large majority.

24. The whole letter is reproduced in Frank, W.: *Op. cit.*, pp. 318 ff.

25.
> Sunday after Sunday this impudent liar
> Profanes God's House,
> We see him administer the Holy Sacrament
> And no one throws the scoundrel out.

(*Kladderadatsch*, November 10, 1895.)

26. *Neue Evangelische Kirchenzeitung*, February 1896.
27. Oertzen: *Op. cit.*, p. 378.
28. According to the report of *Das Volk*, February 8, 1896. Quoted by Oertzen: *Op. cit.*, p. 383.
29. *Reichsbote*, January 5, 1898. Cf. Oertzen: *Op. cit.*, pp. 492 ff.
30. Stoecker's letter to the Protestant minister Braun. Quoted from Oertzen: *Op. cit.*, p. 397.
31. The Kaiser's telegram of February 28, 1896, to Geheimrat Hinzpeter. It was "by Imperial order" conveyed to Baron von Stumm. Stumm, with the Kaiser's approval, published it in his newspaper *Die Post*, May 5, 1896.
32. Quoted from Frank: *Op. cit.*, pp. 267 ff. Frank quotes from an undated letter by Stoecker to his wife which he assumes to have been written in reaction to the decree: "The answer of the Protestant Church's Superior Council to Stumm is shameless and dishonorable, a clanking chain on the leg of the State church. Where are we heading?"
33. Krause (*Zum Austritt Stoeckers*) disclosed that Stoecker had been willing to give *in camera* a binding promise that he would break with the left wing of the Christian Social Party, grouped around *Das Volk*; but that he had refused to do so openly for reasons of political expediency. Krause further cast aspersion on Stoecker's integrity by referring to the latter's attempt to save Hammerstein despite the immorality of his conduct.
34. Mehring, Franz: "Der Fall Hammerstein," *Neue Zeit* (1895–96), vol. XIV, No. i, pp. 2 ff.

CHAPTER IX

1. Stumm won in the newly created election district of Ottweiler the industrial center of which, Neunkirchen, was the seat of his largest steel works.
2. Before the Catholic Center Party was organized and the *Kulturkampf* brought the Free-Conservatives in conflict with political Catholicism, the Catholic element within the Free-Conservative Party was considerable. Among others, Carl Friedrich von Savigny, one of the founders of the Center Party, originally belonged to the Free-Conservatives. The Center Party later succeeded in conquering many Free-Conservative districts, especially in the Rhineland, and thereby modified the heavy-industrial character of the party.
3. Quoted from Hellwig, Fritz: *Carl Ferdinand Freiherr von Stumm-Halberg* (Heidelberg-Saarbrücken, 1936), pp. 238 ff.
4. *Ibid.*, p. 441.
5. *Ibid.*, p. 492.
6. Ziekursch, Johannes: *Das Zeitalter Wilhelms II.*, *loc. cit.*, p. 57.
7. *Die Reden des Freiherrn Carl Ferdinand von Stumm-Halberg*, ed. by A. Tille, 12 vols. (Berlin, 1906–1915), vol. VIII, p. 463.
8. When Adolph Wagner dared to speak against Stumm in the Reichstag debate on the sedition bill, Stumm challenged him to a duel. See Wagner, Adolph: *Mein Konflikt mit dem Freiherrn von Stumm-Halberg* (Berlin, 1895). In a Phillipic against the "socialism of the pulpit, the chair and the street" (April 12, 1896) Stumm abused Protestant ministers of the Saar who sympathized with the Stoecker movement, and Stoecker himself, to the point where Stoecker had to sue him for libel. Stumm had a stenographic record of his speech submitted to the Kaiser and made known through the *Neue Saarbrücker Zeitung* (July 19, 1896) that the Kaiser had approved of it "without reservation." Stoecker consequently also sued the newspaper's editor for libel. In this trial Stumm was called as a witness. He announced that the Kaiser had authorized him to testify before the court. "Upon my inquiry as to whether the approval of His Majesty included also that part of my speech dealing with Stoecker, His Majesty replied: 'Particularly so!'" Thereupon Stoecker withdrew the suit against the editor. But he won his case against Stumm who was sentenced for libel. The court's decision amounted to a sentence against the Kaiser and cooled the friendship between Wilhelm II and Stumm.
9. Reactions against this solid opposition of the ruling groups to every kind of social critique were not lacking. After Stumm's attack on Adolph Wagner, the faculty and students of the Berlin University honored their

professor by a demonstration in which even old Treitschke participated. Against Stumm's opposition, Wagner was in 1895 elected *Rektor* of the Berlin University. Two years later the same thing happened: Stumm's diatribe in the Prussian upper chamber against *Katheder*-socialism in general and Professor Schmoller in particular assured Schmoller the annual rectorship of the Berlin University.

10. *Preussische Jahrbücher,* vol. 82 (1895), p. 183.
11. Fürst Chlodwig zu Hohenlohe-Schillingsfürst: *Denkwürdigkeiten der Reichskanzlerzeit,* ed. by Karl Alexander von Müller (Stuttgart–Berlin, 1931), p. 63.
12. *Briefe Wilhelms II. an den Zaren,* ed. by Walter Goetz (Berlin, 1920), p. 8.
13. The 1898 elections, however, failed to reestablish a *Kartell* majority in the Reichstag. The Catholic Center Party and the Social Democrats, with 102 and 56 seats respectively, returned in greater strength. Together with the oppositional groups of the Poles, Alsatians, and Hanoverian Welfs, the Catholics and Social Democrats could in the new Reichstag frustrate all undesired legislation. It was essential to the government to prevent Catholic-Socialist cooperation.
14. In colloquial German, "white collar worker" is *Stehkragen-Prolet* (starched-collar proletarian). It was the favorite epithet with which organized industrial labor ridiculed the aloofness of the salaried employees from the socialist movement. Much more obvious symbols of social differentiation were the hat and the cap.
15. See the outstanding study of Hans Speier: *The Salaried Employee in German Society* (New York, 1939, mimeographed).
16. The German National Federation of Salaried Commercial Employees, the Pan-German League, and the Agrarian League were organized in the same year. They were part of the opposition against the policies of Caprivi and Wilhelm II. The stunning Social Democratic victory at the polls had given a strong lift to the oppositional movement which was guided by the retired Bismarck. The Hamburg group of employees set itself up in conscious opposition to the Social Democrats who had begun to agitate among the salaried employees. (Cf. Zimmerman, Albert: *Der Deutschnationale Handlungsgehilfen Verband* (Hamburg, 1921), p. 8.
17. Anti-Semitic nationalism suspected the national loyalty of the Jewish group on account of Jewish relations with the West. Before the Russian October revolution, German anti-Semitism rarely accused Jews of treacherous relations with the East.
18. Lambach, Walther: *Was wir sind; von Wesen und Art des Deutschnationalen Handlungsgehilfenbandes* (Hamburg, 1926), p. 5.
19. Schack joined Liebermann von Sonnenberg's Reichstag group of German Social Anti-Semites. Soon afterwards his career was ended by a criminal investigation and a jail sentence for moral turpitude.
20. Cf. Lederer, Emil, and Marschak, Jakob: *Der Neue Mittelstand. Grundriss*

der Sozialökonomik, 9. Abtg., 1 Teil (Tübingen, 1926. Transl. by E. Ellison, New York, 1937), p. 14.

21. In 1897, four years after the German National Federation, the Central Federation of Commercial Employees (*Centralverband der Handlungsgehilfen*) was founded by the Jewish bookkeeper Max Josephson. The Central Federation affiliated itself with the Social Democratic trade union movement. Most of its officers and members were Social Democrats. By 1911 it had organized about 15,000 commercial employees as compared to the German National Federation's 111,000. The sociologist Emil Lederer (*Die Wirtschaftlichen Organisationen,* Leipzig-Berlin, 1913, p. 62) summarized the essential differences between the two organizations as follows:

> While the German National Federation of Salaried Commercial Employees has particularly paid attention to, and considered exclusively effective, the *mittelständische* element which is undoubtedly present in the employees' situation, the Central Federation has stressed the proletarian element (coming from the occupation's lack of independence). This is the reason why the Central Federation is small. It is [the result] not of its radical language but of those ideological elements which interpret the employees' class situation as one-sidedly proletarian.

22. Buch, Willi: *Op. cit.,* p. 26.
23. Giese, W.: *Die Herren Raab und v. Liebermann in der deutschsozialen Reformpartei* (Berlin, 1901), pp. 108 ff. Cf. Lange, Paul: "Der neue Mittelstand," *Neue Zeit,* (1907), vol. XXV, 2, pp. 360–361.
24. Rosenberg, Arthur: "Treitschke und die Juden. Zur Soziologie der deutschen akademischen Reaktion," *Die Gesellschaft* (Berlin, 1930), vol. II, pp. 78 ff.
25. Kehr, Eckart: "Zur Genesis des königl.-preussischen Reserve Offiziers," *Die Gesellschaft* (Berlin, 1928), vol. II p. 495.
26. Cf. Ziekursch, Johannes: *Das Zeitalter Wilhelms II, loc. cit.,* p. 11. Ziekursch comments that "a man who held such an opinion and wondered why German youths thought only of civil service careers to satisfy their ambition for leading positions in the state must have been devoid of the least vestige of a political instinct."
27. On the political transformation of the Prussian civil service see Puttkamer, Albert von: (ed.) *Staatsminister von Puttkamer. Ein Stück Preussischer Vergangenheit 1828–1890* (Leipzig, 1929), pp. 80 ff.
28. In his famous speech on "Science as a Vocation," Max Weber warned the German students of the hazards which a teaching career entailed. "When a young scholar comes to seek advice about habilitation, the responsibility which one takes in advising him is heavy indeed. If he is a Jew, one naturally tells him: *lasciate ogni speranza.*" (*Wissenschaft als Beruf,* München, 1919. Reprinted in Weber, Max: *Gesammelte Aufsätze zur Wissenschaftslehre,* Tübingen, 1922, pp. 524 ff.).
29. Cf. Werner, Lothar: *Der Alldeutsche Verband 1890–1918* (Historische Studien, Berlin, 1935, Heft 278), pp. 64–65.

30. Alfred Hugenberg in his address for Carl Peters. Cf. Bonhard, Otto: *Geschichte des Alldeutschen Verbandes* (Leipzig and Berlin, 1920), p. 244.

31. *Alldeutsche Blätter* (Berlin) 1894, no. 1.

32. *Handbuch des Alldeutschen Verbandes für 1918* (Mainz), 22nd ed., p. 5.

33. Hasse, Ernst: *Deutsche Weltpolitik* (München, 1897), vol. 1, Heft 4, p. 46.

34. Kuhlenbeck, Ludwig: *Rasse und Volkstum* (München, 1905), p. 24.

35. *Alldeutsche Blätter,* 1908, no. 38.

36. Class, Heinrich: *Wider den Strom, Vom Werden und Wachsen der nationalen Opposition im alten Reich* (Leipzig, 1932), p. 130.

37. Class attributed his anti-Semitism to the influence of his teacher Heinrich von Treitschke. "His phrase, 'the Jews are our misfortune,' became a part of my body and soul when I was twenty years old; it essentially influenced my later political work." (*Ibid.,* p. 16.)

38. *Ibid.,* p. 17.

39. *Ibid.,* pp. 88–89.

40. Under the pseudonym of Daniel Frymann, Class published in 1912 a book, *If I Were the Kaiser,* of which five editions appeared until World War I. In it Class expounded his anti-Semitic program which was based on the racial theory. He called the Zionists as his star witnesses: "Those who regard the Jews as belonging to a foreign race which, despite its participation in all the products of our culture, did not become German because it cannot become German on account of its basic differences, must rejoice over the fact that among the Jews, themselves, the national movement, called Zionism, is gaining more and more adherents. One must take off one's hat to the Zionists; they admit openly and honestly that their people are a people of its own kind whose basic characteristics are immutable and could not be destroyed by living almost two thousand years without a state of their own and among foreigners; they also declare openly that a true assimilation of the Jewish foreigners to the host nations would be impossible according to the natural law of the race which is stronger than superficial conformity to the circumstances of foreign surroundings. The Zionists confirm what the enemies of the Jews, the adherents of the racial theory, have always asserted; and though they may be only a small group in relation to their entire people—the truth they preach cannot be denied. Germans and Jewish nationalists are of one opinion in regard to the indestructibility of the Jewish race—who then wants to deny the Germans their right to draw the necessary political conclusions?" (Frymann, Daniel: *Wenn ich der Kaiser wär',* Leipzig, 1914, 5th ed., p. 78.) The necessary conclusions are drawn in Class' program for a solution of the Jewish question. He puts forth the following demands (*Ibid.,* p. 76):

Jews are to be barred from all public offices.
They are not to be admitted to military service in army and navy.
They are not to have either active or passive franchise rights.

The professions of lawyers and teachers are to be closed to them. So is the management of theaters.

Newspapers which employ Jews must declare this fact.

Other newspapers which may generally be called "German" can neither be owned nor written by Jews.

Banks which are not purely personal enterprises are not to have Jewish directors.

Rural property may, in the future, neither be owned nor mortgaged by Jews.

As a compensation for the protection which Jews as aliens enjoy, they are to pay twice as much in taxes as the Germans.

Together with this program, Class proposed a reform of the constitution. The general franchise in the Reich should be replaced by a class-franchise similar to the Prussian three-class franchise, based on the amount of taxes paid by the citizen, but improved in so far as the educated should be favored. Property and *Kultur* should be combined to define a new élite.

Class knew very well that these and similar "reforms" could only be achieved in the course of a major political upheaval. War was the great chance. If Germany was victorious, the execution of his plans would be facilitated and if the war was lost, the prospects appeared equally good. Internal dissension and chaos would bring about a call for a dictator. From as early as 1914 he was engaged, in his own words, "in awaiting the Führer."

After World War I, a new edition of his book appeared. His reform plans, he conceded, had been insufficient. But he placed his hopes on a dictator who, "blessed with the greatest force of soul and mind," would arise to lead the German people. "He will enforce the reform of the Reich and he will build the *völkisch*-German state headed by a new Kaiser." (Cf. Jung, Dietrich: *Der Alldeutsche Verband*, Inaugural Dissertation, Würzburg, 1936, p. 18.)

The new Kaiser was Adolf Hitler. The Pan-German League was one of the few organizations that was not dissolved when the Nazis came to power. Justizrat Class and Geheimrat Alfred Hugenberg, whom Class calls the father of the Pan-German League, were appointed by Hitler to honorary membership in the German Reichstag.

41. George N. Shuster and Arnold Bergstraesser (*Germany, A Short History*, New York, 1944), call the Pan-Germans "narrow-minded and chauvinistic political amateurs" and believe that the League "remained for decades without much influence on political action" (p. 108).

Mildred S. Wertheimer in her fine study *The Pan-German League 1890–1914* (New York, 1924) comes to the conclusion that "the Kaiser had no connection with the League, and except as a symbol of the monarchic principle, in which it firmly believed, the League had no regard for the Kaiser. Nor did the League have any connection with the German government. No documentary proof has come to light that the government ever made use of the League, except as it used any political agency which supported its policies. . . . There was no such thing as a great 'Pan-German plot'" (pp. 215–216).

Hans Delbrück wrote in 1911: "The Pan-Germans are, it is true, a very active but completely powerless sect" (*Preussische Jahrbücher*, 1911, p. 338). He changed his opinion two years later and at that time considered the League a greater menace to the future of the German Reich than the Social Democrats or the Catholic Center.

Franz Neumann (*Behemoth, The Structure and Practice of National Socialism*, 2nd ed., New York, 1944) stresses the League's "extraordinary propaganda apparatus" and invests the Pan-Germans generally with great political importance. They were in his opinion the propagandists of big industrial interests, "whatever may have been the motives of the other members of the League." This point of view neglects the *mittelständische* composition of the League and the great number of intellectuals among its members, facts which Neumann is inclined to regard as "not very revealing" (pp. 206–207).

Some German and foreign observers attributed a power to the League which it clearly did not possess. Thus the French writer Paul Vergnet: "It is, in fact, easily proved that the Pan-Germans, apart from some exaggerations in their speeches and demands, received, in the last analysis, everything they asked for from the people, the Reichstag and the imperial government." (Quoted from *Alldeutsche Blätter*, April 12, 1913, p. 114.)

During the first World War the German Socialist Kurt Eisner wrote that for a quarter of a century the Pan-Germans exerted a decisive influence on the course of German foreign policy. "They have in the course of time achieved more than all the political parties and all the parliamentary groups of Germany taken together." (*Treibende Kräfte*, Berlin, 1915.)

The Democratic Reichstag member Conrad Hausmann (*Geheimbericht no. 7*, of February 1917, *Die Innenpolitik Deutschlands als Instrument der Aussenpolitik Frankreichs*) goes even further: "The history of the diplomacy of the last years before the war is, as far as Germany is concerned, nothing else but a permanent capitulation of the leaders in foreign affairs to the demands of the Pan-Germans."

The soundest evaluation of the League seems to be Eckhart Kehr's, who called the League "a sort of political-ideological holding company which furnished 'spiritual' weapons for the other propaganda outfits—the Colonial Society, the Naval Society, and later, the Association for Defense (*Wehrverein*)." (Kehr, Eckhart: "Grundlagen der Tirpitzschen Flottenpropaganda," *Die Gesellschaft*, vol. II, 1928, p. 225.)

42. Werner, Lothar: *Op. cit.*, p. 71.
43. Bachem, Karl: *Op. cit.*, vol. VI, p. 181.
44. See, for instance, Hohenlohe's diaries of March 2, 1898: "All kinds of rumors and intrigues are current again. Holstein and Marschall [both in the Foreign Office] accuse [Prussian Minister] Köller of trying to play the lead-

ing role in the Cabinet, while Köller complains that Marschall carries on a hostile campaign against him in the *National-* and *Kölnische Zeitung*. Köller says that he asked the gentlemen of the National Liberal Party, among them Marquardsen, why they worked against him and the latter answered that the initiative did not come from the editors but from higher circles. Marschall, in Köller's opinion, works against him through Levysohn of the *[Berliner] Tageblatt*. I told this to Marschall who wants to have it out with Köller and [Prussian Minister] Miquel, too. The latter has put Köller on Marschall's trail. Marschall says that Miquel has always done this kind of thing and used the press to work against Caprivi." (*Denkwürdigkeiten der Reichskanzlerzeit, loc. cit.*, p. 49.)

45. These thoughts were systematically developed in Naumann's book *Demokratie und Kaisertum* (1900).

46. Naumann's best-known book, *Mitteleuropa*, was published during World War I (1915). It envisaged an economic empire, dominated by Germany, that would include the whole of Central Europe and secure the material resources for Germany's expanding industry.

47. Quoted from Gothein, Georg: *Warum Verloren Wir den Krieg?* (Stuttgart and Berlin, 1920) p. 41.

48. Pascal, Roy: *The Growth of Modern Germany* (London, 1946), p. 75.

49. From the Franco-German war of 1870 to the First World War, Imperial Germany enjoyed four decades of peace. With regard to anti-Semitism this period may be divided into two parts of almost equal length. Political anti-Semitism was rampant from 1875 to 1895. After the mid–nineties it lost its momentum and vehemence.

The spans of growth and decline of German political anti-Semitism coincide with periods of economic depression and recovery. The period 1873 through 1894 was one of stagnation, including fifteen years of economic depression and only six years of recovery. During the years 1895–1913, German capitalism experienced, but for two short recesses in 1901–02 and 1908–09, continuous advance in business activity, accumulation of wealth, high employment, and enormous technological progress. In contrast to the preceding two decades, this was a period of great prosperity. The same coincidence of "high-low" occurred in the Weimar Republic. The years of greatest economic disintegration, 1919–23 and 1930–32, were years of flourishing political anti-Semitism. In the period of recovery, 1924–28, the anti-Semitic wave receded.

This concurrence of economic depression and increase of hostility to Jews in Germany should not hastily be interpreted to mean that the immediate causes of modern German anti-Semitism were economic. In order that resentment and aggression released by economic hardships turn to a specific target, the target must be present in the minds of the embittered. Only because anti-Semitism already had had a place in the political and cultural life of the nation, was it bound to be intensified with every intensification of socio-economic conflicts. Only in this restricted sense is the concurrence of economic depression and rising anti-Semitism meaningful.

CHAPTER X

1. For a detailed history of labor's political separation from liberalism see Mayer, Gustav: *Die Trennung der proletarischen von der bürgerlichen Demokratie in Deutschland 1863–1870* (Leipzig, 1911).
2. The Socialists recognized this dilemma of the German middle classes. Few of them, however, saw as clearly as the Russian anarchist Bakunin the portent the liberal compromise with Bismarck held for the future of Germany and Europe. At the threshold of Germany's national unification, Bakunin wrote:

> Like doctor Faustus, these excellent [liberal] patriots pursued two goals, two contradictory tendencies: a mighty national unity and liberty. As they wanted to reconcile two irreconcilable elements, for a long time they hampered the realization of one by insisting on the other until finally, warned by experience, they decided to give up one in order to achieve the other. And thus they are now about to erect their great Prusso-Germanic Empire, not upon the rubble of freedom —they never were free—but upon the ruins of their liberal dreams. By their own will they will build from now on a terrible state and a nation of slaves. (Michael Bakunin: *Gesammelte Werke*, Berlin, 1921, 2 vols., vol. I., pp. 69–70.)

   Bakunin has often been called a fanatical hater of everything German. Such a judgment needs qualification. His passionate outbursts against the "Knouto-Germanic" regime were directed against the ruthless ambition of Prussian-German nationalism and against the servility of the German middle classes. He saw no signs of a truly anti-authoritarian spark in the German bourgeoisie. On the contrary, it was in his opinion the willing tool of nationalism and imperialism. "Scarcely five years have passed," he wrote shortly before Bismarck united Germany, "since Prussia was looked upon as the last among the five big powers of Europe. Today she wants to become the first and she undoubtedly will become the first. And woe, then, to the independence and freedom of Europe! Particularly woe to the small states which have the misfortune to possess Germanic or formerly Germanic people, as for instance the Flemish. The appetite of the German bourgeois is as big as his submissiveness is monstrous, and relying upon this patriotic appetite and this wholesale German servility Herr von Bismarck . . . might very well be tempted to undertake for his master the realization of the dreams of Charles V." (*Ibid.*, pp. 56–57.)
3. Mehring, Franz: *Geschichte der deutschen Sozialdemokratie*, 4 vols., 11th ed. (Stuttgart-Berlin, 1921), vol. III, p. 30.

4. The literature on Lassalle's extraordinary life is large; outstanding is the biography of the historian Hermann Oncken: *Lassalle, eine politische Biographie* 1st ed. (Stuttgart, 1904).

5. Lassalle, Ferdinand: *Offenes Antwortschreiben an das Central-Comité zur Berufung eines Allgemeinen Deutschen Arbeitercongresses zu Leipzig* (Zürich, 1863).

6. As early as 1847, Marx and Engels had advised the revolutionary workers as to the position they should take in the fight between the liberal middle classes and the bureaucratic government. "[The proletariat] asks whether the present . . . rule of bureaucracy, or the rule of the bourgeoisie which the liberals are seeking, will furnish it with more opportunities to realize its own aims. One only has to compare the political position of the proletariat in England, France and America with that in Germany in order to see that the rule of the bourgeoisie not only gives to the proletariat entirely new possibilities for fighting the bourgeoisie but also an entirely new position, the position of a recognized party." (*Deutsche Brüsseler Zeitung*, no. 73, September 12, 1847.)

To this statement Marx and Engels referred in 1865 when they refused any cooperation with the *Socialdemokrat,* the Lassalleans' paper, in which Lassalle's successor, Schweitzer, had just published a series of articles glorifying Prussianism and its skillful servant Bismarck. They had expected, they wrote, that the *Socialdemokrat* "would use at least as bold a language in the criticism of the cabinet and the feudal-absolutistic party [of the Conservatives] as of the liberals." (Quoted from Bebel, August: *Aus meinem Leben,* 3 vols., Stuttgart, 1919, vol. II, p. 21.)

7. The controversy over Lassalle's negotiations with Bismarck kept German labor in a high state of excitement for decades. Marx and Engels saw in the relations between the two men proof of Lassalle's treason. "Slowly but surely, our brave Lassalle discloses himself as a downright scoundrel (*ganz kommuner Schuft*) . . . Subjectively, his vanity might have made the affair plausible to him; objectively it was a dastardly trick, a sellout of the whole labor movement to the Prussians," wrote Engels in 1865, after Lassalle's death. (Letter to Marx, January 27, 1865. *Briefwechsel zwischen Marx und Engels, Gesamt-ausgabe,* III, 3, Berlin, 1930, p. 219.)

Only in 1928 were Lassalle's letters to Bismarck published. (Mayer, Gustav: *Bismarck und Lassalle, ihr Briefwechsel und ihre Gespräche,* Berlin.) They proved that Lassalle indeed had envisaged the possibility of a pact between the monarchy and the workers.

8. "Das neueste Zerwürfnis des Liberalismus über die soziale Frage," *Historisch-Politische Blätter für das katholische Deutschland* (1863), 2nd vol., pp. 56 ff.

9. Schweitzer, J. B. von.: *Lucinde oder Kapital und Arbeit. Ein sozial-politisches Zeitgemälde aus der Gegenwart,* 3 vols. (Frankfurt a.M., 1863).

10. Mayer, Gustav: *Johann Baptist von Schweitzer und die Sozialdemokratie* (Jena, 1909), p. 89. In Mayer's opinion Schweitzer caricatured the Jews

"only in the style of the *Fliegende Blätter*," a popular weekly, "not in the grim anti-Semitic way later for a while made fashionable in the Lassallean party by Hasselmann," editor of the Lassallean paper, *Socialdemokrat*, and admirer of Bismarck.

In 1880 Hasselmann was expelled from the Social Democratic Party. He shared with Johann Most, who was expelled at the same time, a violent hatred of the middle class and a disdain for intellectuals who as theoreticians, editors, writers, and speakers exerted a strong influence on the young labor movement. Particularly noticeable was the resentment which the overpowering intellect and knowledge of Marx evoked, not only in self-taught men like Hasselmann and Most. This antipathy against intellectuals was unmistakably associated with anti-Semitism. It seems as if the adherents of "direct action," of a philosophy of power, viewed Jews in the labor movement as influences making for caution, negotiation, *Verbürgerlichung*, and betrayal. The anarchists, Michael Bakunin and Eugen Dühring, were passionate haters of Jews.

The opponents of socialist labor frequently aired their anger about the prominent part intellectuals had in the leadership of the Social Democratic Party. Such attacks usually had an anti-Jewish slant. Stoecker, for instance, attacked the Social Democrats for sailing under the colors of a workers' party while really being led by "journalists and Jews," and called upon a supporting witness who shared his contempt for the liberal bourgeoisie. In a Reichstag debate, turning to the Social Democratic deputies, he exclaimed: "I challenge your claim to be representatives of the workers. . . . You always act as though all it takes to be a spokesman of labor is to put the label 'friend of labor' on one's back. . . . I've looked up the Reichstag register and taken notice of your occupation. Well, what are you really? Four of you are genuine workers, eight are journalists, six are employers. You [claim to be the] spokesmen of labor? Lassalle once said: 'There are two things I hate, journalists and Jews. Unfortunately, I am both.' This has remained so with you. Whether you are today still saying 'unfortunately' I do not know. But a party which has 'institutionalized' such a state of affairs—to use a fashionable term—such a party is certainly not a labor party." (Quoted from Oertzen: *Op. cit.*, p. 251.)

11. The Marxist organization, the *Sozialdemokratische Arbeiterpartei*, was founded in 1869, at a congress in the Thuringian city of Eisenach. Until the Lassallean "General Workingmen's Association" and the Marxist "Social Democratic Workers' Party" were fused at Gotha (1875), the Marxists were commonly referred to as the *Eisenachers*.

12. Leopold Sonnemann, a prominent South German democrat, founder and later owner of the *Frankfurter Zeitung*, was anxious to prevent the separation of the workers' associations from the liberal movement. Until 1869, when the Marxists founded their own party, he was a leading figure in these associations and on friendly terms with Marxist leaders, particularly August Bebel. After the congress of Eisenach which Sonnemann still at-

· tended as a delegate, he parted company with the *Eisenachers*. "The class character of the party repelled him," Bebel states. (Bebel, August: *Aus meinem Leben, loc. cit.*, vol. II, p. 91.)

To the Lassalleans, however, Sonnemann was an arch-representative of moneyed liberalism. In contrast to Bebel's friendly appraisal of Sonnemann's work, Frank Mehring, who never missed an opportunity to come to the defense of Lassalleanism, had only scorn for his role in the workers' associations. (See, for instance, Mehring: *Geschichte, loc. cit.*, vol. III, pp. 14, 70, etc.) In his appraisal of Schweitzer's novel *Lucinde* Mehring writes that "a few types, drawn from life, are very well done, like the liberal banker Itzinger for whom Sonnemann stood as model. . . ." (Mehring: *Op. cit.*, vol. III, p. 86.)

13. Mayer, Gustav: *Schweitzer, loc. cit.*, p. 31.
14. Meyer, Rudolph: *Der Emancipationskampf des Vierten Standes, loc. cit.*, vol. I, p. 217.
15. Marx's *Zur Judenfrage* grew out of a review of his friend Bruno Bauer's pamphlet, *Die Judenfrage* (Braunschweig, 1843).

    At the same time, the Christian and Jewish religions had been attacked by another leading philosopher of the young-Hegelian school, Ludwig Feuerbach. Feuerbach saw in the Jewish religion the religion of egoism which was indifferent to anything but the individual's personal gain and therefore fundamentally irreligious. Every emancipation of the Jews was in his opinion condemned to be superficial and futile as long as the Jews themselves were not free of a belief that set the individual against society and prevented his identification with the general good.
16. Translated from the German.
17. *Aus dem literarischen Nachlass von Karl Marx, Friedrich Engels und Ferdinand Lassalle*, ed. by Franz Mehring (Stuttgart, 1902).
18. Franz Mehring: "Kapitalistische Agonie," *Neue Zeit* (1891–1892), vol. X, no. 2, p. 548.
19. One could speculate whether this did not, in Marx's mind, constitute a specific responsibility of the Jews.
20. It is noteworthy that Marx, after having settled his account with the Jewish question at the age of 23, never came back to it. In his personal writings to intimate friends, biting anti-Jewish remarks may be found, especially in his letter to Engels concerning Lassalle. He liked to air his irritation over political and theoretical disagreements with Lassalle in invectives often used by Gentiles and Western Jews to express their displeasure with alleged or real cultural characteristics of Eastern European Jews.

    Those who are interested in Marx's personal relations to Jewry will find an excellently documented and balanced study in Solomon F. Bloom's "Karl Marx and the Jews," *Jewish Social Studies*, vol. IV, no. i, pp. 3–16.

    Of German Social Democratic writers, Franz Mehring did most to bring *Zur Judenfrage* to the attention of the Socialists. (Franz Mehring: *Karl Marx, Geschichte seines Lebens.* 4th ed., Leipzig, 1923, pp. 71–78;

Geschichte der Deutschen Sozialdemokratie, vol. I, pp. 169–177; and his introduction to the reprint of *Zur Judenfrage* in the *Nachlass-Ausgabe*.)

Wilhelm Liebknecht's attempt to attribute the bitterness of Marx's essay to an early childhood experience is not convincing. Writes Liebknecht: "Shortly after the birth of the boy an edict was issued leaving all the Jews no other choice but to be baptized or to forego all official positions and activity. The father of Karl Marx, a prominent Jewish lawyer and notary public at the county court, submitted to the inevitable and with his family adopted the Christian faith. Twenty years later, when the boy had grown to be a man, he gave the first reply to this act of violence in his pamphlet on the Hebrew question and his whole life was a reply and was the revenge." (Liebknecht, Wilhelm: *Karl Marx, Biographical Memoirs*, Chicago, 1906, pp. 13–14.)

Bloom points out that long before the father's conversion "the household had ceased to be significantly Jewish" (*op. cit.*, p. 5). On the other hand, Bloom is inclined to see in Marx's often displayed contempt for the middleman "a diminished echo of the not-too-distant age when commerce was socially disreputable and even disgraceful." He cautiously suggests that Marx may on such occasions have spoken "in a measure for the old agrarian, Christian and aristocratic society" (*ibid*, p. 16).

The young Marx was certainly influenced by the romanticists. But can one really believe that the author of *The German Ideology* was partial to the values of agrarian, Christian, aristocratic society? The term *Schacher* is often loosely used in Marx's and Engels' writings to characterize the essence of capitalist society, not only the function of commercial capital and of the middleman. Their attack upon the new forms of production and distribution did not stem from a predilection for the old ones. The ideologists of the liberal order claimed that it would free man forever. Marx and Engels made this claim the object of their critique.

21. Address and Provisional Rules of the Working Men's International Association, in *Karl Marx, Selected Works*, ed. by V. Adoratsky, 2 vols. (London, 1942), vol. II, p. 443.

22. August Bebel, in his report on "The Social Democratic Party and Anti-Semitism," at the Cologne party convention of 1893. *Protokoll über die Verhandlungen des Parteitages der Sozialdemokratischen Partei Deutschlands, Köln, 22–28. Oktober 1893* (Berlin, 1893), p. 224.

23. Kautsky, Karl: "Das Massaker von Kischineff und die Judenfrage," *Neue Zeit*, vol. XXI, no. 2, p. 307.

24. Bernstein, Eduard: "Das Schlagwort und der Antisemitismus," *Neue Zeit*, vol. XI, no. 2, p. 234.

25. Actually a large part of officialdom is poorly paid and in order to keep up a prescribed standard of living (*standesgemässes Auftreten*) an official may be forced to go into debt. Since he cannot give adequate security to the legitimate loan institutions, he borrows from the loan sharks who more often than not are Jews. It is easily seen how anti-Semitism takes root in a debt-ridden officialdom. . . .

Another contributing factor is the fear that borrowing from loan sharks may be the beginning of the end for the *Junker* estate. His Jewish creditor may finally take it over, lock, stock and barrel.

(Bebel, August: *Protokoll* etc., *loc. cit.*, pp. 236 ff.)

26. The decaying artisan fights against big industry and jobbers; the little retailer against the department stores; the deeply indebted farmer against the loan shark and trader, especially the cattle and grain dealer. By the decay of these economic groups their sons are driven into a profession instead of entering their fathers' businesses, with the result that the professions get more and more swamped. All these groups attack the Jews who appear to them as the real exponents of money and commercial capitalism and who, furthermore, are represented among the professions by numerous and efficient individuals. What better way could these groups figure out to make an end to their distress than to eliminate the Jews?

(Kautsky, Karl: *Neue Zeit*, vol. XXI, no. 2, p. 304.)

Similarly, Heinrich Cunow in a review of Otto Freiherr v. Boenigk's *Grundzüge zur Judenfrage* (*Neue Zeit*, vol. XIII, no. 1, p. 824):

The anti-Semitic movement is not a racial but an economic movement, accentuated by ethnic and religious divergencies. It is a reaction of certain lower middle-class groups, threatened in their existence, against modern big business and its money economy. As it is often headed by Jews, they regard them as the essential representatives of the oppressive conditions. One must add to these groups part of the peasantry, indebted to Jewish usurers, as for instance in Hesse, and part of the salaried employees in the big cities who complain about bad pay and long hours in Jewish department stores. . . .

Franz Mehring thought it "quite natural and in a way even unavoidable that the peasant gains the first understanding of social interdependence through the person of the Jewish usurer, who as the executor of capitalism, drives him from home and land." (*Neue Zeit*, vol. XI, no. i, p. 363.)

Bebel saw a cause-and-effect relation between the first anti-Semitic wave after the collapse of the speculation boom in the 1870's, and the prominence of Jewish speculators:

Now, it is indisputable that the Jews have taken an important position in the foreground of our economic development after they received full emancipation and our new social and economic legislation . . . opened new and surprisingly successful avenues for capitalistic activities. Since among the Jews were quite a few big capitalists (bankers or directors of banks), they could be seen everywhere in the foreground of many new business ventures which sprang into being during 1871 to 1874 and which often were of a highly dubious quality. They controlled and still control many commercial enterprises in the most different fields.

(Bebel, August: *Sozialdemokratie und Antisemitismus*. Rede auf dem sozialdemokratischen Parteitage in Köln, Berlin 1906, pp. 12 ff.

This is a revised and supplemented version of Bebel's speech at the party convention of 1893.)

27. Kautsky, Karl: "Das Judentum," *Neue Zeit,* vol. VIII, pp. 27–28. The idea is further developed in Kautsky's book *Judentum und Rasse,* 2nd ed. (Stuttgart, 1921), translated into English under the title *Are the Jews a Race?* (New York, 1926). The American author Lewis Browne has used the same concept in his novelistic treatment of anti-Semitism.

28. "Anti-Semitism is by nature reactionary because it wants to abolish general civil equality before the law by depriving Jewish citizens of this equality, although Jews do nothing else but what civic law and civil institutions enable and permit them to do." (*Die Sozialdemokratie im Deutschen Reichstag. Tätigkeitsberichte und Wahlaufrufe aus den Jahren 1871–1893.* Berlin, 1909, pp. 515 ff.)

Occasionally, however, socialist writers, too, would refer to unfair Jewish business practices, trickery, and cunning as irritants for which there was no longer any excuse. They diagnosed such lack of business ethics as a survival of habits commonly found in precapitalist modes of exchange and, in the case of the Jews, favored by the oppressed conditions of their existence. But such anachronistic vestiges were unsuited to the technical and psychological requirements of modern business, and, therefore, bound gradually to disappear. Bernstein, for instance, found it unconvincing to argue that shortcomings attributed to Jews could also be found among non-Jews. ". . . it does not refute the fact that certain unpleasant characteristics may indeed be encountered more often in Jews than non-Jews, although not to the extent the anti-Semites claim this to be true." (Bernstein, Eduard: "Das Schlagwort und der Antisemitismus," *Neue Zeit,* vol. XI, no. 2, p. 236.)

29. Kautsky pointed out that Russia, unlike Western Europe, did not have an "overproduction of intelligentsia but an underproduction." This might be the reason why "in Russia a woman student in a university is not met with hostility by the masters of the intelligentsia as a competitor but welcomed as a friend and comrade. In Western Europe, the same groups of the intelligentsia which are most anti-Semitic, are also the most narrow-minded opponents of higher education for women." (Kautsky, Karl: "Das Massaker von Kischineff und die Judenfrage," *Neue Zeit,* vol. XXI, no. 2, pp. 305 ff.)

30. In tracing the history of this opinion, one finds a good many Russian Jewish Socialists as its active propagandists.

31. There was, however, at least from the nineties on, no socialist consensus of opinion as to what bearing such assimilation would have on anti-Semitism. The idea that in the further course of capitalist development the class struggle would supersede the struggle against the Jewish group was not shared by a group within the Social Democratic Party which began to question the tenets of orthodox Marxism. The "revisionists," led by Eduard Bernstein, were inclined to doubt that the Jewish group could hope to placate

its enemies by dissolving into the various economic classes of capitalism. On the contrary, Bernstein foresaw a further deterioration in Jewish-Christian relations, due to the narrowing opportunities for the occupational groups into which Jews were forced to move. Capitalist society could no longer be expected to provide a solution. "In view of the violent competition which today dominates all spheres of economic life," Bernstein wrote, "the Jews cannot choose any occupation without provoking the anti-Semites. The emancipation of the Jews happened at a time when bourgeois society still believed in its unlimited possibilities. It can only be completed in a new society." (Eduard Bernstein in 1894, reviewing C. Lombroso's "Der Antisemitismus und die Juden im Lichte der modernen Wissenschaft," Neue Zeit, vol. XII, no. 2, p. 407.)

32. Kautsky, Karl: "Das Massaker von Kischineff," etc., loc. cit., p. 307.
33. Bebel, August: Protokoll, etc., loc. cit., pp. 236 ff.
34. Kautsky, Karl: "Das Massaker von Kischineff," etc., loc. cit., p. 307.
35. Bahr, Hermann: Der Antisemitismus, loc. cit., pp. 28 ff.
36. Mommsen's answer to Treitschke's Ein Wort über unser Judentum was polemically entitled: Auch ein Wort über unser Judentum (Berlin, 1880).
37. Despite Mommsen's strong feeling about the futility of all appeals to reason, he suggested an international declaration of protest issued by outstanding men of good will.
38. Vorwärts, April 11, 1893.
39. Mehring, Franz: "Kapitalistische Agonie," Neue Zeit, vol. X, no. 2, pp. 545 ff.
40. Bebel, August: Sozialdemokratie und Antisemitismus, 2nd ed. (Berlin, 1906), p. 38.

    A survey of popular Social Democratic periodicals might yield interesting findings on the possibility that the socialist fight against liberal "philo-Semitism" disseminated anti-Jewish stereotypes among workers. Liberal periodicals like Kladderadatsch and Simplicissimus definitely contributed to the dissemination of anti-Semitic caricatures. See Fuchs, Eduard: Die Juden in der Karikatur (Munich, 1921).
41. Reviewing the first election that took place under the conditions of the anti-Socialist bill, the Social Democratic Party stated:

> Only after the bill against the Social Democratic Party had been passed did the scandalous nuisance of the anti-Semites become possible. That it did not grow into a general persecution of the Jews is the merit solely of the Social Democratic Party which warned the workers not to get involved in this shameful movement which had its roots in the meanest motives . . . To sum up: only the era of the Sozialisten-Gesetz produced the excesses of the Stoecker clique.

(Die Sozialdemokratie im Deutschen Reichstag. Tätigkeitsberichte und Wahlaufrufe aus den Jahren 1871–1893. Berlin, 1909, p. 209.)

CHAPTER XI

1. "The endeavors of Stoecker and Adolph Wagner as well as the furious articles of the 'Staatssozialist' against the 'Roman concepts of property and law' left no doubt that Herr Bismarck's government was not at all concerned with suppressing socialism, the cause of so many headaches for Herr Bamberger, but that it simply intended to deprive the socialist labor movement of its democratic character and to make use of it to intimidate the liberal bourgeoisie." (Auer, Ignaz: *Nach Zehn Jahren, loc. cit.,* pp. 80–81.)

2. In his memoirs August Bebel (*Aus meinem Leben, loc. cit.,* vol. II, p. 396) writes about the period:

   "In those days, [Johann] Most, with all the passion of his temperament, had begun to agitate for leaving the church. The public meetings he called were overcrowded and feverishly tense. The excitement grew when the newly founded Christian Social Party, led by the Court Chaplain Stoecker, also started to hold meetings and sent their speakers into Most's meetings where, as was to be foreseen, they came off second best to the delight of the audiences. This agitation created enormous excitement among the nation's pious. . . . Even the old Kaiser . . . thought it necessary to warn that religion must be saved for the people. (*Die Religion muss dem Volke erhalten bleiben.*)"

   See also Bernstein, Eduard: *Geschichte der Berliner Arbeiterbewegung, loc. cit.,* vol. I, pp. 350 ff. Mehring critically views Most's agitation as a windfall for Stoecker and attributes the small number of workers who left the church to their indifference toward religion. (Mehring, Franz: *Geschichte der deutschen Sozialdemokratie, loc. cit.,* vol. IV, p. 132.)

3. Bernstein, Eduard: *Geschichte der Berliner Arbeiterbewegung, loc. cit.,* vol. II, p. 60.

4. Bernstein reports (*ibid.,* vol. II, pp. 164 ff.):

   "[In government circles] the hope was nourished that a conflict might yet develop between the workers' trade union movement and the Social Democratic leadership. Every incident was welcomed that seemed promising in this respect. But each time the pleasure proved short-lived. . . . Whenever a union leader gave an indication that he was tempted to cooperate politically with those anti-Semitic procurers (*Zutreiber*) of the government who called themselves Christian Social, he was called to order by the rank and file and had no other choice but to retract or lose all influence. This is what happened in 1884 to the leader of the carpenters' organization, Gustav Rödel. Unquestionably gifted and a popular speaker, it seemed for a moment that he might win the fight against the combined union leaders. But once he started to use the anti-Semites' terminology and went into cahoots with the [anti-Semitic] '*Staatsbürgerzeitung*,' he was a dead man."

5. *Norddeutsche Allgemeine Zeitung*, November 12, 1881.

6. *Volkszeitung* (Berlin), November 19, 1881.

7. The *Jahrbuch für Sozialwissenschaft* (Zürich, 1879), financed and edited by the wealthy Jewish Socialist Karl Höchberg, succeeded the bi-monthly, *Die Zukunft*, which the government had suppressed in 1878. *Die Zukunft* (not to be confused with Maximilian Harden's later publication) had been the first scientific journal of Social Democracy. During the thirteen months of its existence (October, 1877–November, 1878) the bi-monthly had tried to further the cause of socialism by appealing to all men of good will not to stand in the way of reason and justice. It had been under constant attack by the Marxists.

The passages of the *Jahrbuch* referred to appeared in a summary on "the socialist movement in Germany" and read (quoted from Kautsky, Karl: Introduction to the *General-Register* of the *Neue Zeit*, Stuttgart, 1905, p. V.):

> Fortunately, it cannot be denied any longer that in Germany, too, socialist ideas are asserting themselves in the circles of the educated and well-to-do. All the students who have read or listened to Dühring, Schäffle, Adolph Wagner, have become infected by the socialist "poison." The appearance of the clergymen Stoecker and Todt, even the attitude of Prince Bismarck toward men of such firm socialist, although not Social Democratic, convictions as Geheimrat Wagener and Lothar Bucher, makes it evident that the new truth is irresistibly capturing German minds.

8. Speech of September 11, 1883. Quoted from Bernstein, Eduard: *Geschichte der Berliner Arbeiterbewegung, loc. cit.*, vol. II, p. 116.

9. *Ibid.*, vol. II, p. 137.

10. Frank, Walter: *Op. cit.*, pp. 79–80.

11. Mehring, Franz: "Knechtseliges," *Neue Zeit*, vol. XIV, no. 2, p. 227.

12. A moderate wing, with strong support within the Social Democratic Reichstag group, had been steadily working for a course of action which would help the party to break "the iron ring" which, while it supported, also isolated the organization. Especially after the Imperial Message of 1881, inaugurating the government's program of social reform, "parliamentarianism," and "Lassalleanism" gained ground in the organization, to the disgust and dismay of the orthodox Marxists who saw the monster of the Lassallean "social kingdom" under Hohenzollern-*Junker* domination raise its head again.

13. "During the whole period of the *Sozialisten-Gesetz* we made sure to prevent any general secret organization, covering all Germany, from being built up. We were convinced that such an organization would be unearthed

very quickly and lead to general persecution of the worst kind." (Bebel, August: *Aus meinem Leben, loc. cit.*, vol. III, p. 137.)

14. Quoted from Mayer, Gustav: *Friedrich Engels,* 2 vols. (Haag, 1934), vol. II, pp. 349 ff.

15. See, for instance, Engels' letter to F. A. Sorge of April 12, 1890: "Since the official friendship for labor goes together with the desire for military dictatorship (you see how all present-day government becomes Bonapartist *nolens volens*) we must see to it that [the government] does not get a chance [to set up a dictatorship]." (Quoted from Mayer, Gustav: *Friedrich Engels,* II, p. 496).

16. In 1879 Engels had sharply criticized the account which the Social Democratic Reichstag group had just rendered to the Social Democratic voters. The report, in Engels' opinion, had made "unpleasant concessions to the German philistine"; had quite unnecessarily bowed to "public opinion which in Germany will always be that of the beer-drinking simpleton"; and had "completely blurred the class character of the movement." (Letter to Bebel, November 14, 1879. Quoted from Bebel, August: *Aus meinem Leben, loc. cit.*, vol. III, pp. 71–72.)

Bebel defended the report; he pointed out that the party, while having no illusions about the nature of "public opinion," nevertheless could not ignore the fact that other groups but workers had cast their vote for it. "We had in mind also the petty bourgeois and peasants who in the last few years have joined us in greater numbers and who in the last elections [the first elections under the anti-Socialist act] have in many a district saved the honor of the party. . . ." (Letter to Engels, November 18, 1879, *ibid.,* p. 77.)

Engels replied:

"That petty bourgeois and peasants are joining the movement is certainly a symptom of the rapid progress it is making but also a danger if one forgets that these people have to join and do so only because they can't help it. Their joining is proof that the proletariat really has become the leading class. But since they bring along the ideas and wishes of petty bourgeois and peasants, it should not be forgotten that the proletariat would throw away its leading historic role were it to make any concessions to such ideas and wishes." (Letter to Bebel, November 24, *ibid.,* p. 81.)

17. Engels had a concrete concept of the revolutionary strategy which the historical situation demanded. In March, 1893, at the time of Caprivi's army reorganization bill, he published a series of articles in the *Vorwärts* entitled: "Kann Europa abrüsten?" Couched in cautious language, the articles contained the outlines of a master plan for the coming revolution. The plan was based on the premise that a new economic crisis was near which would engulf all of Europe; and that, as a result, the precarious peace of Europe would come to an end. In order not to be caught helpless in an unwanted European war, the Social Democrats should endeavor to prevent it or to assure that, if it came about, it would end in the defeat of German semifeudalism. The opportunity to act, in Engels' opinion, was

given by the fight for the reduction of the period of military service, an issue of great concern to millions of Germans. Germany should propose to France that both nations simultaneously shorten the training period of their standing armies. If France agreed, peace was secured. If she refused, Germany would not only fight with world opinion on her side, the war would also put her in a position to rid herself of the Hohenzollern regime and to establish the democratic republic which the revolution of 1848 had failed to bring about.

Engels' reasoning is comprehensible only if we remember certain axioms of his thinking. A national war, he was convinced, would not supersede the class war. On the contrary, the war could be fought as a national one only by a shift of power at home. As early as 1864, during the constitutional conflict, he had criticized the Liberals for their refusal to grant the budget for the reorganization of the army which the government had requested. They should have given more, not less, than what was asked for, he argued, and insisted on the introduction of universal military conscription, which would transform the army from a tool of crown and conservatism into an instrument of the people which could not be used any more for antidemocratic designs. In 1893, this same idea was behind his suggestion to reduce the term of military service. If accepted, it would mean a larger army with a stronger element of antifeudal officers. If not, the preparation for war and the war itself would force German "semi-feudalism" to create a modern military organization, to arm "the people." The necessities of modern warfare would wrest from the old groups the military monopoly, the chief weapon with which they defended their privileges. The economic depression which he predicted for the end of the century would bring the national war but also create the sociopolitical conditions for establishing the democratic republic, which Engels considered a necessary phase of the socialist revolution. Finally, a victorious German democracy should of its own volition return Alsace-Lorraine to France, thus cementing friendly relations between the German and French working classes.

18. *Handbuch der Sozialdemokratischen Parteitage von 1863 bis 1909*, ed. by Wilhelm Schröder (München, 1909), p. 540.

19. The distinctive feature of "revisionism" is its opposition to orthodox Marxism rather than a consistent theory and program of action of its own. The "revisionists" questioned the validity of basic elements in Marx's philosophic and economic system, from the philosophy of dialectic materialism to the theory of class struggle and proletarian revolution. Germany's prosperity after the middle of the nineties favored the growth of "revisionism" which aimed at a policy of adjusting labor's struggle to the new economic conditions. Prosperity would gradually make for class cooperation. Cartels and trusts, the organizations of capital, in cooperation with the trade unions, would be able to bring some order into the chaos of the capitalist market, thereby decreasing international political tensions as well as the chances of business slumps. Future depressions could be softened, if not

entirely prevented. The idea of labor's emancipatory mission was dropped. Instead "revisionism" tended to emphasize labor's stake in the state, in industrial expansion, active colonial policy, and Germany's world power politics.

"Revisionism" attracted followers of various conviction and temperament, pacifists and "social imperialists," democrats and nationalists. Some of its adherents clearly realized the dangers which Social Democracy incurred by a sterile radical phraseology and an unimaginative policy of opposition. It would be wrong, therefore, to look upon "revisionism" only as a force aiming at the liquidation of the revolutionary aspirations of labor. In its attempts to enlarge the class basis of the Social Democratic Party by winning over *Mittelstand* groups, some "revisionists" revealed more political insight into the specific nature of Germany's social conflicts than the radicals. How consistently the latter were deceived as to the real political developments may be seen from their arguments against the "revisionists." Rudolf Hilferding, an outstanding member of the orthodox Marxists, thought in 1912 that "revisionism" within the party had been decisively beaten. Commenting on the eclectic nature of "revisionism" as a theory and program he wrote: "It is doomed before it can even be defined. The events of the last years illustrate how it is falling apart." (*Neue Zeit*, vol. XXX, no. 2, p. 1003.) Less than two years later the Social Democratic Party voted for the imperial government's war credits.

20. The socialist contribution to the sociological and political theory of anti-Semitism was made during the few years when racial anti-Semitism was at its height. The *Neue Zeit*, founded in 1883, did not publish a serious analysis either of the anti-Semitic movement or the situation of the German Jews until 1890, but devoted in the following five years more than thirty articles to these topics.

21. The Austrian Socialist Heinrich Braun, editor of the *Archiv für soziale Gesetzgebung und Statistik*, himself a Jew, was known in the party as an independent mind. He stood on the side of the revisionists against Marxist orthodoxy, leaning even toward the state-socialism of the *"Katheder-*socialists." But he, too, shared the opinion that the anti-Semitic movement was a trail-blazer for Social Democracy. In 1893 he evaluated the anti-Semitic movement as follows ("Zur Lage der deutschen Sozialdemokratie," *Archiv für soziale Gesetzgebung und Statistik,* 1893, pp. 513–514.)

> Its rapid growth is not unlike that of Social Democracy. . . . There can be little doubt that we have to deal in anti-Semitism with a strong social movement and that a radical anticapitalistic tendency of a general nature is ever more clearly and consciously trying to assert itself, along with the attacks upon Jewry. Thereby, however, anti-Semitism is moving toward Social Democracy. Chancellor Caprivi rightly called it the seed of Social Democracy. In this respect anti-Semitism represents social trends which are all the more significant as it succeeds through a brutal and stupid agitation in reaching and shaking out of their lethargy groups of the population

which are not yet mature enough for Social Democratic propaganda. The sociopolitical job which anti-Semitism is doing today in overcoming the century-old idiocy of the peasants; in creating passionate commotion in this most indolent stratum of the population; in propagandizing the small artisans, the petty officialdom, and other groups not easily accessible to the Social Democracy—this job can, in the perspective of a revolutionary development of society, hardly be overestimated. It is very likely that anti-Semitism, by the law of social gravitation, one might say, will be attracted into the greater and more powerful Social Democratic movement.

22. *Protokoll über die Verhandlungen des Parteitages der Sozialdemokratischen Partei, Halle 1890* (Berlin, 1890), p. 48.

23. Bebel was one of the reporters assigned to speak on the topic. When his motion to postpone the discussion "in consideration of the advanced hour and many pending matters" was carried, he expressed his satisfaction but also stated that "in order to meet the wishes of those who want to have a thorough report on the subject matter, Liebknecht and I have decided to take it up in popular meetings which we will call in the nearest future, here in Berlin, and to have our speeches stenographically recorded and printed to get them before the public at large." *Protokoll über die Verhandlungen des Parteitages der Sozialdemokratischen Partei Deutschlands, Berlin, 14.–21. November 1892* (Berlin 1892), pp. 248–9 and 293–4.

24. Engels, Friedrich: "Die Bauernfrage in Frankreich und Deutschland," *Neue Zeit*, vol. XIII, no. 1, pp. 292–306.

   In an aside on the revisionist aberrations of the *Parti Ouvrier*, the French Marxists who in Marseilles (1892) and Nantes (1894) had adopted a reformist agrarian program, Engels commented: "Had the French a noisy anti-Semitic demagogy as we have, they'd have hardly committed the mistake of Nantes." The implication seems clear. Engels interpreted political anti-Semitism in Germany as a symptom indicating that the same group of small property owners whom the French Socialists were trying to win over by promises which they could not honor, was already in full economic and ideological disintegration.

25. *Protokoll über die Verhandlungen des Parteitages der Sozialdemokratischen Partei Deutschlands, Köln, 22.–28. Oktober 1893* (Berlin, 1893), p. 228.

26. *Ibid.*, p. 224. The resolution was formulated and presented by Bebel.

27. *Vorwärts*, November 4, 1893.

28. When *Germania*, the Catholic daily, indignantly took issue with Ahlwardt for an article in which he had lumped together princes, *Junkers*, clerics (*Pfaffen*), and the bourgeoisie, "liberally sprinkled with Hebrews," as the ruling groups whose pretended concern for the masses was "pure hypocrisy and fraud," the *Vorwärts* remarked: "Our readers know what we think of Ahlwardt. But we grant him that he has made progress since his 'Jewish Rifles' affair." (*Vorwärts*, July 4, 1894.)

29. Quoted from *Vorwärts*, December 22, 1894. The *Vorwärts* report notes

that the audience greeted with "enthusiastic bravos" Ahlwardt's demands for unlimited credit for [non-Jewish] trade and handicraft, and for the appointment for life of civil servants, but that the suggested nationalization was strongly opposed from the floor.

30. Quoted from *Vorwärts*, May 13, 1894.
31. Bahr, Hermann: *Der Antisemitismus, loc. cit.,* p. 25.

In the same year the *Vorwärts* (June 26, 1893), dealing with the results of the run-off elections which brought the anti-Semites their main successes, wrote:

> Capitalism is sinking into barbarism and wants to drag mankind with it. It has found its most worthy representatives in the anti-Semites. The best illustration of capitalist culture is the fact that the Conservative and National Liberal parties have endorsed anti-Semitism. It is only logical that within the bourgeois camp the anti-Semites have taken the leadership in the battle of capitalism against Socialism. Soon the remnants of the National Liberal and Conservative parties will have been absorbed by anti-Semitism which, together with police-socialism, its twin brother, represents the last phase of the dying capitalist society.
>
> Go right ahead! Fortunate that the process of putrification and decomposition is so swift. Anti-Semitism itself must further it. Barbarous as it is, it is a bearer of culture against its will—cultural manure for socialism in the truest sense of the word. Let us, therefore, rejoice over the successes of anti-Semitism, a heavy blow for all other capitalist parties, almost as much as we do over our own.

CHAPTER XII

1. Mehring, Franz: *Die deutsche Sozialdemokratie,* 2nd ed. (Bremen, 1878), p. 7. This critical history of Social Democracy is not to be confounded with Mehring's later work, *Geschichte der deutschen Sozialdemokratie,* 2 vols., (Stuttgart-Berlin, 1897–98) which to this day has remained the best-known single work on the history of German socialist labor in the nineteenth century. The hostile version was written in Mehring's "black period," as his adversaries in the Social Democracy later called the years of his life during which he was an opponent of the party and attacked it in several publications. His second *Geschichte* was published by the party's publishing house, thereby receiving the stamp of official approval. Nevertheless, there was strong disagreement in the party with Mehring's way of presenting controversial issues, particularly with his outspoken bias for the Lassalleans. In Bebel's memoirs *Aus meinem Leben* one finds so many implicit refutations of Mehring's *Geschichte* that one must infer them to have been written with the intention of correcting Mehring in mind.
2. Mehring, Franz: *Herr Heinrich von Treitschke, der Sozialistentöter* (1875).
3. Quoted from Kautsky, Karl: "Franz Mehring," *Neue Zeit,* vol. XXII, no 1, p. 103.
4. Mehring, Franz: *Kapital und Presse. Ein Nachspiel zum Fall Lindau* (Berlin, 1891), p. 110.
5. This early controversy with liberalism—Jewish liberalism in this case—sounds the keynote of Mehring's later fight against what he considered the basic weakness of all liberalism: political, social, and cultural irresponsibility.
6. Mehring, Franz: *Herr Hofprediger Stoecker der Sozialpolitiker* (Bremen, 1882).
7. *See* Kautsky, Karl: "Franz Mehring," *Neue Zeit,* vol. XXII, no. 1, p. 98.
   The party's central organ, the *Sozialdemokrat,* which during the *Sozialistengesetz* had to be published in Switzerland, praised the *Berliner Volkszeitung* under Mehring as "a fearless publication" which spoke out against Bismarckian reaction "in a manner no bourgeois paper has risked for decades." (*Sozialdemokrat,* March 21, 1899. Quoted from Mehring's *Kapital und Presse, loc. cit.,* pp. 65–66.)
8. The details of the controversy are of no particular interest today. Lindau and his friends disliked and systematically ruined the career of an actress whom Mehring considered a victim of the Lindau clique.
9. Mehring quit when one of his co-editors, Georg Ledebour, who had taken

his side in the controversy, was fired. Ledebour also joined the Social Democratic Party, was from 1900 to 1918 a Reichstag member, and during World War I, as one of the leaders of the party's left wing, organized the oppositional Independent Social Democratic Party. He took an active part in the revolution of 1918. After the left wing of the Independents had merged in 1920 with the Communists and the right wing in 1922 with the Social Democrats, he tried to build a radical organization independent of the Social Democrats and Communists but failed. In 1947, 92 years old, he died as a refugee in Switzerland.

10. Mehring, Franz: *Kapital und Presse, loc. cit.*, p. 64.
11. Mehring, Franz: "Anti-und Philosemitisches," *Neue Zeit*, vol. IX, no. 2, p. 587.
12. Mehring, Franz: "Kapitalistische Agonie," *Neue Zeit*, vol. X, no. 2, pp. 545–6.
13. Buschhoff, a Jewish butcher at Xanten (Lower Rhine) had been charged with the murder of a five-year old child. The anti-Semites tried to trump up the case as a ritual murder. Although acquitted by the courts, the trial ruined Buschhoff financially; a group of liberals came to his rescue by taking up a public collection for him.
14. In the case of Bleichröder versus Ahlwardt, Mehring wrote: "The rough pamphlets of the anti-Semitic *Rektor* Ahlwardt about the 'Aryan Peoples' Battle of Despair against Jewry' contain, after all, not a few small grains of salt for capitalism. Especially the fact that a Jewish big capitalist committed perjury in order to avoid paying alimony to a dismissed *maîtresse* and that some police officers assisted him in his dirty private affair of getting rid of the inconvenient witness, has been verified to such a high degree of probability that it is not quite comprehensible why there is no official investigation of the evidence which, after all, is a little disparaging for the 'God-fearing Empire of piety.'" (*Neue Zeit*, July 27, 1890, p. 585.)

On the occasion of Ahlwardt's "Jewish Rifles" attack upon the company of Ludwig Löwe, Mehring commented that decent people would of course turn with disgust from the "slanderous nonsense" about German army equipment having been deliberately spoiled by Jewry in order to secure Germany's defeat in the next war. But the conclusion seemed to him inescapable "that these or those military jobholders who were charged with conducting the negotiations with the firm Löwe had upheld their curved palms [accepted bribes]." (*Neue Zeit*, vol. X, no. 2, p. 324.)

Mehring's *History of the German Social Democracy* contains comments like these: "During the 'swindle period' moneyed Jewry had put on airs which inevitably had made it the center of unpleasant attention; in Berlin particularly, Judaization (*Vermauschelung*) of public life had reached such proportions as to make even the most intrepid admirers of the wise Nathan feel ill at ease." (*Geschichte, loc. cit.*, vol. IV, p. 96.) After the financial crash of 1873, Manchester liberalism tried to defend the swindles with arguments which convinced no one, Mehring states. "Least of all was the 'socialism of the dolt' disarmed by an artificially bred philo-

Semitism which was not more intelligent but still more disgusting than the peasants' and artisans' indigenous (*naturwüchsig*) Jew-hatred." (*Ibid.*, p. 98, see also vol. III, pp. 276, 358, etc.)

15. Bernstein, Eduard: "Das Schlagwort und der Antisemitismus," *Neue Zeit*, vol. XI, no. 2, pp. 228–237.

It is significant that it was Bernstein who cautioned the Social Democratic Party against ambiguity of language and attitude in the Jewish question. His protest anticipated the disagreement with the "orthodox" interpretation of Marxism which, a few years later, he systematized in his book *Die Voraussetzungen des Sozialismus und die Aufgaben der Sozialdemokratie* (1899). Although at the time of his writing (1893) he still shared the party's official viewpoint of anti-Semitism as "the intermediary link that is being put between socialism and the reactionary parties— seemingly as a dam against the former, in reality as an approach to it" (*ibid.*, p. 234), the coming theoretician of "revisionism" was even then at variance with the "radical" leadership on basic questions of capitalistic development and socialist strategy.

Bernstein had joined the *Eisenachers* in 1872 and had during the years of the anti-Socialist act edited the party's paper, the *Sozialdemokrat* in Zürich. What line the paper under his editorship had pursued is excellently summarized by no other than Mehring.

"It was then [under the *Sozialistengesetz*] no longer of primary importance to imbue the harassed, oppressed and persecuted workers with the passion to fight, and to use a revolutionary language commensurate to the fury of reactionary persecution. It became more important to spoil the schemes of official social demagogy, to educate the party about the socio-economic forces in society and state, to put in their proper light misleading catchwords, such as 'fighting against Manchesterism,' a slogan which once had made sense and might again become meaningful [sic] but which in those years threatened to bring the German working class into a shady alliance with the shadiest elements of the ruling system of exploitation. None of these problems could with sufficient candor be discussed in the German labor papers without their falling under the ax of the *Sozialistengesetz*. Thus the *Sozialdemokrat* in a series of illuminating articles tore to shreds the fairy-tale of the social kingdom, the empty juggling of Stoecker and [Adolph] Wagner, the stupid notion that each act of 'nationalization' was a step toward socialism. It showed that at the time when the state was in the hands of the worst enemies of labor, the economic task of the Social Democracy could not be to increase the state's influence, to enlarge the area of its power but only to further and protect the proletarian class interests. Under the given conditions the class-conscious proletariat had to direct its efforts toward conquering [more] political power and political rights." (Mehring, Franz: *Geschichte der deutschen Sozialdemokratie*, vol. IV, p. 226.)

Bernstein's anti-authoritarian (and, therefore, also anti-Lassallean) convictions were strengthened by the economic and political observations he made during the many years which he spent in Western Europe. Few German Social Democrats were as conscious as he of the political and psychological consequences it might have for the labor movement when it insisted on bringing about socialism single-handed, against the opposition of all other social groups.

16. *Neue Zeit,* vol. XI, no. 1, p. 363.
17. *Neue Zeit,* vol. XI, no. 2, p. 548.

CHAPTER XIII

1. The history of Social Democracy has been widely discussed and is still far from being clarified. The reader is forewarned that our selection of evidence and interpretation leaves ample scope for controversy.
2. After the elections of 1903 Eduard Bernstein had suggested that the Social Democratic Party should claim the right to nominate the vice-president of the Reichstag. Socialist participation in government had become a practical problem since 1899 when the French Socialist Deputy Alexandre Millerand joined the cabinet of Waldeck-Rousseau as minister of commerce.
3. *Protokoll der Verhandlungen des Parteitages der Sozialdemokratischen Partei Deutschlands, abgehalten zu Dresden, September 13–20, 1903* (Berlin 1903), p. 418.

   The revisionists, incidentally, supported the resolution. Their stand may have been dictated by tactical reasons, so as not to disclose their numerical weakness. Perhaps it expressed a cynical awareness that the future course of the party would not be determined by radical pronunciamentos and that the majority was more concerned with upholding the radical ideology than pressing for a radical course of action.
4. Luxemburg, Rosa: "Geknickte Hoffnungen," *Neue Zeit*, vol. XXII, no. 1, p. 37.
5. The orthodox Marxists in order to refute evidence that seemed to contradict their theory of capitalist development spent much ingenuity on analyzing the less obvious changes in social stratification. With regard to the fate of the lower middle classes Kautsky (Introduction to Karl Marx's *Revolution und Contre-Revolution in Deutschland*, Stuttgart, 1896, p. XXIV) argued thus against the revisionists:

   > Statistics may sometimes prove that these small enterprises in industry, trade and agriculture do not decrease in number but it will not succeed in proving that the petty bourgeoisie and the peasantry are not going down, that the insecurity and misery of their existence are not constantly growing. And on top of it, there is the strong increase of the 'liberal professions' which has already led to a numerous and rapidly growing 'intellectual proletariat.'

6. Bamberger, Ludwig: *Wandlungen und Wanderungen in der Sozialpolitik* (Berlin, 1898), p. 18.
7. Kautsky, Karl: "Der Kongress von Köln," *Neue Zeit*, vol. XXIII, no. 2, p. 314.

8. A year later (1906) the problem of the mass strike was once more put on the agenda of the national convention, much against the will of the party leadership. It was forced upon it by the publication of the contents of a secret discussion between trade union leaders and members of the party's executive board, in which party leaders had agreed with union leaders that a general strike was out of the question since it would end in certain defeat. Again, the party convention did not on principle rule out a general strike as a legitimate defense of labor but resolved by a great majority to make such a strike dependent on the agreement of the trade unions—which had condemned it a year ago! The party's desire for maintaining the organization was no less impelling than that of the unions.

9. Called to task by the national Social Democratic convention, the united South German delegates declared the national convention not authorized to decide in this matter which, in their opinion, came under the jurisdiction of the various Social Democratic state organizations. The party leadership did not force the issue.

10. A Social Democratic coalition with the most parliamentary of all German parties, the Catholic Center, did not materialize, partly on account of ideological conflicts, partly on account of the Catholic Center Party's role in the era of imperialism.

11. The total Social Democratic vote remained stable but the parliamentary seats were lost in the run-off elections where the Social Democratic candidates faced a united opposition from the anti-Semites to the Progressives.

12. *Internationaler Sozialistenkongress zu Stuttgart, August 18–24, 1907* (Berlin, 1907), p. 83.

13. Kautsky, Karl: "Der Essener Parteitag," *Neue Zeit*, vol. XXV, no. 2, p. 856.

14. Gustav Noske became in the Weimar Republic the first Minister of the *Reichswehr* which he helped to organize. He took an eminent part in the suppression of the revolutionary left, making use of illegal organizations of armed officers and soldiers, the notorious Free-Corps.

15. *Parteitag zu Essen* (Berlin, 1907), p. 258.
    Kurt Eisner, of Jewish descent, became Prime Minister of the first Bavarian Socialist Republic in 1918 and was murdered in 1919. Upon his death the ill-fated Bavarian Soviet Republic was proclaimed.

16. Bebel, August: *Sozialdemokratie und Antisemitismus, loc. cit.*, p. 38. Our italics.

17. Scheidemann, Philipp: "Wandlungen des Antisemitismus," *Neue Zeit*, vol. XXIV, no. 2, p. 632.

18. Bebel's statement did much to help the rulers of Germany bring about the solid front with which the nation went into the First World War. When, in the crucial July days of 1914, Albert Ballin asked the Chancellor v. Bethmann-Hollweg, "Why such haste to declare war on Russia?" Bethmann answered: "If I don't we sha'n't get the Socialists to fight." See *Memoirs of Prince von Bülow*, 4 vols. (Boston, 1931–1932), vol. III, p. 187.

19. In an article on "Poalei-Zionismus," *Neue Zeit* (vol. XXIV, no. 1, pp. 804 ff.) attacked the new Zionist currents in the Jewish socialist movement of Russia. Bankrupt political Zionism, the article maintained, was forced to make concessions to the revolutionary tendencies within Jewish labor and the Jewish petty bourgeoisie which had come under revolutionary influence. "The revolutionary tinge of the Zionist Socialists stems from the Russian movement for freedom. Once absolutism is gone and persecution of the Jews has ended and the freedom movement has reached its aim, Poalei-Zionism will lose its basis and sink hopelessly into the sea of oblivion."

The criticisms of Zionism which appeared in German Marxist literature seem to have come chiefly from Russian socialist circles. For the German Social Democrats the whole issue was of minor interest, and was dealt with in a detached and dogmatic manner. There were no sharper critics of Zionism than Jewish Marxists. See J. Stern's review of Theodor Herzl's *Judenstaat*, Document No. XI.

20. Kautsky, Karl: *Rasse und Judentum* (Stuttgart, 1921), p. 105.

21. The *Sozialistische Monatshefte* appeared from 1898 until Hitler's rise to power. The monthly was not recognized by the Social Democratic Party as an official party publication. Contributors were leading revisionists, among them Eduard Bernstein, Ignaz Auer, Georg Vollmar. The founder and editor was the Zionist Josef Bloch.

Bloch's Zionism was part of his theory of modern imperialism which brought him and his disciples into conflict with British policies on the European continent and made them look to France as the leader of a European Continental Empire, including North Africa. During the Weimar Republic, Bloch's friends agitated for a rapprochement with France and "continental policy," opposed to England's interference.

22. Anin, Maxim: "Ist die Assimilation der Juden möglich?" *Sozialistische Monatshefte*, 1908, vol. II. May–August, pp. 614–619.

23. Bauer, Otto: *Die Nationalitätenfrage und die Sozialdemokratie* (Vienna, 1907).

24. An article like Karl Leuthner's "Junker und Juden" (*Sozialistische Monatshefte*, 1908, vol. II, pp. 912–22) which questioned the radicals' premise of a steadily advancing political maturity of the masses, may serve as an illustration. To prove his point, Leuthner chose the phenomena of liberal hatred of the *Junkers* in Prussia, and of anti-Semitic hatred in Vienna. In both instances, the popularity of the negative stereotypes seemed to him rooted in their psychological service of satisfying a deep-seated desire to hate. The search for subjective, evil motivations replaced the analysis of objective factors and social forces. The persistence of such stereotypes cast doubt on the progress of political rationality which Marxism claimed to have brought about among the people. Leuthner saw the great attraction of anti-Semitism in the gratifications to be gained from hatred, in the self-satisfaction to be derived from indignation.

25. Hannah Ahrendt's thoughtful study on the Dreyfus Affair deals with the

moral devastation brought about by, and revealed in, its course. French socialist labor, Ahrendt shows, did not keep free of guilt. (Ahrendt, Hannah: "From the Dreyfus Affair to France Today," in *Essays on Anti-Semitism*, ed. by Koppel S. Pinson, New York, 1946; first published in *Jewish Social Studies*, New York, July 1942.)

26. The significance of prevailing economic concepts for the status of the Jewish group is excellently analyzed by Louis B. Boudin: "Recent Developments in Economic Theory and the Resurgence of anti-Semitism," *ORT Economic Revue* (New York), June and September 1947, March 1948.

27. Michels, Robert: "Die deutsche Sozialdemokratie, deren Parteimitgliedschaft und soziale Zusammensetzung," *Archiv für soziale Gesetzgebung und Statistik* (1906), pp. 471–566.

Michels mentions as the only case of overt anti-Semitism that he found in Social Democratic publications a booklet written by Richard Calwer, editor of a provincial party newspaper, the *Braunschweiger Volksfreund* (*"Das Kommunistische Manifest und die heutige Sozialdemokratie,"* Braunschweig, 1894). Calwer deplored the intrusion of a "petty-bourgeois radicalism" into the party which in his opinion was "fed and incited by a few Jews who make slander their business" (p. 18). He criticized the party literature for going so far in combatting anti-Semitism as to create an impression "that we were philo-Semites" and to give the party's opponents the opportunity to call the Social Democracy *"durch und durch verjudet"* (p. 39).

Calwer stood at the extreme right of the party. On the role of this "social-imperialistic" wing of revisionism see Neumann, Franz: *Behemoth, loc. cit.*, p. 212.

28. In 1906 Robert Michels in his analysis of the membership and social composition of the Social Democratic Party (*loc. cit.*) mentioned as prominent Jewish members in the field:

1. of social theory: Eduard Bernstein, Adolf Braun, Jakob Stern, Simon Katzenstein, Bruno Schönlank;

2. of journalism: Georg Gradnauer, Kurt Eisner, Josef Bloch;

3. of party organization: the expert in municipal administration Hugo Heimann; the specialist for electoral law Leo Arons; the organizer of youth Ludwig Frank.

The list could be continued. Important contributions in economic theory and political analysis were made by Rosa Luxemburg, Rudolf Hilferding, Heinrich Braun, Parvus-Helphand.

In 1912, 12 of the 100 Social Democratic Reichstag members were of Jewish descent. They were Eduard Bernstein, Oscar Cohn, Georg Davidsohn, Ludwig Frank, Georg Gradnauer, Hugo Haase, Josef Herzfeld, Otto Landsberg, Gustav Hoch, Arthur Stadthagen, Georges Weill, Emanuel Wurm. Three of these, Cohn, Davidsohn, and Haase, professed Jewish religion. (According to the *Reichstagshandbuch, 13. Legislaturperiode*, edited by the Office of the Reichstag, Berlin, 1912.)

The total number of Jewish Social Democrats cannot be obtained. The

Social Democratic Party, for which religion was "a private affair," never registered the denomination of its members; besides it must be assumed that most Jewish intellectuals, when joining the Social Democratic Party, formally or informally severed their association with the Jewish community and declared themselves *konfessionslos*, conforming to the party's code in the matter of religion.

29. Liebknecht, Wilhelm: *Über den Kölner Parteitag* (Bielefeld, 1893), p. 33.
30. In *Der Aufbau*, (New York, Oct. 13, 1944). Max Osborn died in New York in 1946.
31. Among the most impressive testimony of the socialist workers' loyalty to their leaders was the way they honored them in death. For decades the workers of Breslau observed the anniversay of Lassalle's death by proceeding to his grave in the cemetery of the Jewish community. The workers of Berlin made the funeral of Paul Singer in 1911 a demonstration of which the *Berliner Tageblatt* (February 5, 1911) wrote that none of the mighty of this earth could be buried as he was. The procession of mourners lasted from morning to night and even the conservative *Deutsche Tageszeitung* spoke of a human sea that defied all standards of measurement.

In the early years of the Weimar Republic there were similar manifestations of labor's loyalty to its dead, for instance to the murdered Rosa Luxemburg and Karl Liebknecht. The funeral of the murdered Walter Rathenau who, although not a Socialist, was considered an exponent of a democratic Germany, became the occasion of a protest against the enemies of the Republic at which more than a million people participated.
32. The underestimation of the potential violence of anti-Semitism was tied up with the concept of the lower middle classes as anachronistic elements in the developed industrial society, weak, unstable, and permanently at the brink of social and economic disaster.

A discerning student of German socialism once remarked to the author that the attitude of the orthodox Marxists toward the "archaic" social classes which had largely disappeared in England, stemmed from injured national pride. The existence of such classes was proof of Germany's "backwardness."

It would be worthwhile to study the semantics of the term *Kleinbürger*, as used in the socialist vocabulary. We would not be surprised if it evoked associations of mental, moral, and physical qualities that added up to the image of a natural species. Timid, servile, of small stature and general meekness, the *Kleinbürger* could never be suspected of having the physical energy and the determination to kill and burn.
33. It was perhaps to the moral, though not to the political credit of Social Democracy that it was incapable of believing its enemies would resort to crime and utter ruthlessness when the stakes were high enough. From the nineties to Hitler's rise to power, the Social Democrats refused to learn the sad lesson that all professed values, ideals, and norms by which Western civilization usually abides, were at crucial times withdrawn from

circulation. "I don't believe in the innocence of the French captain Dreyfus. . . . The leaders of the campaign [for Dreyfus] assert that the general staff had knowingly sentenced an innocent man. A simply monstrous presumption! It could only have been to the interest of the general staff to find the culprit and to bring him to justice. That the Jew Dreyfus was sent to Devil's Island simply out of anti-Semitic hatred, is a presumption which clashes with all psychology and common sense. . . . No one will suspect me of being an anti-Semite, but as high an opinion as I have of the Jew-hatred of Messrs. Liebermann von Sonnenberg, Boeckel, Ahlwardt and their ilk, I would never believe that they, as judges, would be capable of declaring a Jew guilty of a capital crime only because he is a Jew."

The man who wrote this indeed could not be suspected of anti-Semitism. In the Reichstag, at party conventions, at public meetings and in his writings, he had fought the vileness of the anti-Jewish agitation. He was Wilhelm Liebknecht. (Liebknecht, Wilhelm: "Nachträgliches zur Affaire," *Die Fackel*, Vienna, April-September, 1899, end of September, pp. 1–10.)

DOCUMENTS

DOCUMENT NO. I

The Anti-Semites' Definition of Capital

LIEBERMANN VON SONNENBERG ON "USEFUL" AND "HARMFUL" CAPITAL*

We anti-Semites are opposed to neither Jewish capital nor to capital in general. We distinguish, however, between useful and harmful capital. We seek to promote the useful and to restrain the harmful. Useful capital, in our opinion, is that which is put to work in agriculture and in industry, where it creates livelihoods for millions of workers. Useful capital operates in honest trade the function of which is to collect the world's goods and offer them for sale everywhere thus enabling the whole of mankind to participate in the progress of civilization. Useful capital, we think, is present in the form of savings which represent the fruit of an industrious life. Useful capital increases on a modest scale only after real labor has been spent on increasing it.

But harmful capital grows beyond all limits without doing real work, setting the stage for frauds and swindles that rob trusting people. Such capital may be found at the stock exchanges, and it is certainly no fault of *ours* that this capital is mostly in Jewish hands.

* *Reichstag, Stenographische Berichte,* December 7, 1893, p. 322.

DOCUMENT NO. II

Adolf Stoecker's First Anti-Semitic Speech:

"WHAT WE DEMAND OF MODERN JEWRY"*

For a long time the Jewish problem has been a burning question, but in the last few months it has burst out into an open conflagration. It is not fed by religious fanaticism nor by political passion. The orthodox and the freethinkers, conservatives and liberals, all talk and write about it with the same vehemence. All alike consider the Jewish problem not a question of contending religious beliefs but a disturbing social problem. "The social problem is the Jewish problem," writes Glagau. "Don't vote for a Jew!" exclaims W. Marr, in his third pamphlet. "The end of Germany has come," he concludes his passionate appeal to our people.

Well, we do not believe the end of the German spirit to be so near. Peoples as well as individuals can be reborn. Germany, and Berlin too, will recover and rid themselves of the foreign spirit. But there are symptoms of the presence of a disease: our national body is plagued by social abuses, and social hostility never exists without reason. Christians as well as Jews should be seriously concerned lest this enmity turn into hatred. For the rumbling of a far-off thunderstorm can already be heard. It is strange indeed that the Jewish liberal press does not have the courage to answer the charges of its attackers. Usually it invents a scandal, even if there is none. It sharpens its poisonous pen by writing about the sermons in our churches and the discussions in our church meetings; but it hushes up the Jewish question and does everything to prevent its readers from hearing even a whisper from these unpleasant voices. It pretends to despise its enemies and to consider them unworthy of an answer. It would be better to learn from the enemy, to recognize one's own defects, and work together toward the social reconciliation which we need so badly. It is in this light that I intend to deal with the Jewish question, in the spirit of Christian love, but also with complete social truthfulness.

Occasional comments of mine on this topic at Christian Social meetings have been disseminated in the general public, often for partisan purposes, and always in distorted, exaggerated, poisoned form. The reporters of certain papers, a disgrace to this city of the intelligentsia, are as ignorant as they are

* Speech delivered at the Christian Social Workers' Party rally of September 19, 1879. Stoecker, Adolf: *Christlich-Sozial, Reden und Aufsätze, loc cit.*, pp. 143 ff.

untruthful. They misrepresent a great deal from ignorance, but mostly from sheer spite.

An incident which happened last year is quite instructive and typical. During my absence there was more talk about Jews in our meetings than there should have been. The Jewish press wrote that the Christian Social movement was filled with hatred of the Jews and itched to persecute them. When I returned, I took the opportunity to declare publicly and solemnly: We hate no one, not even the Jews; we respect them as our fellow citizens and love them as the people of the prophets and apostles that brought forth our Savior. But when Jewish papers assail our faith and the Jewish spirit of Mammon corrupts our nation, our love should not prevent us from pointing out this danger. This statement, too, has been distorted. I am supposed to have said that all Germany's misery has been brought about by the Jews. I was flooded with letters. A Berlin Jew whose name is known to me wrote that his people were God's favorites and when Christians professed their love for the chosen people, it was the same as when courtesans—I prefer to use this more decent expression—gave their hearts to noblemen. Another sent me a pamphlet in which an unbelieving baptized writer describes and exaggerates the role of the Jews in the field of medieval science. The dedication reads: "To the Jew-baiter, with contempt." A third one from Frankfurt am Main, who signs himself "Unfortunately a Jew," congratulated me on revealing the German plight so frankly.

This incident, insignificant in itself, is a clear example of the lies, the arrogance, and the hatred which confuse the issue as soon as the Jewish question comes up for discussion. People who are in the habit of pouring out the most biting criticism of State and Church, men and events, become highly incensed when anyone takes the liberty of directing even so much as a searching glance at Jewry. They themselves hatefully and sneeringly assail any non-Jewish endeavor. But as soon as a mild word of truth is uttered about them and their doings, they put on an act of injured innocence, of outraged tolerance, of being the martyrs of world history. Nevertheless I shall dare to speak up openly and candidly about modern Jewry tonight. And I am quite prepared for the distorted reports that will come back.

I do indeed consider modern Jewry a great danger to German national life. By this I mean neither the religion of the orthodox nor the enlightenment of the reformed. Orthodox Judaism, this ossification of the Law, the Old Testament without a temple, without priests, without sacrifice, without a Messiah, is neither attractive nor dangerous to the children of the nineteenth century. It is a form of religion which is dead at its very core, a low form of revelation, an outlived spirit, still venerable but set at nought by Christ and no longer holding any truth for the present. Reformed Judaism is of even less religious significance. It is neither Judaism nor Christianity, but a pitiful remnant of the age of enlightenment. Its ideas did not originate on Jewish soil but in a wretched period of the Christian church, a period long since overcome by the church itself. Both factions boast, of course, that the Jews are the bearers of the loftiest religious and moral ideals for mankind and the world and that it is the mission of Jewry, now and in the future, to maintain those ideals, to develop and spread them. On this point the Jewish press, from right to left, stands united.

The incense which the Jews lavish on themselves in the synagogues of both schools is quite overpowering. When recently the centenary of the noble Moses Mendelssohn was celebrated, the solemn gathering was confronted with the slogan: "From Moses to Moses there is none to compare" (*Von Moses bis Moses ist niemand wie dieser*). The gracious personality of Moses Mendelssohn can hardly be said to have exercised an overwhelming influence on the development of mankind. Yet he is now being invoked in a peculiar way. At the commemoration of the anniversary of his death in 1870 the *Landesrabbiner* Dr. Adler uttered these glowing words: "The Jewish State has perished, but Jewry lives on and carries on its mission. Its existence is an important factor in the history of mankind, in the progressive culture of man. Our mission has been, is, and will be: the victory of the progressive spirit of man, the victory of humanity. Even the vanished Jewish State is not dead to us. What perished was only the shell of a life everlasting, of a people vested with a great mission of historic importance."

Here you see that mankind is actually only a pedestal for the imperishable tribe of the Jews. This is the way of almost all Israelites who meditate about their people. Philippson sees the great mission of Israel in the spreading of monotheism, in the exchange of international communication, in the achievement of religious equality and freedom. He writes as follows: "Struggle in every field assures Jewry a great future. This is true of professing Jews as well as for all mankind in its gropings. It is Judaism alone that in the midst of chaos offers thoughts and ideas which accord with the history of mankind, with reason and emotion." And in complete agreement with this notion the orthodox Israelite says: "The Jew is the incarnation of mankind. Any progress within mankind is progress for Israel; any discovery, any advance—they all take place, first of all, for the benefit of our people."

"It is Israel's mission," they say in the Jewish orthodox camp, "to bring salvation to the world, and the time is near, for the cross is disintegrating, the crescent is going down, and the pagan peoples of Asia and Africa no longer care for their traditional idols!"

"The day the temple was destroyed Messiah was born; on that day began Israel's enlightened progress as the savior of the world from delusion and error," Rabbi Levin preached naively in Nürnberg at the consecration of a synagogue, before Christian representatives of the town. Spreading his arms he cried out to the gathering: "This kiss to the whole world." That is going a little far.

S. Meyer, editor of the *Jüdische Presse* writes: "We cannot permit the indisputable fact to be challenged that Judaism is the source of all the lofty ideas on which the moral order of the world is based, which form the intellectual content even of modern culture and civilization and the basis of true charity." And again: "Nothing that is good in the Gospels is new, but stems from Judaism, and all that is new is not good."

Dr. Adler writes in a similar vein: "Israel's religion is the eternal inexorable truth; Christianity and Islam are preliminary stages which had to be attained before the whole truth could be revealed." The Reformed Rabbi Nascher joins the chorus: "It is Israel's mission and endowment to be a beacon on the sea of mankind's ideas. You are called upon," so this vain man told his vain listeners in a sermon, "to shine like the stars to your fellow men." Lest anyone believe these are exaggerations on the part of individuals, let him read the resolutions of the Augsburg synod of 1871 which state among other things: "The spirit of true awareness of the divine and of ethical purity more and more pervades the consciousness of the peoples. Jewry joyfully recognizes this as a step toward the goals which it has striven for throughout its historic development."

Here we wish to make our first request. We ask: *please, be a little more modest!* We do not deny that Israel carried the knowledge of the one and only God through ancient times like a sacred flame until Christ came and brought the more perfect faith, the richer conception of God, and the higher truth. But it is a historic fact that the people of Israel time and again relapsed into the grossest idolatry, that God was able to suppress apostasy for short periods only by sending outstanding personalities. It is God's grace rather than Israel's merit that the doctrine of the one God has been preserved for mankind. It is just as indubitable that the ideas of freedom of religion, of tolerance in the modern sense, do not fit into the character of the Old Testament. Whoever violated the sabbath was stoned; the priests of Baal were slaughtered. This was inherent in the Jewish legal institutions and we are far from blaming the Old Testament for it.

But it is quite out of order when Jews claim as their own ideas which were historically altogether unknown to their religion. And furthermore they are quite aware of the fact that they had a caste of priests—certainly the opposite of equality; that they had slavery—certainly the opposite of freedom; that they indulged in polygamy—certainly the opposite of ideal family life. Only Teutonic-Christian life put an end to these abuses. It is true, Israel had an enlightened economic legislation; social forms of property ownership, the prohibition of usury, and the greatest charity toward the poor. But we have only to mention these things to realize the fearful chasm between the Old Testament and modern Jewry. It was German law alone that protected the concept of common property, the Christian church alone that decreed the prohibition of usury; it is precisely here that the faults and sins of modern Jewry are plainly revealed.

Even if we presume for once that this lofty mission really is Israel's permanent task, who, then, are those thinkers and poets, who, inspired by the divine spirit, preach, praise and honor the living God? Perhaps the editors of the *Tageblatt*? Or the scholars of the *Kladderadatsch*? Where is the school of the prophets of the Holy Spirit which trains young men for their world mission? Where are the missionary posts? Where are the missionaries? Perhaps at the stock exchanges of Berlin, Vienna and Paris? Alas, the Jews should not be told such foolishness. For it is their ominous fate that, having failed Christ, they have lost their divine course, have abandoned their sublime mission. Confronted with the Lord's sharp-edged alternative: 'Thou canst not serve both God and Mammon," they now worship the idol of gold, having forsaken the path of God.

The old prayers in which the Jews yearn for God and Zion are moving. "Because of our sins we have been driven from our country and exiled from our soil; we cannot fulfill our duties in your chosen dwelling and in your great and sacred temple in which your name is invoked. . . . Let us gather together from the far ends of the world. Lead us to Zion, your city, with rejoicing, and to Jerusalem, your sacred temple, with everlasting jubilation." But those who play a role in modern Jewry know nothing of this; they prefer to live in the *Jerusalemerstrasse* rather than in the streets of Jerusalem. A devout Christian once pitied a Jewish brother for not having a high priest and a temple. Oh, was the reply, our temple is the synagogue and our high priest is the *Herr Oberrabbiner.*

The religion of the Old Testament requires worship by sacrifices and services in the temple. Without them Judaism is a dry well and a withered tree. And barren it is, indeed, nothing but the shadow of the Christian church within whose sphere it is located: in Germany enlightened and torn apart in factions; in the Latin countries split between strictest Talmudism and unbelief; in the Slav nations petrified in formulas and again in the grip of wild frenzy; under the Crescent devoid of spirit and rotting like Islam itself. This is the picture of Judaism on earth. Lacking any creative religious force, it lives on nothing but its fantasies.

Occasionally, a ray of insight into the full extent of their own misery falls upon Jewish writers. You may read them in their magazines: "Religious fervor is declining in the elder as in the younger generation. Let us not be deceived by the symptoms of active participation in the interests of Jewry and Judaism, for it is not always religious conviction that inspires those men; they strive for external things rather than for the improvement of the spiritual life."

In Vienna a noble Jew complains: "The modern system of credit creates deep unrest, ethical frivolity, religious indifference; the teachers and spokesmen of our religion lack the courage to call these things by their right name!" In their sober moments even men like Philippson will say: "The younger generation is overcome by doubts that man can attain any firm convictions. All ideals have evaporated and nothing seems worth striving for save that which promises material benefits and wealth, honor, power, and pleasure. . . . Hence this mad spirit of speculation and this striving to become rich quickly, at the expense of others. There is an ebb tide in all the domains of art. We have neither poets, painters, sculptors, musicians, nor actors of original and lasting importance; those few who are left are gradually dying out without being replaced. Where are they to come from in a materialistic world deprived of any spiritual impetus? These are the consequences of atheism and materialism, as proved beyond any doubt by history and experience."

Even the reformed Israelitic weekly considers it worth while to present its readers with the following verse:

Überall wo es gilt zu sehn und zu hören,
Scheint die Zahl der Juden sich täglich zu mehren
In Promenaden, Theatern, Konzerten and Bällen
Siehst du meist Juden in allen Fällen.
Willst du wo mehr Christen als Juden sehn,
Musst du Freitag abend in die neue Synagoge gehn.

(Wherever there is something to be seen and heard,
The number of Jews seems to increase every day;
On promenades, in theaters, at concerts and balls
You are certain to see mostly Jews.
But if you want to see more Christians than Jews,
You'd better go to the new synagogue on a Friday night.)

"It is quite certain that in Berlin less than a quarter, probably hardly more than one tenth of all Jewish *Gymnasiasten und Realschüler* (high school pupils) over 13 ever hear a word of religious instruction." "Morality is limited to this precept: Whatever the criminal law does not forbid or whatever is beyond the reach of the judge in a criminal court is permissible, useful, shrewd." These Jewish voices date back to 1871; things have grown much worse in the meantime. The Jews fight our religion, but they know very well that man cannot live without religion. "A repulsive generation is being raised," says one of the reformers. "Even in its swaddling clothes it greedily craves pleasure and money, money and pleasure, and from adolescence on worships only the golden calf. Its only God is Mammon. The name and memory of Israel are thus delivered up to scorn, a scorn and hatred well deserved. Go on raising Jews without Judaism, and you will have Jews to whom that meaning of the word fully applies which fanatical hatred attributes to it."

And in spite of this truth, in spite of their utter lack of religious creativeness, they stick to their delusion of being a religious power. The truth is that modern Jewry is most certainly a power against religion; a power which bitterly fights Christianity everywhere, uproots Christian faith as well as national feeling in the people, in their stead offering them nothing but the idolatrous admiration of Jewry such as it is, with no other content but its self-admiration. Berthold Auerbach said quite correctly in his novel *Waldfried*: "The educated Jews are non-Christians rather than Jews." That is why they are fond of affecting free thought. Their credo is written on the empty page between the Old and the New Testament. But they never dream of openly conceding their poverty. They fashion a regal mantle from the rags of un-belief and manage to impress the undiscriminating mass of readers. For even today the Jew must pose as being vested with a task of historic importance. Even the most liberal reformer wants to remain a Jew. "May our Judaism be-come for us and remain for our children and our children's children what it was to our forefathers, a beloved, precious jewel. Every day anew we should be proud and happy to be Jews, followers of a religion that includes the origin and the final goal of humanity." This is what the leader of the congregation in Dresden wrote to the Jewish communities years ago.

They persist in remaining Jews. Yet it is obviously incongruous to refuse to believe in anything Jewish and at the same time remain a Jew, or to be a Jew in the narrowest sense of the word and at the same time to throw about utopian ideas of universal happiness (*Menschheitsbeglückungsideen*). The initiate everywhere cannot fail to notice how ridiculous these doings are. It becomes downright absurd, for instance, when a Dr. Berliner during the French war looks at world history through Jewish glasses. "I consider the last quarter of the fifteenth century to be the termination of the Middle Ages. It was then that the Jewish press started to operate, and a Jew, Tipsiles, of Augsburg, was said to have invented gun powder, with which, at last, the powerful fortresses of the Middle Ages could be breached." Did anyone of you know that Tipsiles invented gun powder? Does anybody really believe that it was the Jewish press rather than the renaissance, the discovery of America, and the reformation which initiated the modern age? Indeed, once this standpoint is adopted, it is easy to understand why they hold similar beliefs with regard to the future, culminating finally in the opinion that the world belong to the Jews. Cremieux said at a meeting of the Israelitic Association in Paris: "A new Messianic empire, a new Jerusalem, must arise in place of the emperors and popes." And a certain Dr. Rosenzweig recently suggested quite seriously that circumcision be made generally obligatory.

All this may have contributed to make the Jews, especially the Jewish newspaper boys, intolerant to such a degree as to become quite intolerable. We really mean it if we address our second request to the Jewish press: *please, be a little more tolerant!* Unlike many others who have dealt with this topic, we shall not quote the Talmud with its contempt for foreign peoples and its hatred for human rights. We do not feel that present-day Jewry in its totality can be made responsible for books which were written thousands of years ago. Otherwise we should also have to hold the Catholics responsible for the persecutions of heretics and the trials of the inquisition which no pope has ever disavowed. And a change in this respect has really occurred. The strict Jews still accept the Talmud as infallible, like the law. Some of them quite unreasonably declare that the whole Talmud, including all the vengeful and savage passages, is sacred to them. But it appears, nevertheless, that many years of living together with Christians and maintaining business relations with them, and the kinder spirit of modern times have caused the hatred of Christians to decline greatly in the synagogue.

The official hatred has ceased; the first Jewish synod even passed the following decision: "In the new prayers (*Gebetsstücke*) and in those which remain to be revised, all utterances which might be interpreted as expressions of bitterness or vindictiveness should be avoided." Yet the Jewish press exhales a hatred against everything Christian that is loathesome indeed. Articles are not signed in our papers and journals, and thus the objection may be raised that there is no way of knowing whether the anti-Christian articles have really been written by Jews. We even know that there are enough baptized scribblers on the editorial staffs of the papers to carry out the sorry task of reviling their church. But it is a fact that the worst Berlin papers are in the hands of Jews and that the Jewish element completely dominates the editorial staffs. The most convincing evidence, however, is the fact that religious disputes among the Jewish factions are scarcely ever mentioned, that the rigors of Jewish orthodoxy are never touched upon, and that literary attacks against Jews are not to be found. Orthodox Jewry is never criticized: let it reject the nondenominational (*konfessionslose*) school and threaten unwed couples with excommunication—no liberal paper ever takes notice. But let such a thing happen in Christian meetings and the bloodhounds of the press are out in full cry. Our sacred institutions are constantly dragged into the dust; the synagogue is protected by the tacit agreement of all liberal newspapermen. Show us in the liberal press one single article which treats the day of atonement or the Talmud Associations as ignobly as the *Tageblatt* derides this year's Day of Repentance, one of our holiest days, or as the Berlin Jew press ridiculed our August conference. Christianity alone has to put up with such indignities. The Jewish chairman of the City Council of Berlin recently made a public statement on church matters which do not concern him at all and spoke in this connection about "real inquisitors who ardently desire to burn heretics at the stake." Who gives him the right to sow discord and incite hatred in the Christian population? This intolerance is unbearable.

As early as 1873 the paper of the reformers wrote: "The Jewish press is regrettably marred by bad taste and venom. A slanderous, bitter and aggressive tone sounds from every page. This has corrupted the public which has now developed a taste for spicy little stories." And how much worse the Jewish press has grown since! Where, in the Protestant, in the conservative press, would you ever find a trace of such ruthlessness? Whoever dared ridicule a Jewish holiday, the Jewish dietary and purification laws? The most elementary sense of decency should forbid desecrating what is sacred to a people. It is these continuous attempts at undermining the very foundation of a people's faith, morals, and national honor that are criminal and vile. The Social Democratic press has occasionally been more obscene; but some publications which are among the most widely read in Berlin are even more dangerous because they are less crude and much more venomous. Unless these wells of poison are cleaned out, the situation cannot improve. Benzenburg wrote as early as 1816: "Germany's splendor may perish with the Jews." If the Christians continue to expose themselves constantly to the influence of the Jewish spirit which deprives them of their German and Christian character this prophecy will certainly come true. But perhaps—and this is our hope—Germany's splendor will arise with new life after this period of decline. We should be indeed a nation without honor if we did not break these chains of a foreign mentality, if we really became Judaized.

Every sensible person must realize that the rule of the Semitic mentality means not only our spiritual but also our economic impoverishment. The German is a great idealist; for a time he will stand for others exploiting his love of ideas to their own profit. But in the end the figure of *Nathan der Weise* whom Lessing created out of Christian humanitarianism is bound to disappear behind that of Shylock, and the warning judgment of the Jews voiced by our best men—Kant, Fichte, Herder—will prove its validity.

The Jews are and remain a people within a people, a state within a state, a separate tribe within a foreign race. All immigrants are eventually absorbed by the people among whom they live—all save the Jews. They pit their unbroken Semitic character against Teutonic nature, their rigid cult of law or their hatred of Christians against Christianity. We cannot condemn them for this; as long as they are Jews, they are bound to act in this way. But we must, in all candor, state the necessity of protecting ourselves against the dangers of such an intermingling. There are 45,000 Jews in Berlin alone, as many as there are in all of France, in all of England. That is too many. If they had a real bond with us, there would be nothing wrong with this figure. But this half of a hundred thousand lives by itself, in easy circumstances, with increasing power, equipped with a very profitable mind, and without any concern for our Christian-German interests. Therein lies the real danger.

We are approaching the Polish ratio in the Christian-Jewish population, save for the fact that the Berlin Jews are much richer, much more clever and influential than the Polish Israelites. They control the arteries of money, banking, and trade; they dominate the press and they are flooding the institutions of higher learning. The latter is certainly a beautiful trait; it has often moved me deeply to see how poor Jews sacrificed all they had to give their children an education. But this development is ominous. We are moving toward the point when public opinion will be completely dominated and labor completely exploited by the Jews. The process of disintegration is under way; nothing will stop it, unless we turn about and make the Jews turn about too. And this is where we make our third request. Modern Jewry must take part in productive work: *a little more equality, please!*

It used to be said that emancipation would push the Jews into other occupations. Now they are emancipated, but the opposite has happened. More than ever, they cultivate those trades where they can get rich quickly and easily. Lately they have been trying to squeeze into the judiciary, a matter that has not reacted well upon justice. They take almost no part at all in handicraft and little in industrial labor. That means that they do not enjoy work and that they do not believe in the German concept of the dignity of labor. To a great extent we have to thank them for the slogan "cheap and shoddy." They are to be found wherever misery and the instinct of gambling can be exploited. The launching of shady enterprises (*Gründungen*) and usury are undeniably their favorite occupations. They love to reap where they have not sown. If the big social question is that of a just division between wages and profits (*Arbeits- und Kapitalsertrag*), then those who systematically and immoderately exploit labor in the interest of capital represent the worst element in this question. It is true, the Jews, through Marx and Lassalle, have seen to it that they have their friends in the ranks of the Social Democrats as well; the nihilists in Russia are partly Jews. Nevertheless, their one-sided financial interests entail dangers for them too. For me the Jewish problem centers in the question as to whether the Jews who live in our midst will learn to participate in all aspects of German labor, including the hard toil of artisans, factory workers, and peasants. We should ask nothing more of them.

Even the general press of Jewry has not been able to forego some warnings in this respect. "It must be admitted that there are a number of Jews among the stock jobbers and swindlers, and more than the ratio of the population would warrant." "The inclination to learn a trade is disappearing more and more and even the youth in grammar schools and orphanages want almost exclusively to go into business. Many persecutions in the Middle Ages," they cannot help but admit, "were brought about because princes, nobility, and burghers were indebted to Jews, and tried to rid themselves of their obligations by exterminating all Jews, at least those who lived in their districts." One even finds the advice that "the tide of hatred of the Jews would recede more quickly, if the Jews learned the lessons of the past better and struggled to work and build on solid ground."

The question is: what shall be done? We believe that Jews and Christians must try to establish a proper relationship with each other. There is no other way. Hatred of the Jews is already flaring up here and there, and this is repugnant to the Gospels. If modern Jewry continues to use the power of capital and the power of the press to bring misfortune to the nation, a final catastrophe is unavoidable. Israel must renounce its ambition to become the master of Germany. It should renounce its arrogant claim that Judaism is the religion of the future, when it is so clearly that of the past. Let not foolish Christians continue to strengthen the self-conceit of this people. Jewish orthodoxy with its circumcision is decrepit, while reformed Judaism is not a Jewish religion at all. Once Israel has realized this, it will quietly forget its alleged mission and stop trying to rob of their Christianity people who offer it hospitality and civil rights. The Jewish press must become more tolerant—that is the first prerequisite for improving the situation. The social abuses which are caused by Jewry must be eradicated by wise legislation. It will not be easy to curb Jewish capital. Only thoroughgoing legislation can bring it about. The mortgage system in real estate should be abolished and property should be inalienable and unmortgageable; the credit system should be reorganized to protect the businessman against the arbitrary power of big capital. There must be new stock and stock-exchange regulations; reintroduction of the denominational census so as to find out the disproportion between Jewish capital and Christian labor; limitation of appointments of Jewish judges in proportion to the size of the population; removal of Jewish teachers from our grammar schools, and in addition the strengthening of the Christian-Germanic spirit—these are the means to put a stop to the encroachment of Jewry on Germanic life, this worst kind of usury.*

Either we succeed in this and Germany will rise again, or the cancer from which we suffer will spread further. In that event our whole future is threatened and the German spirit will become Judaized. The German economy will become impoverished. These are our slogans: A return to a Germanic rule in law and business, a return to the Christian faith. May every man do his duty, and God will help us.

* Untranslatable play on the words *überwuchern* and *wuchern*.

Anti-Semitism, Liberalism, and the Prussian Government

DEBATE ON THE JEWISH QUESTION
IN THE PRUSSIAN DIET
MARCH 21 AND 22, 1890*

A discussion on education generally and the value of classical education and the *Gymnasium* in particular preceded the debate of March 20 during which Stoecker took the floor first to defend classical education and the true spirit of learning (*wahre Gelehrsamkeit*). Antiquity, he argued, was the basis of the unique German *Bildung* (culture) and, together with Christianity, it will remain so. He then went on to praise the German school system, criticizing it only for overloading the student with academic knowledge.

"To me the ideal school system would be one that attempted to make the mind so eager and able to learn that it would be able to apply the capacities it has acquired by training in one field to some other field as well. This is certainly a serious shortcoming of our German character training. . . . Many highly educated and distinguished persons are yet unable to penetrate to the heart of a question. They learn nothing and forget everything. The joy of learning, the capacity for probing deeply have not been sufficiently developed."

Stoecker then praised the Prussian Minister of Public Worship and Instruction for furthering physical education and passed on to the problem of religious instruction. He considered it a mistake and a degradation to treat religious instruction as but one subject among many others in the school curriculum. The spirit of religious education either "permeates all instruction, in which case it somehow dominates each subject, or it is reduced to the position of just one more item in the curriculum, and not even a major one. . . ." But, Stoecker continued, this was not the main reason why he had asked for the floor.

"I wanted to say a word about the disproportionate Jewish element in some of our secondary schools (laughter on the left. Cries of 'Hear, hear!' on the right). . . .

"We consider it our political duty to draw attention to the fact that certain aspects of our secondary school system are marked by intolerable abuses which

* Excerpts from speeches by Adolf Stoecker, Heinrich Rickert, and von Gossler, Prussian Minister of Public Worship and Instruction. *Die Judendebatte im preussischen Abgeordnetenhause anlässlich der zweiten Beratung des Kultusétats am 20. und 21. März 1890.*

hamper the thorough moral and religious character training so necessary in our schools."

To demonstrate how serious the situation was Stoecker quoted statistics:

"I want to begin by reading a few figures to you, otherwise you may not realize how great is the harm that has been already done. Naturally I am not referring to conditions throughout the country but only to those prevailing in certain regions and cities, mainly Berlin, Breslau and Upper Silesia, and Frankfurt am Main. I shall deal with Berlin in detail. In 1887, according to the latest statistical yearbook, there were in all the *Gymnasiums* of the capital, state as well as municipal, 1,898 Jewish, 6,904 Protestant, 278 Catholic, and 26 nondenominational students. . . .

"But the picture becomes even more revealing when you consider each *Gymnasium* separately. There is, for instance, the *Französische Gymnasium* in which there are 193 Jewish compared to 222 Protestant and 12 Catholic students (cries of 'Hear, hear!' on the right), the *Wilhelmsgymnasium* with 201 Jewish compared to 541 Protestant pupils . . . in the *Köllnische Gymnasium* 180 compared to 340, in the *Friedrichsgymnasium* 202 compared to 349.

"These are the highest figures, but in the other schools as well the Jewish element is pretty strong. The matter gets even worse when you consider the upper grades; there the Jewish element is even greater. By Easter of 1886, for instance, there were in the *Oberprima* [high school senior class] of all *Gymnasiums* 52 Jews, compared to 132 Protestants, by Michaelis [fall term] 48 Jews, compared to 141 Protestants. In 1887 this proportion somewhat declined. . . . But even these figures are child's play compared to the percentages at some schools. As you know, the Jewish element congregates mainly in the business and high-class residential sectors of the city, and it is in the *Gymnasiums* of such neighborhoods that conditions prevail of which the honorable gentlemen who are not from Berlin certainly have not the slightest idea. At the *Französische Gymnasium*, for instance, there are 32 student in the *Obersekunda* [high school sophomore class] of whom 22 are Jews (cries of 'Hear, hear!'). At the last Easter term ten pupils were promoted from the *Untersekunda* to the *Obersekunda* [from freshmen to sophomore] of whom the class leader was—I state it with satisfaction—a Gentile, while the rest were Jews —which is much less to my satisfaction. At the *Wilhelmsgymnasium* 13 boys passed their *Abitur* [university entrance examination] including nine Jews. You will admit that this is really going too far (cries of 'Very true!'). It is precisely this enormous percentage that is so dangerous. . . .

"In the higher schools for girls (*höhere Töchterschulen*) things are even worse. In 1887 Berlin counted 1,639 Jewish students, compared to 3,446 Protestant, 63 Catholic, and 12 nondenominational girls. If you take the schools separately, you have the following figures: 239 Jewish, compared to 565 Protestant students, 256 compared to 586, 319 compared to 518, 308 compared to 589, 316 compared to 386. This is a situation which will eventually develop into a kind of Judaization (*Verjudung*) of the higher schools for girls (cries of 'Very true!')."

Stoecker then quoted some figures on the proportions in the *Volksschulen* (elementary schools) where in his opinion the danger was not so great. However, here too there were many Jews.

"In the Gipsstrasse, for instance, another sector overcrowded with Jews, there is an elementary school which as long as three years ago had 131 Jewish boys and another with 151 Jewish girls. Here the solution should be simple. If in two public schools which are so close together there are 131 Jewish boys and 151 Jewish girls, a Jewish elementary school should be organized, under the constitution and the legal provisions (cries of 'Very true!' on the right)."

The problem in the high schools was such that Stoecker considered

". . . a solution quite difficult. But it should be possible if we approach the problem with the impartiality and clear mind required by the danger. In Frankfurt am Main Jewish high schools have existed for a long time; they were established before the Prussian time. There our Israelitic fellow citizens established their own high schools, from a sound and sensible awareness of the state of affairs. If Jews could do that for their *own* purposes, why should we not have the courage to do the same for *them* and for ourselves at the same time? (Cries of 'Very true!'). . . .

"Such proposals are by no means unconstitutional! The Jews will continue to enjoy equal rights; they can attend Christian schools just as Christians can go to their schools. . . . There exists full equality of rights. But that Christian schools in the German capital, the main scene of the intellectual struggles that must secure our future, should admit such a percentage of elements which preclude a Christian National education—that is certainly not equality of rights. I should rather call it preferential treatment (cries of 'Very true!' on the right). And that our Jewish fellow citizens have no right to claim. . . .

"I know how difficult it is to pick out in the so-called Jewish question those points that have reached the stage of development where they can be dealt with politically. I will admit that so far I know of but two factors that are, in my opinion, ready for action. Something can be done about the administration of justice, especially unrestricted legal practice . . . and about the growing preponderance of the Jewish element in our high schools. Something can, something must be done to protect our German people. Therefore, Herr Minister, permit me to tell you: *Videant consules, nequid detrimenti res publica capiat.*" (Vigorous applause on the right.)

Rickert:[*] "I really do not think that this inflammatory speech by a Protestant minister (cries of 'Oho!' on the right), as delivered here by Herr Stoecker, directed as it is against a considerable group of our fellow citizens, is a very worthy chapter in Germany's parliamentary history. . . .

"Should not a man whose vocation it is to preach Christian charity and tolerance ask himself the question what effect such speeches might have on the tender minds of school children? Gentlemen, I just overheard a teacher

---

[*] Heinrich Rickert was a leader of the Progressives and a prominent opponent of anti-Semitism. He was one of the founders of the Defense League Against Anti-Semitism (*Verein zur Abwehr des Antisemitismus*), a non-Jewish liberal organization.

next to me saying: 'I should not be surprised if those poor Jewish children now got beaten into the bargain' (laughter on the right).

"If such religious intolerance is preached even here in the House of Representatives, no wonder the boys and girls, the children of these men, put this doctrine to practical use in their relations with their Jewish classmates. . . . I believe Herr Stoecker has stored up enough fuel for that purpose. . . .

"The second point, however, which pains me just as deeply, is that the Herr *Kultusminister*, though the speech was addressed to him—Herr Stoecker made this clear—did not have a single word to reply to this speech. Gentlemen, I must confess: I have a different conception of the duties of a Prussian *Kultusminister* (cries of 'Aha!' on the right) and I believe that his predecessors, even those who were Conservatives, would have felt the obligation, confronted by such an oration, to protest against a speech which can have but one effect, to disturb the harmony that has hitherto prevailed among the children in school. Gentlemen, the Herr *Kultusminister* is the guardian of peace, he is the man to whom the care of the schools, and especially of religious peace, is entrusted, and I should like to ask him: Was this a speech he could afford to ignore, even if he agrees with Herr Stoecker's aims? I do not believe it. And I ask the Herr *Kultusminister*—of course, it is up to him whether or not he will vouchsafe me an answer—whether he agrees with the bias that emanates from every word of that speech?

"As for the facts, gentlemen: You cannot bear the idea that your children sit beside Jewish children in the high schools (cries of 'That is not the point!'). No? *What else then is the purpose of the speech?* After all, that was its only purpose. . . .

"It is amazing to see two souls dwelling within a single breast. Gentlemen, as a rule you are not at all so terribly opposed to Jewish capital (laughter on the left). When a member of the *Junker* party is to be taken care of, or a splendid career is to be prepared for him with the help of Jewish capital, then the Jews are good enough, then they are exalted, introduced into society, fussed over (cries of 'Very true!' on the left). And when certain Jewish bankers give money for political purposes which serve your interests, then the Jew is a fine fellow. For the rest, you don't wish to have anything to do with him, and even want to prevent his children from sitting on the same school bench as your children.

"I do not think such conditions are *unbearable*: On the contrary, they are a rather gratifying indication of the urge for education that inspires our Jewish fellow citizens. . . . What gives you the right to try to *force* the Jews into *special Jewish schools?* Is that perhaps constitutional and lawful? . . . I say no! You don't have any legal basis for satisfying your desire, and I wonder whether the Herr *Kultusminister* will agree with you that these ideas of Stoecker, which are clearly those of the Conservative Party, can be adopted.

"Gentlemen, you will not succeed in separating the Jewish spirit, in so far as it is German, from the national spirit. On the pages of German history there are inscribed many great deeds, mainly in the domain of the intellect, accomplished by our Jewish fellow citizens. . . . Gentlemen (addressing the right), what would your party have been if Stahl, who was a Jew, had not been your champion and preacher—a Conservative worth ten Stoeckers? . . .

"Herr Stoecker is particularly worried about the fact that there are 22, I repeat 22 students among the 32 pupils in the *Obersekunda* of the *Französische Gymnasium* (exclamations on the right). . . .

"That is really frightening. A friend of mine has just sent for the directory and looked up the names of the teachers. For I thought that there might really be a danger that all the teachers were Jewish. To judge by the names, however, there may actually be one Jew among them! I really do not understand Herr Stoecker's horror at having 22 Jewish children taught by Protestant teachers. Is that, perhaps, a proof of his confidence in the power of persuasion of the 'Christian National' spirit? If you were not afraid of having Jewish children taught by Christian teachers and if you had more confidence in the 'Christian National' spirit, you should be proud of the fact that these children are being taught by Christian teachers. But far from being proud, Herr Stoecker is afraid. He does not believe in the power of the Christian National spirit, and this is the reason that he pleads for religious segregation. . . .

"Herr Stoecker talked a great deal about the moral spirit of Christianity. Well, Herr Stoecker, if the moral spirit of Christianity consists in acting in so unkind, unjust, and reprehensible a manner against the children of our Jewish fellow citizens then the Prussian people will certainly not embrace it. They will turn away from Stoecker's narrow-minded bigotry."

Kultusminister Dr. v. Gossler: "I did not find in Herr Stoecker's speech all those outrages censured by the previous speaker (cries of 'Very true!' on the right). I think that the character of the speech delivered by Herr Stoecker was a different one, and if I take the floor, it is mainly in order to express my belief that *Herr Rickert has attacked a speech by Herr Stoecker he would have preferred to have heard, but not the speech actually delivered* (cries of 'Very good!' on the right).

"The problem raised by Deputy Stoecker—*how to adjust the denominational structure of our high school system*—is one of the thorniest confronting the administration of education; it is complex because of the relation between the two major Christian faiths, and it is no less complex because of the Jewish and the nondenominational elements, regardless of tolerance. I recall to your mind the legal stipulations, according to which everybody, regardless of creed and religion, has access to the public schools. He has no right, however, to demand that the doctrines of his creed should be taught in schools which have a denominational character, in accordance with the law. . . . Beyond that it is clear, however, that if extensive denominational intermixture results, this entails considerable difficulties for the educational authorities. The question of nondenominational schools (*Simultanschulen*) has often been discussed here. We cannot exclude the nondenominational school entirely from the public school system, though you know that I have always tried to dispose of this eternal bone of contention, supported in this endeavor by a large fraction of the House, including the Liberals. For wherever the nondenominational schools have disappeared—because there was no need for their existence—peace among the creeds has been established.

"The problem becomes much more involved in the field of higher education. . . ."

The Minister explained that in big cities separation into strictly Catholic or Jewish *Gymnasiums* was not feasible on account of the great distances and then quoted figures on the shifts in the denominations. He stressed the difficulties for the school administration which resulted from the fact that Jews have different holidays which often interfere with the curriculum. Therefore, a more widespread denominational separation appeared to be desirable.

"In view of the fact that the questions that have been raised here are of considerable importance I should like to point out that, according to a statistical survey of 1885–86, there were 72 per cent Protestants, 17.6 per cent Catholics, and 9.7 per cent Jews in the student body of the high schools— that is, the number of Jews amounted to more than half the number of Catholics (cries of 'Hear, hear!'). A statistical survey for the Prussian universities in 1886–87 revealed approximately the same percentages—almost 70 per cent Protestants, a little over 20 per cent Catholics, and about 9½ per cent Jews.

"If one compares this figure with the population of the Prussian State, it will be seen that the male population of Prussia consists of 64¼ per cent Protestants, a little over 34 per cent Catholics, and only about 1.29 per cent Jews (cries of 'Hear, hear!').

"Well, gentlemen, that is a fact! I am not drawing any conclusions from it, but it certainly is a rather relevant fact that we have in Prussia about 1.29 per cent male Jews, while we have 9.58 per cent Jews at the universities (exclamation: 'But why?').

"The reasons given by the author of this statistical survey are rather weighty. They may be described as a greater native ability—one gentleman spoke in that sense here today—a greater desire for education, large financial means; but what surprised me greatly when I was studying these figures was the great influence of the place of residence. Eighty-two per cent of all Jews live in cities, while only 40 per cent of the Protestants and 31 per cent of the Catholics live in cities. . . . One gains the impression that the Gentile creeds supply the large masses of workers, homesteaders, and farm laborers, while a large part of our Jewish fellow citizens do not care to settle in the country but prefer to live in cities. That is the reason for the disproportionate increase of the Jewish element in our high schools and universities. . . . Gentlemen, I really do not know what conclusions you wish me to draw from that fact. The question in itself is quite important, it is important to make clear how the denominations are distributed within a state. . . . It is quite an important fact that a sector of the population which represents only about 1 per cent of the total population, supplies about 10 per cent of the educated classes (cries of 'Very true!' on the right). . . .

"The only conclusion I can draw is to say: the distribution of the denominations is of objective interest to the administration of education. I followed Herr Stoecker's speech attentively and my own findings are rather the same.

I did not gain the impression that he intended to force the administration of education to adopt specific measures (cries of 'Very true!'). I had rather the impression that he wanted to point to a phenomenon which exists in our public life (cries of 'Very true!'). Some of you may approve of the situation, others may want to have it altered. But that is not new to the administration of education. I can only say that I have accumulated much more material since 1883, some of which I have here in my hands, but to my knowledge I have not infringed upon the rights of any Jew as yet! (Laughter.)

"I owe it to my country that the administration of education should be able to turn its attention to this matter without being told every moment that I intend to take some step or other. I would not know what kind of a step I should take in this connection."

DOCUMENT NO. IV

THE CATHOLIC CENTER PARTY'S ARGUMENT AGAINST ANTI-JEWISH LEGISLATION

AS STATED IN THE 1895 REICHSTAG DEBATE ON MOTIONS FOR A BILL TO STOP FURTHER IMMIGRATION OF FOREIGN JEWS.[*]

The Catholic speaker, Deputy Lieber,[†] first pointed out that the passage of laws prohibiting further Jewish immigration would violate existing agreements on trade and residence rights which the Reich had concluded with other countries. Moreover, such Reich legislation would conflict with constitutional privileges held by German states, for instance Bavaria. He then continued:

"For these reasons alone, I and my political friends are not in a position to support these motions, and I earnestly beg you not to underestimate our scruples with regard to any violation of treaties and constitutions.

"When I now turn to the matter itself, I must emphasize that today as before we hold the view in this as well as other questions that we do not want discriminatory laws of any kind. We do not want any discriminatory laws against certain classes of our fellow citizens, against political or economic parties, nor do we want discriminatory laws against certain creeds nor—as certain people put it so delicately—against certain races. I shall not trouble at this time to inquire into the purity of the Teutonic or Aryan blood of those who today speak rashly about the Jewish or Semitic race.

"Gentlemen, it has been repeatedly emphasized, in particular last Wednesday by Deputy Dr. Paasche[‡] and in earlier phases by my political friends, that we do not fail to recognize that our Jewish fellow citizens—and I must include them in my consideration since these motions are meant to be but the first step toward a general solution of the Jewish question—have repeatedly given us cause for serious complaints.

[*] *Reichstag, Stenographische Berichte,* March 6, 1895, pp. 1286 ff. The motions were made by members of the Conservative and Anti-Semitic groups.

[†] Although the Reichstag minutes record Lieber as "farmer, Saxony, Catholic Center Party," it is most likely that the speaker was identical with the Catholic parliamentarian Ernst Lieber who, after Windthorst's death in 1891, became a leader of the Catholic Reichstag group.

[‡] Professor Hermann Paasche, economist and spokesman of an active colonial policy, was a member of the National Liberal Party.

"Those of us in particular who bore the brunt of the *Kulturkampf* will never forget how viciously and brutally Jewish pens attacked, dragged into the mud, reviled, ridiculed and insulted all that is sacred to us and that we were called on to defend so strenuously and painstakingly. Even today we see with great sorrow and just indignation those pens that continue to fight not only us and all that we Catholics respect but—one must state it candidly when one thinks, for instance, of the *Zukunft*,* I mean the periodical, not the times to come —that do not even shrink from attacking most viciously the highest values in the life of our nation and people. We also deplore a number of abuses in our economic life, for which the Jews are greatly to blame.

"However, while we do not close our eyes to this fact, we cannot but recognize that it is not the Jews alone who are to blame. Centuries of discrimination have left them virtually no other occupations than those in which the defects we deplore thrive most easily and manifest themselves most grievously.

"Viewing the problem from all angles, we consider it the task of just legislation, honestly devoted to the fatherland, to strive for the general removal of general abuses through general legal stipulations.

"You will never lure us into supporting discriminatory legislation, if only for reasons of justice. . . .

"As a minority in the Reich, we have not forgotten how we were treated and for this reason alone, not to speak of higher considerations and deeper motives, we shall never lend a hand to forge weapons to be used today against the Jews, tomorrow against the Poles, the day after tomorrow against the Catholics. . . .

"Don't expect our support in making it possible for you to exult: 'We got rid of the Jews. Now *bon voyage* to the Catholics!' "

* Maximilian Harden's weekly, which, incidentally, was often highly critical of the Jewish group. Underlying Lieber's attack on the *Zukunft* was probably less Harden's Jewish origin than his support of Bismarck, the old adversary of the Catholic Church.

DOCUMENT NO. V

Social Democratic Criticism of Anti-Semitic "Reform"

WILHELM LIEBKNECHT IN THE REICHS-
TAG, NOVEMBER 30, 1893.*

Answering the speeches of Liebermann von Sonnenberg and Zimmermann who had presented anti-Semitism as a "cultural movement," Liebknecht declared:

"First of all anti-Semitism is not a cultural movement (*Kulturbewegung*) and secondly the movement which it represents does not exist in other civilized countries. An attempt in this direction was made in France, but the whole anti-Semitic gang foundered in the muck of the Panama affair. There is no anti-Semitic movement in England, nor is there one in America or in Italy. The movement is limited to Germany, and here it has become possible only as a result of the unsound political conditions that prevail in our country, though I do not at all deny the economic basis of anti-Semitism.

"A movement that wants to tax machines claims to be a *Kulturbewegung*? You want to help the little man by attacking the machine? You are aware that the machine ruins the little man but you don't see that behind the machine looms the whole system of modern capitalism, the whole bourgeois society, and to a certain extent the whole culture whose representative you wrongly pretend to be. How can you help the little man? By smashing capitalism! You can achieve that not by imposing a tax on machines, but by destroying modern big industry, modern large-scale agriculture, the big trusts, in short everything on which modern culture is founded. In this respect we Social Democrats hold views that differ sharply from those you represent. We too recognize the evils you indicate and want to eradicate them. But *you* say you want to cure them by breaking with modern civilization and returning to the conditions of the Middle Ages—that would be the consequence of the measures you advocate. *We* say: the present capitalist form of society is a necessary period of transition; we must go through that period, we must preserve all the advantages which capitalism has given us and save the culture which it no longer is able to represent, in order to establish a *higher form of society*, founded on justice, reason and equality. We are a *Kulturpartei*, something that cannot be said of you at all. You are the representatives of anticulture.

* *Reichstag, Stenographische Berichte*, November 30, 1893, pp. 180 ff. The debate on the "Jewish question" developed in the course of the Reichstag discussion of the budget for 1894–95.

"You insinuate that there is some method behind our 'peculiar' attitude toward the taxation of stock-exchange transactions, that a secret is involved which may be revealed at some later date. The only thing 'peculiar' about our attitude is that we reject any kind of new tax. What of the secret, Herr Zimmermann,* which you have proclaimed so loudly? Go ahead, speak up! You have blurted it out a hundred times and have shouted it from the rooftops: the 'secret' is that we are paid by the Jews. The whole of Social Democracy is in the pay of the Jews. We will not bother to answer such charges; the Social Democrats are a popular party, indeed. I have, at the moment, a letter in my pocket which refers to the Jesuit bill† and insists that we have sold ourselves to the Jesuits."

Liebknecht then went on to enumerate a number of other groups and people to whom the Social Democrats were said to have sold themselves, and continued:

"Those gentlemen will never be able to cure what they seek to cure, because, true to the practice of quacks, they do not dream of getting at the roots of the evil. Instead of fighting the causes, they stick to the symptoms and incidental factors. You have not helped and you will not help the small craftsman and the small peasant whose main advocate you claim to be. You are unable to help them because you do not understand what is at stake. When one pays some attention to the practical aspects of your proposals, your social cure turns out to be on about the same level as the old Schulze-Delitzsch‡ gospel for the lower middle classes and craftsmen. You want to preserve the so-called *Mittelstand* and think you can do it by using petty palliatives such as the organization of credit, cooperative stores, etc. Why don't you study the history of the social movement in Germany since Schulze-Delitzsch? . . . The small craftsman is going to the dogs with ever-increasing rapidity, and with all your remedies you are not going to save a single peasant. Well, you say, at least we can hit capitalism, which is dangerous to the little man, in *one* of its expressions, in the form of the Jew—let's get at Jewish capitalism! [You say] that it is above all Jewish capital which is to blame for the disintegration and ruin of handicraft, the peasantry, and agriculture in general. But that's a fallacy! I have told you so before: Look at England, at America! There Jewish capital has never played a part, there a Rothschild can never play a part, because bourgeois society there has developed on a grand and gigantic scale. If you ask about the peasant class in England, people will laugh at you. For generations there have been no peasants in England. They have been wiped out by big capital, by big capitalist concerns which are almost exclusively in Christian hands. And what about America? I told you on a pre-

* Anti-Semitic deputy elected to Reichstag in 1890, friend of Boeckel.

† The Jesuit order was outlawed in 1872, as one of Bismarck's first measures in the *Kulturkampf*, but the Catholic Center never tired in its fight to have the ban repealed. The Social Democrats, opposed to all oppressive legislation, backed the Catholics. Under Bülow's chancellorship (1904) the anti-Jesuits Act was partly rescinded, during World War I (1917) it was fully repealed.

‡ Schulze-Delitzsch, a social reformer, saw in the organization of producers' cooperatives the best way of raising the living standards of the workers and craftsmen.

vious occasion that the farmers in the United States who had developed under the most favorable economic conditions—and who were considered an ideally happy peasantry, are today debt-ridden; that according to official statistics the American farmers are encumbered with mortgages amounting to eight billion dollars. Well, almost no part of this gigantic sum is stored in the vaults of Jewish capitalists who play as little a part in America as they do in England. The capitalists who have swallowed the peasant in England and who are now swallowing him in America are Christian Anglo-Saxons, they are just as Teutonic as our own anti-Semites and at least as Christian, for the English and the American capitalist conscientiously goes to church twice every Sunday.

"So you see, gentlemen, that Jewry has nothing to do with the decline and fall of the peasant class. We Social Democrats know it and we do not tell the peasant: it is the Jew who ruins you. But we may say something else: it is the *Junker*, who calls you brother—brother peasant—who embraces you with the tenderness of a boa constrictor coiling around its victim, who loves you enough to eat you, as the saying goes, and who actually gobbles you up. The *Junker* has swallowed more peasant farmsteads than the Jew. Look at the list of those who have driven off peasants in Prussia, especially in the eastern provinces! How many *Junkers* do you have there and how many Jews? . . . But the *Junker* no more ruins the peasant in his capacity as a *Junker* than does the Jew in his capacity as a Jew. He does it, just like the latter, because he is richer, because he has more money than the little farmer. He ruins the small peasant according to the same iron laws of economics which make Herr Krupp, another friend of the little man, ruin the little craftsman, namely through his greater capital—even if he personally is the most humane man in the world. This is simply in the nature of economic development, of laws it is no more within your power to alter than in mine, which can be suspended only by changing the foundation of our present society. . . .

"You [anti-Semites] tell the peasants that you can save them by your absurd remedies. We tell the peasants: in our present society you cannot be saved; it is not the Jews who ruin you, as the anti-Semitic gentlemen are trying to tell you; don't believe the words of men who appeal to your prejudices, who appeal to stupidity; your enemy is the present social system; your enemy is capitalism and if you want to save yourselves, there is only one means—not capitalism, not running after false prophets, but the transformation of capital-ist society into a socialist society. Instead of fighting us, help us to fight your enemy and ours. We do not make promises which cannot be kept, whereas every word you say is immediately given the lie by the test of practical ap-plication."

DOCUMENT NO. VI

Hermann Ahlwardt on
the Semitic Versus the Teutonic Race

EXCERPTS FROM HIS REICHSTAG SPEECH IN FAVOR
OF LEGISLATION TO CLOSE GERMANY'S BORDERS TO
"ISRAELITES WHO ARE NOT CITIZENS OF THE
REICH."*

"It is certainly true that there are Jews in our country of whom nothing adverse can be said. Nevertheless, the Jews as a whole must be considered harmful, for the racial traits of this people are of a kind that in the long run do not agree with the racial traits of the Teutons. Every Jew who at this very moment has not as yet transgressed is likely to do so at some future time under given circumstances because his racial characteristics drive him on in that direction. . . .

"My special political friends—well, I admit their number is none too great in the House, but that their number is not quite so small in the country some of you will realize, in spite of your laughter, when you lose your seats—well, these gentlemen share my views. When one of the previous speakers, Herr Hasse,† asserts that we anti-Semites are fighting the Jews on account of their religion, then I say:

"My political friends do not hold the view that we fight the Jews because of their religion. Religious feelings are much too delicate to withstand the rude grasp of politics. We would not dream of waging a political struggle against anyone because of his religion. For this reason we support, for instance, the repeal of the law against the Jesuits, although I personally cannot claim to have any particular liking for the Jesuits. We hold the view that the Jews are a different race, a different people with entirely different character traits.

"Experience in all fields of nature shows that innate racial characteristics which have been acquired by the race in the course of many thousands of years are the strongest and most enduring factors that exist, and that therefore we can rid ourselves of the characteristics of our race no more than can the Jews. One need not fight the Jew individually, and we are not doing that, by the way. But, when countless specimens prove the existence of certain

* *Reichstag, Stenographische Berichte*, March 6, 1895, pp. 1297 ff.
† Professor Ernst Hasse, National Liberal, was a charter member and the first president of the Pan-German League.

racial characteristics and when these characteristics are such as to make impossible a common life, well, then I believe that we who are natives here, who have tilled the soil and defended it against all enemies—that we have a duty to take a stand against the Jews who are of a quite different nature.

"We Teutons are rooted in the cultural soil of labor (*Kulturboden der Arbeit*); each of us seeks to work for others and demands in return that others work for him. It is on this soil of culture that we have worked our way up from past barbarity to our present state of civilization. It is different with the Jews. The Jews do not believe in the culture of labor, they do not want to create values themselves, but want to appropriate, without working, the values which others have created; that is the cardinal difference that guides us in all our considerations.

"The Jews want to grab what others have produced by their work; we ourselves would be content, if we could only get what we have labored for. If you take this point of view into account and examine whether it is justified, you will certainly judge our views less disparagingly than you are doing now.

"Herr Deputy Rickert* here has just expounded how few Jews we have altogether and that their number is steadily declining. Well, gentlemen, why don't you go to the main business centers and see for yourselves whether the percentages indicated by Herr Rickert prevail there too. Why don't you walk along the Leipzigerstrasse [in Berlin]† or the Zeil in Frankfurt† and have a look at the shops? Wherever there are opportunities to make money, the Jews have established themselves, but not in order to work—no, they let others work for them and take what the others have produced by their labor. The other day, when I was walking along the Zeil in Frankfurt am Main, I felt very sad indeed. I said to myself, how terribly did it suffer in the Thirty-Years' War, in the Seven-Years' War, in the Wars of the French Revolution and in the Napoleonic Wars! But whatever they may have suffered, they did remain citizens of their town, they had not been driven from the homes their fathers had built. But the Jews have achieved what no foreign enemy was ever able to achieve: They have driven the people from the city to the suburbs. And that's how things are wherever Jews have settled in numbers.

"Gentlemen, the Jews are indeed beasts of prey, they work like beasts of prey. You cannot alter this fact and only by proving that the Jews are just as productive as the Germans can you marshal a serious argument against us. All the empty phrases that have been uttered here are to no avail.

"When Deputy Hasse says that the anti-Semitic movement is pointless, I beg to disagree. When a serious wrong exists which may lead to ruin—and you will not deny that this is the case—then the fight against such wrong is never pointless, provided it is waged with sufficient thoroughness. And you may be assured that we are going to be thorough. What matters is that you should understand the inner substance of our endeavors—even though certain aspects may still be immature and faulty. I feel sure that eventually all of you will adopt our views.

* About Rickert see Document No. III.
† Main business streets.

"Deputy Hasse attempted to explain anti-Semitism by saying that the peoples of the world are now steering a somewhat nativist course. I shall not deny that fact but the gentleman has committed the grave mistake of putting the Jews and other peoples on the same level, and that is the worst mistake that we could possibly make.

"The Jews have an attitude toward us which differs totally from that of other peoples. It is one thing when a Pole, a Russian, a Frenchman, a Dane immigrates to our country, and quite another thing when a Jew settles here. . . . Once our [Polish, etc.] guests have lived here for ten, twenty years, they come to resemble us. For they have stood with us on the same cultural soil of labor. . . . After thirty, forty years they have become Germans and their grandchildren would be indistinguishable from us except for the strange-sounding names they still bear. The Jews have lived here for 700, 800 years, but have they become Germans? Have they placed themselves on the cultural soil of labor? They never even dreamed of such a thing; as soon as they arrived, they started to cheat and they have been doing that ever since they have been in Germany. . . .

"The Jews should not be admitted, whether or not there is overpopulation, for they do not belong to a productive race, they are exploiters, parasites."

Answering Rickert's arguments that there was already too much, not too little legislative interference, and that it would be a shame if fifty million Germans were afraid of a few Jews, Ahlwardt continued:

"So we are to leave the Jews alone, because we already have too many laws! Well, I believe if we did away with the Jews, we could also do away with half the laws now on our books.

"Herr Rickert, who is just as tall as I am, is afraid of one single cholera bacillus—well, gentlemen, the Jews are just that, cholera bacilli!

"Gentlemen, the crux of the matter is Jewry's capacity for contagion and exploitation. . . . How many thousands of Germans have perished as a result of this Jewish exploitation, how many may have hanged themselves, shot themselves, drowned themselves, how many may have ended by the wayside as tramps in America or drawn their last breath in the gutter, all of them people who had worked industriously on the soil their fathers had acquired, perhaps in hundreds of years of hard work. . . . Don't you feel any pity for those countless Germans? Are they to perish unsung? Ah, why were they foolish enough to let themselves be cheated? But the Germans are by no means so foolish, they are far more intelligent than the Jews. All inventions, all great ideas come from the Germans and not from the Jews. No, I shall tell you the national difference: The German is fundamentally trusting, his heart is full of loyalty and confidence. The Jew gains this confidence, only to betray it at the proper moment, ruining and pauperizing the German. This abuse of confidence on the part of the Jews is their main weapon. And these Jewish scoundrels are to be defended here! Is there no one to think of all those hundreds of thousands, nor of those millions of workers whose wages grow smaller and smaller because Jewish competition brings the prices down? One always hears: you must be humane toward the Jews. The humanitarianism of our century, this humaneness of beasts of prey* is our curse. Why aren't you for once humane toward the oppressed? You'd better exterminate those beasts of prey and you'd better start by not letting any more of them into our country.

"Herr Rickert is of the opinion that the situation of the Jews was not so bad in the East, because there they were carrying out a cultural mission. I would like to tell you that the day before yesterday I made a trip to the East to the Russian border to have a close look at the real Jews. If you come to a city like Flatow, Meseritz, Bomst, etc., you will hardly find any German shops at all. Business is completely in Jewish hands, and the Jew exploits everybody at will! And you speak of a cultural mission! How does he carry out this mission with regard to the peasants? Why don't you go and ask them what they are getting for their grain? They work from 3 A.M. until 9 P.M. until they drop, and you ask who derives the profit from the crop! Most of the people are so poor that they cannot wait until the harvest is in. They must ask for advance payment, and the Jew gets the poor people's grain for next to nothing. Without the Jew no one can sell cattle or grain, no one can buy a pair of shoes. The Jew carries out his cultural mission by maintaining these regions in a state of barbarism (*Unkultur*). The people there are all poor. Wherever the Jews put in their appearance, the Germans become poor. Once they are completely impoverished, the Jews leave. Yes, Herr Deputy Rickert, where there is nothing to grab, you won't find any Jews. But they are here, and now they are sitting in the big cities, especially in Berlin.

"If you walk out of this building, you are right in Berlin's west side. Have a good look at what you see there! Do you see those splendid villas? It has been said that we are just jealous and that we would sing a different tune if we owned those villas. No anti-Semite is jealous as an individual, but we would like to see members of our people live in those villas, and not Jews. And come along with me to the neighborhood where I live. Two, three families in a single room . . . [describes the squalor of their living conditions]. Here live the useful people, there the scum that does not work but uses the labor of others to lead a luxurious life.

"Now Deputy Rickert declares that tramps, beggars and such nuisances should be dealt with ruthlessly, but that we cannot put the Jews on the same level with these people. . . . I do not want to put the Jews on the same level with these people. For these tramps, these beggars are, from a Christian viewpoint, our brothers. They are Germans like us. They have been ruined, partly through their own fault, partly as a result of unfortunate circumstances. Many of these people could still be saved if you offered them work, if you were to take care of them, but do you really believe you could save a Jew? Do you really believe you can break a Jew of the habit of cheating? . . .

"The fight against Catholicism is a serious symptom of growing pains (*schwere Kinderkrankheit*) in the new German Reich, for which we have had to pay dearly. Politics should keep hands off religious matters and the state

* The psychologist will find it noteworthy that *Rektor* Ahlwardt uses the term *Raubtierhumanität* (humaneness of beasts of prey) instead of *Humanität für Raubtiere* (humaneness towards beasts of prey).

should give complete freedom to all religious communities. But the part the Jews have played in inciting Catholics and Protestants against each other— that is another story. . . . During the twelve years in which we, Protestants and Catholics, have been fighting each other, the Jew has been dipping his hands in the pockets of both of us. . . ."

The opponents of the proposed anti-Jewish bill had appealed to the Christian spirit of human brotherhood, to which Ahlwardt replied:

"All men are our fellows but above all the oppressed, the exploited. This means that the Germans are our nearest brothers, and only then the Jews. Only when we have saved the Germans from the Jews, only when the Jews no longer can harm us, only then may the Jew also become our fellow. . . .

"We do not want discriminatory legislation against Germans at all, and particularly not against people who do productive work in our fatherland,* but these parasites must be made harmless by a special law . . ."

Taking issue with the liberals' argument of Jewish achievements in the arts, Ahlwardt declared:

"Art in my opinion is the capacity for expressing one's innermost feelings in such a way as to arouse the same feelings in the other person. Now the Jewish world of emotions (Gefühlswelt) and the Teutonic world of emotions are two quite different things. German art can express only German feelings; Jewish art only Jewish feelings. Because Jewry has been thrusting itself forward everywhere, it has also thrust itself forward in the field of art and therefore the art that is now in the foreground is Jewish art. Nowadays the head of a family must be very careful when he decides to take his family to the theater lest his Teutonic feelings be outraged by the infamous Jewish art that has spread everywhere.

"The Jew is no German. If you say, the Jew was born in Germany, he was nursed by a German wetnurse, he abides by German laws, he has to serve as a soldier—and what kind of a soldier at that! let's not talk about it— he fulfills all his obligations, he pays his taxes—then I say that all this is not the crucial factor with regard to his nationality; the crucial factor is the race from which he stems. Permit me to make a rather trite comparison which I have already used elsewhere in my speeches: a horse that is born in a cowshed is far from being a cow.†

"A Jew who was born in Germany does not thereby become a German; he is still a Jew. Therefore it is imperative that we realize that Jewish racial characteristics differ so greatly from ours that a common life of Jews and Germans under the same laws is quite impossible because the Germans will perish.

"Gentlemen, many hundreds of thousands have been degraded to the proletariat; those who still hold out are in the end bound to follow suit. Therefore

* Allusion to the anti-Socialist act which had expired in 1890 but which the die-hards tried to revive.

† Julius Streicher's Stürmer used the same kind of metaphor, substituting a pig for Ahlwardt's horse.

I beg you from the bottom of my heart not to take this matter* lightly but as a very serious thing. It is a question of life and death for our people. . . .

"We wouldn't think of going as far as have the Austrian anti-Semites in the Federal Council (*Reichsrat*) and to move that a bounty be paid for every Jew shot or to decree that he who kills a Jew shall inherit his property. We have no such intention. We shall not go as far as that. What we want is a clear and reasonable separation of the Jews from the Germans. An immediate prerequisite is that we slam the door and see to it that no more of them get in."†

* Prohibition of Jewish immigration.

† The attitude of the Conservatives was expressed in classic fashion by Deputy von Manteuffel, who was one of the movers of the resolution to close the German frontiers to Jewish immigrants. Said he: "This motion should not be at all interpreted as having an anti-Semitic tendency . . . or, worse, as inciting anti-Semitic bias. . . . It would above all . . . serve the interests of the Jews who are now living in Germany." (Reichstag, *Stenographische Berichte*, March 6, 1895, p. 1303.) At the end of the debate a vote was taken, with 218 representatives present. Of these, 51 voted for, 167 against the motion.

The Racists' Decalogue

"TEN GERMAN COMMANDMENTS OF LAWFUL SELF-DEFENSE"*

I. Be proud of being a German and strive earnestly and steadily to practice the inherited virtues of our people, courage, faithfulness and veracity, and to inspire and develop these virtues in thy children.

II. Thou shalt know that thou, together with all thy fellow Germans, regardless of faith or creed, hast a common implacable foe. His name is Jew.

III. Thou shalt keep thy blood pure. Consider it a crime to soil the noble Aryan breed of thy people by mingling it with the Jewish breed. For thou must know that Jewish blood is everlasting, putting the Jewish stamp on body and soul unto the farthest generations.

IV. Thou shalt be helpful to thy fellow German and further him in all matters not counter to the German conscience, the more so if he be pressed by the Jew. Thou shalt at once take into court any offense or crime committed by the Jew in deed, word or letter, that comes to thy knowledge, lest the Jew abuse the laws of our country with impunity.

V. Thou shalt have no social intercourse with the Jew. Avoid all contact and community with the Jew and keep him away from thyself and thy family, especially thy daughters, lest they suffer injury of body and soul.

VI. Thou shalt have no business relations with the Jew. Never choose a Jew as a business partner, nor borrow nor buy from him, and keep your wife, too, from doing so. Thou shalt sell nothing to him, nor use him as an agent in thy transactions, that thou mayest remain free and not become slave unto the Jew nor help to increase his money, which is the power by which he enslaves our people.

VII. Thou shalt drive the Jew from thy own breast and take no example from Jewish tricks and Jewish wiles, for thou shalt never match the Jew in trickery but forfeit thy honor and earn the contempt of thy fellow Germans and the punishment of the courts.

* Fritsch, Theodor: *Antisemiten-Katechismus* (Leipzig, 1893), pp. 358 ff.

VIII. Thou shalt not entrust thy rights to a Jewish lawyer, nor thy body to a Jewish physician, nor thy children to a Jewish teacher lest thy honor, body and soul suffer harm.

IX. Thou shalt not lend ear nor give credence to the Jew. Keep away all Jewish writings from thy German home and hearth lest their lingering poison may unnerve and corrupt thyself and thy family.

X. Thou shalt use no violence against the Jews because it is unworthy of thee and against the law. But if a Jew attack thee, ward off his Semitic insolence with German wrath.

Autobiographical Explanations of Anti-Semitism

---

a. THE JUNKER*

Up to my thirtieth year I was an anti-Semite; first by instinct, then by conviction, and, finally, I was plagued by doubts. Each human being is in the beginning the product of his environment and education. Someone who grew up in an arch-conservative castle in the most conservative election district of Prussia cannot very well be expected to have the mentality of the *Verein zur Abwehr des Antisemitismus*. As a child I saw Jews only as rawhide and rag Jews who came to our estate to buy and sell. They were poor devils of a most embarrassing servility, the kind of people who if they are thrown out at the front door, will return by the back door. Nobody hated them but they were despised. Inferior race!

That was altogether the belief in which I was brought up: The Jews are different from us and beneath us. They don't want to work but only to haggle. They know no principle of ethics but that of making money at all costs. That's why one should be careful with them. Best to avoid them altogether—for *qui mange du juif, en meurt*.

At high school, I proceeded according to this formula. We had at most a half-dozen Jewish schoolmates. We did not beat them up—the "tough fighters" are the product of Hitler spirituality—but we snubbed them. The few harmless Jewish comrades were jailed, so to speak, into a spiritual-social ghetto. Later I became a rational anti-Semite, if the term is permissible, by the education I received in the *Verein deutscher Studenten*. . . .

The only student organizations, which in the 1890's engaged in politics, were the *Verein deutscher Studenten* on the right and the *Freie Wissenschaftliche Vereinigung* on the left. For me, as *Junker*, of course, only the organization on the right counted. . . .

The *Verein deutscher Studenten* was anti-Semitic because Jewry was considered un-German—race theory; unpatriotic—the Jews stood almost without exception in the camp of the opposition; and asocial—they were believed to be the pillars of Manchesterism. Court Chaplain Stoecker and Professor Heinrich von Treitschke were the two gods of the *Verein deutscher Studenten*. . . .

The main reason for the anti-Semitism of my first thirty years of life was that I hardly knew a Jew. Why should I bother with the representatives of an inferior race? Especially since these people ranked below par morally,

* Gerlach, Hellmut von: *Von Rechts Nach Links, loc. cit.*, pp. 108-110, 115.

but unfortunately above par intellectually so that one was apt to lose out in contact with them. Was not all the power of this so numerically limited alien tribe based on this combination of shrewdness and moral unscrupulousness?

That is what I heard daily in the *Verein deutscher Studenten*, in my own social group, and in the anti-Semitic meetings, but above all from the right-wing press—"Jewish sheets," of course, I would not touch. The literature that was read in our circles made its contribution. For me, who hardly knew a single Jew, the image of Jewry was all the more firmly fixed: a people of crassest materialism, only out to make money, shirking hard work, unproductive, exclusively devoted to trade, unprincipled as to the means employed and therefore especially strongly represented in the statistics of crime; destructive by inclination, cynical, lewd—all in all Mephistopheles incarnate in a people.

[Gerlach did not remain an anti-Semite. He attributed his change of mind to personal experience, reason, and taste. Heinrich Heine, Karl Marx, Eduard Bernstein are among the men of Jewish descent whose intellectual or artistic achievements impressed him. So did the civic-consciousness and social-mindedness of prominent Jewish families. Finally, the mediocrity of the anti-Semitic leadership repelled him to such a degree that, as he declared, the anti-Semites cured him of anti-Semitism more quickly than the Jews.]

b. THE RACIST*

The impulse came from a pamphlet which I found in my parents' home. One of my brothers, ten years older than I, had brought it home. Locked in the privy (*auf verschwiegenem Örtchen*) I started to read and stumbled over a sentence: "The Aryan and the Semite represent two inassimilable contrasts, like fire and water." It was a pamphlet of the national youth organization, united in the *Wartburgbund*, since 1899 *Jungdeutscher Bund*.

That Semite stood for the Jew I knew. But the Aryan gave me a headache. Gradually by my asking around, the fog lifted. However, I only grasped later why the Aryan should be the complete opposite of the Semite. It is true, already then, we boys did not like the Jew, we disliked him emotionally and put up with Jewish classmates only when we were forced to.

Finally, but not least important, a present from my mother contributed to my aversion; she put O. Glaubrecht's novel *Das Volk und seine Treiber* (The People and Its Drivers) under the Christmas tree for me. . . . This novel appeared in the first third of the nineteenth century and is, just as Polenz' novel, *Der Büttnerbauer*, excellently suited to enlighten the German people as to the foreign attitude of the Jew and his injurious activities.

Around 1893 I became more fully aware of the Semitic way and its Aryan opposite. My mother had sent me to Gutschow in the southern part of Friedrichstrasse to get some flour. In one of these buildings there was housed Dewald's Anti-Semitic Book Store. It exhibited Jewish caricatures, anti-Semitic newspapers, and other related writings. Attracted by the pictures I

* Willi Buch, "Wie ich Antisemit wurde," *50 Jahre antisemitische Bewegung, loc. cit.*, pp. 28 ff.

read everything my eyes could reach, from the first to the last letter. One periodical especially caught my fancy; it carried the queer title *Personalist und Emanzipator*. I am sure that at least nine-tenths of its title and contents were incomprehensible to me at the time, but the publication intrigued me sufficiently to make me trudge from now on once a week from Bülowstrasse in the west to Friedrichstrasse and to read the periodical and everything else I could make out through the window pane.

Eagerly I bought the *Mitteilungen aus dem Verein des Antisemitismus** (Bulletin of the Society of Anti-Semitism) at the newsstands on Belle-Alliance Square and the corner of Bülow- and Potsdamer Streets. And, this may sound like a bad joke, but through this miserable sheet (*dieses elende Schandblatt*) I became a rabid anti-Semite in earliest boyhood and through this and other publications that I bought when I could afford them with the few pennies I was given, I gained a sizeable knowledge of the men who then were active in the anti-Semitic movement.

Besides, other Jewish newspapers like the *Berliner Tageblatt* and the *Freisinnige Zeitung* worked in the same direction as the philo-Semitic defense publications. The defense against anti-Semitism was so reckless, the attacks against its representatives so full of hate and obvious lies that their effect upon the sober and realistic German was mostly contrary to the intended one. They proved to be part of that power which schemes evil but creates the good.

Before long I started to spend my pocket money on subscriptions to anti-Semitic periodicals which I had sent to my parent's home address. First, of course, deceived by the title, *Das Freie Wort*, which came from a southwestern city. Then followed Dr. Boeckel's *Reichsherold*, Berlin, the *Deutsch Soziale Blätter*, Hamburg, the *Deutsche Reform*, Berlin, the *Sachsenschau*, Magdeburg, the *Unverfälschte Deutsche Worte* (Unadulterated German Words) which came from Vienna, the *Alldeutsche Tagblatt*, *Kikeriki*, the comic paper devoted to Lueger's cause, and similar periodicals. I kept changing the subscriptions and finally settled for the *Deutsche Reform* and the *Deutsch Soziale Blätter*. It so happened, however, that my father did not approve of them. He railed against "vile Jew-baiting" and forbade me to subscribe to them. When I did not cancel the subscription, he one day silently tore up the papers the letter carrier had brought. This outraged my boyish heart and I dared say something about tampering with the mail. Well, inconsiderate as fathers are at times, he hit me on my insolent mouth and for days afterwards my ears were burning.

Not that it helped, for now I claimed my mail at General Delivery. There, at the post office West 57, I had a fellow reader. Many a time I caught the postal clerk reading my papers. I did not mind it at all as I hoped to see him thus also converted to anti-Semitism. Benevolently he then always handed me the newly arrived shipment.

[Buch remained an anti-Semite throughout his life. Later experiences only confirmed the convictions he had acquired at the age of ten!]

* Apparently a publication which attempted to fight anti-Semitism by ridiculing it.

DOCUMENT NO. IX

*A Private Letter of Friedrich Engels**

. . . However, I must ask you to consider whether you will not do more harm than good through anti-Semitism. Anti-Semitism is a characteristic feature of a backward culture and can be found therefore only in Prussia, Austria, and Russia. He who would try to practice anti-Semitism here in England or in America would be laughed at, and M. Drumont in Paris creates with his writings—which are infinitely superior to those of the German anti-Semites —only a minor, ineffective one-day sensation. Moreover, now that he has become a candidate for the city council he is forced to admit that he is against Christian capital just as much as against Jewish! And M. Drumont would be read even of he advocated the opposite opinion.

In Prussia, it is the low nobility, the *Junkers,* who earn 10,000 marks and spend 20,000 and therefore fall prey to the usurers, who go in for anti-Semitism; and in Prussia and Austria it is the petty bourgeois, doomed to extinction by the competition of big capital, the craftsman and small business-man, who join the chorus. However, in so far as capital ruins *these* classes of society, which are reactionary through and through, it fulfills its mission and is useful, whether it be Semitic or Aryan, circumcised or baptized; it helps the backward Prussians and Austrians advance to the modern point of view where all old social differentiations dissolve in the one great conflict between capitalists and workers. Where this point has not yet been reached, where no strong capitalistic class exists *yet*, and therefore no strong working class, where capital is still too weak to take possession of the entire national production, and where the stock exchange is the main arena of its activity; where production is still in the hands of the peasants, the landowners, the craftsmen and similar classes, taken over from the Middle Ages—only there is capital predominantly Jewish, and only there does anti-Semitism thrive.

In all North America with its millionaires whose wealth can be hardly expressed in our shabby marks, florins, or francs, there is *not a single Jew* among those millionaires, and the Rothschilds are real beggars compared to

* On May 9, 1890, the Social Democratic *Arbeiter-Zeitung* of Vienna published these parts of a letter by Friederich Engels, with the following note: "Surely, we do not have to mention explicitly that we reprint this letter with the approval of the sender as well as of the receiver." It is not clear to whom the letter was addressed. Although included in the collection of Victor Adler's articles, speeches and letters which the governing body of the Austrian Social Democratic Party published in honor of its leader, the letter was not addressed to Adler. We quote from *Victor Adlers Aufsätze, Reden und Briefe* (Vienna, 1922), pp. 6-8.

those Americans. And even here in England Rothschild is a man of modest means compared, for instance, with the Duke of Westminster. Even on the Rhine, where, 95 years ago, with the assistance of the French, we chased the aristocrats out of the country and have created a modern industry, where are the Jews?

Thus, anti-Semitism is nothing but a reactionary movement of decaying, medieval, social groups against modern society, which is essentially composed of capitalists and workers, and therefore anti-Semitism serves only reactionary purposes underneath its socialistic disguise; it is a variety of feudal socialism, from which we must stay away. If it can thrive at all in a country, it is only proof that not enough capitalism exists in that country. Today capitalism and labor are inseparable. As capitalism grows stronger so does labor. Therefore, I wish us Germans—and I count the Vienese among them—a rapid development of capitalism, and certainly not its stagnation.

Moreover, anti-Semitism distorts the entire picture. The anti-Semites do not even know the Jews against whom they howl; otherwise they would know that here in England and in America—thanks to the anti-Semites from eastern Europe—and in Turkey—thanks to the Spanish Inquisition—there are thousands and thousands of *Jewish proletarians*; and as a matter of fact, these Jewish workers are the most exploited and the most miserable ones. Here in England we have had *three* strikes of Jewish workers during the last twelve months, and then we are supposed to practice anti-Semitism in the struggle against capital?

In addition, we owe a great deal to Jews. Not to mention Heine and Börne, Marx was of purely Jewish origin; Lassalle was a Jew. Many of our best people are Jews. My friend Victor Adler, who is now paying in a prison in Vienna for his devotion to the cause of the proletariat; Eduard Bernstein, the editor of the London *Sozialdemokrat*, Paul Singer, one of our best men in the Reichstag—people of whose friendship I am proud, and all of them Jews! I myself was made a Jew by the [conservative weekly] *Gartenlaube*. To be sure, if I had to choose, then rather a Jew than "Herr *von*"! . . .

Friedrich Engels

London, April 19, 1890.

DOCUMENT NO. X

On the Intellectual History of Franz Mehring

Mehring's development illustrates the impact of the revolutionary theory on the evaluation of political anti-Semitism. The pre-Marxist Mehring saw in Stoecker a miserable and dangerous demagogue. Mehring the Marxist appraised Stoecker as almost a second Luther. The early Mehring feared the effects anti-Jewish rabble-rousing might have on the Jewish group. Later, Mehring no longer believed that there was a Jewish problem; nor that anti-Semitism was actually directed against the Jews. The phenomenon interested him exclusively as a manifestation of the class struggle.

a. THE HUMANITARIAN CONSERVATIVE*

In the Germany of the 1870's, Mehring believed, a genuine Jewish question existed, as did a movement of popular anti-Semitism. However, it had not, as he explains, been created by Stoecker.

"To charge him with such a thing would be to give far too much credit to this miserable demagogue. All he did was to poison this question as he has attempted with all his might to poison and inflame all our public life. The Jewish question was bound to arise of its own accord, especially in Berlin, and there was nothing anyone could do about it. In Berlin the Jewish element between 1780 and 1880 became an important and inseparable part of the population, just as the French colony had become between 1680 and 1780. As long as a hundred years ago, the good and bad elements of Jewry formed a sharp contrast. On the one side were ranged Lessing's friends Herz and Mendelssohn, on the other the money-changer Jews Ephraim and Itzig. In the same characteristic way the Jewish scholars of our universities today face our Jewish stockbrokers. The grandeur and misery of Berlin's history in the last century are unthinkable without the traces Jewry has left on each of its pages. But throughout this long period the alien, unpleasant or at least unaccustomed features of the Jewish character never impressed themselves so painfully on the great majority of Berlin's population as during the last ten years. This is said neither by way of indictment nor even of complaint: the phenomenon is so perfectly normal that it would be astonishing if it had *not* occurred. When the dikes were breached that since time immemorial had forced a strong and deep stream into an unnaturally narrow channel, an inundation

* Mehring, Franz; *Herr Hofprediger Stoecker der Sozialpolitiker* (Bremen, 1882), pp. 64–69, 75–76.

was bound to happen. And a gifted, shrewd, tough-fibered race that has been suffering for hundreds and even thousands of years under despotic oppression will, at the moment of liberation, develop an expansive and explosive force which is hard to imagine for anyone who has not seen it with his own eyes. It will generate this power all the more readily when it has been able to acquire, despite all oppression, the mightiest weapon of our time [money], and when it has ample opportunity to advance with this conquering sword.

"This was the particular situation at the beginning of the 1870's. Victory, so long hoped for and finally won, intoxicated the Jews, and when in the full flush, one is anything but modest and sensible, thoughtful and cautious. In those days the more mischievous elements among Berlin's Jews participated, in an abnormally high proportion, in bogus stock and stock-company swindles. Jewish writers and speakers delighted in criticizing the internal state of affairs of our Christian churches—and frequently with an effrontery that was in inverse proportion to the understanding their criticism revealed. Each day produced new evidence of that strange lack of *verecundia* which Schopenhauer rightly or wrongly imputes to the Jewish people. As a result, there arose among the cultured groups of Berlin society, irrespective of political, religious and social beliefs, a deep animosity against the Jewish character. Whoever denies this has either not spent the last ten years in Berlin or disputes the truth.

"It was a serious political obligation to bring into the open the hatred that was smoldering under the ashes, before its invisible ravages had affected the noblest parts of our national organism. To have done this, and in the only dignified manner possible, namely with manly frankness and scientific seriousness, is the great and unforgettable contribution of Treitschke. This patriotic deed did not only meet objective opposition, often from equally honorable motives—I mention only Cohen's* high-minded, serious rebuttal; it also had to suffer the most disgusting vilification. This was a wretched attempt at intellectual terrorism (*Gesinnungsterror*), all the more contemptible since it tried to sail under a 'liberal' flag and usually originated with people who for their part made the most extensive, not to say intemperate, use of the right of free speech. It is an ironic fact that one may publicly speak and write about God and the world, about Church and State, about everything twixt heaven and earth—except the contemporary effects of Jewish emancipation, or rather its bad effects. For enthusiastic praise of its good effects is considered the highest flower of 'liberalism' in those circles. Some of these people seem to believe in good faith that, once the civil emancipation of the Jews has been written into our laws, the historical concept and the historical fact of Judaism had thereby ceased to exist and that it would be a grave mistake to revive them. These worthies manifest such a complete lack of historical and political sense that they have not the slightest claim to be heard publicly. After all, the success that attended Treitschke's pluck is the most telling justification for his action. For who can deny that a good many Jewish vulgarities

* The neo-Kantian philosopher Hermann Cohen replied to Treitschke's attack in *Ein Bekenntnis in der Judenfrage* (Berlin, 1880).

and ill-manners no longer flourish in our national life today as they did even two years ago. . . ."

Mehring then quotes from the writings of an anonymous Jewish author "*Was müssen wir Juden tun?*" to show the concern of "an intellectual and informed" Jew with the Jews' own responsibilities.

"That serious and patriotic Jews speak today in such a way, that a broad basis for understanding is thus being gained on which the painful question may gradually be brought to a settlement—that is Treitschke's merit which cannot be overestimated. The fortunate turn toward clarification which the situation has taken becomes clear when one thinks of certain events of the last years: on the one hand the League of Anti-Semites, the Petition of the Anti-Semites, and similar horseplay (*Bierulk*); on the other hand the mania for denunciation and chastisement; the eternal cry for the police whenever a drastic word against the Jews was uttered; the raising of every insignificant street brawl to the level of a treasonable act against Crown and State; the malicious gloating when veritable conspiracies deprived of their livelihoods people who were suspected of anti-Jewish feelings; the way personalities who by the simplest principles of constitutional law should stand above political conflicts were endlessly dragged into the feuds of the day; the irresponsible exploitation of the Pomeranian riots*—enough, all these ugly events which the liberal parties will unfortunately never be able to brush off altogether from their coattails. (As for the anti-Jewish riots, I happened to be visiting my Pomeranian home when they occurred. I took care to look into the matter and can only say that the news about them was in part incredibly exaggerated, in part lies cut from whole cloth, and that in more than one little town the nuisance started only because so much ado had been made about the affair.)"

Mehring goes on to appraise the right and wrong methods of dealing with the stiuation, sharply taking issue with the anti-and philo-Semitic scandal sheets (*Schandblätter*) "which represent only the opposite poles of the same lack of intellectual and ethical integrity," and then returns to the attack on Stoecker.

"When Herr Stoecker began to strike up this particular tune he discovered to his joy that he was at last able to fill a hall. Such a success, as everyone knows, goes to the heads of demagogues and clowns alike. The tiger had tasted blood. Within two years the Jewish question became the core of 'Christian Social' agitation and Herr Stoecker finally achieved what he had been unable to gain through either the real or the fictitious content of the Christian Social program: a certain power over the Berlin masses. The Jewish question, as now treated by him, took on quite a different appearance. For it is evidently one thing to analyze the Jewish question as a contemporary phenomenon under scientific, historical, psychological, social aspects; and another to make it the substance of political party strategy, of political mass agitation, carrying it as an immediate issue into groups who can react to it only emotionally and not with reason. Any half-way responsible agitator will resort to such a step only under the pressure of extreme necessity. For the danger

* Incidents of violence against Jewish property and life.

of 'unleashing the beast' is nowhere greater than here. The Jewish question brings into play the three most potent sources of hatred known in history: a religious, a racial, and a class conflict. The inherent dangers are made infinitely greater because of the fact that the Jewish question in Germany no longer really permits of a solution through legislation, the apparent goal of anti-Semitic party agitation. For the crux of the problem lies in the fact that the fusion of Teutonic and Semitic elements has not progressed far enough and at the same time already too far—not far enough to eliminate sharp friction and too far to allow a line of demarcation to be drawn that would be politically recognizable and definable by law; we suffer from the discomforts of such a transitional period. These aspects of the problem ought to give pause to every agitator who has preserved even the faintest sense of political responsibility, before he makes the Jewish question the cornerstone of a mass movement. . . ."

Mehring then attacks Stoecker for the ambiguity of his criticism of the Jews and for failing to state clearly what he proposes to do in order to remedy the situation.

"Side by side with a good many defects in modern Jewry it is perhaps its highest glory that there is today not one person of culture in Germany who is not linked in intimate relations of heart and intellect with one or more Jews. It is from their outlook that Stoecker's anti-Jewish agitation is so unspeakably depressing. Hearing this wretched fanatic, eyes piously raised, mouth drooling with unction, make his incendiary speeches against the Jews until the mob, goaded into a frenzy by demagogic tricks, breaks out into the howling cry 'To the stake with the Jews!'—no man of feeling can think without the deepest pangs of those many honorable and high-minded fellow citizens who, hurt to the quick, must become obsessed by the devilish thought that their life and work among the German people, the best and deepest part of their earthly existence, is after all nothing but a snare and a delusion."

b. THE THEORETICIAN OF THE CLASS STRUGGLE[*]

"It is almost exactly eight years since that tempest in a teapot, the campaign of vilification against Stoecker, reached its climax in the liberal press.[†] He was then Chaplain to the Court, and he withstood this storm, as he subsequently did many others, as the bold and God-fearing man that he was. Little did he dream then that less than a decade later the howling mob of his own followers was to rage over him, mercilessly trampling their erstwhile leader. We now bear daily witness to this unhappy process of destruction,[‡] and whatever Herr Stoecker's future in Church and State, his career as a demagogue is over for good and all.

[*] Mehring, Franz: "Das Ende eines Demagogen," Neue Zeit, vol. XI, 2 (1892-3), pp. 545, ff.

[†] Reference to public reaction to Stoecker's court suit in 1885 which boomeranged.

[‡] Reference to the violent opposition Stoecker received from Ahlwardt's racial anti-Semites.

"Yet the demagogue in him was his better part, for despite everything he was one of the better demagogues. He was endowed with native wit, the gift of ready repartee, quickness of thought, an indestructible good humor that helped him over the roughest spots, and an unshakable belief, less in his cause, than in himself. He was by no means the mendacious fellow the liberal press sought to make him out. Prevarication in the cowardly and contemptible sense of the word was quite alien to him. He did, however, have that happy-go-lucky carelessness in asserting and retracting facts that is of the essence of the demagogue. It was this aspect of his character that was exploited to the utmost by the hired scribblers of moneyed Jewry to present Stoecker as a scarecrow of untruthfulness. His admirers came much closer to the truth when they celebrated him as a 'second Luther.' Much in Stoecker, good and bad, recalls Luther—but with a slight difference. Stoecker lacked what made Luther a historic personage—the revolutionary period in his life. And this difference may perhaps be reduced to another. Luther was born the son of a proletarian; Stoecker of a Royal Prussian sergeant in the Halberstadt Cuirassiers.

"The so-called petty bureaucracy, military and civil, is among the most solid props of reaction, as embodied in the Prussian State. By social position, by its pitifully poor living standards and frugal mode of life, it belongs to the masses. Actually it is not only aloof from them, but in sharp hostility to them, by virtue of its many privileges which, while they do not fill its belly, make it into a collection of vest-pocket despots over the population that has nothing. In Prussia the poor man may come into his right before God, but never before the policeman. The subalterns, on their part, are slavishly submissive to the officials in the upper brackets before whom they dare not even bat an eye on pain of instant dismissal; on the other hand, while the way into high office and honor is closed to themselves, it is open to their offspring. This is one of the main sources of the vitality which the fossil ruin of the Prussian mandarin system has still managed to retain in the modern world. The whole social background of the petty bureaucracy makes it inevitable that its second generation partakes of a goodly portion of proletarian strength and proletarian defiance—in other words, a considerable creative potential. But these young people are suckled on contempt for the masses, and their sense of proletarian solidarity is at the outset adulterated into that 'proletarian' ambition that seeks to match in abuse of those of lower position the arbitrary treatment their own class suffers at the hands of higher officialdom. Any glance at the history of higher Prussian officialdom will show that its best minds stem chiefly from the families of the petty bureaucrats, from which the bourgeois liberal, to say nothing of the proletarian revolutionary, movement gains virtually no recruits. At least not until now, for in recent years social ferment has managed to penetrate even into the ranks of Prussia's petty bureaucracy.

"Once this social background from which Stoecker rose is understood, it is also clear why he became a 'second Luther,' but only at the expense of all that made Luther what he was. Stoecker started out by betraying the proletariat—a betrayal into which Luther, after revolutionary beginnings, was pushed only by the force of history and not without vehement resistance.

Stoecker's ambition was limited to rising from the ranks of the oppressed into the oppressor class as quickly as possible. And he succeeded with surprising speed. While still at a relatively tender age, he was appointed to the influential Court chaplaincy in Berlin. To be sure, chance was partly responsible—that chance, which in the wise words of Albert Lange always plays its part in the lives of meteoric upstarts. Stoecker married money, which freed his energies for 'politics on a higher plane,' to use his own term. As Divisional Chaplain in Metz he attracted the attention of Field Marshal Manteuffel, who was shrewd enough to see that the man might be useful and commended him to the aged Emperor Wilhelm. Yet undoubtedly Stoecker also owed his brilliant career largely to a native endowment that distinguished him from his kind; or, to our way of thinking, to the rugged capacity for defiance his proletarian origins had given him.

"For Stoecker was never a climber and sycophant in the ordinary sense. This merit can hardly be denied the man whose expulsion from Berlin was at one time seriously considered when martial law was imposed. His rigid orthodox faith springs precisely from his rigid character traits. For under Bismarck orthodoxy was not living on the fat of the land, and men who craved the good things of life were poorly advised, in the seventies, to flirt with traditional Catholicism or organized Protestantism. Indeed, Stoecker's first public appearance was a bold move against Bismarck. A week to the day after Bismarck had bargained with Bennigsen in Varzin about forming a National Liberal cabinet, Stoecker, in January, 1878, opened his campaign against Social Democracy, specifically against the Social Democratic movement as the offspring of liberalism. It was a shrewd gamble on the sentiments and convictions of the octogenarian Emperor, and how well it paid off, how deeply the Emperor was infused with the significance of that important affair of state, is shown in the recently published letters he wrote to Roon on the subject. Since that day Stoecker was the old Emperor's fair-haired boy, whom even Bismarck could never unseat—though the Emperor's favor applied only to Stoecker's person. On the political side, the dubious attempt [upon the Emperor's life] by the imbecile Hödel, coming a few months after the onset of the Christian Social agitation and at a time, by the way, most welcome to Bismarck, showed the Prussian leadership that only *Junker* brutality rather than religious unction could be depended on to 'destroy' socialism.

"But if Stoecker was no climber and sycophant in the current sense, neither did his whole development stamp him as a man to pursue a policy independent of the interests of the exploiting and oppressing classes. No sooner had the anti-Socialist laws cleared the way for the impoverishment of the masses à la Bismarck, when Stoecker quickly trimmed his sails to the new wind. Perhaps his vilest demagogic trick occurred on November 22, 1880, in the Prussian Diet when he declared that Bismarck's 'protective tariff' was identical with what he had demanded in his Christian Social program as 'workers' protection,' had expressly elaborated as abolition of work on Sunday, introduction of the standard work day, etc. This dangerous mischief was meliorated only by the fact that Stoecker's Christian Social program had

never received the slightest notice from the working class. It was one of the
lucky chances in his career that in his attack on Social Democracy he ran
smack into Most, who became embroiled in a spectacular duel of oratory with
him. But the leadership of the Social Democratic Party then in office, and the
good sense of the German workers made short shrift of the matter. As early
as the elections of 1878 the utter failure of Christian Social agitation was revealed. The three candidates it ran in Berlin polled less than 1,500 combined
votes. Though Stoecker was finally granted the boon of putting on his farce
about the identity of 'workers' protection' and 'protective tariff' before the enlightened statesmen of the Prussian Chamber of Deputies, he knew full well
that he could not fool the workers with this brazen fraud. Consequently, he
threw himself into his anti-Semitic agitation.

"Today we need not fear that we shall be misunderstood when we say
that here, too, he proved to have a certain proletarian instinct. In the late
seventies and deep into the eighties the anti-Semitic movement presented a
wholly senseless and undisciplined picture. It seemed like a furious outburst
on the part of those who had drawn the short end of the bargain against those
shrewd enough to beat them, a cheap joke no one was bold enough to credit
with a future. To see in it a historic symptom of permanent social dis-
franchisement at least requires a little more social and political sense than to
rant about the 'shame of the century.' It is to this relative superiority that
Stoecker owed the fact that he emerged with equanimity from the ceaseless
torrents of moral and political indignation that poured in upon him. He had
the good fortune to watch the hatred of his opponents transcend all the
bounds of reason, and it was not without skill that he exploited this advantage.
He had the good fortune to arouse Bismarck's displeasure—Bismarck who
was far too seasoned and sturdy an exploiter himself to look upon even
partial opposition to Jewish capital as anything but a heinous assault on the
sacredness of exploitation itself. He had the good fortune, finally, to find foils in
other anti-Semitic demagogues—of whom the sober sycophant Adolph Wagner
was not the least—against whom he stood out sharply.

"But even in this agitation he found no cause to hold aloof from the interests of the ruling classes. He could never tell the ruined peasants and petty
bourgeois: It is bourgeois society that is the cause of your decline, nor is
there any salvation for you in such a society. Indeed, he could not even
propose to the sinking petty bourgeoisie a single palliative nostrum that might
have cut into the body of feudal and capitalist exploitation. The more clarity
the anti-Semitic movement attained about its own nature, the more did the
agitation of its leader degenerate into idle and senseless prating. Stoecker's
sense of insecurity became plain when the Court Chaplain appealed to the
courts for protection against the reverses the demagogue could no longer fend
off. These unworthy tactics met their deserved reward when Emperor Friedrich, whom he had bitterly insulted, refused during his hundred days' reign
to have him disciplined, denying him the cheap glory of the martyr that
might have revived his political prestige for some time.* The most grievous

* Cf. our interpretation, Chapter IV, p. 56.

blow of all was inflicted by Stoecker on himself when the new policy confronted him with the choice of surrendering either his office or his anti-Jewish agitation. He frantically clung to his office. The 'second Luther' could not do otherwise.* It was not long before he was thrown out of office, unsung and unlamented as he deserved to be. The more the anti-Semitic movement stood revealed as the social rebellion of the petty bourgeoisie, the more rapid became Stoecker's decline. . . .

"Those who today draw and quarter him are his disciples and pupils. They are no whit better than he, perhaps a whole lot worse—at best cheaters cheated. Herr Stoecker is quite right in looking down with contempt on these 'oafs' (Fatzkes), as he tastefully calls them. He reveals one more flash of his proletarian origins when he proclaims Social Democracy the true heir of the anti-Semitic agitation. The Kölnische Volkszeitung sees in this a 'curious agreement' between Herr Stoecker and the Neue Zeit. Why 'curious'? A bad conscience is a powerful pair of glasses through which even Herr Stoecker may come to see what we have long since recognized in the light of socialist knowledge."

* Reference to Luther's famous statement before the Diet in Worms: "Hier stehe ich. Ich kann nicht anders."

DOCUMENT NO. XI

The Marxist Appraisal of Zionism

A REVIEW OF THEODOR HERZL'S *Der Judenstaat**

A droll project, just as utopian as Theodor Hertzka's bankrupt Free-Land (*Freiland*) and conceived in the same spirit of negative courage. Struggle must be avoided; there the struggle of class and here of race. The latter, by the way, is only the mask for a special and reactionary form of class struggle, petty bourgeois-corporative and feudal-clerical. On this behalf the feuilletonist Th. Herzl publishes an appeal for the creation of a Jewish State in Palestine or Argentina. He expounds the details of his plan in this booklet. According to the newspapers he has already held a meeting at the London Society, "Maccabaeus," to promote his idea, but with very little success. The Jewish capitalists will be careful not to be taken in. They know only too well that anti-Semitism would follow them into the new Jewish State; of course, it then would drop the name and character of the 'socialism of the dolt' and appear as the unadulterated and unmasked struggle of the exploited masses against their exploiters. (How little racial and tribal kinship and community of religion prevent Jewish capitalists from exploiting Jewish proletarians, could be witnessed again at the International Socialist Congress a short time ago.) [The Jewish capitalists] would much rather stay in civilized countries where "the strong power of the state" holds its protective aegis over them. Incidentally, it is a pity that the poet Robert Hamerling did not live to learn of his compatriot's project; it surely would have given him some piquant material for a few additional touches in the eighth song of his satirical epos, "Homunculus," which deals with a similar Jewish State.

* J[akob], S[tern]: "Theodor Herzl, *Der Judenstaat. Versuch einer modernen Lösung der Judenfrage*," *Neue Zeit*, Vol. XV, i (1896–97), p. 186.

A Jewish Socialist on Jews and German Social Democracy*

Widely varying opinions exist concerning the role of the Jews in the German Social Democratic Party. In the anti-Semitic press one finds the statement that Social Democracy is a Jewish invention and, behind the scenes, is run by Jews; that Jews are the hidden wire-pullers of the party. At times, one can also hear the opposite opinion: that the Social Democratic workers have discovered the Jew to be the exploiter and are, therefore, trying to rid the party of Jewish influence. Zionists and those similarly minded also often speak of an anti-Semitic tendency in the Social Democratic Party.

It is not necessary to say much about the ridiculous legend that the Social Democratic Party is a Jewish invention. The legend stems from the fact that the two greatest spiritual leaders of German Social Democracy, Karl Marx and Ferdinand Lassalle, were of Jewish origin. But even before Marx and Lassalle, there were radical socialists in Germany. . . . Moreover, before the party was organized in Germany, both England and France had socialist movements in neither of which Jews played a prominent part.

The legend that the Jews are the inventors of German Social Democracy is childish. Nevertheless there is a problem tied up with the personalities of Marx and Lassalle, namely, how these two men have influenced the attitude of the German Social Democratic Party toward Jews and the Jewish question.

Both Marx and Lassalle unintentionally influenced the attitude of the Social Democratic Party in favor of the Jews. The mere fact that these two great men who stood up so wholeheartedly for the workers were of Jewish origin, must naturally have strengthened socialist opposition to anti-Semitism. The same fact also aided the spread of socialist propaganda among Jews. The writings of Marx and Lassalle about Jews, however, probably had an opposite effect.

There is a special treatment of the Jewish question by Marx, printed in the *Deutsch-Französische Jahrbücher*, 1844, under the title "On the Jewish Question," in which he discussed Bruno Bauer's two tracts on the same subject. As in all of Marx's work, there is much that is deep and inspiring but the treatment of the main theme is unsatisfactory. In this analysis more than in his other works Marx is influenced by the Hegelian method of drawing

* Bernstein, Eduard: "Jews and German Social Democracy," translated from the Yiddish, *Die Tukunft*, vol. XXVI (New York, March, 1921), pp. 145 ff.

general conclusions. He considered the Jews a nation composed entirely of traders; therefore he favored postponement of the question of equal rights for Jews, then a vital question in Germany, until the coming socialist revolution which would eliminate trade. . . .

The article elaborates on the theme that the Jew is the embodiment of egoism and that his faith is that of a money-minded person. It states: "The ideal which is found in the Jewish faith: the dislike of science, of art, of human history as a goal in itself, is truly the well-known position of the money-minded person." In brief, the Jewish money-minded person is the average Jew. This statement of Marx's was not applicable to the Jews of Western Europe, still less to those of Eastern Europe. Nevertheless, it was useful to the anti-Semites, and Socialists with anti-Semitic leanings accepted the interpretation. Among other things this is what happened to W[ilhelm] Hasselmann, the editor of the Lassallean wing. For a long time there was a noticeable tendency in the literature of the party to show that the capitalist and the Jew were synonymous.

Ferdinand Lassalle, from whose diary we know that in his youth he was enthusiastic about Jews, in his later years displayed a very unfriendly attitude toward Jews whenever he wrote about them. His most able pupil, J. B. Schweitzer went even further. In his socialist novel *Lucinde*, which appeared in Russian under the title *Emma*, the Jewish banker appears as the embodiment of the exploitation and betrayal of the common people. Also, in his dramatic work, *Die Schwalbe*, the evil manufacturer is a Jew. In this respect, Hasselmann, Schweitzer's pupil, excelled his teacher. After 1871, in the *Neue Socialdemokrat* which he edited very ably, the Jew and the exploiter were identified at every possible opportunity. And although Hasselmann was strongly opposed to Marx, he couldn't resist the temptation to reprint the above-quoted article in order to prove the correctness of his own opinions about Jews. Had Marx seen this article, he would undoubtedly have opposed it because his article had been written for an educated public which could be trusted to see the sociological implications: that the capitalistic nature of society had historically imbued the Jews with these acquired characteristics. But Hasselmann's paper was mainly circulated among poorly educated workers. . . . He often used the people's naive dislike of Jews as propaganda against a political opponent regardless of whether he belonged to one of the bourgeois parties or to the socialists. It is a well-known fact that the *Neue Socialdemokrat* derisively designated the Social Democrats of the Eisenach program [the party of Bebel and Liebknecht] "the thirteen Jews of Mühlendamm," because they had a fairly large number of Jewish members. Mühlendamm was then the home of the Jewish trade in second-hand goods and there used to be constant bickering about prices between the Jews and the passers-by to whom they sold their wares. They were considered of low moral character and were therefore heartily disliked.

Despite such anti-Jewish propaganda, there was no lack of Jewish members among the Lassalleans. . . . Even after Lassalle's death the entrance of Jewish members into the party did not cease. When the movement split in 1869,

most Jews went over to the opposition and helped build the Social Democratic Workers' Party of the Eisenach program. It would be wrong to attribute this split to the stand taken by the old party on the Jewish question.
At that time there was as yet no Jewish question in the modern sense of the
word. It was the era of rising liberalism which opened continually increasing
new possibilities of endeavor to the Jews. And those Jews who entered the
Socialist party took a very philosophic attitude toward the anti-Jewish bias of
Schweitzer's articles. The articles were directed against the bourgeoisie with
whom the Jewish Socialists themselves had broken. The opposition arose over
Schweitzer's dictatorial policies and his friendship with the Prussian conservatives. . . .

The first Socialist of Jewish origin to enter the Reichstag was the writer
Max Kaiser, who was elected in 1878 from the Saxon district of Freiberg. . . .
A characteristic example of his attitude is supplied by the following episode.
Shortly after his election, a Jewish newspaper asked him for a photograph
and biographical material in order to print a directory of the Jewish deputies
in the Reichstag. To this request he replied that since he was elected as a
Socialist and not a Jew, he must deprive himself of the honor of appearing in
the directory. . . .

The second Socialist of Jewish origin to enter the Reichstag was the world-
famous Paul Singer. He was, himself, a merchant and manufacturer and a
member of the middle-class democratic group. He had joined the socialist
group of the Eisenach persuasion and been on friendly terms with such leading
Socialists as Bebel long before he openly embraced socialism in 1884. . . . In
the Reichstag Singer at once became the man most hated by the reactionaries
and when, in one of his speeches, he sharply criticized the dishonest policies
of one of the Ministers, the latter took revenge and expelled him from Berlin under the provisions of the anti-Socialist law. This caused Singer heavy material
losses. He had to leave the business which he had built up and developed.
But for the Social Democratic Party it was a great gain because from then on
he devoted himself to party activities. . . . In questions of tactics and politics,
he belonged to the radical wing of the party, and he often appeared to be
more to the left than Bebel. . . . He and three other party members were
the first Socialists to enter the Berlin City Hall. In city administration his
abilities showed in their full brilliance, which even his opponents finally recognized. In 1910, on the twenty-fifth anniversary of his membership in the
Berlin City Council, the bourgeois government sent a deputation to his home
to express its thanks for his useful work.

His real greatness became evident in his private activities. In opposition to
the city asylum, he established the Berlin Asylum for the Homeless, where the
police had no control. The exemplary facilities and kindliness of the administration in his asylum were his pride and joy. . . . Although the anti-Semites
slandered him outrageously, no one achieved such popularity among the Berlin masses as Paul Singer. In this respect he can be compared only with
August Bebel. Singer's funeral was the most impressive Berlin had even seen.

Two other Socialists of Jewish extraction entered the Reichstag during the last decade of the nineteenth century: the lawyer Arthur Stadthagen and the chemist and writer Emanuel Wurm. Stadthagen. . . . showed his solid knowledge and critical abilities in the commission which prepared the new codification of German civil law. . . . His book on labor law which went through many editions and is often cited is a very able work. . . . Emanuel Wurm lived to see the revolution and during the early months of the German Republic was Minister of Food. . . . With Karl Kautsky he became one of the editors of the party's weekly *Die Neue Zeit*. Like Paul Singer and Arthur Stadthagen, he was a member both of the Reichstag and the City Government. And he, too, was given the highest praise for his work in local government. . . .

A few more Social Democrats of Jewish origin must be mentioned who served in the Reichstag before the revolution: Max Cohen, Oscar Cohn, Georg Davidsohn, Georg Gradnauer, Hugo Haase, Josef Herzfeld, Gustav Hoch, Otto Landsberg, and the author of this article. Gradnauer and I were chiefly writers. Haase, Herzfeld, and Landsberg were lawyers. . . . Through his courageous attitude Oscar Cohn became known abroad. Gustav Hoch is little known abroad, but he was one of the most able and diligent members of the Social Democratic Reichstag group. . . . The high esteem in which Georg Gradnauer was held in Saxony can be seen from the fact that immediately upon the establishment of the Republic, he was elected Minister President. . . .

Of the eleven Jewish Social Democratic Reichstag members, seven—Cohn, Haase, Herzfeld, Hoch, Stadthagen, Wurm, and Bernstein—were opposed to the war budget. On the question of the war budget an oppositional minority developed in 1916 which called itself the Independent Social Democratic Party. Six of the above-mentioned, except Gustav Hoch, joined the opposition. . . . It has been said that when the six Jewish deputies left the group, one of the non-Jewish members called out: "Thank God! Now we are rid of the Jews!" I mention this because much was written about it at the time. Even if such a statement had really been made, it would not reflect on the attitude of the party toward the Jewish question. It only shows how strong the feeling of nationalism was among the German workers during the war. Friedrich Engels had predicted something like this during the eighties when he warned me not to think lightly of a war with Russia. A war between Germany and Russia, he wrote, would automatically draw in France on the side of Russia. Should Germany get into a war of national existence with France and Russia, the nationalistic passions would get hold of the workers. This would happen regardless of whether the Socialists wanted it. To many Social Democrats the war really seemed to be one for national existence; and to many passionate natures the opposition of so many Jews to the war credits might have seemed to betray un-German or anti-German thinking. How little such feeling had to do with anti-Semitism can be seen from the fact that those Jews who voted for the war loans were more highly esteemed and sought after than ever.

Moreover, one must not think that because seven of the Jewish Social Democrats in the Reichstag were opposed to the war credits and [only] four in favor, the same proportion prevailed among Jewish Social Democrats outside the Reichstag. Just the reverse was true. In the circle of the *Sozialistische Monatshefte*, which included many Jews, I was for a long time the only one opposed to the granting of credits. Even I was not against the war credits until I had become convinced that the imperial governments of Berlin and Vienna were responsible for the war; that every attempt of the proletariat to protest against the war would be useless as long as the Social Democratic Party continued to vote the imperial government the means with which to carry it on. Such an attitude, unfortunately, was misunderstood by a great many of the German workers but it had nothing to do with a lack of interest in the fate of the German people.

With regard to the circle around the *Sozialistische Monatshefte*, one must first speak of the periodical's editor, Dr. Josef Bloch. He is an exceptionally gifted East Prussian of Jewish origin. He is so Prussian-minded that at times he may be mistaken for a German nationalist. Before the war, he favored the defense and colonial policies of the German empire. To him, England was the power which German foreign policy must strive to conquer. During the war he was one of the most enthusiastic defenders of the war credits; today he is the guiding spirit among the socialist proponents of the so-called continental policy, that is, a policy which would tie together Germany, Russia, and France against England and, if necessary, also against the United States. This is not as a result of dislike of the English but because he believes that such a policy is necessary in the interest of Germany's world mission. As a Socialist he is a revisionist and as a Jew he is close to the Zionists.

Also in this group may be mentioned Bruno Borchardt, a City Councillor of Charlottenburg and division chief in the Ministry of Education; Max Cohen, who before the war was a member of the Reichstag and has since been a member of the Presidium of the Central Council of the Workers' and Soldiers' Councils in Germany; Julius Kaliski, a well-known journalist and authority on finance; and Vally Zepler, one of the most talented and devoted workers of the women's socialist movement. The group had a most unusual friend in the noted physicist Dr. Leo Arons who died a year ago. For years he supported the journal and even saw to it that after his death it would not get into financial difficulties. He is a descendant of a Berlin family of wealthy bankers. Even before he became a member of the Social Democratic Party, the Prussian government deprived him of the right to lecture in the Prussian universities. He devoted a large part of his fortune to socialist propaganda and to the aid of needy Socialists. As he was especially friendly to the trade union movement, he gave during the nineties a large sum of money for the building of the Berlin Trade Union House. This was the first large building in Berlin for the exclusive use of the workers. . . .

A third important organization for the Berlin workers was also built up and maintained as a result of the endeavors of a Socialist of Jewish extraction, Hugo Heimann. It is the Public Library and Reading Room which is outstanding for its literary treasures among similar institutions in Berlin. . . .

No profession is so well represented among the Jewish Social Democrats as medicine. If no Jewish physician has thus far been a Social Democratic representative in the Reichstag, it is because there have been altogether few physicians in the Reichstag. However, many Social Democratic physicians of Jewish origin are found in municipal governments. In Berlin, one of the first was Dr. Ignaz Zadek, the brother of the late New York comrade Julia Zadek-Rome. Ignaz Zadek belonged to the Social Democratic Party for over forty years; he is one of those socialist students whom the anti-Socialist law against party activities could not frighten. . . . Zadek is responsible for the sanitary conditions of Berlin. During the nineties, when cholera spread through Germany, he organized the Workers' Sanitation Commission in Berlin, which was composed of public-minded workers and doctors. Its job was to uncover the unsanitary conditions of the tenements in the poorest sections, bring them to the attention of the proper officials, and propose plans for remedy. The Commission received eager cooperation from the workers. . . . Dr. Hermann Weil, who was then Chairman of the City Council of Greater Berlin and the leader of the non-partisan group in the Council belonged to it. Especially helpful to Zadek was . . . Dr. Alfred Blaschko, founder of the German Society to Combat Venereal Diseases and as a dermatologist well-known outside of Germany. . . .

Regarding the profession of teaching and writing, it is necessary to remember that before the [1918] revolution there were very few Jewish professors in Germany. Only those who were converted to Christianity and thus showed their political subservience, were invited to become professors. As a result, a Socialist of Jewish origin who became a professor was an exception to the rule. Such an exception was Emil Lederer, professor of economics at Heidelberg University, who in 1918 was chosen as a member of the Socialization Commission. Even before the war, the great mathematician Albert Einstein received an invitation from the then Royal Academy of Science in Berlin. His Judaism had to be accepted. The Berlin Academy could find no excuse for rejecting a man whom all authorities in his field had recognized as one of the greatest thinkers of his day. But Einstein is not only a Jew; he is also a Social Democrat. Recently the University of Frankfurt am Main honored Hugo Sinzheimer. For many years a jurist and active lawyer, he is a member of the Social Democratic majority and was, in January, 1919, elected to the National Assembly. . . . He was also a member of the committee investigating the conduct of the war. In this committee he showed unusual Jewish cleverness and sharp-wittedness. Among others, he and Oscar Cohn questioned the venerated generals, Hindenburg and Ludendorff, and were not overawed by them. This gave the German anti-Semites new opportunities for irrational attacks.

Until recently a similar situation [as in the universities] existed in the intermediate and secondary schools. Under the *Kaiserreich* the *Gymnasiums* were schools of ingrained nationalism; since the war they have been nests of dark anti-Semitism. The Social Democrat of Jewish origin who made teaching his career has until now been solely dependent upon the free workers' educational institutions and upon his writings.

In the list of Social Democratic writers and journalists we find a considerable number of persons of Jewish origin. From the days of the anti-Socialist law may be mentioned: Adolf Hepner, who was Liebknecht's coeditor on the

Volks-Staat; Karl Kirsch; Max Kaiser, who is mentioned above; Samuel Kakasky; and Maximilian Schlesinger. During the period of the anti-Socialist law, the author of these lines also became a professional writer and acted as editor of the Zürich *Socialdemokrat*. Somewhat later, Dr. Heinrich Braun started to edit the *Archiv für Soziale Gesetzgebung [und Statistik]* and the *Sozial-Politische Central-Blatt*. Also journalistically active were Moses Oppenheim and Reinhold and Bruno Schoenlank in Munich. Schoenlank was for a time editor of the Berlin *Vorwärts* and ended his career as editor in chief of the *Leipziger Volks-Zeitung*, which he helped to establish. He was a member of the Reichstag and for many years the leading political editor of *Vorwärts*.

Kurt Eisner, of Jewish extraction, was a writer with a broad philosophic and literary background, a talented poet and excellent stylist; as a politician he had the fortunate gift of being able to get at the core of a complicated situation. Nevertheless, his idealistic spirit led him into errors. His first decrees and speeches as Minister President of Bavaria were examples of far-seeing *Realpolitik*. But when, in opposition to the united middle-class parties, the workers, stirred up by Moscow, organized to convert Bavaria forcibly into a soviet republic on the bolshevist pattern, Eisner was no longer on solid ground. The assassin's bullet which killed him in March, 1919, rescued him from a very complicated situation.* A year earlier he had delivered a courageous speech against war. Fully knowing that the speech would put him in jail, he was willing to sacrifice his freedom to set an example to those who fought to end the war. It was he who made public the dispatch by Count Lerchenfeld which revealed the tragic double-dealing of Berlin and Vienna which led to the war.

Friedrich Stampfer, who during the war and today is the leading political editor of *Vorwärts* is likewise of Jewish origin. . . . His articles at the time when the German armies were crumbling and during the early days of the November Revolution made *Vorwärts* the most popular paper in Berlin. . . . He is strongly nationalist-minded and probably no one was more responsible than this "Jew" for the fact that the Socialists voted for the war budget in 1914.

Another writer of Jewish origin—Austrian-born—who had a great influence upon German Social Democracy was Dr. Rudolf Hilferding. He was the leading editor of *Die Freiheit*, the fighting organ of the Independent Social Democrats. Hilferding is the author of *Das Finanzkapital*, one of the most eminent economic works written from the Marxist point of view. Through this work he gained a position of such eminence in the academic world that he was elected to the Socialization Commission in 1918 and even the present coalition government of the [Weimar] Republic appointed him to the Economic Council. . . .

The gallery of writers and journalists of Jewish origin could be indefinitely increased by persons who are well above average. From this one should not conclude, as the anti-Semites do, that the Social Democratic press is controlled by Jews. There is not a particle of truth in this. It must not be forgotten that there are in Germany today at least two hundred daily Social Democratic

* The Bavarian Soviet Republic was announced only after Eisner's assassination.

newspapers which employ at least five hundred journalists and writers. Even
if fifty of them were of Jewish origin, [the figure] would amount only to one-
tenth. Statistics on this question do not exist because the party does not inquire
into the ancestry of its members; besides, the Jewish Social Democrats pay
little attention to their faith and generally give their religion as "unaffiliated"
or "dissident." There are very few converted Jews among the Social Democrats,
and those few were converted in their youth at the request of their parents
or were converted before they became Social Democrats. Zionism does not
have any strong adherents among the ranks of the German Social Democrats.
Nevertheless, the increase of anti-Semitism in schools has increased the influence of Zionism and Jewish nationalism among the younger generation of
Jewish Social Democrats.

The percentage of Jews as compared to non-Jews in the party can be seen
at conferences and conventions. It is seldom that more than ten per cent of
those present are Jews. Actually, the number of Jewish participants is even
smaller. In the present Reichstag, eight or nine of the one hundred and thirteen
majority* Socialists are of Jewish origin. Of the fifty-nine deputies belonging
to the right wing of the Independent* Socialists, six are Jews; of the twenty-
four deputies of the newly united left wing of the Independent Socialists and
the Communists, only two are of Jewish origin.

This is a larger proportion than the number of Jews in the population at
large. However, it is hardly necessary to point out that as a result of historical
factors for which the Jews were not responsible, they are almost entirely city
dwellers and engage in urban occupations. Since the members of the Social
Democratic Party are largely city dwellers, it is logical that Jews should have
joined the party in proportionately larger numbers than their ratio to the entire
population. Besides, it would be undue modesty not to point out that because
of certain historical facts, Jews are intellectually more alert and take a larger
part in communal life than do the non-Jewish masses. This also helps to account for the larger percentage of Jews in the Social Democratic Party.

In the German Social Democratic Party an outspoken anti-Semite is an im-
possibility. Here and there in the party or in the socialist trade unions one
finds a certain amount of anti-Jewish feeling but this does not affect the distribution of positions or privileges. I have belonged to the Social Democratic
Party for almost fifty years and I know of no instance when a person was not
chosen as a candidate for office or defeated [as candidate] for a party post
because he was a Jew. The workers especially show themselves to be objective
and interested only in whether the candidate is true to his principles and
possesses the qualifications for the job. . . .

In spite of the fact that during the 1918 Revolution many Jews were appointed as Ministers and to other high posts, it must once more be stressed
that it is stupid and wrong to speak of Jews dominating the Social Democratic

* In 1921, when this article was written, the old Social Democratic party was
split between the moderate "majority" and the "Independent Social Democrats."
In 1922, after the left wing had already in 1920 gone over to the Communists, the
"Independent Social Democrats" reunited with the "majority."

Party. But in the Reichstag and its predecessor, the National Assembly, in the Landtag, the communal governments, and the party organizations, over ninety per cent of those elected to office are non-Jews. And it should be sufficient to mention just a few of the long list of non-Jewish leaders, like Gustav Bauer, Hermann Molkenbuhr, Hermann Müller, Philipp Scheidemann, Robert Schmidt, Rudolf Wissell of the Social Democratic majority; Rudolf Breitscheid, Wilhelm Dittmann, Hermann Jaeckel, Fritz Kuhnert, Georg Ledebour, and Louise Zietz of the Independent Socialists; and Emil Eichhorn, Adolf Hofmann, and Klara Zetkin of the Communist Party, in order to prove that these are people who take orders from no one. The Jews in the Social Democratic Party are not a cohesive group. There are as many differences of opinion among them as among the non-Jews. The Jewish influence in the party is that of individuals. The Jews in the party never acted as Jews, and there was never any reason to do so. In this respect, too, the Social Democratic Party showed itself as the party of equal rights for all, without discrimination as to origin or race. I do not believe that the non-Jewish members ever regretted it.

INDEX

INDEX

Adler, Victor, 312

Agrarian League, 72, 90, 119, 191, 244; anti-Semitic parties and, 139; Boeckel denounces, 89; campaign of 1893 and, 70; Catholic Center and, 69-70; founding and program of, 67-69

Ahlwardt, Hermann, 100, 167, 168, 179, 187, 235, 263; anti-Semitic parties disown, 240; Bleichröder and, 93; career of, 92-96 *passim*; Conservatives and, 65-66, 105, 106; on Jewish success, 79; on Jews and the law, 96; Ludwig Löwe and, 93; Mehring on, 266; on master nation, 83; on Semitic *vs.* Teutonic race, 300-305; socialist tendencies of, 182-183; tactics and arguments of, 95, 96, 106

Alldeutsche Blätter, 145

Alldeutscher Verband. *See* Pan-German League

Allgemeine Deutsche Arbeiterverein. See General German Workingmen's Association

Alliance Israélite Universelle, 93

Ammon, Otto, 142

Anin, Maxim: on assimilation of Jews, 199-200

Anti-Catholic legislation of 1873, 16

Anti-Chancellor League, 15

Antisemiten-Katechismus, 77, 79

Anti-Semites' Day, 90

Anti-Semites' Petition, 39-40, 216, 315; Stoecker and, 232

Anti-Semitic German Progressive League, 87

"Anti-Semitic group" (in Reichstag), 91, 113

Anti-Semitic People's Party, 91

Antisemitische Correspondenz, 91

Anti-Semitism; American, 235; areas of, 75; autobiographical explanations of, 308-310; Bahr on, 99; Bebel on, 254-255; Bernstein on, 161; Bismarck and, 37, 42; Braun on movement of, 262-263; Caprivi on, 105; Christian Socialists and, 29, 30; Cunow on, 255; de-

cline of capitalism and, 264; Conservatives and, 64-66, 77, 88, 104-105, 229; economic fluctuations and, 103, 249; Engels on, 311-312; gain in prestige of, 66; *Germania's* theory of, 15; German Workingmen's Ass. and, 155-156; historical role of, 14, 27, 113, 115; imperialism and, 147-148; Kautsky on, 163-164, 255; labor unions and, 171; liberalism and, 166, 167; Liebknecht on, 297-299; Marxist theory of, 160-161; Mehring on, 158-159, 187-189; Mommsen on, 168; nature of, 256; Naumann on, 118; Oertzen on preachers of, 232-233; Oppenheimer on, 148; Outbreaks of violence of, 108; Pan-German League and, 143; peasants and, 101; periods of, 103, 249; provincialism of, 133; Prussian government's reply on, 40; Reichstag members preaching, 236-237; Russian, 164-165, 196-197; Scheidemann on, 197-198; sex envy and, 234; Social Democrats and, 151, 170-171, 204-205, 257; Socialist theory of causes of, 162-163, 166; Stoecker and, 29-30, 76-77; Treitschke on, 76; *Vorwärts* on, 70; "white collar" workers and, 136. *See also* Anti-Semitism, racial, Berlin Movement

Anti-Semitism, racial: aspects of, 82-83; Characteristics of movement and followers, 77, 79, 84, 100-103, 108; Christian Social anti-Semitism and, 237; decline of, 191, Social Democrats and, 174-183 *passim. See also* Anti-Semitism, Berlin Movement

Anti-Semitism, radical. *See* Anti-Semitism, racial

Arbeiter-Katechismus. See Catechism for Workers

Arons, Dr. Leo, 220, 272, 326

Auer, Ignaz, 271; on Progressives, 173

Auerbach, Berthold, 283

Auguste Victoria, 46

Bachem, Julius, 216
Bachem, Karl, 145; on Catholic Center, 69
Bahr, Hermann, 167-168; career of, 236; interpretation of anti-Semitic movement, 99
Bakunin, Michael, 250, 252
Ballin, Albert, 270
Bamberger, Ludwig, 4, 10, 14, 44, 78, 192, 221, 258
Baron, Salo W., 212
Barth, Theodor, 187; on decline of liberalism, 230
Barzun, Jacques: on racist ideologies, 80
Bauer, Bruno, 253; on Jews, 157
Bauer, Otto; on assimilation, 199
Bavarian People's Party, 222
Bebel, August, 87, 161, 162, 171, 179-184 passim, 202, 215, 222; on anti-Semitism, 254-255; Engel's correspondence with, 176-178, 260; on Jewish capital, 169; on Stoecker, 173; reply to Stoecker, 172; on Social Democratic position, 181, 260; on Social Democrats and war, 195, 196; on Russian anti-Semitism, 196-198
Bennigsen, Rudolf von, 210; letter to Miquel, 52
Bergsträsser, Ludwig, 31
Berliner Tageblatt: Lindau and, 186
Berliner Volkszeitung: Mehring and, 184-185, 265
Berlin Movement, 172, 203; Bernstein on, 40; Bismarck and, 18, 42; description of, 30, 54, 221; Frank on, 175; Kaiser's audience with leaders of, 175
Bernhard, Georg, 200
Bernstein, Eduard, 162, 179, 188, 193, 219, 256-257, 271, 272, 309, 312; on anti-Semitism, 40; on Berlin anti-Semitism, 161, career and convictions of, 267-268; on Jews, 256-257; on Jews and the German Soc. Democracy, 322-330
Bethmann-Hollweg, 145, 270
Bismarck, Herbert: reaction to Agrarian League, 68; on Stoecker, 39
Bismarck, Otto von, 169, 213, 220-221, 222, 259; Agrarian League and, 68; anti-Polish policy of, 230; anti-Semitism and, 37, 42; Bakunin on, 250; Berlin demonstration against, 173; Caprivi and, 70; Conservatives and, 63; Harden and, 184; Jews and, 4, 42-43; on Jews, 213-214; Kardorff information to, 131; Lassalle and, 154, 251; Marr's

attack on, 9; Meyer on, 214-215; National Liberals and, 33-34; political position of, 3-20 passim, 55; political strategy of, 3, 33, 34, 144, 154; Prince Wilhelm-Waldersee meeting and, 54-55; Progress Party and, 210; letter to Puttkamer, 38-39; on Reichsglocke, 214; resigns, 57; Russian treaty of, 61; Saar mines and, 127; Schweitzer on, 156; Social Democrats and, 34-35, 170-172, 176, 227; Stoecker and, 42, 53, 56, 121-122, 223-224, 318-319; Stumm and, 127-128; on protective tariffs, 31; Wilhelm II and, 73; letter to son Wilhelm, 42, 223-224
Bismarck, Wilhelm, letter from father, 42, 223-224
Blaschko, Dr. Alfred, 327
Bleichröder, Gerson von, 39, 206; Ahlwardt's charge against, 93; Bismarck and, 4; letter to Kaiser, 38; Kreuzzeitung attack on, 14, Stoecker's attack on, 38
Bloch, Joseph, 200, 271, 272, 326
Bochum anti-Semitic convention, 65
Boeckel, Otto, 95, 167, 179, 182, 234; on capitalism, 183; career and program of, 87-91 passim, 113, 114; on conversion to anti-Semitism, 96; Gerlach on, 88; on Jews, 88; later years of, 239-40
Bonapartism, 12
Borchardt, Bruno, 326
Börne, Ludwig, 312
Boulanger, General, 52
Braun, Heinrich, 162, 179, 272, 328; on anti-Semitism, 262-263
"Breaking the Slavery of Interest," 13
Brentano, Lujo von, 186, 218
Bruhn, Wilhelm, 100, 101
Buch, Willi, anti-Semitic argumentation of, 96-97; on decline of anti-Semitism, 113; on later years of Boeckel, 239-240; on Fed. of Salaried Comm. Employees, 139; why he became an anti-Semite, 309-310
Bucher, Lothar, 254
Bülow, Prince, 135, 144
Bund der Landwirte. See Agrarian League
Bundesrat, function of, 19
Busch, Moritz, 84, 88
Buschhoff: trial of, 168, 188, 266

Calwer, Richard, 272
Capital, Stoecker on, 12, 24; types of, 12; "useful and harmful," 270
Caprivi, Leo von, 105, 222; Ahlwardt's

charge against, 93; Chancellorship of, 60-74 *passim;* Pan-German League and, 142; Polish policy of, 230; Stumm's letter to, 130

Carlyle, Thomas, 80

Carnot, Sadi: assassination of, 73

Catechism for Workers, 117

Catholic Center Party, 216-217, 222; Agrarian League and, 69-70; anti-Semitic campaign of, 17; argument against anti-Jewish legislation, 295-296; Bismarck and, 6, 15-16, 51; Bülow and, 135; Caprivi and, 61; election results of, 17, 35, 71, 227, 244; history of, 211, 226; legislative action of, 51, 134; liberalism and, 36; Social Democrats and, 270

Catholic People's Association, 211

Catholic-Conservative a l l i a n c e , 15-18 *passim*

Central Federation of Commercial Employees, 245

Centralverein d e u t s c h e r Staatsbürger, jüdischen Glaubens. See Zentralverein

Chamberlain, Houston Stewart, 142, 144

Christian Social Party, 13, 29, 34, 54, 58, 124-125, 134; anti-Semitism of, 29, 77, 79; Bismarck and, 42; Conservatives and, 116-121; Elections and, 52, 71; Mehring on, 184; Naumann and, 117-118; new program of, 120-124; Stoecker and, 52, 56; *See also* Christian Social Workers' Party

Christian Social Workers Party, 23-29 *passim*

Class, Heinrich, 143; anti-Jewish demands of, 246-7; on Zionism, 246

Cohen, Hermann, 314

Cohen, Max, 325, 326

Cohen-Reuss, 200

Cohn, Emil, 186

Cohn, Oscar, 272, 325

Cologne convention, resolutions of, 182

Conrad, Johannes, 218

Conservative Central Committee, 41, 86; functions of, 30

Conservative Citizens' League, 41

Conservative Party, 13, 16, 27, 52, 128, 133, 197, 264; Agrarian League and, 68-69; anti-Semitism and, 64-66, 77, 88, 104-105, 229; becomes opposition party, 62-63; Bismarck and, 6; Boeckel and, 89; Caprivi and, 61, 62, 93, 105; Catholic Center and, 17; Christian Social and, 116-123 *passim*; Harden on, 69; history of, 210-211; *Kartell* and,

51; legislative stands of, 134, 227; liberalism and, 36; National Liberal coalition with, 90; peasant organizations and, 90; Stoecker and, 27-28, 58-59, 122-123; Tivoli convention of, 64-67; *Vorwärts* on, 70. *See also Kartell*

Cremer, Joseph, 18, 44

Cremieux, 284

Cunow, Heinrich, 162; on anti-Semitism, 255

David, Eduard, 181

Davidsohn, Georg, 187, 272, 325

Defense League against Anti-Semitism, 290

Delbrück Hans, 117-118; on Pan-German League, 248

Deutsche Eisenbahnzeitung, 15, 214, 215

Deutsch-Französische Jahrbücher, 157

Deutschnationaler Handlunsgehilfen Verband. See German National Federation of Salaried Commercial Employees

Deutscher Volksverein, 86

Deutsche Volkszeitung, 87, 220

Dreyfus Affair, 80, 200, 271-272; Liebknecht on, 274

Drumont, Eduard, *La France Juive,* 80; Engels on, 311

Dubnow, Simon, 4-5, 211

Dühring, Eugen, 100, 172, 219, 252, 259

Duncker, Franz, 127

Einstein, Albert, 327

Eiskeller Hall, Stoecker's speech in, 24-25

Eisner, Kurt, 195, 270, 272, 328

Elbogen, Ismar, 211, 216

Elections: of 1874, 17; of 1878, 28, 35; of 1881, 41, 43-44, 171; of 1884, 173, 177; of 1887, 51-52, 173; of 1890, 57, 91, 227; of 1893, 70-71, 91, 113; of 1898, 244; of 1903, 190; of 1907, 194

Emancipation law of 1869, 3-4, 107

Emigration: 1876-1890, 60-61; table of, 228

Employers' Committee to Combat Social Democracy, 129

Engels, Friedrich, 154, 203, 215, 219; on anti-Semitism, 311-312; on French Socialists and anti-Semitism, 263; on Lassalle's negotiations with Bismarck, 251; predictions and philosophy of, 176-177; attack on reformists, 181; revolutionary strategy of, 260-261; advice to revolutionary workers, 251; on Social Democratic policy, 260; on war with Russia, 325

Eulenburg, Count Botho von, 73, 231; anti-sedition bill of, 73-74
Evangelisch-Sozialer Congress. *See* Protestant Social Congress

Feder, Gottfried, 13
Feuerbach, Ludwig, 253
Fichte, Johann Gottlieb, 14
First International: declaration of, 160
Forckenbeck, Max von, 156, 237
Förster, Bernhard, 39, 86, 87, 100, 114, 237
Förster, Paul, 90, 100, 113, 240
Förster-Nietzsche, Elisabeth, 114
Fortschrittspartei. *See* Progress Party
Franchise: three-class, 220; universal, 19, 26-27
Franco-German War, 5, 15
Frank, Ludwig, 272
Frank, Walter, 30, 126, 213, 220; on Berlin Movement, 175; *Hofprediger Adolf Stoecker* of, 218-219; on Jewish problem, 107
Frankfurter Zeitung, 52, 184
Frantz, Constantin, 18, 212, 216
Free Conservative Party, Catholic element of, 243; Conservatives and, 211; in elections, 35, 52, 227; *Kartell* and, 51; platform of, 128, 135; Stumm and, 128
Friedrich III, Ahlwardt's description of, 105; reign of, 55-56; Stoecker's letter to, 23, 28; Stumm and, 130
Freisinnige Party, 224
Fritsch, Theodor, 14, 87, 90, 97, 113, 114; charges against Jews, 77-78; on success of Jews, 79
Fuchs, George, 220

Gartenlaube, Die, 10-11, 212
General German Workingmen's Association, 116, 153, 252
Gerlach, Hellmut von, on anti-Semitic leaders, 114-115; on Ahlwardt, 95; on Boeckel, 88; career of, 116, 117, 124; on conspiracy against constitution, 230-231; on Stoecker, 22; why he became an anti-Semite, 308-309
German Anti-Semitic Alliance, 87, 89
German Citizens' Party, 86
"German Industrialists' Central Association," 21
German National Federation of Salaried Commercial Employees, 137-140, 244, 245
German Reform Party, 87
German Nationals, 86

German People's Association, 86
German Social Anti-Semitic Party, 91
Germania, 14-15, 17, 18, 213, 263
Giese, W., 139-140
Glagau, Otto, 10-12, 212
Gneist, Rudolf von, 218
Gobineau, Joseph Arthur de, 144
Gobineau Society, 142
Göbbels, 86
Goethe, 14
Göhre, Paul, 119, 147
Gossler, Gustav von, debate on Jewish question, 288-294 *passim*
Gradnauer, Georg, 272
Graetz, Heinrich, 213
Grüneberg, Emil, 23, 219
Guesde, Jules, 200

Haase, Hugo, 272, 325
Hamerling, Robert, 321
Hammerstein, Baron Wilhelm von, 64, 72, 117, 132, 231; on Conservative provocation of Social Democrats, 116; scandal of, 121
Hammerstein-Stoecker combination, 115
Hänel, Albert, 216-217
Harden, Maximilian, 184; on anti-Semitic hatred, 91; on social change, 69, *Zukunft* of, 146
Harnack, Adolf, 117, 122, 241
Hasenclever, Wilhelm, 171, 241; on Stoecker, 174
Hasse, Ernst, 142, 300-305 *passim*
Hasselmann, Wilhelm, 156, 192, 252, 323
"Heidelberg Declaration": terms of, 51
Heimann, Hugo, 272, 326
Heine, Heinrich, 309, 312
Henrici, Ernst, 39, 77, 85-87 *passim*, 100, 107, 113-114, 237
Hepner, Adolf, 327
Herder, Johann Gottfried, 14
Hermes, Otto, 186
Hertzog, Rudolf, 44, 224
Herzfeld, Josef, 272, 325
Herzl, Theodor, 321
Hilferding, Rudolf, 262, 272, 328
Hindenburg, 86
Hinzpeter, Geheimrat, 242
Hitler, Adolf, 13, 83-84, 86, 106, 205, 219; on Jews, 234; Pan-German League and, 247; on World War I, 219
Hoch, Gustav, 272, 325
Höchberg, Karl, 259
Hödel, 225
Hohenlohe-Schillingsfürst, Prince Chlodwig zu, 37, 74, 107, 134, 135, 215

Holstein, Friedrich von, 248
Huber, Franz Aimé, 154
Hugenberg, Alfred, 142, 247

Imperial Message, 44
Industrial law of 1869, 5
International Congress of Anti-Semites, 107
International Socialist Congress (1907), 194-195

Jaurès, Jean, 181, 195, 200
Jena Convention, 193-194
"Jewish Capital," Caprivi on, 105; Dubnow on, 5; Rickert on, 291; Socialists on, 169; Stoecker's fear of, 22
"Jewish Liberalism," 6, 8, 133, 216
"Jewish Press," 34, 78; Stoecker on, 277-287 passim
"Jewish question," 133, 170-171, 206, 240-241; Bauer on, 199-200; Bismarck and, 39; Boeckel on, 88; Class on, 107, 246-247; Conservatives and, 64, 85, 105; debate in Prussian Diet on, 288-294; Dubnow on, 5; Frank on, 107; Glagau on, 11; Liebknecht on, 297-299; Manteuffel on, 66; Marr re-defines nature of, 7-8; Marx on, 157-159, 253; Mehring on, 184, 313-320 passim; Russian anti-Semitism and, 198; Social Democratic pessimism regarding solution of, 256-257; Socialist evaluation of, 151; Stoecker on, 277-287
Jewish Religion, Feuerbach on, 253; Marr on, 6-7
"Jewish Rifles," 93, 263, 266
Jewry's Victory over Teutonism, 10, 78, 80, 84, 211, 212; quotations from, 6-9
Jews, 3-4, 138, 143; Ahlwardt on, 92, 300-305; attributes ascribed to, 79-84, 224; Bauer on, 157, 199; Bernstein on, 256-257; Bismarck and, 42-43, 213-214; Boeckel on, 88; Catholics and, 18, 81, 217; Class on, 246; Eisenbahnzeitung on, 15; Fritsch on, 77-78; Germania's program against, 14-15; Henrici on, 85; Hitler on, 234; Kaiser's attitude toward, 37; Kautsky on, 163-164; Lassalle on, 252; Law and, 96, 97; Marr on, 7-9; Marx on, 157-159; Marxist theory of assimilation of, 163-166; Mehring on, 187-188; Mittelstand concept of, 12-13; mixed marriages with, 106-107; in National Assembly, 210; Nazis and, 109; periods of hostility to, 249; Social Democrats and, 174,
202-203, 322-330; Socialist attitude toward, 162; Stoecker and, 30, 46, 277-287; Ten German Commandments against, 306-307; Treitschke on, 246; urban migration of, 108, 238; violence against, 101, 108
Josephson, Max, 245

Kaliski, Julius, 200, 326
Kaiser. See Friedrich III, Wilhelm I, Wilhelm II
Kaiser, Max, 324, 328
Kakasky, Samuel, 328
Kant, 14
Kardorff, Wilhelm von, 131
Kartell, 51, 59; Bismarck and, 55; in elections, 52, 57; Stoecker and, 52, 121-122, 227; Wihelm II and, 59
Kathedersozialisten. See "Socialists of the chair"
Kautsky, Karl, 162, 179, 181, 193, 195; on anti-Semitism, 163-164, 167, 255; Engels and, 177; argument against revisionists, 269; on Russian anti-Semitism, 165-166; on Russian intelligentsia, 256; on Zionism, 198
Katzenstein, Simon, 272
Kehr, Eckart, 222
Ketteler of Mainz, Bishop, 154
Kiderlen-Wächter, Alfred von, 145
King Albert of Saxony, 72
King Wilhelm of Württemberg, 72
Kirsch, Karl, 328
Kischineff, pogrom of, 165
Kladderadatsch, 122
Klasing, Heinrich, 65
Knapp, Georg Friedrich, 218
Köller, Ernst Matthias von, 134, 248-249
Konservative Korrespondenz, 45, 122
Konservative Monatsschrift, 124
Krause, Colonel von, 126, 242
Kreuzzeitung, 64, 213; anti-Semitic articles of, 13-14; on resignation of Bismarck, 58; Conservatives and, 65, 211; Germania and, 18; Stoecker and, 22, 41, 123
Krupp, Friedrich, 131
Kuhlenbeck, Prof. Ludwig, 143
Kulturkampf, 14-17, 81, 214

Lagarde, Paul de, 80
Landsberg, Otto, 272, 325
Lange, Albert, 318
Lasker, Eduard, 4, 13, 44, 78; Catholics and, 18; Glagau on, 10; Kreuzzeitung on, 14

Lassalle, Ferdinand, 12, 203, 273, 312, 322-330 *passim;* Bismarck and, 251; on Jews, 252; Mehring and, 184; program of, 153-154
League of Anti-Semites, 85, 315
Ledebour, Georg, 265-266
Lederer, Emil, 327
Leipziger Volkszeitung, 186
Lensch, Paul, 186
Leuss, Hans, 117
Leuthner, Karl, 271
Levi, Paul, 203
Levin, Rabbi, 280
"lex Arons," 135
Liberalism, 6, 12, 36, 81; anti-Semitism and, 82, 159-169 *passim;* Barth on decline of, 230; Bismarck and, 34-35; Kautsky on, 198; Mehring on, 265
Liberalism, economic, Glagau on, 11; Mehring on, 187; Stoecker and, 29
Liberal Union (*Liberale Vereinigung*), 44
Lieber, Ernst, on anti-Jewish legislation, 295-296
Liebermann von Sonnenberg, Max, 34, 86, 87, 91, 236, 297; on Ahlwardt, 240; on capital, 276; Anti-Semites' Day platform of, 90
Liebknecht, Karl, 273
Liebknecht, Wilhelm, 162, 171, 181, 184, 202, 263; on Dreyfus affair, 274; Engels and, 177; on Jewish socialists, 203; on Marx and Jews, 254; on anti-Semitic "reform," 297-299; Stoecker and, 172-173
Lindau, Paul, 186, 265
"little anti-Socialist act," 135
Löwe, Isidor, 93
Ludwig Löwe, industrial firm of, 93-94
Luxemburg, Rosa, 186, 188, 190, 272, 273

Manchesterism, 11, 184
Manteuffel, Count Otto von, 116, 305; on Jewish question, 66
Marquardsen, Heinrich von, 249
Marr, Wilhelm, 78, 80, 155; Bismarck and, 9; on Jews, 6-8; origin and background of, 10, 211-212
Marschall von Bieberstein, Adolf Hermann, 248-249
Martineum, 122, 241
Marx, Karl, 12, 176, 184, 203, 213, 309, 312; Bernstein on, 322-330 *passim;* on Jewish question, 157-158, 253; Lassalle and, 154; Liebknecht on, 254; advice

to revolutionary workers, 251; formulation of theories of, 178
Marxism, 152-153; economic adjustments and, 140; France and, 157; on Jews and anti-Semitism, 100-102, 161-169; Lassalle and, 153, 157; Mehring and, 184, 189; religion and, 151; Stoecker and, 22-23, 116; theories of, 159-160, 180, 201, 205. *See also* Social Democratic Party
"mass movement from the right," 28, 67-70, 85, 220
Maurenbrecher, Max, 147
Maurras, Charles, 80
Mayer, Gustav, 155; on anti-Semitism in Lassallean movement, 251-252
Mehring, Franz, 117, 126, 162, 184-189 *passim,* 253, 255, 313-320 *passim;* on writings of Ahlwardt, 266; on anti-Semitism, 95, 158-159, 175; on Buschhoff trial, 168; *Geschichte der deutschen Sozialdemokratic* of, 265, 266-267; on *Politische Gründer,* 215
Mein Kampf, 84, 213, 219
Meyer, Rudolph, 214-215
Michels, Robert, 202
Millerand, Alexandre, 269
Miquel, Johannes, 51, 52, 241
Mission, Berlin City. *See Stadtmission*
Mitteleuropa, 249
Mittelstand, Ahlwardt and, 95; Conservatives and, 17, 64, 66, 70; definition of, 209; description of, 10-12; Jews and, 75-76; Kuhlenbeck on, 143; Scheidemann on, 198; Social Democrats and, 91, 204; status and loyalties of, 28, 47, 100, 106, 136-137, 140-141; Stoecker and, 21-22, 41
Mommsen, Theodor, 167-168, 187, 257; on Jews, 83
Mosse, Rudolf, 187
Most, Johann, 24-25, 170, 184, 192, 219, 252, 258

Nasse, Erwin, 218
National Assembly: Jewish members of, 3
National Liberal Party, 5-19 *passim,* 28, 43-44, 51, 134, 211, 264, 397; Bismarck and, 19, 33-34, 51; Caprivi and, 61; in elections, 17, 35, 52, 70-71, 91, 141, 194, 227; Harden on, 69; Liebermann on, 90; objectives of, 19; Pan-German League and, 144; Social Democrats and, 35, 227, 73; Stumm and, 128; *Vorwärts* on, 70. *See also Kartell*
National Social Association, 147

National Socialism, 11, 12, 27, 71, 86, 94, 98, 227, 237; Institute for the Study of the Jewish Question, 14; Jews under, 109

Nationalverein, 152

Naumann, Friedrich, 117-118, 147; *Mitteleuropa* of, 249; letter to Stoecker, 121; Stumm and, 132

Neue Zeit, 93, 117, 126, 181, 184, 186, 197, 198, 215, 262; on Ahlwardt, 93; on Buschhoff trial, 168; on Zionism, 271

Neu-Germania, 114

Neumann, Franz, 248

Neunkirchener Tageblatt, 128

Nitzsche, Max, 221, 222

Norddeutsche Allgemeine Zeitung, 52, 54, 171, 241

North German Federation, 4, 15

Noske, Gustav, 195

Oberwinder, Heinrich, 116, 124

Oertzen, Dietrich von, 124; on Stoecker, 30, 77, 232-233

Offenes Antwortschreiben, 153

Old Conservatives. *See* Conservative Party

Oppenheim, Heinrich Bernhard, 218

Oppenheimer, Franz, 148

Osborn, Max, 203-204

Paasch, Karl, 113, 114

Paasche, Prof. Hermann, 295

Pan-German League, 72, 141-146, 244, 247-248

Papen, Franz von, 86

Paris Commune, 23

Parvus-Helphand, 272

Pastor, Ludwig, 217

"penitentiary bill," 135

Peters, Carl, 142, 143

Pinkert, Alexander, 87

Pless, Prince of, 128

Polish Party, 230

Pomeranian riots, 315

Preussische Jahrbücher, 134

Progressive Association, 71

Progress Party, 5-6, 40-52 *passim*, 141, 147, 197, 211, 217, 224; Caprivi and, 61; in elections, 35-36, 52, 57, 71, 91, 171, 194, 226, 227; Harden on, 69; history of, 210; *Neunkirchener Tageblatt* and, 128; Social Democrats and, 171, 173

Progressive People's Party, 71

Protestant Social Congress, 117-119 *passim*, 125, 147

Protestant Workers' Associations, 119

Proudhon, Pierre Joseph, 157

Public Answer, 153

Pückler, Count, 101

Puttkamer, Robert von, 38-39, 53, 173, 223

Racial theories, 80-84, 102-103

Rathenau, Walter, 273

Ratibor, Duke of, 128

Reichensperger, August, 216

Reichensperger, Peter, 216

Reichsbote, Der, 41, 122, 220, 223

Reichsherold, Der, 88, 183

Reichstag, 5, 13, 16, 35, 41, 44, 70; anti-Semitic members of, 236-237; *Fraktionen* system of, 230; function of, 19; Jewish members of, 329; voting record in, 229

"Reinsurance treaty" with Russia, 61

Renan, Ernst, 212

Reventlow, Count Ludwig, 236

"Revisionism," 261-262

Richter, Eugen, 37, 71, 134, 211

Rickert, Heinrich, 71, 301-305 *passim*; debate on Jewish question, 288-294 *passim*

Riemann, Robert, 222

Riesser, Gabriel, 3, 210

Rodbertus von Jagetzow, Karl, 154, 215

Rodel, Gustav, 258-259

Romanticism, German, 82

Roon, Count, 120

Roscher, Wilhelm, 218

Savigny, Carl Friedrich von, 243

Schack, Wilhelm, 138, 244

Schäffle, Albert, 254

Schemann, Prof. Ludwig, 142, 144

Scheidemann, Philipp, on anti-Semitism, 197-198

Schlesinger, Maximilian, 328

Schlesische Volkszeitung, 18, 216

Schmoller, Gustav, 184, 186, 244

Schönlank, Bruno, 272, 328

School bill, defeat of, 62

Schulze-Delitzsch, Hermann, 298

Schweitzer, Johann Baptist von, 155-156, 251; Mayer on, 251-252; Bernstein on, 323

"Secessionists," 44, 224

Semi-Gotha, 107, 238

Septenat act, 34

Simson, Eduard, 4

Singer, Paul, 164-165, 312; Bernstein on, 324; funeral of, 273; "Jew-Paul" and, 203-204

Sinzheimer, Hugo, 327

Social Democratic Party, agrarian question and, 180; attitude toward anti-Semitism, 100, 157, 159-161, 174-183 *passim*, 257, 297-299; theory on causes of anti-Semitism, 162-163, 167; Bismarck and, 34-35, 227; Caprivi and, 61-63; Conservatives and, 90, 115; beliefs of, 201-202; in elections, 28, 44, 52, 57, 70-71, 91, 94, 226, 227, 241, 244; Engels and, 176-178; Essen convention of, 195; functions of, 19-20; Göhre and, 147; Grüneberg and, 24; intellectuals in, 252; International Socialist Congress and, 195; Jena convention of, 193; Jewish members of, 272, 286, 322-330; Jews and, 157, 202-204; becomes legal reform party, 190-193; Liebermann and, 90; Mehring and, 184-189 *passim*; militarization and, 195; on "philo-Semitism," 169; political transformation of, 69, 72, 119, 190-193; religion and, 201, Russian anti-Semitism and, 196-197; Russian revolution and, 193, 196; sedition bill and, 134; Singer and, 173; *Sozialisten-Gesetz* and, 35, 94, 222, 259-260; Stoecker and, 22, 23, 25, 29, 41, 46, 170-174 *passim*, 286; Stumm's program against, 129; union movement and, 258; voting record of, 60; weaknesses of, 204-205. *See also* Marxism

Social Democratic Workers' Party, 156, 252

Sozialdemokrat, 156, 251, 265, 267

Social insurance program, 67-68

"Socialists of the chair," 21, 186, 218

Social question, the, 21, 58; Naumann and, 118; Stoecker and, 23; Stumm and, 130

Social Reich Party, 85

Sonnemann, Leopold, 156, 184, 252-253

Sozialisten-Gesetz, 35, 51, 57, 222, 259-260

Sozialistische Monatshefte, 199, 200, 270

Stadthagen, Arthur, 272, 325

Stadtmission, Berlin, 22-23, 53-55

Stahl, Friedrich Julius, 216, 292

Stampfer, Friedrich, 328

Stern, Jakob, 272

Stock Corporation Law of 1870, 5

Stoecker, Adolf, 12, 13, 22-31 *passim*, 37-45 *passim*, 78, 79, 87, 88, 89, 99, 215, 220, 223, 241, 258, 259, 308; agreement to renounce politics, 56; on agricultural economy, 68; Ahlwardt and, 92; anti-Semitism of, 76-77; Anti-Semites' Petition and, 232; biographies

of, 218; Bismarck and, 38-39, 42, 53, 224; Bleichröder and, 38; on influence of Boeckel, 87; criticism of Caprivi government, 62; Christian Social Party and, 26-29, 52-53, 120, 124-125; Conspiracy against constitution, 231; Conservatives and, 27-28, 63-64, 90, 120, 123-124, 126; the Youth Faction and, 196; economic liberalism and, 29; *Eiskeller* hall speech, 24; on Franco-German war, 219; letter to Friedrich III, 23; Grüneberg and, 24; Hammerstein scandal and, 121-123; on Imperial Message, 44; debate on Jewish question, 288-294 *passim*; "What we demand of modern Jewry," 30, 277-287; on Jews, 30, 84, 107; *Junker* and, 89, 132; Kaiser and, 30, 37, 39, 44; *Kartell* and, 52; Krause on, 242; size of meetings (table), 31; London speeches, 45, 224-225; Mehring on, 184, 313-320 *passim*; Most and, 258; *Norddeutsche Allgemeine Zeitung* and, 52; Oertzen on, 232-233; breaks political retirement, 57-58, 227; racists and, 84, 103; Social Democrats and, 41, 169, 170-174 *passim*, 252; Stumm and, 132, 242, 243; Treitschke on, 64; on Waldersee meeting, 54; letter to Wilhelm II, 28, 46

Stumm-Halberg, Carl Ferdinand von, 175, 242, 243; letter to Caprivi, 130; career of, 127-131; "penitentiary bill" and, 135; Social Democrats and, 129, 132, 134; solution to social question, 130; Stoecker and, 243; Wagner and, 243

Superior Church Council: degree of, 125-126

Tariff, protective, 31-33

Ten German Commandments, 83, 234, 306-307

Todt, Rudolf, 21, 215, 259

Treitschke, Heinrich von, 184, 232, 244, 308; anti-Semitism of, 76; on Jews, 246; Mehring on, 314; on Stoecker, 64

Ujest, Duke of, 128

Verein für Sozialpolitik, 118, 218

Verzweiflungskampf der arischen Völker, 84, 92-93

Virchow, Rudolf, 40, 41, 127, 173, 187, 213, 223

Volk, Das, 116, 123, 124; on Stoecker, 57-58

Vollmar, Georg von, 179-180, 181, 271

Vorwärts: on decline of anti-Semitism, 183; on political anti-Semitism, 70; on Ahlwardt, 263; on decline of capitalism, 264; attack on Mommsen, 168; publishes Stoecker's letter, 121

Wagener, Geheimrat Hermann, 13, 18, 213, 259
Wagner, Dr. Adolph, 44, 117, 171, 172, 186, 218, 243, 258, 259
Waldersee, Alfred von, 61, 134; meeting with Prince Wilhelm, 53-55
Wawrzinek, Kurt, 18, 115, 214, 216, 220
Weber, Max, 117, 119, 141, 245
Weil, Dr. Hermann, 327
Weimar Republic, 43; anti-Semitic periods of, 249
"What are the Jews really guilty of?", 77-78
"What we demand of Modern Jewry," 30, 277-287
Wilhelm I, Kaiser: letter from Bleichröder, 38; Bismarck and, 55, 121-122; death of, 55; attempts on life of, 35, 222; Stoecker and, 30, 37, 39, 44, 46, 121-122, 318; Stumm and, 130; Prince Wilhelm's letter to, 45-46

Wilhelm II, Kaiser: Bismarck and, 54, 55, 57; Caprivi and, 72, 230; constitutional system and, 72, 134, 231; letter to Czar, 134; oratorical outbursts of, 73; Pan-German League and, 247; new policy of, 58; sedition bill and, 134; Stoecker and, 45-46, 58-59, 125; Stumm and, 130, 243; Waldersee and, 53-54
Wilmanns, Judge C., 218
Wilser, Ludwig, 142
Windthorst, Ludwig, 16, 211
Wurm, Emanuel, 272, 325

Zadek, Dr. Ignaz, 327
Zedlitz-Trützschler, Robert von, 62
Zepler, Vally, 326
Zentralverein deutscher Staatsbürger jüdischen Glaubens, 96-97, 235
Zentral-Verein für Sozialreform, 21, 38
Zimmermann, 113, 240, 297-298
Zionism: Class on, 246; Jewish socialists and, 199; Kautsky on, 198; Marxist appraisal of, 321; *Neue Zeit* on, 271
Zukunft, Die, 146, 296
Zur Judenfrage, 157-159, 253

Date Due